Routledge Revivals

Christianity and Educational Provision in International Perspective

Published in 1988. Christianity has been one of the most potent forces in the development of education. This book critically examines this influence and discusses its political implications.

Christianity and Educational Provision in International Perspective

Witold Tulasiewicz and Colin Brock

First published in 1988
by Routledge

This edition first published in 2018 by Routledge
2 Park Square, Milton Park, Abingdon, Oxon, OX14 4RN
and by Routledge
711 Third Avenue, New York, NY 10017

Routledge is an imprint of the Taylor & Francis Group, an informa business

© 1988 Witold Tulasiewicz and Colin Brock

All rights reserved. No part of this book may be reprinted or reproduced or utilised in any form or by any electronic, mechanical, or other means, now known or hereafter invented, including photocopying and recording, or in any information storage or retrieval system, without permission in writing from the publishers.

Publisher's Note
The publisher has gone to great lengths to ensure the quality of this reprint but points out that some imperfections in the original copies may be apparent.

Disclaimer
The publisher has made every effort to trace copyright holders and welcomes correspondence from those they have been unable to contact.

A Library of Congress record exists under LCCN: 89118431

ISBN 13: 978-1-138-58812-7 (hbk)
ISBN 13: 978-0-429-49248-8 (ebk)
ISBN 13: 978-1-138-58813-4 (pbk)

CHRISTIANITY AND EDUCATIONAL PROVISION IN INTERNATIONAL PERSPECTIVE

CHRISTIANITY AND EDUCATIONAL PROVISION IN INTERNATIONAL PERSPECTIVE

Edited by
WITOLD TULASIEWICZ
and COLIN BROCK

ROUTLEDGE
London & New York

First published 1988 by
Routledge
11 New Fetter Lane, London EC4P 4EE

Published in the USA by
Routledge
in association with Routledge, Chapman & Hall, Inc.
29 West 35th Street, New York NY 10001

© 1988 W. Tulasiewicz and C. Brock

Printed and bound in Great Britain by Mackays of Chatham PLC, Kent

All rights reserved. No part of this book may be reprinted or reproduced or utilised in any form or by any electronic, mechanical, or other means, now known or hereafter invented, including photocopying and recording, or in any information storage or retrieval system, without permission in writing from the publishers.

British Library Cataloguing in Publication Data

Christianity and educational provision
   in international perspective.
   1. Western world. Education. Role of
Christian church
   I. Tulasiewicz, Witold II. Brock, Colin
377′.8′091812

ISBN 0-415-00568-X

Library of Congress Cataloging-in-Publication Data
   ISBN 0-415-00568-X

CONTENTS

Acknowledgements

Contributors

1. WESTERN CHRISTIANITY, EDUCATIONAL PROVISION
   AND NATIONAL IDENTITY: AN EDITORIAL
   INTRODUCTION
   Colin Brock and Witold Tulasiewicz ... 1

2. CHRISTIANITY AND EDUCATIONAL PROVISION IN
   SCOTLAND
   Ian Findlay ... 17

3. RELIGIOUS DICHOTOMY AND SCHOOLING IN
   NORTHERN IRELAND
   Margaret Sutherland ... 38

4. 'SENSUS FIDELIUM': THE DEVELOPING CONCEPT
   OF ROMAN CATHOLIC VOLUNTARY EFFORT IN
   EDUCATION IN ENGLAND AND WALES
   Vincent A. McClelland ... 61

5. EDUCATION, RELIGION AND CULTURAL CHANGE IN
   THE REPUBLIC OF IRELAND
   Seamus Dunn ... 89

6. CHRISTIANITY - NATIONAL IDENTITY AND
   EDUCATION IN POLAND
   Stanislaw Litak and Witold Tulasiewicz ... 117

7. CHRISTIANITY: CULTURAL POLITICS AND
   EDUCATION IN GERMANY
   Winfried Bohm ... 170

Contents

8. SCHOOLING, IDENTITY AND DENOMINATIONALISM:
   THE AMERICAN EXPERIENCE
   Ron K. Goodenow 192

9. THE ROLE OF DENOMINATIONAL BODIES IN
   EDUCATION IN THE DEVELOPMENT OF EDUCATION
   IN THE COMMONWEALTH CARIBBEAN
   M. Kazim Bacchus 217

10. CHRISTIAN DENOMINATIONS AND THE DEVELOPMENT
    OF PRIVATE EDUCATION IN CHILE
    Ruth Aedo Richmond 270

11. A SCHOOL SYSTEM FOR AN INDIGENOUS RELIGIOUS
    MINORITY: THE KIMBANGUISTS OF ZAIRE
    William J. Rideout, Jr. 316

12. AFRIKANER IDENTITY AND EDUCATIONAL POLICY
    IN SOUTH AFRICA
    Alan Penny 345

    Index 375

ACKNOWLEDGEMENTS

The editors acknowledge with thanks the collaborative effort of all contributors to this volume, with several of whom it has been their pleasure to discuss topics relevant to the theme of this book.

They would also particularly like to thank Dr Wolfgang Mitter of the International Institute for Educational Research, in Frankfurt, and Dr Jozef Miaso of the Polish Cabinet of Sciences, Warsaw, for their advice on some contributions.

The editors' thanks are due to Mrs Monika Shepherd and Miss Elizabeth Ashurst for help with the translations, Mrs Shirley Brock for preparing the index and Mrs Jennifer Webster for typing the drafts.

CONTRIBUTORS

Colin Brock is Senior Lecturer in Education and Chairman of the International Educational Unit at the University of Hull.

Witold Tulasiewicz is University Lecturer in Education at Cambridge University, Fellow of Wolfson College and Guest Professor at the University of Mainz.

....

M. Kazim Bacchus is Professor of Education and Director of the Centre for International Educational Development at the University of Alberta.

Winfried Bohm is Professor of Education at the University of Wurzburg.

Seamus Dunn is Senior Lecturer in Education, University of Ulster at Coleraine.

Ian Findlay is Principal Lecturer in Education at Aberdeen College of Education.

Ron Goodenow is Associate Professor of Education at Boston University.

Stanislaw Litak is Professor of Education in the Catholic University of Lublin.

Vincent A. McClelland is Professor of Education and Dean of the School of Education at the University of Hull.

Alan Penny, King Alfred's College, Winchester, was formerly Professor of Education at Rhodes University, South Africa.

Ruth Aedo Richmond is a visiting lecturer at the University of Hull.

Contributors

<u>William J. Rideout Jr</u> is Professor and Chairman, Department of Education Policy, Planning and Administration at the University of Southern California.

<u>Margaret Sutherland</u> is Emeritus Professor of Education, University of Leeds.

WESTERN CHRISTIANITY,*
EDUCATIONAL PROVISION AND NATIONAL IDENTITY: AN EDITORIAL INTRODUCTION

Colin Brock and Witold Tulasiewicz

With the exception of some countries of the Asian continent, formal educational provision is in most parts of the world dominated by the European model, whose educational traditions derive from two main formative influences: Graeco-Roman culture, and institutionalised Christianity. The former may well have been influenced by African elements, acknowledgement of which would seem to have been suppressed. The latter, in its turn deriving from near Eastern roots, together with centres of Arab learning, kept education alive in Europe through the 'barbarian' period following the decline of the Roman Empire.

For most of Europe, the arrival of Christianity coincided with the generation of learning. Colonisation leads to conversion, and just as the spread of the Christian message throughout medieval Europe required the reading of scripts and scriptures so did the message of European missionaries more recently in the former colonial territories of European powers. Although at times conversion was characterised more by the use of the sword - for example of the Old Prussians by the Teutonic Knights - it is a truism that organised religion and formal education go hand in hand.1 Learning Christian religion normally required the learning of a new language. For most of

---

* Though many of the following comments apply to the whole of Christianity, the respective roles of the State and Church have assumed somewhat different aspects, not least in the provision of schools, in Orthodoxy.

medieval Europe, this meant Latin, although the much more accommodating acceptance of the converted nation's native language in the form of Church (Old) Slavonic in south-eastern Europe was also possible.

It also required the provision of an orthography, a newly codified grammar, as well as an extended lexis for the indigenous language which could function as one vehicle for the converted country's art. Thus, the early Christian missionaries became teachers and historians, even statesmen if the right accommodation could be found.

While it is difficult to find examples of theocracies within post-classical Europe, though the more fundamentalist evangelical sects of Christianity come close to this model with their views of their role in societies, there is no doubting the fundamental part played by the Christian Church in the formation of nation states in that continent. Just like the famous examples of Boniface, Bede and Patrick, ordinary priests, monks and nuns have been teachers and advisers, thus maintaining the dynamic link. From the remote 'Man of God' to an instructor and catechist, the shift in the status of the priest is reflected in the changing style and mode of worship: sermon rather than sacrifice. Though fully associated with the free Protestant ministry, this change in status also applies to a large extent to the Catholic and Orthodox denominations.

But the cumulative influence of Christianity cannot be seen merely as the summative outcome of the spiritual and secular work of thousands of individual priests. It has provided the framework for a wider concept of culture of each converted nation, when the pre-Christian elements were variously superseded, and which determines its national - not just religious - identity: an aspect which has recently come to occupy the attention of a number of academic disciplines, eg. Church history.

To what extent Christianity has shaped national identity is of interest not only in the question 'How Catholic or Protestant are Southern and Northern Ireland respectively in strictly religious terms?' for example, but 'How is this reflected in their social, artistic and political climates?' The Christian framework of the formal model of European

Christianity and Education

education is a significant part of the wider culture and it is this broader dimension that is the focus of the present volume.

The Christian Church, having subsumed much of the earlier Graeco-Roman educational traditions, became the expected provider of formal schooling at all levels in the converted nations. Religious schooling, in fact, did not have to be provided exclusively in denominational institutions maintained by secular or monastic clergy within a cathedral or chapter. It could and did take place in schools founded by individuals, many linked with the secular rulers, which thus provided an additional or alternative source of Christian teaching. State intervention in education in the western world is, in fact, a relatively recent phenomenon, associated with the foundation of modern industrial nations whose initial medieval emergence was in most cases brought about by Christianity. In taking over education from the Church, the State has inherited and retained many of the characteristics of Christian schooling, a system which resulted from a close collaboration, an acquiescence to its presence on the part of the converted ruler.

It is possible to distinguish between three types of education provided by the Church:

a) **Firstly**, education for the good of the soul (eg. catechism); that is to say, schooling exclusively designed to assist salvation with articles of faith and rules of conduct, although from the very outset associated with basic literacy and numeracy. So while the texts were used to strengthen belief, this kind of formal Christian schooling - the first on offer - was inevitably mixed with general educational, non-religious, elements.

b) **Secondly**, education as preparation for secular administrative service in the converted society in which the Church was either all powerful or was allowed to hold power by a secular ruler, whose ancestors, in fact, may have been invited to rule by the Church.2 This form of education is ostensibly less overtly concerned with spiritual matters, though elements of these would be imparted in religious

3

Christianity and Education

denominational instruction lessons. It provides the basic skills and knowledge required for the organisation and administration of society within a Christian ambience.

c) Thirdly, education for the priesthood, historically the first consideration but in varying degrees including elements of the second form as well as subsuming the first. This form of education is important in that the output of its seminaries replenishes the stock of clergy and thereby maintains institutionalised Christianity.

Each of these forms of Christian education has influenced the others, to different degrees at different times. The first type was the widest in availability and the simplest in structure. But with increasing sophistication of society and the fragmentation of denominations, it inevitably became more complex over time, encroaching on the second type or being taken over by denominational schools. The third form, the training of priests, would also seem to be straightforward with a long tradition of content and style, not to mention enviably clear objectives. Yet this too has had to accommodate a rapid and wide-ranging social change in the modern context. With the general level of education rising, the priests, to function, had to become better schooled themselves - that is to say in the second form above, but also in doctrine, so as to be able to take part in theological dispute. Indeed, it can be difficult at times to distinguish between the interests and influence of the secular State and the spiritual requirements of the Church, so closely connected were the various strands of European Christianity with the rise and nature of the nation States and their emergent systems of education.

Each of the three types may or may not include the provision of formal schooling. Though catechist education might proceed in the least formal educational environment, it could after all be given by parents at home or obtained by attending religious services, missionary education seen as a religious cult could be made to require a respectful stance by pupils learning and attending it. Mass secular education too would be possible in an informal setting, though the teaching of skills to a disciplined workforce could also require a 'school'. The selective schools of the second type certainly developed a sophisticated structure earliest and their teachers had received the longest professional preparation; while theological seminaries increasingly tended to assume a formal aspect for the education of peasant entrants who had to be initiated into both an academic and hierarchical religious routine. Indeed, the second and third types have, with the course of time, terminated with the attainment of certificated achievements and exhibit thereby, as well as through their selective entry, a formal and often elitist stamp.

In general, the 'mode three' described above provided a legacy of bookish, male dominated models of schooling with a selective intake. The forms of elitism varied, however. In predominantly Catholic states, for example France, 'state elitism' operated in that the Church was close to the state and strongly associated with selection of pupils for secondary schooling on behalf of the community at large. The Anglican Church, founded by a monarch, remained tied to the aristocracy in England and later, the establishment, operating a dual system of private boarding schools for the elite and mass education at primary level. This has been termed 'private elitism'. The Protestant churches of Scandinavia and northern Europe developed a 'popular elitism' in that although selective, a wide range of population had, and still has, some chance of selection.

In all denominations, the establishment of second type secondary institutions which developed with the stronger position of the Church in the country was a higher priority than that of mass elementary education, and the curriculum that emerged provided the structure of knowledge as well as the standards of entry towards which all education was directed. Thus, the curriculum of all three types of education would include a strong denominational component, not just of formal catechist activities but the moral, ethical and philosophical systems of the Church especially in the third type, which increased with the rise of an educated clerical graduate class who could advise the ruler of the day on secular and spiritual matters.

Administrative, legal, computing, linguistic and similar subjects would be dominated by the Church's world view. Details emerge clearly in a comparison of the Polish Commission of National Education's secular syllabuses with those of the earliest Piarist schools. Elementary local education was concerned with useful vocational (agricultural, craft), military and civic skills in all the countries. A variegated curriculum offered in the secondary school was important when the Church established a network of schools serving the State administration.

When the schools became secularised, countries which first developed a State-supported system, eg. Prussia, operated 'education for military and commercial purposes' or the 'three R's' as in England; while the religious components decreased. Therefore, the Church made efforts to re-establish influence in denominational church or partly state-supported schools, which in some cases in this century has been described as trouble fomenting (in Northern Ireland), giving rise to moves for a secular syllabus to which all Churches together could agree, as in Scotland in the late 1980s.

Through their elitist schools, the various denominations played significant political roles in the emergence of, and relationships between, the distinct nation states of Europe. They have had, too, distinctive pedagogical effects on school styles and traditions, though the Church is not necessarily directly involved in the secular curriculum. When expedient, it adapted according to the requirements, not least as the denominational churches themselves adapted.3

Some denominations in some countries would be more concerned with developing secondary education, others concentrated more on mass education, like the Protestant sects in south-west Germany or the churches in England and Wales in the nineteenth century.

However, Church/State relationships over education have always been sensitive and sometimes extremely acrimonious as both parties are aware of

the significance of controlling public knowledge.
All three types of education mentioned above aim at preserving the status quo in society. They do, therefore, keep the body of knowledge taught reproducing the values the society has been built on, and therefore on which the schools were founded. The civic knowledge and skills included in the curriculum of Church controlled or influenced schools would tend, at least in the formative period, to be conservative. For example, the medieval Church schools taught a pre-Copernican astronomical/ geographical system long after it had been disproved. Such an approach has consolidated and confirmed the power of the Church through maintaining known traditions and limitations in respect of syllabus and discipline Those receiving an education are socialised into society as it is. The Church and education are seen as part of the same type of superstructure.4 The State may go along with this approach - often the State itself is a compliant product of the Church - or it may decide to wrest power over education from the Church. If the Church is successfully challenged, the educational outcome may well be equally conservative but legitimised by a secular ideology rather than by a religious monopoly,5 that is to say not shared by the entire population as the medieval Church had been. Once more, however, the new provider provides its own intellectuals. In the field of science education, school syllabuses have been shown to lag behind new scientific developments.6 In the maintenance of customary curricula indeed, the two agents State and Church may come together. For example, in respect of the teaching of religion in schools during and after the Industrial Revolution, the policy could be interpreted as the bourgeoisie's use of the Christian tradition in an effort to contain the rising working class.

The State would intervene, too, in the event of a fragmentation of power over schooling as between a number of denominations. The object would be to replace a potentially disruptive variety with a new orthodoxy and maintain control over what is deemed to be legitimate knowledge. Fundamental sects since early on in the Church's history have tried to re-establish a Church world view by introducing literal interpretations of the Bible or banning certain scientific cosmogonies; their believers made out to be a chosen elite destined to proselytise.

A number of approaches are possible, from neutrality and co-existence, mutual toleration, to dictatorial anti-clerical or anti-church systems, even to the point of complete secularisation. The trend has, in fact, been in favour of the secular State, at least in Christian societies, concerned to control the second category of schooling outlined above. The Church may still be left with power over types one and three. But in its most extreme form, such as in the Soviet Union, the Church may be denied the right to provide any religious education at all, though vestigial forms may linger on even there. This is because the three types are never completely self-contained; indeed a religious education received through church services may propagate 'innovative' secular nationalistic elements as in occupied Poland, though in situations of constraint at the hands of the State, perhaps precisely then, the hierarchies of Christian Churches tend to be conservative in order to preserve their position of influence. The religious establishment, with its longstanding links with the political establishment does not for example support liberation theology movements which, by definition, seek change. It may be that the Church does not wish to alienate a population or section of a population that is conservative in religious terms, even though disadvantaged, as in parts of Latin America. Or it may be that the political establishment has succeeded in using a Church to maintain it in power, as in South Africa. Different denominations have different policies in this respect, indeed the same denomination may use different policies locally as the Catholics in South America. This may affect their relations with the Vatican as seen during the 1987 visit of the Pope to Chile and Argentina. Another illustration of this contrast would be the relationship between Church and State in El Salvador and Nicaragua in recent years. Whereas in the former, the Archbishop was murdered during Mass in his own cathedral, in the latter Catholic priests occupy ministerial posts in the government.

Christianity and Education

There are usually less extreme circumstances, as represented by several examples in this volume, where some sort of modus vivendi has been reached between Church and State over education. By accepting certain regulations and restrictions the various denominations may maintain a degree of influence through schooling and teacher education, even universities. In present-day secular states, the Church's position is always dependent on the acquiescence of the State. Should the Church-controlled elements of a national system challenge the conventions by introducing radical denominational curricula, the Church's remaining power over schooling would most likely be abrogated. In fact, the 'nationalisation' of schools in the more authoritarian governments, as in Zaire, has done exactly that.

So there is a dilemma here for Christian providers of schooling wishing, for example, to support greater awareness of Third World deprivation and by doing so incurring the displeasure of a State intent on maintaining Third World dependence for the benefit of an advanced economy. Having lost influence over schooling, as in communist states, the Church carefully seeks a way back, a move often facilitated by the secular rulers, who, as Castro in Cuba recently, seek to harness the influence of the Church as a resource in their own policies. Thus, the religious element in education obtains a reprieve.

In periods of Church ascendancy, it was the Church which would block secular innovations by the State through its control of the second type of educational provision. In modern Christian societies, this is not likely to be found often though there are religious enclaves of the fundamentalist variety where the secular State has limited entry. In some versions of Islam, the State and Church have coincided even more closely. Nonetheless, the historical role of the Christian Church in the development of European nations' political structures and education systems, makes the Christian tradition a powerful agent shaping cultural and national identity. Through its continued support of prestigious components of the education system, such as many of the independent schools in England, the Church continues to exert some indirect influence in social terms though the purely religious ethos in them has declined. This factor is also evident at the present time in France and much of Latin America, though the religious factor there is stronger. In direct support of the State and its government in this respect much depends on whether the Church initiates or follows in the potentially fluid relationship between it and the State. When the State needed the capacity of the Church to absorb a significant part of the cost of educational provision, then the latter was in a relatively strong position. This does not mean, however, that the Church necessarily used such power in any radical or even liberal way. The Irish Republic is a case in point. Indeed, education can make an indirect, at times direct, contribution to the maintenance of authoritarian systems of government, eg. in Franco's Spain.7 As against that, the social policies of the Church of England in the 1980s are ahead of those of the State. According to Luckman, Christianity can only exist in a community.8 This is a situation which schooling can help to maintain. Recently the majority of the Church has been in the process of relinquishing its educational rights to the State (the number of Church of England schools has been declining), though, as in the U.S.A., the minority denominations have been encroaching and gaining power vis-a-vis the State.

Viewed historically, we may construct a typology of Church/State relations in respect of education. At one extreme would be a situation of unity where the Church is the State. The coincidence of civil and religious authority in the person of the rulers of some medieval German states, and also the County Palatine between England and Scotland, did represent a merger of Church and State that went beyond mere accommodation. In certain non-Christian religions, this may operate once more. At the other extreme, there are purely secular states where Church influence has been abolished as in the U.S.S.R. In between, there are various intermediate stages exhibiting a degree of tension between religious and civil power in Europe, and in its extensions overseas, that range from moderate to extreme.

This volume discusses the impact of Christianity

on education in respect of the second type of education, though the encroachment of the first is seen in some places through the action of fundamentalist groups. Some chapters are predominantly historical studies that illustrate the complicated relationships between Church and State, of which the pattern of educational control is some sort of index fluctuating within the range of the suggested typology. However, all trace developments in their countries to the present day. The same denomination can, of course, be very differently represented as between one country and another, and this contrast is well illustrated in the chapters on England and Chile in respect of the Roman Catholic Church. In the former, though a minority, it occupies an outspoken pro-education position, a situation also seen in the chapter on Zaire, though with reference to a Protestant group. In both cases, the cause and position of the denomination is strongly related to formal education. The chapter on the Commonwealth Caribbean is also historical, and explains the background to the colonial powers' denominational pattern that accounts for the present situation.

The majority of the contributions concentrate on contemporary examples, though with significant historical analysis, and their current implications for schooling. These range from the dominant role of the Church in the Irish Republic to its deliberate removal from that position of official influence in Poland, and with a variety of patterns in between.

With respect to the legacies of European colonialism in this regard, there is also an infinite variety of Church/State relations in education. It is possible to contrast the formative role of minority sects in the British settlement of North America with the role of monolithic Christian missions in the European colonisation of Africa and Latin America. The Caribbean represents a half-way house. In the former, the link between the colonising Church and the civil power was not a major influence whereas in the latter the colonisation was a collaborative effort between the major denomination and the respective States. This difference has obviously had its effect on the historical and contemporary patterns of educational provision, culminating in current regulations and operations. The cases of the U.S.A. and the West Indies exemplify this contrast, but that of the Kimbanguists of Zaire illustrates the capacity of a minority denomination to gain disproportionate political influence through the relative strength of its school system.

In attempting to place our chapters on the spectrum of Church/State relations in education alluded to above, we find a mosaic rather than a broad band. While certain traditions are clearly maintained and represented, they interrelate differently in each case. In the Protestant/British or British-derived examples, the secular party is clearly the main provider of education in what are described as 'broad' Protestant schools in the U.S.A., with the Church being allowed, traditionally, to maintain its presence by certain agreements: religious lessons in maintained schools in the United Kingdom or partly supported or entirely private Church schools of various kinds. The major denominations have not sought to increase their share of provision. The influence of Protestant minority groups or non-Protestant denominations has been strong however, and their share of education has been growing: Roman Catholic schools in England, fundamental sects in the U.S.A.

In the Catholic examples there is a stronger, distinctive Church presence, with crucifixes in schools, unless there is separation of Church and State. Other denominations are represented but with a lower profile, as in Chile. However, throughout the Catholic world, schools too would be secular, with religious education available, indeed often compulsory, but taught separately by priests or increasingly assuming a 'social science' syllabus outlook. However, the separation of Church and State can leave the Church in different positions of influence, if one compares France with Poland or Germany. On the other hand, the Catholic Church is often likely to be identified with State politics, especially in parts of Latin America, or the State with the Church as in the Republic of Ireland.

None of the chapters in the volume attempts a detailed examination of the school syllabuses of the subject of religious instruction. What is shown are the different forms religious education by agreement can assume, from doctrinal instruction by clergy, to general socio-moral education provided in ecumenical sets with lay teachers, and its scale. After the age of 14 or earlier in some cases, students may opt out of the subject, sometimes parental permission is needed, as in Federal Germany. The move led by the State seeking to reconcile or rationalise provision towards a broadly non-denominational religious instruction in which all Christians and other students can take part is gaining ground. In several countries, as in Scotland or in Poland, courses of 'study of religion', moral and personal education too, for example in the Federal Republic of Germany, are found the curriculum emphasising the social and spiritual areas of students' experience. However, in all countries discussed in this volume, denominational religious instruction is available in establishments of the first type, on church premises or catechist points. Such education is not compulsory, of course, and school students cannot be compelled to attend by the threat of the application of the usual sanctions against truants or their parents. In some fundamentalist Christian sects, these moral pressures are applied by the community, eg. the Amish, without State support. Where the Church and State do work closely together, as in the case of the Dutch Reformed Church and the National Party in South Africa, religious and civic education are both taught with the syllabuses showing a degree of overlap, the agreed civics teaching social, moral and spiritual syllabuses mutually supporting each other. Specifically, Christian elements are absent in the syllabuses of the 'nationalised' Zaire schools. On the other hand, the Church's continuing influence in some communist countries is due in no small measure to the social dimension of its doctrinal instruction syllabus, as taught in establishments of the first and third type. Here and in the few remaining denominational schools, as in Hungary, teachers have to be rather circumspect in their treatment of social and moral problems. The experience of PAX in Poland illustrates the situation. In the West, interpretations of the curriculum are more diverse.

Each country represents its own distinctive

contribution to the mosaic of collaboration/co-existence. Christian religious schools can be available for purely prestigious or generally 'superior' upbringing, which usually leads to socio-political advancement. The public schools in the United Kingdom perform that function. The rapid growth of Steinerian anthroposophic schools in Federal Germany, where the private sector has never enjoyed the prestige of its British counterpart, may lead to this too. The U.S.A. chapter also provides interesting material in this respect. Purely denominational religious education may seem less important, especially in Protestant countries, though there is no doubt that a subtle Christian education takes place in 'general' religion or study of religion lessons. However, the results may be counter-productive on occasion.

The number of 'non-believers' or indifferent Christians among school leavers is on the increase. This is more noticeable in the Catholic Christian societies usually considered to be more religious, in Poland or Germany. If therefore the State in the examples given in this volume has been at least tolerant of the Church's influence on education, this may be partly because the end product of such schools in recent years has rarely turned out to be so religious as to be anti-State. However, this result is not impossible, and it is now the secular State's turn to determine the limits of tolerance where there is separation from or distrust of the other party. The State can be generous. Even in the U.S.S.R. there has recently been a minimal abatement of the atheistic and anti-religious education programmes.

The present volume does not attempt to provide detailed statistical information of religious education. Rather, as a continuation of the editors' previous work, <u>Cultural Identity and Educational Policy</u>,9 it examines the relationship between the parties' policies which has led to the continuing provision of religious education within specific religious education identity patterns in each of the case studies presented. This identity includes the ecclesiastical party's own plans in respect of the simple question of the introduction and desirability of religious education and a plea for it, but extends to something more than mechanical instruction in doctrine and literacy, affecting the whole socio-political reality of society. The question of freedom of manoeuvre to produce a legitimation to the Church's continuing claims to the right to provide such education is a complex one.

Issues relevant to the country in which they occur at the moment may, of course, in the ever narrowing ecumenical world, appear in the other countries too, at different times, in different forms and scales of dimension. How denominational is the English agreed syllabus and why do the Catholics clamour for their own schools? One denomination may grow at the cost of another and its world view spread with it. How successful Christianity is in respect of legitimising its own presence in schooling is a question which assumes particular importance with the ascendancy of non-Christian religion in the traditionally Christian sphere of influence.

The order in which the chapters appear in this volume represents neither an order of merit nor importance. Nor does it reflect the typology suggested, since there is no Soviet chapter in the book, nor one reflecting the extreme fundamentalist position, which cannot co-exist with the State. These would have required chapters on the secular State on the one hand and the theocratic type of society, intolerant of the State, on the other hand. The eleven chapters in the volume are case studies deliberately chosen to show the range and dimension of tensions, characteristic of Church and State relations, between the extremes suggested. Though some societies are more in favour of religious upbringing and education than others, this is counterbalanced by the critical assessment of the results of such policy by either Church of State, or indeed both. In this respect the chapters are self-contained and unique. However, the possibility of some situations capable of being replicated in other countries in the right conditions exists. Though the Church's initiative in bringing them about on the whole is reactive rather than active, in some circumstances, in parts of the British Isles (N. Ireland) as well as in more exotic areas (Zaire), it has shown signs of vigour with varying results for society at large. In at least one extreme case, South Africa, the close link between religious and civic state upbringing is worth noting as a deterrent.

NOTES AND REFERENCES

1. Compayre, Gabriel, The History of Pedagogy, London: Swan Sounenschein & Co., 1904.

2. The Pope presented the Polish King, Boleslaco, with the gift of a royal crown signifying the Pope's approval of a new Catholic ruler. Similar gifts have been recorded to other kings and emperors; cf. the colourful accounts of Charlemagne's relationship with the Pope.

3. Hans, Nicholas, Comparative Education, London: Routledge and Kegan Paul, 3rd edn, 1964.

4. Gramsci, A., The Modern Prince, London: Lawrence and Wishart, 1947.

5. Berger, Peter L. and Luckman, Thomas, The Social Construction of Reality, London: Allen Lane, 1967.

6. This is no longer concerned with the Church, but symptomatic of the education system as a whole. See Turner, Ken, in Bentley, D. and Watts, M. (eds), Practical Alternative, Open University, 1987.

7. Miclescu, Maria, Die Spanische Universitat in Geschichte und Gegenwart, Koln-Wien: Bohlau, 1985.

8. Luckman, Thomas, The Invisible Religion: The Problem of Religion in Modern Society, London: Collier Macmillan Ltd., 1970.

9. Brock, Colin and Tulasiewicz, Witold (eds), Cultural Identity and Educational Policy, London: Croom Helm, 1985.

2

CHRISTIANITY AND EDUCATIONAL PROVISION IN SCOTLAND

Ian Findlay

INTRODUCTION

It is perhaps best at the outset to assert that Scotland does indeed, even today, have a strongly and separately recognizable, in fact <u>distinctive</u> cultural and religious identity, despite the perception of most of the rest of the world to the contrary. That the average American uses the term 'England' when meaning in reality the United Kingdom, stems from nearly three centuries of political unification of a number of nations within the United Kingdom. Scotland, which constitutes the northern third of the Great Britain land mass, is relatively imperceptible in cultural, religious and educational terms to the world at large, since in the media, foreign policy, cultural exchange and similar contacts British culture is represented in terms of the component culture of the heavily populated southern neighbour. That there is a different established church, a totally separate legal system and a very largely independent machinery of education, not to mention customs, habits - all of these things are not generally known to most uninitiated visitors to the country. They are in fact the result of the 1707 Act of Union which created the dual Kingdom. All the institutions mentioned existed before that Act, and had done so for some 150 years, many of the customs for much longer. The institutions were guaranteed a separate existence after 1707, this continues until the present day in return for Scottish agreement to the loss of the formerly existing Scottish Parliament and its merger with the Westminster assembly in

London. That church, law and education continue to be different 'north of the Border' arguably constitutes a basis for a confident assertion that Scotland is a "nation within a political union" and maintains even in the twentieth century its own 'personality'. Anyone who studies Scottish history, or music, or the Gaelic language or 'old Scots' dialect would confirm the many other facets to this separate cultural claim. This chapter will attempt an analysis of how this situation emerged, with special reference to the religious component and trace how it has remained and yet changed in centuries past.

THE PRE-1872 EVOLUTION

The intention in this section is to give brief coverage of earlier centuries of Scottish evolution and to take 1872 as a kind of watershed, since it was the year in which state control replaced church provision of education, though by no means eliminating church concern and interest.
    It is conventional practice in such an historical survey to take the arrival of St. Columba in the island of Iona in 563 AD as the beginning of at least traceable religious involvement in Scottish education. Immediately, a point of continuity can be drawn to attention, in that Iona in the twentieth century has again emerged as a centre of religious involvement in the social, industrial and general aspects of Scottish life.1 During the following six hundred years or so, the educational influence of this Celtic church extended throughout Scotland, and indeed internationally to England, Ireland and Scandinavia.
    From the twelfth to sixteenth centuries, the Roman Catholic church became the dominant and substitute form of Christian influence. Crucially, it brought with it forms of diocesan and parish organization, which in turn laid a foundation for the post-Reformation "school in every parish" ideal (at least in Lowland as opposed to Highland areas) so very characteristic of sixteenth to nineteenth century school Protestant provision. By 1500 there had evolved a network of cathedral schools, abbey

Denominational Scotland

schools, collegiate schools, parish schools and 'song schools' for choristers. Most towns in Scotland had all of these by then, and many of these religious foundations became some of the longer-standing grammar schools, as distinct from later 'burgh' schools.2 As far as university education is concerned, from late twelfth to early fifteenth centuries, Scots went south to Oxford and southeast to Paris, Bologna and elsewhere. But in the space of the fifteenth century, three of the 'traditional' four Scottish universities were founded by religious agency. Edinburgh by contrast in the sixteenth century was a town initiative.

However it was the Protestant Reformation of the second half of the sixteenth century in Scotland which was the powerhouse of the tradition, philosophy, practice and provision of the ensuing three centuries. It is indeed arguable that elements of this tradition have had a continuing influence within the last century of state education - in the 'immediate geographic availability' of schooling or the reasonably widespread acceptance even now, of a 'religious dimension' to curriculum in the shape of an assessable subject of Religious Education,3 the latter having gone through varying states of strength until the 'new deal' described below in the 1980s.

The "First Book of Discipline" of the Scottish Reformers in 1560 set forth a blueprint for a national Scottish system of education. Legislation of the Scottish Parliament (before 1707), and later Acts passed in London for Scotland can be seen simply as 'fleshing out the skeleton'. In contrast no such systematic planning characterizes the contemporary English scene.

Some idea of the system proposed in 1560 may begin to indicate the style and ethos, which has conditioned tradition until very recently. The pattern suggested was:

Age 5-8: elementary schools in country parishes, with the twin basic aims of 'literacy and godliness':

Age 8-12: grammar schools in 'towns of any repute' for the teaching of Latin grammar:

Age 12-16: high schools (or colleges) 'in important towns' (possibly diocesan centres under the previous dispensation for Latin, Greek, logic and rhetoric):4

Age 16-19: a three year Arts course at university:

Age 19-24: a five year medicine, law or divinity course as the ultimate professional preparation also in the university.5

This system was essentially a ladder available to talent, an open door, and not a suggestion that somehow all should attain to the ultimate. It had the clearly stated aim of the moral good of the individual and his (not 'her' in the sixteenth century!) service to the community. The type of talent in mind was of course academic talent only, but it aimed, it must be said in its favour, at all classes with no rich/poor distinction whatever. This has been described by at least one Scottish educational historian as a tradition of 'democratic meritocracy'!6 It might be noted in passing that the university in the sixteenth-century scheme of things was seen as providing both 'general upper secondary' education as well as the more usual and expected postsecondary professional/vocational preparation.

This arguably created the cultural frame of reference, common psychological consensus and value system which has dominated Scottish education for four centuries, and which is now undergoing significant change in the late twentieth century. It established deep in the Scottish psyche the involvement of the church in education. It enthroned academic and intellectual standards as paramount (later perhaps 'of higher status' would be a fairer estimate) in education at the expense of the practical, the aesthetic, the technical domestic or physical. It tended to exalt selection hurdles at the expense of encouragement to limits of potential. In ensuing centuries, it made possible numerous rags-to-riches examples of poor boys from humble beginnings 'making it' to the top echelons of national and international life (by a testing, self-sacrificial academic path of course!). The 'lad o' pairts' (boy of talent) is a revered figure of semi-mythology in any reputable history of Scottish education. No doubt social historians could show in detail that the class composition of Scottish society, with a much lesser social distance than in England between aristocracy and peasantry, made such a process a widespread social phenomenon north of the Border.

We refer to the bibliography7 for greater detail, suffice it to say that, throughout the seventeenth, eighteenth and early nineteenth centuries, this 'parish system', if one may describe it thus in shorthand, spread in the way that the Reformers had intended. It was supplemented in the early 1700s by private provision, but the advance of the eighteenth century - especially after the Jacobite-Catholic cause was defeated in 1745 and with the rapid development of industrialization, urbanization and shift of population in the last quarter of that century brought about an imbalance of geographical availability of schools and a need for rationalization. This was attempted in an Act of Parliament: a Westminster Act for Scotland in 1803.8

In the nineteenth century some major developments contributed to further educational change. Firstly the 1803 Act dealt to some extent with teachers' salaries, restated in detail the control of the Presbyterian Church of Scotland over teacher appointments and provided for the spread of parish schools into areas of need. It heralded a period of seventy years of struggle between Church and secular sources of school financing, culminating in state take-over of schools in 1872.9 In 1843 a huge 'Disruption' within the Church of Scotland,10 produced two energetic churches whose provision of schools competed and proliferated in the last period of frenetic activity before final state entry in 1872. In the same period the Scottish Episcopal Church expanded its own, relatively minor, school provision for the children of those who belonged to a 'branching church tradition' which one hundred and fifty years before had been forced to yield establishment status to the Presbyterians.11 In the late seventeenth century, presbyterianism became the form of worship in the established Church of Scotland, as against its alternative, Episcopalianism. Irish immigration in the same period, motivated by work in industrially expanding Scotland, introduced a large Roman Catholic segment into the population. As this church grew it provided its own schools - a sector which became of considerable size, although remaining a minority.12 Intensifying sectarian bitterness in some areas - especially west and southwest - ensured the continuing separation of provision, although this was an inevitable consequence of the genuine desire for religious freedom in such schools. In 1867, a national Commission revealed a veritable kaleidoscope of denominational provision. This included among others 519 Church of Scotland schools, 617 Free Church of Scotland schools, 74 Scottish Episcopal schools and 61 Roman Catholic schools in the country.13

The 1872 Act gave the state full control of all presbyterian schools, while the Roman Catholic and Episcopalian schools remained staunchly separate until a further and very major postwar Education (Scotland) Act of 1918.14 But the 1872 Act created almost 1000 School Boards15 on which there continued to be deeply involved presbyterian church representation. Such representation has continued to the present day in the three stages of reorganized local education authorities, viz: a) 1918-1929 *ad hoc* - (ie education-specific) local/county level authorities; b) 1929-1975 *ad omnia* (multi-purpose) county level authorities and c) post-1975: nine Regional and three Island authorities. On these last mentioned present-day bodies, the Education Committee - responsible within a corporate management structure to a full Regional or Island Council - usually has two or three church representatives, probably covering the full spectrum of Church of Scotland, Roman Catholic and Episcopal churches.

Denominational Scotland

THE RELIGIOUS SETTLEMENT OF THE 1918 ACT

One main historical question remains to be discussed, without which the current situation would be less than comprehensible. In the period from 1872 to 1918, successive educational legislation had placed ever increasing burdens of social and physical welfare commitment upon all schools, and no less on the still separate Catholic and Episcopal schools. The result of this was that in the immediate pre-World War One period, especially after a major Act of 1908,16 the financial crisis was acute for such schools. In the ten ensuing years - with a break of activity during the first part of the war - ca 1914-16, for obvious reasons, but with surprising reintensification during the 1916-18 period, prolonged, detailed, difficult and delicate discussions took place between the 'Scotch' Education Department (after 1918 'Scottish') and the churches. Research carried out in the 1970s shows just how hard the work of finding a satisfactory religious solution in those years was.17 But a solution was found - unique nowadays not only within the United Kingdom but in world terms: a church-state agreement on schooling placing Roman Catholic schools under secular control in all but religious matters. What the agreement did, essentially, was

> a) to transfer the provision of church schools (buildings, curricula, payment of staff) to the control of the state (in the form of the new local authority) and
> b) on the other hand, to guarantee freedom of religious instruction, appointment of teachers, and access by the priest to the school, to supervise religious instruction.
> c) To require education authorities to establish new denominational schools, if necessary.

Since 1918, therefore, Scotland has retained a very large sector of denominational schools within its state system. Initially these were Catholic and Episcopal. However, Episcopal schools have within the last seventy years almost disappeared (in the late 1980s, two Episcopal primary schools remain).

Denominational Scotland

The Catholic Church by contrast has maintained a robust presence within the system both at primary and secondary level - with a predominance towards the west and southwest of the country. In the northeast the presence is small but continuing. To complete the picture, however, it should be mentioned that there are, nevertheless a small handful of (highly prestigious) Catholic private secondary schools in different parts of the country, with a socially 'upward-biased' intake.

In the last seventy years, of course, the situation has changed. The 1980s are relatively blessed with an absence of the sectarian bitterness characteristic of 1918. This in turn raises the question of the future of the Catholic schools within state provision. This may however be better discussed along with other facets of the total contemporary scene.

THE CURRENT SITUATION

It must be emphasized that the denominational schools question is often a bone of contention. In a recent article contributed to the 'Scotsman' some of the issues discussed on these recurrent occasions are usefully highlighted and in fact put in very comprehensible 'nutshell' dimensions. The author, Councillor Brian Meek of Lothian Region, identifies the 1970s as the period in which the 1918 Settlement began to need reform to meet new social conditions. To justify his argument he quotes the following facts:

To follow his argument:

a) the birth rate took a very steep dive, in the Catholic as much as among the general population - despite the Church's traditional stances on contraception - within a climate of economic recession;
b) between 1975 and 1984 Roman Catholic secondary population dropped by 16.5 per cent in comparison to a general secondary drop in the same period of 2.7 per cent;

c) between 1975 and 1984, primary Roman Catholic population dropped by 40.4 per cent in comparison to a general drop of 26.7 per cent.18

He sees therefore considerably "...fewer Catholic children in Scotland altogether, and fewer still in Catholic schools..." and concludes that "some Catholic parents are ignoring the Church's strictures on birth control and others are simply opting to send their children to non-denominational establishments..." The Church's four defensive arguments in reply are: 1) that the schools' intake suffers from shift of population; 2) that local authorities have refused to provide (despite the requirement of the 1918 Act that is) new schools in new housing areas; 3) that the benefits of Catholic education are in a secular world, consistently under-played (some recent research, indeed, did show the value of a Catholic school ethos);19 and 4) evidence is available that birth rates will rise again. They quote figures showing some rise at primary first and second year-level ages.

However, as Meek points out, the huge drop in the primary sector will now immediately hit the secondaries, and this poses a serious problem of the viability of Catholic secondaries in the mid-1990s. One might add that the welter of new demands, from reports on secondary curricula, especially the widening range of 'modular provision' at 14-18,20 will intensify this problem for the Catholic Church. The move of Catholic teachers to non-denominational schools in recent years certainly does not help. Two solutions are suggested: The first, the closure of some Roman Catholic schools and the centralization of other schools; and the second, the integration within secular schools, the latter coupled with a 1918 style 'religious guarantee'; viz: access of clergy, a say in promotions, and an 'input' to the curriculum. Councillor Meek is confident that the second solution, given time, could work if underpinned by a reform of the 1918 Act.

It must be mentioned that a further complicating factor in the Catholic problem is that since 1918, parents in Scotland (as in the rest of the United Kingdom) have the right to choose the school to which they send their children. If the above trend, of Catholic parents choosing secular schools for their children that is, continues, presumably guided by criteria other than religious ones - then the percentage drop will logically accelerate in denominational schools and make the question of their viability as separate institutions acute indeed. Of course a possible change in the late 1980s to a United Kingdom government other than Conservative would probably herald the abolition of the Conservative "Parents' Charter", part of which led to the 1981 Education Act, a return to a school zoning principle, and thus place a check on the haemorrhage from Catholic schools to some extent. Nevertheless the birth rate trend, population shift in a time of high unemployment and lack of funding for local authorities to build too many new schools for 'general' new areas, let alone Catholic populations, would continue to present a complex issue to the Church. It is as much a fact of Scottish socio-political life in the 1980s as in 1918 that the Catholic hierarchy (if not all rank and file Catholics) "fiercely opposes any hint of school closures" to use Councillor Meek's words again.

It could be argued that the time is coming, if it is not already here, for a recasting of the 1918 Settlement in modern terms. If in 1918 state and church could come after much negotiation to a "principled agreement" motivated by the economic circumstances of the first twenty years of the present century, they could again do so, within the context of the last twenty, in suitably modified terms. This implies, within the state sector at any rate, not separate Catholic schools, but a 'protected Catholic presence' within secular schools - or at least a presence in those areas where the number of Catholic children justified such a solution. In such a dispensation, a change would probably take place more quickly in the north and northeast and later in the south and southwest, where most non-Catholics live. It only remains to add that other denominational schools virtually do not exist now in Scotland except for one or two regional Episcopal schools. This solution would, just as in 1918, put Scotland in the vanguard of reform of state/church relations.

However, the problem is rather more complex than this, so that even a modification might not outlast the twentieth century. The reason for this is the fundamentally changed nature of Religious Studies within Scottish state secular schools since ca 1972. Until that time and for the previous hundred years ever since the Education (Scotland) Act of 1872 religious instruction was a protected subject (and still is, in the absence of any expressed public consensus to the contrary) as the only part of the state curriculum required by law. This underlines the point made above about the churches' continued interest in the schools, even after state takeover.

In 1972 and subsequent years, assembling an influential committee and a series of national bulletins on Religious Education and Moral Education provided a response to a general tacit consensus that Religious Instruction in schools had become an undoubted 'disaster area'.21 In the wake of suffering the ministrations of unmotivated non-specialists for the most part, the subject had fallen on very bad days. The Scottish Central Committee on Religious Education (known within Scotland as SCCORE) advocated as the basis of an educational contribution to state secular curriculum by Religious Education - the following five aims:22

> to explore the phenomenon of religion as part of human experience;
> to enable pupils to consider and discuss questions about the nature and meaning of existence and the answers that religions give to these questions;
> to help pupils to understand the nature of commitment within both a religious and a secular setting;
> to help pupils to appreciate the importance of coming to a considered stance;
> to enable pupils to understand the wider social and cultural impact that religions have had.

Immediately, new elements were officially introduced into Scottish Religious Education syllabuses: a) an emphasis on investigation; b) an objective analysis of a variety of religions; c) an acceptance of the co-existence of the religious and secular in society: in the context of the plurality of religions within modern society; all these to be examined in an historical/social/contemporary context approach.23 SCCORE in the later 1970s evolved this rationale further by increasing the emphasis on starting from the individual pupil's current state of awareness and seeing the curricular purpose of Religious Education as part of a general search for meaning and purpose in personal life.

In the 1980s some extremely significant developments of Religious Education as a subject have taken place. Building on the recognition of RE as a subject in its own right within the state secondary sector since 1975 by Regional Authorities, and the simultaneous commitment, yet to be honoured by some Regions, to staffing all secondary schools with at least one specialist, trained teacher of the subject, a committee took up the question of its examinability at national level.24 Scotland was in fact the last constituent nation of the United Kingdom to provide such an examination for school pupils, any Scottish pupils having had to resort to the Newcastle Examination Board and others in England for such an option in the past. The Committee produced an O Grade examination, in Religious Studies available at age 16, in the fourth year of secondary schools, and this has now been an objective for an increasing minority of fourth-year pupils in the last few years. To this has subsequently been added a Higher paper for the more able and motivated fifth-year students. This paper was claimed half-seriously by some25 to be excessively testing and verging upon university level studies. Perhaps this is inevitable in the early days of striving for status for the subject within the secondary school system.

The crucial points for this study, however, are that both these assessment levels are connected with a Religious Education curriculum that is essentially 'multifaith' in its approach. Secondly, the Roman Catholic Church was represented on, and made constructive contribution to, the committee work which produced this national multifaith curriculum. It should be said that the options available in the examinations tend to provide for 'majoring' in Christianity and 'minoring' in another world religion of the student's own choice.26

To indicate even further the direction being taken, Education Council within the context of the new Scotvec National Certificate catalogue package of '16 plus' short, flexible, 40-hour courses initiated in Scotland in 1983, there is a small number of Religious Studies Modules covering such areas as: Religion and World Conflict; Religion in the Local Community; and Ethics. The multifaith/social context and the multicultural approach are clearly visible.27 Some of the latest thinking on these courses asks questions about their 'cross-curricular' links with Music, Drama, the media, and their vocational relevance to work in the caring professions serving a multifaith/multicultural community. And if the message is not yet clear, it will certainly be emphasized by the report directed at Multicultural Education itself - expected in 1987,28 which must inevitably imply an assessment of the contribution that Religious Studies among other curricular areas, can make to preparation for life in a multicultural society.

The reader must forgive this insistence on providing some detail of the evolution (revolution?) in style, direction and objectives of Religious Studies in Scottish schools. The purpose of such a discussion is to show that - whatever the pros and cons of separate Catholic schools, or indeed separate Catholic provision within schools, the classic 'Catholic hierarchy' position on this issue is, in view of the social trends described by Councillor Meek, and the multifaith emphasis outlined above, inevitably going to be exceedingly difficult to justify in years to come. The same must apply of course to any other group likely to ask for separate provision. A recent initiative has been taken by Strathclyde Moslems to have single sex education provision for Moslem girls.

Perhaps the last area of contemporary education to be mentioned in this chapter is what one might call the growth of the secular comprehensive school and the churches reaction to it. Here the historical context is the period from the mid-1960s to the present day. In that time three other significant movements have paralleled the confessional religious instruction and the resurgence of Religious Education in the curriculum as an examinable subject. The new movements may be listed as follows:

> a) guidance and counselling have evolved from small beginnings in the late 1960s to a much more sophisticated pastoral care system involving training and careful deployment of teaching personnel in the provision of pastoral, and increasingly individualized care for students;
> b) social and moral education have been the subject of recurrent initiatives in the period, reaching now the position where most secondary schools have a planned programme of Social Education - covering personal/social development, sex education, drugs education, alcohol abuse and others. Some of this education verges towards education for international understanding and multicultural education;
> c) student Personal and Social Development as part of the curriculum has been a topic of concern in reports on primary, secondary first, second, third, fourth, fifth and sixth year levels with a growing discussion in that context of "aspirations and values", "life skills", "spiritual development" and the like.29

All the major churches (Church of Scotland, Catholic Church and Scottish Episcopal Church) have national and local diocesan committees on education, which in the 1980s are showing distinct signs of ceasing to concern themselves exclusively with Sunday Schools, Youth Fellowships, and similar denominational issues - and turning their attention outwards to trends in the secular schools system and society, such as have been listed above. It is not inaccurate to say that there is a growing awareness that areas which might, for shorthand purposes be entitled Values Education are areas of potential partnership between the churches and state education. Increasingly, both school and church are asking the same question namely, "what sort of young people or people generally do we wish to produce for today's/tomorrow's

Denominational Scotland

society?" Questions of unemployment, new forms of employment, the effect of high technology, the changing nature of the 'work ethic', ethical problems posed by medical and scientific advance, the need for caring attitudes in a society with increasing numbers of older people, the trend towards integrating the handicapped, all of this happening within a rapidly changing life and work scene - all of these complex issues are beginning to persuade church and school (with other agencies) of the need to pool their educational resources.

CONCLUSION

Since our main concern in this study is the "religious contribution" factor, the final question is: what part does or will religion play in Scottish society?

It is all too easy for a nation to be perceived in terms of stereotypes by others. In the case of Scotland, the image is perhaps a curious mixture of kilt, haggis, urban deprivation, Red Clydeside and such factors with a semi-mythological awareness that "education is good there", the sabbath is strict, the law is 'somehow' different north of the Border. All this is generated, one supposes, by a combination of English 'distance', American films, and the sanitization of the awful realities of the eighteenth century Highlands via Sir Walter Scott in the nineteenth century into a twentieth-century myth (outside Scotland at least) of 'romantic Scotland'.

In fact Scotland in the late twentieth century is a society which - taken nationally - shares in proportion with Western Europe a secularism of a 'post-Christian' kind: has seen a decline of heavy industry and its replacement by both 'glens' of high technology and more than its share of United Kingdom unemployment with established churches striving to retain credibility in educational, social, and cultural terms: a central region moving more and more to the kind of multiethnic population found throughout England: a northern area which has suffered the culture shock of boom and recession generated by oil: a cultural revival, despite economic recession, of the Gaelic language in the Western Isles since 1975.

It is within this social mix that the new Religious Education syllabus makes sense. Such provision has not yet had time to prove itself in the few years of its existence, but if recent moves by Strathclyde Region to increase awareness in its police and fire service of the ethnic minorities are any indication of the future, such a syllabus may indeed have more impact.

It would not really be correct in the 1980s to say the Scots are a 'religious nation'. Church attendance as a statistic has dwindled as in similar areas elsewhere in the United Kingdom. But it is fair to say that, in the northwest Highlands and Western Isles, there still exist very strong influences, particularly in the Free Church of Scotland, towards the retention of strict sabbatarianism. It would also be true to say that there also still remain in many areas individual congregations of all denominations well known far and wide for their lively and active and relevant Christian outreach - often, significantly, attracting students 'like flies'. Within education also there has been some growth of a healthy 'Christian values' philosophy, such as the Association of Christian Teachers, Scotland. To sum up: Scotland is a generally secular nation with a 'religious northwest' a still respected, largely fossilized but here and there very live, church establishment. This is turn means the shifting of influence upon the child from the once paramount Church - in a majority of cases - to the school and its guidance and other subsystems. However, official reports on education are stressing increasingly the need for a partnership between parents and school in the education of the child.

This chapter discussed the half fact, half mythology of Scottish educational standards as "high and respected around the world". To achieve such 'high standards' in the late twentieth century (and the twenty-first) must involve a discussion among all interested parties, religious and secular alike, about the kind of values, persons, responsible decisions, spiritual development and a faith of stance for living. Such discussions are taking place as has been shown. Their successful outcome will depend on whether the churches will retreat into a kind of spiritual ghetto, or grasp the opportunity to use their spiritual insights to share with the schools in fostering the fullest development of individuals - within the range of openings being provided by state curricular trends. One hopes it will be the latter.

NOTES AND REFERENCES

1. Iona Abbey has been renowned over the last half century as a place of worship, and in the postwar period, the Iona Community, the brainchild of Rev. George McLeod has been developed as a centre for ecumenical worship, peace and reconciliation, and the relinkage of the Church generally with the "real world of industry, leisure and people in the mass".

2. Burgh schools in the Scottish context are schools of longstanding tradition supported by the Scottish city and town councils (for example, the Royal High School of Edinburgh).

3. Generally speaking, the SCCORE REPORTS (see n.22) following the Millar Report (see n.21), created a climate in which in the 1980s it proved possible to create an O Grade examination in Religious Education - since followed by a Higher Grade. The subject can also be 'inspected' by Her Majesty's Inspectors.

4. Since there was not a total destruction of old style Roman Catholic education in 1560, some of the earlier provision was adapted to fit the new Protestant system.

5. Taken from Scotland, J. *History of Scottish Education*, University of London Press, 1969, vol. I, p. 45.

6. Davie, G.E. *The Democratic Intellect*, London: English Universities Press, 1961.

7. Scotland, J., op. cit., vol. I, 1969.

Knox, H.M. *Two Hundred and Fifty Years of Scottish Education 1696-1946*, Oliver and Boyd, 1953.
Morgan, A. *Rise and Progress of Scottish Education*, Oliver and Boyd, 1927.

8. Education Act of 1803 ('An Act for making better provision for the Parochial Schoolmasters, and for making further regulations for the better Government of the Parish Schools in Scotland') - consult ED Records, Scottish Record Office, West Register House, Edinburgh.
National Library of Scotland ED Records Public Record Office, London ED Records Public Record Office, Hertfordshire for availability.

9. Education (Scotland) Act 1872.

10. The 'Disruption' in 1843 of the established Church of Scotland into a smaller established Church of Scotland and the new Free Church of Scotland took place over deeply felt issues of ability or inability to subscribe to confessional statements. As a result in many communities, there was schism into two church congregations and two schools, often physically quite near to each other.

11. This refers to 1690, when after thirty bitter years of post-Restoration religious strife and bloodshed in Scotland, Presbyterianism eventually triumphed over Episcopalianism as the form of government of the Established Church of Scotland.

12. Cf. n. 13, below.

13. Report of Argyll Commission 1867. See Scotland, op. cit., vols 1 and 2, for detail.

14. The 1918 Act - among many other major initiatives affecting Scottish education until the present day - created an internationally unusual situation as regards denominational schools. It effectively made these schools state schools, while setting apart certain important privileges and rights such as Church decision on Religious Instruction within them, the access of the priest to give

instruction, and the appointment of staff; Brother, Rev. Kenneth, The Education (Scotland) Act, 1918 in the making, Innes Review 19, 1968.

15. The School Board pattern of the 1872 Act was closely, but not exclusively geared to the existing Church of Scotland parish structure. By 1918 this form of control was felt to be parochial in the 'attitudinal' sense, affecting social conditions - as well as modernization of travel - produced the possibility of a larger unit. The ad hoc nature of 'county level control' is indicative of the importance attached by society and church to education as a special issue, so much so that a more rationalized form of integrated public service was held off until 1929. The Regions of 1975 are merely a continuation of the 1929 view, but in larger and more management-integrated units.
    Scotland, J. The Centenary of the Education (Scotland) Act 1872, British Journal of Educational Studies, 20, 6, 1972.

16. The Act of 1908 was crucial in that it imposed much more of a physical and social welfare burden on the school system (in the light of major examinations of the physical fitness of the nation at the time of the Boer War in 1902). This meant that, for the religious schools, the financial writing was then on the wall.
    Smith, J. The Church and her place in Education, Edinburgh and London: Blackwood, 1822.

17. Findlay, I.R. 'Sir John Struthers, KCB, Secretary of the Scotch/Scottish Education Department 1904 - 22 Doctoral Thesis, University of Dundee, 1979. See chapters on the negotiations leading to the settlement of 1918, of which Struthers was the architect.

18. Meek, Brian, 'Two Choices for Catholic Education', 'Scotsman', Edinburgh, 23 June 1986 - reference made with Meek's permission.

19. Macpherson, Andrew, 'Certification, Class Conflict, Religion and Community: A Socio-Historical

Explanation of the Effectiveness of Catholic Schools' in Kerckhoff, A. (ed.) <u>Research in Sociology of Education and Socialization,</u> <u>6</u>, 1986, Connecticut and London: JAI Press.

20. The Technical and Vocational Initiative (TVEI) - now spreading through Scotland as through England and Wales - demands resources for 'fleshing out' an increasing range of vocational and personal development courses. Scottish Vocational Education Council (SCOTVEC) courses of a similar nature, which have been aimed at age 16-18 since 1983, will now be extended somewhat to 14-16, thereby increasing the burden.

21. <u>Moral and Religious Education in Scottish Schools</u> (the Millar Report), Edinburgh: HMSO, 1972.

22. Scottish Central Committee on Religious Education (SCCORE), 'Curriculum Guidelines for Religious Education', <u>Bulletin</u> <u>2</u>, Edinburgh: HMSO, 1981, p.3.

23. Both by SCCORE (see n. 22) and by the assumptions since 1981 of ATRES (the Association of Teachers of Religious Education in Scotland), Conferences.

24. Consultative Committee on the Curriculum/Scottish Certificate of Education Examination Board (SCEEB - later SEB): <u>Report of Joint Committee on Syllabus Examinations in Religious Education</u>, Edinburgh: Scottish Education Department, 1981.

25. This refers to no official source, but to the emergent feeling in seminars, discussions and conferences held by ATRES.

26. The options available are, generally speaking, Judaism, Islam, Hinduism, Buddhism and Sikhism.

27. Scotvec National Certificate. Catalogue published by Scotvec, Glasgow.

28. International and Multicultural Education Project. <u>Joint Report: CCC Consultative Committee on the Curriculum and the Scottish Examination Board</u> (unpublished).

29. For details of the movements, see the following reports:
<u>More than Feelings of Concern</u>: Report of the Committee on Guidance, Edinburgh: HMSO, 1986;
<u>Learning and Teaching in the First Two Years of the Scottish Secondary School: Report</u>, Edinburgh: HMSO, 1986.
Macbeth, J., Mearns, D., Rodger, H. and Thomson, B., <u>Social Education - Towards a Definition</u>, Scottish Social Education Project, Jordanhill College of Education, Glasgow, 1981.

3

RELIGIOUS DICHOTOMY AND SCHOOLING IN NORTHERN IRELAND

Margaret Sutherland

Schools in Northern Ireland form a dual system: schools attended mainly by Protestant children and schools attended by Roman Catholic children.1 Inevitably during the present troubles and terrorist activities the question arises whether this school system creates or adds to divisions in the community. There is no easy answer. Education in Northern Ireland shows the complexity of attempts to act on the principles of Christianity, the divisions caused by varying interpretations of Christianity and the involvement of religion with social, political and cultural factors. The study of the segregated school system illustrates this complexity in a fascinating if sometimes depressing way.

EARLY ATTEMPTS TO CREATE COMMON SCHOOLS

Christian principles would suggest that children, irrespective of religious affiliation, should meet together and learn to know and respect those of other denominations. In the nineteenth century, when all Ireland was still under British rule, attempts were made to bring about such 'meeting and learning' by a system of schools attended by children of all religious affiliations. It is important to consider why these and subsequent attempts failed and whether new attempts are likely to be more successful. In the early part of the century, the Society for Promoting the Education of the Poor in Ireland (commonly known as the Kildare Place Society) began to provide schools in which both Catholic and

Protestant children were taught. It adopted the policy of religious teaching by simple reading of the Bible, without commentary. This policy, which has been tried in more than one country, did not prove generally acceptable but the work of the Society, especially in establishing a Model School in Dublin in which teachers could be trained undoubtedly influenced the thinking of the Board of Commissioners of National Education which was set up in 1831. The Board decided to establish a system of Model Schools throughout Ireland,2 to provide exemplary teaching and train teachers: in these schools, the policy was that there should be separate religious instruction of denominational kinds but integration of all religious groups in the other parts of the school curriculum - i.e., a policy of 'combined secular but separate religious education'. Schools transferring to the Board's jurisdiction, to become National Schools, were also to follow this policy. But the principles thus defined failed to retain the support of the Church authorities on either side. Although in the earlier states there was some support from both Catholic and Protestant churchmen (the Presbyterians tended to favour the policy while the Methodists moved from initial disapproval to later acceptance), opposition developed on various counts and in 1863 the Catholic Bishops pronounced the view that the separation of religious and secular education was unacceptable. There were also conflicting views within the Established (Anglican) Church. The withdrawal of Catholic children from various Model Schools made these schools' survival impossible and the Board's provision of new Model Schools ceased, though some of the existing Model Schools continued to flourish for a while and indeed a few, as Protestant, local authority schools, have continued to maintain their proud designation until the present time.

At that point in history, objections to the common school seem to have been based on different denominations' interpretations of what religious education should be and whether secular education was an acceptable policy. Similar controversies were rife in England and other countries at the time. But Ireland was throughout the nineteenth century, as

Dichotomy in Ulster

later, torn by conflicting political aims, some parties supporting the union with Great Britain, others calling for devolution of government and some form of Home Rule.3 These political divisions certainly preceded the development of schooling for all children: whether common schools would gradually have reduced the political tensions is doubtful. At any rate this early attempt to unite children of different religious persuasions in the same school had failed. Schools in Ireland remained, for the most part, clearly denominational in their teaching and in their staff and pupils.

When the Government of Ireland Act of 1920 divided the country into Northern Ireland and Southern Ireland, each having its own parliament but the North remaining part of the United Kingdom and being governed, in some respects, from Westminster, the division of territory inevitably did not separate Catholics and Protestants into two distinct groups. A minority of Protestants lived in the South: a large number of Catholics lived in the North. Hence came continuing problems for education and the potential growth of minority apprehensions for both groups - Protestants perceiving themselves as a minority in Ireland as a whole (if Partition did not continue) and Catholics perceiving themselves as a threatened minority in the North. Certainly in the early years of the new regime Catholic opposition to the establishment of the Northern Ireland government and education system had been made abundantly clear, by various forms of declaration and boycott.4 For some time, some Catholic teachers refused to accept salaries paid by the Northern Ireland Ministry (a move which eventually faded when subsidies from Dublin were no longer made available): some Catholic schools refused to present candidates for external examinations set by the new Northern Ireland Ministry in 1922. Perhaps even more seriously, invitations to have representatives on the Lynn Committee which was set up in 1921 to make proposals for the Northern Ireland education system were refused by Catholic authorities.5

These and other actions no doubt served to convince Protestants in the North of Ireland of Catholic opposition to the new state and may well have stimulated and reinforced their determination to ensure that Protestant children would receive, as staunch citizens of Northern Ireland, a distinctively Protestant education.

A FRUSTRATED ATTEMPT TO ESTABLISH COMMON SCHOOLS

Nevertheless, the Lynn Committee and more especially the Northern Ireland Minister of Education, Lord Londonderry, seem to have hoped for an education which would reconcile and bring together the two religious groups. Under the provisions of the 1923 Education Act, Northern Ireland schools were to be the responsibility of a number of local education authorities who, while providing new schools, could also accept the transfer of schools formerly under church management. For local education authority schools, provided or transferred, it was enacted that the authority must allow opportunity for denominational education in accordance with the wishes of parents and should allow access to the schools by religious teachers at agreed times. However, religious education was not to be <u>provided</u> by the local education authority, i.e., it would not take place as part of the ordinary school timetable and would not be paid for by public funds. Moral education might nevertheless form part of the provided curriculum. There was thus, apparently, some hope by the legislators that the schools might manage to keep religious and secular education separate. Realistically, they could have little hope of producing common schooling in this way. The proposal was clearly unacceptable to Catholics who had proclaimed at a meeting in Dublin in 1921 of Catholic primary school managers that 'the only satisfactory system of education for Catholics is one wherein Catholic children are taught in Catholic schools by Catholic teachers under Catholic auspices.'6 Protestants equally were unwilling to have the religious instruction of their children provided on an optional, voluntary basis. Neither were they content with the Act's other attempt, to have teachers appointed without regard to their religious affiliation. Vehement Protestant agitations during the following decade led to successive amendments to the Act so that legislation in 1930 imposed on local education authorities the duty of providing undenominational Bible instruction if requested to do so by at least ten parents. Teachers were obliged to give this instruction; it was not until 1947 that a conscience clause allowed teachers to opt out. Since this form of provision for religious education was not acceptable for Catholics, Catholic school managers were not willing to transfer their schools. Their interpretation of the situation was that the 1923 Act had been amended to suit the Protestants, and there were some queries as to whether the new provisions contravened the constitutional principle set out in the Government of Ireland Act of 1920 that no religion should be endowed by public funds.[7] Effectively, at any rate, the public/local education authority schools were attended by Protestant pupils, taught by Protestant teachers: hence the practice of referring to them as Protestant schools. Catholic schools remained generally outside the public system and have been provided and managed by Catholic Church authorities with, as we shall later show, increasing financial support from public funds. The 1930 Act did at least empower the Ministry of Education to pay 50 per cent of costs of building, altering, equipping voluntary schools.

Although schools giving what was then described as elementary education thus continued to be divided by religious denomination, schools providing for children with special educational needs were not so divided and have, apparently, avoided sectarian problems. Similarly, institutions giving technical education have been attended by Protestants and Catholics alike. Possibly one finds here a beneficial side-effect of the need to be economical. Where relatively smaller proportions of the population have to be provided for, separate provision becomes unwisely expensive. It may be also that by the age of technical education young people are regarded as already sufficiently well indoctrinated. Given a dual system of education, we find two issues of major concern: (i) do parents incur unfair financial burdens when they choose to send their children to schools providing their preferred education? (ii)

Dichotomy in Ulster

does the existence of the dual system have a pernicious effect in creating divisions within the country as a whole - are children attending separate schools likely to develop attitudes of hostility based on ignorance and stereotyping of those of other denominations? There is also the essential question whether the schools of either type do provide good education. Sometimes the financial burden of voluntary schools is said to militate against good teaching since resources may be inadequate. The real effects of a chosen curriculum are certainly not monitored sufficiently often to let parents and others know whether the intended results are being achieved.

THE FINANCIAL SITUATION OF VOLUNTARY SCHOOLS IN NORTHERN IRELAND

To attempt to estimate the financial burdens cast on parents in Northern Ireland's dual system we have to follow a fairly complicated series of developments. As we have seen, schools attended mainly by Protestant children were, from 1930 onwards, publicly financed. Voluntary schools could receive 50 per cent of capital costs from the Ministry. Further, payment of all teachers' salaries in elementary schools was made by the Ministry. The financial differentiations thus came in the area of additional building and in payment for heating, lighting, cleaning, maintenance, and, later, with regard to national insurance payments by employers and superannuation costs. Now the 1923 Act had provided for a category of voluntary school which could receive further financial aid in meeting such costs. This category was that of the 'four and two committee' school. Such schools accepted a management committee having four members representing the providing church authority and two members representing the local education authority. The school then received from the local authority half the costs of heating, lighting, cleaning, equipment repair, maintenance: and a discretionary capital expenditure grant from that authority. Since representatives of the public authority were clearly in the minority, such committees seemed likely to safeguard the rights of the providing religious authorities: but, for reasons which seem unclear, very few Catholic schools chose to benefit by this arrangement: in the 1960s, of 79 schools under 'four and two committees', only eight were Catholic primary schools.8 Possibly it was suspected by the Church authorities that this was the thin edge of a wedge which would bring in, eventually, interference in the religious teaching of the school and even desegregation of schools. J.J. Campbell argued ingeniously, if not ingenuously, in the early 1960s that if, as Catholics were assured, the public representatives would not interfere in any way and the school would remain unaltered then there seemed no good reason to have the public representatives on the committee.9 One should perhaps note that the participation of lay members on school management committees has been accepted with no great enthusiasm by Catholic Church authorities in the Republic of Ireland in recent years. (Equally, perhaps, that in the various local authority committees of Northern Ireland, Protestant clergymen have occupied a goodly proportion of places.) At any rate, although other voluntary schools did find the 'four and two' arrangement acceptable, their numbers were small: indeed it had little effect on Catholic primary schools.

Changes occurred as a result of post-war legislation. In Northern Ireland, as in other parts of the United Kingdom, secondary education was to be made available to all children. This meant that new secondary schools (originally designated secondary intermediate schools, later known as, simply, secondary schools and similar to the English secondary modern schools of the time) had to be provided by both local education authorities and Catholic authorities, either by the conversion of existing schools or by new building. So far as provision for academically able children was concerned, it would have been uneconomic for local authorities or others to provide new schools when there were already grammar schools giving academic secondary education. These grammar schools were voluntary schools for the most part (67 out of 77 at that time) and while some were Catholic foundations, others were Protestant or non-denominational The distinctive characteristic status of grammar schools, as stated in relevant legislation, was that they were fee-paying. Consequently, a scheme was devised by which local authorities would pay the grammar school fees for children of their area (Catholic and Protestant) who had been declared 'qualified' for grammar school education as a result of the 11-plus selection procedure. Grammar schools which agreed to give 80 per cent of their places to such 'qualified' pupils (retaining the remaining places for children whose parents were prepared to pay the fees) were to receive from the Ministry of Education grants of 65 per cent of capital expenditure: grammar schools offering a lesser percentage of places did not receive this grant, though the 'qualified' children's fees were still paid by the local authority. In the beginning, voluntary grammar schools were wary of the arrangements: but gradually more and more adopted Scheme A (offering 80 per cent of places) until only a very small minority had not accepted it. In parallel to the grant provision for grammar schools, a grant of 65 per cent for capital expenditure was extended to other voluntary schools at primary or secondary intermediate level.

Possibly as a result of these changes, or as a result of more liberal attitudes in the following years, even greater progress was made in financing voluntary schools. Under new provisions made in 1968, for voluntary primary and secondary intermediate schools accepting a one-third local education authority representation on their management committees, the Ministry paid teachers' salaries and 100 per cent of employers' contributions to national insurance and superannuation and 80 per cent grant towards capital expenditure. The local education authority paid 100 per cent of cleaning, lighting, heating, maintenance and equipment costs. These schools became designated as 'maintained' schools. Schools not accepting the local authority representation on the management committee received from the Ministry only 65 per cent of employers' contributions to national insurance and 65 per cent grant towards capital expenditure. From the local authority, they received 65 per cent of equipment costs; for maintenance and other costs, a joint contribution of 65 per cent from Ministry and local authority. Similarly for grammar schools accepting one-third Ministry representation on their Board of Governors a grant of a proportion of teachers' salaries was paid by the Ministry plus 65 per cent of national insurance contributions and 50 per cent of teachers' superannuation. There was also a capitation grant for each pupil and 80 per cent of capital expenditure and equipment. Those not accepting Ministry representatives on the governing body received only 65 per cent of capital expenditure and equipment.

While the new 'maintained' status was initially adopted tentatively by a minority of Catholic schools, it evidently proved satisfactory so that by 1980, 497 of a total of 507 voluntary primary schools were maintained: at secondary level, all the secondary intermediate schools had accepted maintained status.10

The burden of providing financially for voluntary schools giving denominational education has thus been very greatly reduced. It has been estimated that public financing of voluntary schools in Northern Ireland has accounted for 95 per cent of total costs. The system thus compares favourably with other systems which have public and voluntary schools though not reaching the complete equality of arrangements made, for instance, in Scotland or the Netherlands.

DIFFERENCES IN THE CURRICULUM

We come therefore to the other and more worrying problem: does the dual system of schools cause or perpetuate divisions within the community? What occurs within the schools which might have these adverse effects?

There is of course the distinctive difference in the teaching of religion. In the local authority schools the teaching of religion, apart from school assemblies, is normally provided in set periods of the timetable during the week. Catholic authorities and parents have traditionally held that religion must permeate the whole life of the school and should not be confined to specific periods. To what extent

Dichotomy in Ulster

this in fact happens probably varies according to the individual school. Some local authority schools take the teaching of the Protestant form of religion more seriously than others. In the Catholic sector, girls' schools, especially convent grammar schools, probably give more attention than others to religious observances during the school day: lessons may begin and/or end with prayer - the Ave Maria, most commonly. In such schools also, and to a lesser extent in other Catholic schools, the symbols of religion - the crucifix, statuettes, sacred pictures - are likely to be present as a continuing reminder. So far as formal teaching of religion is concerned, the two systems differ in the extent to which the same course texts are used within different schools of the sector. Research in the 1970s,11 showed over 90 per cent of Catholic primary schools using the 'Children of God' course which was commissioned by the Catholic Bishops of Ireland for their primary schools. This course is also presented to student-teachers in Catholic teacher-education and has been the theme of in-service courses. At secondary level, there was less unanimity.12 Over 60 per cent of Catholic schools made some use of the Irish Catechetical Programme which also was produced in the Republic though not, unlike the 'Children of God' course, officially designated to be used throughout Ireland. In the controlled or Protestant sector, there was little evidence of common use of courses at secondary level: at primary level there had been some limited use of the Schools Council (Lancaster University) project on Religious Education in Primary Schools: but in 1979 this participation was discontinued and the N.I. School Curriculum Committee agreed a project to construct a suitable course for primary pupils in the controlled sector, focusing on Christianity, and Bible based.

Different presentations of the Christian religion should not, however, develop divisions by arousing feelings of hostility. Differences in other parts of the curriculum seem more likely to develop or reinforce differences of loyalty or opinion with regard to cultural and political matters. Two areas seem influential here, the teaching of history and the teaching of modern languages.

Dichotomy in Ulster

Catholic schools, it is said, favour the teaching of Irish history: the other schools concentrate on British history, possibly from an English point of view. This is not to say that the local authority controlled schools are uninterested in the history of Ireland: many of their pupils and staff are proud of their Irish heritage and unwilling to lose it: increases in the teaching of Irish history have been noted in these schools during recent years. But differences of emphasis probably remain even though pupils are presented for common external examinations in history as is normal, since the syllabus and examination papers offer options. Progress has been made in the last two decades in producing textbooks which give a more balanced approach to history than some earlier used: and in the late 1960s the BBC series Today and Yesterday in Northern Ireland was acclaimed for providing widely acceptable history teaching for younger children. Nevertheless it is difficult to know how individual teachers present the history they teach. It does seem probable that different backgrounds in the study of history may make agreement in adult discussions harder to achieve.

In the mainly Protestant schools, the modern language most frequently studied is, as in England and Scotland, French. Irish is not normally taught. In Catholic schools, French competes with Irish for many pupils: in 1981-82, only one Catholic grammar school and 25 of 90 Catholic secondary schools were not teaching Irish.13 The teaching of Irish in the Catholic schools is not without pedagogical problems caused by sometimes antiquated methods, by the lack of textbooks adapted to the age range of Ulster pupils and the Ulster dialect and by lack of reinforcement, since the language is not used outside school; though holidays in the Gaeltacht, the area of the South where Irish is used, may help. The relative lack of success of attempts in the Republic of Ireland to have the language more widely used within its own bounds might also give pause. Be that as it may, the Catholic schools' emphasis on the study of Irish reinforces their links with the Irish heritage and presumably encourages pupils' interest in strengthening links with the Republic of Ireland.

Another link with the Irish heritage and with the Republic of Ireland may be found in the choice of games played by Catholic school pupils. Gaelic football and camogie are not played by Protestant pupils. Thus opportunities for contact of the two groups outside schools may be reduced. However there are a number of games which they do have in common - soccer, tennis, basketball, netball, for instance (though rugby and hockey tend to remain Protestant preserves): so some such meetings remain possible. It may be argued that in view of Glasgow's history of strife between Rangers and Celtic supporters, such meetings are not necessarily conciliatory.

Overall, while curriculum differences do exist, the two groups of school have much in common in their teaching. What cannot be assessed is the interpretation given by teachers to their subjects and the attitudes they transmit to the pupils explicitly or implicitly. While probably the great majority of teachers are fair and balanced in their teaching, bigots are occasionally found teaching in both groups of schools. The main problem is most probably the lack of opportunity to mix during school hours which can allow stereotypes to continue unchallenged.

UNIVERSITY AND TEACHER EDUCATION

Though primary and secondary schools are thus divided, university education has no such limitation. Queen's University and the newly established University of Ulster receive students from both groups of schools - so, of course, do universities 'across the water'. There is, however, one interesting division, reflecting attitudes when the University was first established: Queen's has a Department of Logic and Philosophy and a Department of Scholastic Philosophy, the latter intended for the teaching of Roman Catholic students. Generally, at university level, many young people find for the first time in their academic career the opportunity to mix daily with people educated in the other religious tradition: for many this is a refreshing and illuminating experience.

Unhappily there is still some religious segregation for those training to be teachers. Training has been offered for many years in Stranmillis College, the College established under the control of the Ministry of Education for Northern Ireland and thus regarded as the Protestant College: for Roman Catholics there have been the Colleges of St. Mary's (for women) and St. Joseph's (for men). But the Education Department of Queen's University has also long offered training courses of the one year full-time postgraduate type, mainly for those intending to teach in secondary schools. It also provided for many years a part-time Diploma in Education, taken by some who had entered teaching as untrained graduates or had College Certificates. Students of both religious groups were included here. In the immediate post-war years it was unusual for Catholic students to take the post-graduate year of training in the University Department for such students would probably not have found it easy to get teaching posts in Catholic schools in Northern Ireland (though they might well be accepted in Catholic schools in other parts of the United Kingdom). But with the growth of more liberal attitudes, the number of Catholic students taking the University course increased so that intending teachers can meet and discuss freely with those educated in the 'other' schools and planning to teach in them. Yet some differences remain in preparation for primary or secondary school teaching. Although the Education Department of the University offers a course on methods of teaching religious education, both religious persuasions being represented in the tutors and in the students, Catholic students intending to teach in primary schools follow a course in religious education at St. Mary's College, also in order to obtain a separate Certificate in Religious Education.

Liberal attitudes also spread to teaching practice for student teachers: it became possible to send students to do teaching practice in schools of the sector in which they were unlikely to teach - i.e., to send a Protestant student on teaching practice in a Catholic school, and _vice versa_. The uneasy feelings of students making their first entry into one of the 'other' schools can illuminate all

Dichotomy in Ulster

kinds of attitudes developed by the segregated system. But although Catholic and Protestant student teachers may mix freely in training courses in Queen's University and in the University of Ulster, which was recently formed by the merger of the short-lived New University of Ulster and the former Ulster College/Polytechnic, the division at College of Education level continues. Certainly the Institute of Education of the University as the validating body has established common examinations and courses: but the interim report of the Chilver Committee in 1981,14 proposing to merge the Queen's University Department and the Catholic Colleges and Stranmillis College, to form a Belfast Centre for Education on the Stranmillis site, met with determined opposition by the Catholic authorities. While the Committee's proposal was apparently motivated by the belief that, with falling numbers of pupils and consequent reduction in the number of teacher-training places required, concentration on one site would be rational and economical, it was not well received by most of those expected to come together on the Stranmillis site. The Catholic hierarchy especially mounted a strong protest. In spite of provision in the proposals for a kind of federal structure in which 'the distinctive ethos of each of the colleges of education would be retained' it seemed to the Catholic authorities that the characteristic qualities of Catholic teacher education would be lost and this might be a first step on the way to desegregated schooling. In this protest, the Catholic hierarchy pointed out that in England and Scotland separate Catholic Colleges of Education continue to exist. It should also be pointed out that in Scotland there has in fact recently been a merger between the Glasgow and Edinburgh Catholic Colleges, because of falling rolls. At any rate, the pleas of the bishops,15 backed by a petition signed, it was said, by some 300,000 Northern Ireland Catholics, led to the abandonment of the proposal to bring all student teachers together on the one site.

Dichotomy in Ulster

ATTITUDES TO THE SEGREGATED SYSTEM

Is the segregated school system perceived by those in the country as divisive and harmful? The belief that separate schools do have adverse effects is probably widespread. A remarkable fact is that in public opinion polls during the last two decades16 majorities of the population ranging from 62 per cent to 81 per cent have been in favour of desegregating the schools. For example, in 1981 75 per cent of Protestants and 66 per cent of Catholics affirmed support for common schools.17 Paradoxically, this willingness to have common schools would seem proof that the segregated schools have not produced attitudes of hostility between the sectors. Likewise some small-scale investigations among school children have found majorities in favour of integration though there may be differences according to religion and sex, within sub-groups. Catholics and girls are more favourably disposed to integration. During the preparation of the 1973 Burges Report,18 which dealt with the possibility of comprehensive schools (to be truly comprehensive presumably schools should not be divided on religious lines), informal soundings among representatives of the different churches did, however, reveal differences ranging from considerable support by some Protestant groups through to the Catholic Church view which was, in principle, clearly against desegregation.

While the idea of desegregation may attract the casual observer, there are obviously factors which would make its implementation difficult. It has been pointed out that some Protestants, who superficially approve of integrated schools, might have reservations if the teaching staff included members of Catholic teaching orders. Darby <u>et al</u>. found, when investigating teachers' attitudes, that many were cautious about an immediate change.19 In particular, some Catholic teachers were uncertain what their own status would be in an integrated system: they had rather an impression that for them it would mean being admitted on sufferance into a basically Protestant system and they were consequently worried about their professional future in such a system. Darby's investigation also discovered some interest-

Dichotomy in Ulster

ing stereotypes the two groups may have of each other: Protestants saw Catholic schools as Church dominated: Catholic teachers thought of Protestant schools as 'cold', 'rigid', 'academic'. Practical difficulties also stand in the way of desegregation. Complicated financial arrangements would be required to deal with land and buildings which are Church property, though no doubt some reasonable solution could be found here. The location of schools is another basic problem. In rural areas there might be no great difficulty in getting children to one common school: but in the larger urban areas of Belfast, and to a lesser extent in Londonderry, where housing is segregated, the neighbourhood school would naturally tend to be segregated: tinkering with catchment areas or bussing to ensure the 'right' mix are not solutions which seem to have worked very well elsewhere. In country districts in fact it has been not unknown for local authority controlled schools to receive Catholic pupils and for a few Protestant pupils to go to a local Catholic school. There has also been very often a feeling of neighbourliness which has eliminated or much reduced feelings of division in rural communities. But in Belfast or Derry more clearly marked 'territories' have been recognized and movement into the other's territory is unlikely. It has indeed been one of the more appalling effects of recent terrorism that householders who were in a small but well accepted religious minority in their area have found themselves compelled, during the bitterness of increased violence, to move house in order to be safer 'among their own kind'. Couples who are engaged in a mixed marriage are in a particularly unenviable position in these circumstances - one of them must be 'displaced'. Their problems would seem to give a kind of belated justification of an earlier argument of parents against integrated schools, that children attending such a school might there meet, fall in love with and eventually marry someone of another religious faith and so have these problems peculiar to Northern Ireland in times of conflict.

In practice some schools are already desegegated. A number of grammar schools have long prided themselves on being non-sectarian and receiving some pupils and employing some staff belonging to the other religious group. It must be admitted that the proportions of the minorities in such instances are small. Similarly, in country areas, some parents prefer to send children to the nearer school even if it is not of their own religious faith. Possibly there has been lately some increase in the numbers of Catholic, middle-class parents opting for a Protestant grammar school for their children or transferring their children after O-levels into the sixth form of a Protestant school.

At primary level there has been another small-scale tradition of desegegation in schools earlier provided for employees' children by employers, for example, mill owners. These schools are integrated and apparently this is happily accepted by parents and children alike. Recent research showed that within one such school integration was so much a part of normal life that it passed without comment by the children. Within the school, children formed friendships irrespective of religious affiliation, though, possibly because of the location of their homes, the children tended to play when out of school with those of their own religious group.[20] Similarly in another study of an integrated school of this kind, integration was found to be taken for granted and friendship choices were made without religious discrimination.[21] Yet such schools do not necessarily remove all differences: in one such school, though not in another, Catholic children were found to have a more favourable attitude to religion than Protestant children: and a similar study of 'religious attitudes' in such a school concluded that Catholic children had more favourable attitudes, or at least attended church more often than the majority of their Protestant class-mates.[22]

NEW ATTEMPTS AT COMMON SCHOOLS AND REMOVAL OF BARRIERS

In these circumstances it is not surprising that attempts are being made to reduce the effects of segregated schooling. It must be noted that moves by some Catholic parents to send their children to local authority schools in the latter part of the 1970s evoked disapproval from their bishop and the threat that such children might be refused confirmation. Notably, the All Children Together movement, mainly created by Catholic parents, has established in Belfast the Lagan College, a secondary school for children of all religious denominations. The school, founded in 1981, has made good progress and in 1984 achieved recognition as a maintained school, so it is now receiving financial support from public funds rather than being dependent on parental fee-paying. Another secondary school of the same type, Hazelwood Integrated College was more recently founded but hopes soon to acquire maintained status.

Significantly, the Northern Ireland Education Act of 1978 23 provided for a new category of school to be known as a 'controlled integrated' school. These schools can be established if:

> not less than two-thirds of ... the management committee of a controlled school ... make a request to the education and libraries board ... that the school should become a controlled integrated school.

One or more of a group of schools under such a management committee may similarly change status. If such a request is made, the Education and Libraries Board 24 must discover from parents:

> so far as practicable in such a way that their identity is not revealed ... whether they would be prepared to send their children to the school if it became a controlled integrated school.

The Department of Education, Northern Ireland, cannot grant the request:

> unless satisfied that at least three-quarters of the parents of children attending that school whose views have been ascertained would be prepared to send their children to the school if it became a controlled integrated school.

If agreement is given, then a management committee of

the appropriate kind must be established. It is worth noting also that the stated aim of the Act is:

> to facilitate the establishment in Northern Ireland of schools likely to be attended by pupils of different religious affiliations or cultural traditions.

Hazelwood primary school in Belfast has become a controlled integrated school and another Belfast primary school may soon achieve this new status. It remains to be seen whether numbers in this category will increase. Legislation seems to have recognized demands for progress of this kind. Possibly the schools will be more successful than their nineteenth-century counterparts: or they may remain isolated symbols of hopes for reform.

Even if desegregation of schools is not an immediate prospect, various other efforts are being made to overcome barriers set by separate schools. Many charitable organizations have organized joint holiday camps and conferences for children from the two groups of schools and have found amicable relationships developing easily among Protestants and Catholics. Some such friendships may be short-lived if, when home again, the friends find themselves unable to meet easily in 'neutral' territory. But joint activities organized by the schools themselves have also proved rewarding. Recently in Belfast an Inter-schools Union has meant that sixth-formers from both types of school have met together at monthly intervals to discuss 'current issues' alternately in a Catholic and a 'Protestant' school. Granted, such movements may be more common among middle class (or academically able) pupils than among working class.

More systematic projects have also been undertaken to improve attitudes and develop a sense of community. The Schools Cultural Studies Project,[25] from 1973 to 1980, attempted to provide course material of units of work on various aspects of History, Geography, Social Anthropology, Sociology and Political Science which would enhance pupils' understanding of their own community and at the same time, it was hoped, develop the principles of scientific enquiry, values clarification, and the

Dichotomy in Ulster

study of values. Teachers from both groups of schools united in work for this project and thus schools with widely different attitudes towards the ongoing 'troubles' came together in some respects. The evaluation report, <u>Chocolate, Cream, Soldiers</u>, indicates that useful work was done. Yet one episode quoted in relation to a teacher's uncertainty as to the precise amount of neutrality expected of the teacher in class discussions offers a vivid illustration of the real-life situation. In this particular class only two pupils were prepared to accept that Protestants might be 'all right'. It is significant that one of these, a girl, argued by reference to experience when a Protestant neighbour had been helpful in a case of illness in the family. The rest of the class, some of whom claimed to have suffered attack, verbal or physical, by Protestants, were vehement in their opposition. Here we have obviously less a question of religious differences than acceptance or non-acceptance of sterotypes, stereotypes reinforced - more rarely, reduced - by personal experience. It is unlikely that the segregated school, rather than the outside environment, creates such stereotypes. Integrated schools would presumably reduce them. But, given segregation, the teachers' task is daunting. There is also the likelihood that with continuing experience of violence and terrorism attitudes are hardening. People have suffered, or those near to them have suffered, in the 'troubles': and these sufferings - damage to property, threats, injury, death - are not always met with Christian forgiveness or forbearance. Nevertheless, educational effort continues: most recently the Northern Ireland Council for Educational Development has fostered the Education for Mutual Understanding project, which establishes contacts between teachers, so far on a small scale.

CONCLUSIONS

From this survey it is evident that the problems do not originate from within the dual system of schools and that they are not simply problems of religious differences, though religious differences are

Dichotomy in Ulster

accounted of considerable importance. The problems lie in the interlinking of religious with cultural and political choices as well as in demands for the right to practise a chosen religion without disadvantage or discrimination. Whether schools can so educate their pupils in the principles of Christianity or humanism that these pupils grow to understand clearly the attitudes and beliefs of others and recognize the need to respect others' beliefs is uncertain.

Meanwhile we can note some encouraging signs, including the relative stability, patience and tolerance shown by a society which has so long suffered from terrorism. There is also some encouragement to be found in the affirmation of parents' rights and the expression by some parents of a desire to end segregation. Churchmen in the past have not always been the most moderate and wise of counsellors. Perhaps greater attention to the views of parents - and teachers - and of young people themselves - may give guidance as to the best solution to this apparently intractable problem of the schools' dichotomy.

NOTES AND REFERENCES

1. The distinction of Roman Catholic is made here; the term 'Catholic' will be used subsequently to denote Roman Catholics, though it is recognized that other churches consider this term applies to them, and it is regretted that they may find the convention here adopted displeasing. 'Protestant' is also used where sometimes finer differentiations among Presbyterians, Methodists, members of the Church of Ireland (Anglicans) and smaller denominations might have been made.

2. See: Craig, A.R. and McNeill, N., Belfast Model Schools 1857-1957, Belfast: Belfast Local Education Authority, 1957.

3. Kennedy, David, 'Ulster and the Antecedents of Home Rule', in Ulster since 1800, London: BBC, 1954.

4. Akenson, D.H., Education and Enmity: The Control of Schooling in Northern Ireland 1920-50, David and Charles, 1973, Ch. 3.

5. Nonetheless, one eminent Catholic, A.N. Bonaparte Wyse - later Permanent Secretary to the Northern Ireland Ministry - was a member, but he served in a personal, not a representative, capacity.

6. Ibid., p.52.

7. Ibid., PP. 117-18.

8. Campbell, J.J., Catholic Schools: A Survey of a Northern Ireland Problem, Belfast: Fallons Educational Supply Co., n.d., p.29.

9. Ibid., p.30.

10. Northern Ireland Statistics 27, HMSO, 1979; and Ulster Year Book, 1981, HMSO.

11. Sutherland, A.E., Curriculum Projects in Primary Schools, Belfast: Northern Ireland Council for Educational Research, 1981, pp.50-1.

12. Sutherland, A.E., O'Shea, A.T. and McCartney, J.R., Curriculum Prospects in Post-Primary Schools, Northern Ireland Council for Educational Research, Belfast, 1983, p.24.

13. Trew, K., 'The Dual Education System in Northern Ireland' in: McWhirter, I. and Trew, K. (eds), The Northern Ireland Conflict: Myth and Reality, G.W. and A. Hesketh, 1983, p.14.

14. Chilver Committee on the Future of Higher Education in Northern Ireland, Interim Report, HMSO, 1980.

15. Lodge, B., 'Catholics voice protest over proposal to train with Protestants', Times Educational Supplement: Scotland, 12 February, 1982.

16. Darby, J., 'Northern Ireland: Bonds and Breaks',

British Journal of Educational Studies, XXVI, 3, 1978, p.220.

17. *Sunday Times*, June, 1981, cited in Trew, K., op. cit.

18. Advisory Council for Education (Burges Report) *Reorganisation of Secondary Education in Northern Ireland*, 1973.

19. Darby, J., op. cit.

20. Davies, J., 'Hilden: Social and Psychological Perspectives on an Integrated Mill School'; abstract in: *Register of Research in Education in Northern Ireland*, Northern Ireland Council for Educational Research, 1984, p.108.

21. Gamble, R.M., 'An investigation into the social interaction, identity and religious attitudes of Integrated Mill School pupils'; abstract in: *Register of Research in Education*, vol. 5, 1984, p.110.

22. Turner, I.F. and Davies, J., 'Religious attitudes in an integrated primary school: a Northern Ireland case study', abstract in: *Register of Research in Education*, vol. 5, 1984, p.283.

23. *Education (Northern Ireland) Act 1978*, HMSO, 1978, Chapter 13.

24. Since 1973, the Local Education Authorities have been the five 'Education and Library Boards', responsible for different areas of the country.

25. Jenkins, D. et al., *Chocolate, Cream, Soldiers*, The New University of Ulster, Education Centre, Occasional Papers, n.d.

'SENSUS FIDELIUM':
THE DEVELOPING CONCEPT OF ROMAN CATHOLIC VOLUNTARY EFFORT IN EDUCATION IN ENGLAND AND WALES

Vincent A. McClelland

In a best-selling work of phantasy, Gordon Thomas describes how Andrew, one of his characters, found his mother explaining to him at seven years old that being a Catholic was an attitude not an act. This was an extension of an idea she had gently pressed upon all her children from the day they were old enough to understand.1 For anyone wishing to examine the tortuous relationship that developed in the nineteenth century between the Roman Catholic Church and the State in relation to the education and schooling of Catholic children it is a key concept and, indeed, a fundamental one to an appreciation of the emergence of the dual system itself. John Cuthbert Hedley, the long-serving Bishop of Newport and Menevia (1881 to 1915) encapsulated the educational philosophy underpinning it when he explained:

> to educate is to cultivate, develop and polish all the faculties - physical, intellectual, moral and religious - and to give to a boy's whole nature its completeness and perfection, so that he may be what he ought to be and do what he should do, to form him as a man, and to prepare him to do his duty in life to those about him, to his country, to himself; and so, by perfecting his present life, to prepare him for the life to come ...2

Just as a monastery was conceived within the Church as a family in which each member, guided by common purpose and seeking an identifiable end, worked for the good of the community, cherished its ideals and

and supported its beliefs, so any Catholic school of any kind was seen as but a part of the family of the Catholic Church in which common beliefs and interests were developed and where everyone worked for the good of the whole. This philosophy was able to cohere, as Jeffrey von Arx has recently put it, because Catholicism presented itself as the only religious system that claimed to possess an infallible authority received from the Word of God.3 The Divine mandate for the Church to teach was at the heart of its scheme of religious formation. In its foundation, the Church had not only predated the written gospels, it had been the source for defining as canonical the fundamental beliefs enshrined therein. Private judgement directed at the supreme truths of religion was anathema because selectivity in spiritual and moral concepts militated against the Church's subscription to ideals of 'wholeness', 'unity' and 'spiritual integrity'. The Catholic school system was thus destined to become what Bernard Sharratt has recently characterised as 'the sociologically central component of specifically English Catholicism, the major mechanism by which the R.C. community both maintains its group identity and aligns itself to the norms of the wider society'.4 One may add a rider to this opinion: it became the mechanism by which the local Church recognised herself as an ever-renewing, visibly identifiable part of the universality of the Church militant.

Associated with the Catholic school system are two claims that have formed the rallying call of the Catholic Church in England and Wales since 1870: the inalienable right of parents to decide that a child be brought up and educated in accordance with their religious convictions and, secondly, that political and social equity demands the State acknowledge parental rights by not making it more difficult for Catholics to follow their consciences in this matter than it does for Anglicans or Nonconformists. In the eyes of Catholics, these two claims have always appeared to be eminently fair, just and necessary. They were to become entrenched as canons of Catholic orthodoxy by four nineteenth-century developments that had far-reaching consequences for Catholic schooling. The first of these arose out of the newly-found confidence acquired from Emancipation.

Cardinal Wiseman characterised the achievement of Catholic Emancipation in 1829 as the equivalent for Catholics of what the egress from the catacombs was to the early Christians.5 But, as E.R. Norman has argued, Emancipation was much more than simply a matter of the gaining of civil liberties, entailing the entry of Catholics into public life and cementing growing relationships with politicians of national and local import.6 It was the harbinger of the growth of 'an organised and articulate middle class'7 in both Ireland and England, the appearance of an independent-minded group of professional laymen which was to be less inclined to toady to the leadership of the 'old Catholic' nobility and squirearchy and which was anxious to retain a religious, social and cultural identity in harmony with the spiritual leadership of the Vicars Apostolic, the visible local symbols of Catholic unity and cohesion. For this group of laymen, Emancipation was not something which had been attained in a once and for all sense, an <u>event</u> after which Catholics could sink again into comparative seclusion or oblivion. For them, Emancipation could not end in 1829. That year marked but a beginning of an evolving process of religious, social, cultural and political growth in relation to which education, in less than a decade, was seen to be the catalytic ingredient that would enable the process to retain its momentum. Writing in <u>The Dublin Review</u> in the first year of its origin, Thomas Wyse delineated the main strands in a recognisably Catholic philosophy of education:

> Education is not instruction, any more than it is books, boards, or schoolrooms. Instruction, as well as gymnastics, is only a brand of education, and it would be just as great a folly to expect regeneration from one alone, as from the other. Education is literally 'bringing up' - but not one section or fraction of the triple man, but the whole - physical, intellectual, moral - the body, the intelligence, the spirit. Leave out any one portion, and you at once overturn the balance, and produce a mass of distortion - a monster. Educate the body at the expense of the

intellectual and moral being, and you produce a brute lump of animated clay. Educate the intelligence at the expense of the moral and religious feelings, and you give power without virtue to wield it. Educate the moral only, and you leave virtue without her noblest ally, - religion, without understanding, becomes fanaticism ...8

In his plea for the abandonment of the existing laissez-faire system of education and a determination of the need for the State to establish 'a "National System" by which every man in the country, and his children after him, shall be secured, not the husks on which men have hitherto been feeding, but a substantial, applicable, enduring education', Wyse stipulated that education must be based upon the concept of 'wholeness' and pay due regard to all the physical, intellectual and religious needs of man.9 Within two years of Wyse's plea for government support for the furtherance of elementary education, Daniel O'Connell, Michael Quin, Lord Shrewsbury and others had established the Catholic Institute in London aimed at facilitating the cause of Catholic education and indicating the need for self-help. In that same year, Charles Russell, a future President of Maynooth who was to regard his contributions to The Dublin Review as 'a fundamental element of his apostolate' to offset 'the tone of supercilious disregard' with which Catholics were often treated,10 took up the cause of Catholic education which he saw as all the more necessary to offset the prejudice against the Catholic Church whose doctrines 'are misconceived and her morality misrepresented'.11

On the future Cardinal Wiseman's part, the concern for Catholic education was not inspired by any narrow sectional interest. It has to be seen, rather, as an aspect of his more general, all-pervading concern for the poor and the oppressed, a desire that they be enlightened and nurtured intellectually while their faith and spiritual development were being sustained and succoured.

The Dublin urged in 1843 that 'the first step to be taken should be to get together accurate statements of the extent of the wants of the Catholics of their respective dioceses (sic) as to education and religious instruction'. When accurate data were collected and placed before Government 'with that weight and influence which the Catholic Church must possess', then 'no government can resist the appeal'. The journal was somewhat naively convinced that 'our venerable prelates cannot fail in obtaining the UNFETTERED command of such temporal means as would, under the blessing of Providence, be sufficient, in their hands to stop the progress of infidelity, which if unchecked, threatens to overtake an existing generation with anarchy and ruin.'12

Such aid, however, was clearly not to be sought at any price! When the Commissioners appointed to enquire into the state of popular education in England began to report in 1861, the spectre of Church of England hegemony was raised, specifically in the matter of school inspection. 'It would be far better for us not to have any share in the parliamentary grant for education', wrote Canon John Morris at the time, 'than to receive the share of it to which we are justly entitled, on the condition of our schools being rendered subject to Protestant inspection.'13 Religious liberty must always be at the heart of any government measure for education and, in the case of the workhouse children, 'it is absolutely necessary that it should be compulsory upon the Guardians to send children to schools in which the religion is taught which their parents profess, unless the parents expressly name some other school'.14 Furthermore, 'justice and fairness demand that a convenient number of schools should be established, to which the Guardians of certain districts should be obliged to send their Catholic children and maintain them up to the age of sixteen ...'.15 The battlelines were thus early delineated and the struggles of 1870 and beyond clearly prognosticated.

Six years before the advent of Gladstone's reforming first Ministry, the Catholic position on public elementary education was well known. It was a philosophy not predominantly different from that of the Church of England and one equally designed to appeal to the liberally-minded. It was a philosophy justified in terms of freedom of conscience, liberty of choice, and responsible guardianship of the young and vulnerable. There could be no question of the assumption by the State of responsibility for the education of the young if it did not take steps to preserve the voluntary nature of education, to regard the deeply felt religious commitment of the nation, and to understand the nature of parental duties and rights. 'As long as the religion of a nation was one', declared the <u>Dublin</u>, 'State institutions for education could teach religion; but when diversity of creed came to be recognised, for the State to teach any one religion (was) a violation of freedom of conscience; and hence in State systems of education religion was left out ... But in England religion has ever been recognised as an essential part of education; and as education is voluntary, there is no difficulty in its being religious'. It was mainly to uphold the religious character of elementary education that the voluntary element was emphasised. The State must confine itself to assisting the different creeds to educate their own children: 'We need hardly add', the <u>Dublin</u> declared, 'that no other system would be tolerated in England; not only our religious feelings but our love of individual freedom would resist any other'. In a nutshell, 'English education is essentially <u>free</u> and <u>religious</u>; nor could it be the latter without being the former'.16

At the time of the restoration of the Roman Catholic hierarchy in 1850, it is estimated there were about 600,000 Catholics in England and Wales, of whom about 25,000 were 'traditional' English Catholics in the sense that they were descended from the survivors of penal days.17 The rest, apart from converts, were of Irish origin or descent, most of them having arrived during the great famine years of 1845 to 1849.18 The determination to weld together the diverse elements in the 'new' English Catholicism and the need to keep alive the sense of 'belonging', a social need for the Irish, gave added stimulus to the Church's stance on elementary education. The parish school, and the work undertaken to sustain and support it, proved to be an important community-welding agent among Catholics, bringing priests, people, benefactors, rich and poor, together as a tightly-knit social and religious entity. The process of achieving such unity was neither rapid nor trouble-free. John Hickey, for instance, in his study of urban Catholicism in Wales, has shown how four years before the Catholic Poor Schools Committee was established to receive Privy Council grants, the Rev. Patrick Millea had to strive very hard to persuade the Irish in Cardiff of the beneficial effects of sending their children to the parish school he had established for them in 1847. The payment they had to find was, of course, a deterrent but out of the 220 Irish boys and girls he estimated to be of school age in that year, fewer than half of them attended the school. With the establishment of the Catholic Poor School Committee and the educational rigour of the restored hierarchy that situation was destined to be remedied. By 1856, Millea's school had to be enlarged because of demand and, as the process of Irish immigration gathered further momentum after the mid-century, more Catholic schools in Cardiff were needed.19

Wiseman opened the first Catholic Reformatory for boys at Hammersmith in 1855 and the first Industrial School for boys at Walthamstow. In 1850 a training college for Catholic male teachers began work at Hammersmith. After 1865, the chief glory of Manning's work as Archbishop of Westminster was to be the rapidity and success with which he initiated and stimulated the growth of schools for poor children. The tone of urgency was set in Manning's first Pastoral Letter, issued two weeks after his consecration. He pleaded for help 'in gathering from the streets of this great wilderness of men the tens of thousands of poor Catholic children who are without instruction or training'.20

This first appeal was not to be the last. Manning's work was divided into three broad areas: the provision of elementary schools, the setting-up of reformatory and industrial schools and orphanages, and thirdly, the transferring of Catholic children from the workhouses. The philosophy was clear and it underscored the establishment of the Westminster Diocesan Education Fund in 1866. Manning articulated the theory to Gladstone at the very height of the education debate in 1870: 'the integrity of our

Schools as to (i) Doctrine, (ii) Religious management, and the responsibility of the Bishops in these respects, cannot be touched without opening a multitude of contentions and vexations'.21 In these statements, of course, he was endorsing what had been the official government response towards educational provision since the first granting in 1833 of government money for elementary education. The 1870 Act was to enshrine that philosophy in its setting up of the dual system. The subsequent fight for Catholics was not one for recognition of the right to educate but one for parity of resources between Catholic schools and board schools. Indeed, as Norman has observed, 'as the century advanced it became almost axiomatic that where a church was established there must be a Catholic school also: a situation which exactly paralleled the educational expansion of the Church of England in the nineteenth century'.22

In 1839, The Dublin Review was able to record that new Catholic churches had been erected at Uttoxeter, Lytham, Hereford, Stalybridge, Derby and Everingham near Beverley, the latter 'built upon designs prepared in Rome, adorned with rich sculptures, marbles, and other decorations, worthy of any Catholic city ...'.23 These churches were but a small sample of those built recently by the munificence of the Catholic gentry and aristocracy,24 indicating, a decade after Emancipation and a decade before the restoration of the hierarchy, how confident the Catholic Church had grown in England after 'the dejection of three centuries of persecution'.25 The growth in Church construction was but a small indication that the wealth of the 'old Catholic' families had remained as healthy as their sense of patronage was undiminished. Indeed, Luigi Gentili (1801-1848) had written to Rome in protest against what he considered the undue influence still being exerted by the lay aristocracy over the Vicars Apostolic.26 The influence of the great families at the Jesuit College at Stonyhurst, for instance, or at the Benedictine houses of Downside and Ampleforth was paramount, representing an educational system for the aristocracy bred and developed in the years of the penal laws and foreign exile. Such institutions were governed by introspective concerns and were characterised by a system of social exclusiveness that had been much less prominent in Continental days.

In the organisation of the Catholic colleges in the first half of the nineteenth century, however, there was little to attract the newly arrived Oxford converts who felt the institutions epitomised the concept of an aristocratic close borough, resistant to outside influence and adverse to change. The situation was ripe for internal contention and in the ensuing struggle can be detected the fomenting yeast that was to constitute the second of the four developments that have been identified as strengthening a Catholic awareness of the need for a coherent approach to education and to the development of schooling.

The Oxford Movement was based upon a renaissance of intellectualism, allied to a renewal of ideals in personal sanctity and dedication. The yearning for romantic medievalism or for Gothic architecture was merely an outward manifestation of an interior force that had its basis firmly rooted in scholarship. The fact that the Movement was grounded upon the deadly antagonism of Tracts for the Times to Erastianism (or Caesarism, as Manning would have divined it) had itself profound educational implications.27 Following the conversion to Roman Catholicism of John Henry Newman in 1845, at least five hundred converts who were Oxford men were to follow the same path in the years immediately ensuing, as were at least two hundred Cambridge men.28 By the end of the century, W.G. Gorman is able to list the names of three and half thousand influential converts to Catholicism.29 The early converts saw their essential mission as providing intellectual leadership to Catholicism, in order to equip it to play a more open and aggressive role in the fight against State encroachment and secularism. The Census of 1851 had recorded 733,866 Irish in Britain, all of whom had been born in Ireland, a figure that did not include the large numbers born in England and Wales of Irish parentage. Here was a vast field of work awaiting the attention and the zeal of converts. But there was an enemy within! This the leading converts, with the notable exception of Newman and his immediate entourage, identified as the 'old Catholic' families and yeomanry who seemed to be marked by the turpitude and lassitude consequent upon centuries of family in-breeding and social exclusiveness.

J.M. Capes took up the cudgels in the pages of The Rambler, diagnosing the 'old Catholic' political and social weakness as being essentially related to the education they had received. 'The past circumstances of Catholicism in this country', he wrote, 'among their other disastrous effects upon our systems of education, have tended to a practical jumble of the secular and ecclesiastical systems, from which we are now most grievously suffering, and which we humbly conceive to be the first thing that demands eradication, in order to the establishment of sound and successful educational institutions for the middle and upper classes'.30 An attack at this level of frankness took the 'old Catholics' by surprise but made little allowance for that 'esprit de corps' fostered by years of proscription and inter-marriage. The following passage from his book To Rome and Back indicates the sneering tone of Capes' criticism, which was not tempered with time:

> 'And what are the old Catholic families like?' Seymour (alias Capes) asked in an imaginary conversation at Prior Park College where Capes, after his conversion, had gained a teaching appointment. 'One hears nothing of them in the world in general, only that there are some historic names among them, that everybody knows'.
> 'They are as proud as Lucifer', said Maxwell, 'and as ignorant as they are proud. They snub their chaplains to their faces. I have known a house where the priest was never allowed to drink more than one glass of wine at dinner, and another where he was always let in at the back door when he came on Sundays to say Mass'.
> 'But surely this is a most disgusting state of things', I exclaimed.
> 'There's more to be said for it than you imagine, Mr Seymour', he replied. 'Some of the English priests are perfectly unpresentable in a lady's drawing room'.31

The provision of a mixed system of clerical and lay education in the one establishment was not, of course, unique to Catholicism. Before the founding of theological colleges in Chichester and elsewhere in the nineteenth century, the same practice had prevailed in the Church of England, although the admixture was more in evidence at university than elsewhere. The opposition of the Oxford Converts to the prevailing Catholic system was not entirely altruistic. In the 'mixed' colleges, priests and religious tended to occupy the great majority of teaching posts: in a purely lay collegiate establishment, the married clerical converts might have found themselves with a suitable outlet for their energies. The problem for them was also a peculiarly male one. While it is true that over fifty religious congregations of women were engaged in educational work for girls of one sort or another by 1850 - constituting an educational record far better in quality terms than anything else provided at the time in England and Wales - single lay women were still able to find a suitable outlet in teaching.

Capes' Rambler article of 1848 constituted the first substantial evidence of that journal's ultimate development into what has been described as 'an organ of the left wing, critical of tradition, eager in its welcome of modern knowledge and ideas, disrespectful of ecclesiastical authority'.32 The 'mixed system' of education was detrimental to the modernisation of the Church and the journal complained 'we have found the middle of the nineteenth century arrive without the establishment of a single purely ecclesiastical, or purely secular, seminary in Great Britain'.33 Capes warned: 'Vain will be every apparent improvement if we ignore the momentous difference between the life of the priest and the layman, and are content to perpetuate a system which more or less brings them up in one indiscriminate crowd'.34

The debate thus initiated was lengthy and acrimonious and not made any more palatable by the intervention of well-meaning converts such as Frederick Oakeley who, seeking to offset the threatened animosity, wrote that, in his view, 'the difference between the English Catholic idea of education and that to which we (the converts) were accustomed to at Oxford is ... a fundamental one: the one making the formation of (mental) character its great aim, the other, the storing of the mind with a certain amount of valuable facts. Hence our acquirements seem to Catholics "limited", and their intellectual character and habits seem to us shallow and desultory'.35

The tradition of educating Catholic lay boys in the same establishments as clerical students was an old and venerable tradition and destined to die hard. Nevertheless, Wiseman and Manning tried to begin the process of introducing distinct educational provision for clerics by seeking to set up seminaries for the training of priests on a diocesan basis in accordance with the old Tridentine decrees. Before Manning's death in 1892, over two-thirds of the dioceses had local seminaries, a fulfilment of Manning's policy which he began as an Anglican with such a foundation at Chichester. Although the plan of separate diocesan seminaries did not survive long after Manning's demise, it was replaced by a regional provision motivated by the same philosophy. A reintroduction of 'mixed' education within the Catholic colleges was not favoured. In the establishment of the Oratory School in 1859, Newman himself followed the pattern deemed to be most congenial to the converts, even establishing houses superintended by tutors and dames in the old Etonian fashion. A similar venture was undertaken by the thirteenth Lord Petre, a young priest who decided to establish a Catholic Eton for the gentry at Woburn Park, Surrey, in 1877 as a 'sanctuary of our country's youth'.36 The nature of the aristocratic clientele Petre attracted from Catholic families was a sufficient indication that the admixture of social classes in the old clerical/lay colleges was perhaps one of their most objectionable features. This class-based objection was a matter that the future Cardinal Vaughan was to identify as a major weakness in the Catholic Church in England.37 Before Vaughan arrived at Westminster, even Oscott College had decided to dismiss its lay students.

The major outcome of the educational debate of the mid-century was an ever-growing consciousness within the Roman Catholic Church of its duty as an educator, a duty requiring the formation of its own youth in the light of the Sacred Deposit of Truth of which it believed it was the guardian. It is perhaps best described in Manning's philosophy: 'as natural society develops man in the natural order, so the church perfects man both in the natural and in the supernatural order'. Indeed 'it perfects the natural society of man also, in all its relations of public and private life'.38 From 1865 onwards, it was Manning's belief that the true mission of the Catholic Church was to save England from the secular liberalism that was about to engulf it. This could only be achieved from a position of intellectual strength and cohesion. In 1870, he was to see the Vatican Council as the means of freeing the Church from the fetters of the <u>ancien regime</u> and thereby strengthening it to confront the forces of atheistic liberalism. Henceforth, the Church secured by its spiritual independence could engage in genuine dialogue with Democracy.39 It was this belief that led to the third development that strengthened the Catholic position in regard to its educational exclusiveness.

Writing in 1874, Lord Robert Montagu claimed that 'all Catholics held from the first, and were bound to hold, that the gift of Infallibility was inherent in the Church, and was exercised by the Teaching Body of the Church, including the Pope, in all matters relating to Faith and morals'. The Vatican Decrees merely asserted that this Infallibility of the Church was exercised through her Head, when he spoke officially as such. Moreover, the Bull <u>Unam Sanctam</u> 'has been an article of faith since the year 1302, having been promulgated by and in a Council of Rome'.40 There was no doubt that the matter of an infallible teaching authority had been a key factor in a large number of the Oxford conversions to Catholicism. J.M. Capes, for instance, put his own position this way: 'At last I came to the conclusion that the existence of an infallible and intelligible teacher is thus necessarily involved in the nature of a revelation, for that otherwise it would be really no real revelation at all. And such being my conclusion, there seemed no alternative but to betake myself to Rome as the divinely appointed guide'.41

'Protestantism', he argued, 'disowns infallibility; Greece has for centuries and centuries ceased to appeal to any living light; while Rome still stands forth, claiming to be the home of the still living Redeemer, taught by Him and guided into all truth'.42 To Capes, as to many others converted in the mid-century, the Papacy was 'a token of some mighty spiritual power, permanent among all changes of kings and empires, outlasting all stages of civilisation and ruling men's minds by the sheer force of (its) belief in the unseen'.43

Gladstone, of course, though otherwise. He interpreted the work of the Council as, quite simply, a declaration of war upon Democracy and upon the rightful prerogatives of the State. By reasserting its doctrinal and moral independence in such an uncompromising fashion, the Papacy had resurrected the Augustinian concept of the Church at war with the world. Gladstone's reaction was, indeed, but a logical development from his early history and, in particular, from his publication as a young man in his late twenties of <u>The State in Its Relations with the Church</u> (1838). This book, his first, had attempted to offset the disestablishment tendencies of early Tractarians. 'Of course the religious ground of the nationality of the Church', he had written, 'consists in its claim of spiritual and personal descent from its inspired Founder; but the constitutional ground of its title is in the law; and the actual ground, or, so to speak, the efficient or material course of its standing in the law, is to be found in its possession of a preponderance of the social forces, of which the law itself is only one'.44

Gladstone's early book, discreetly forgotten after his enforced disestablishment of the Irish Church, had been savagely reviewed by T.B. Macauley for its lack of logic. 'If Mr Gladstone means that we ought to believe that the Church of England speaks the truth because she has the apostolic succession', he had written, 'we greatly doubt whether such a doctrine can be maintained'. Visibly 'the Church has not unity', he went on, and 'as unity is the essential condition of truth the Church has not the truth'.45 Gladstone had never fully recovered from the onslaught.

Manning, for his part, had approached the Roman Catholic Church from Anglicanism as a result of a lengthy and profound examination of the directive action of the Holy Spirit in preserving the Church from error and in guiding the individual soul in its yearning for assured truth. The nomination of the theologically suspect Hampden to the See of Hereford in 1847 and the institution of George Gorham to the living of Brampford Speke in 1850, in spite of the judgement of Bishop Phillpotts of Exeter as to Gorham's lack of orthodoxy, left Manning with no belief in the energising role of the State, the Royal Supremacy or the Establishment to underpin true doctrine within the Church. For him, the Church of Christ must recognise the ultimate guarantee <u>within herself</u>: the guarantee of the Holy Spirit. Her charge must be 'to imbue each successive generation of her children with the conclusions of the faith, openly tendering, also, the proofs of Holy Scripture; and thus going before us from our childhood, being ever herself of one ripe age, teaching what things are necessary, probable, or doubtful - both what we must, and what we may believe; ever leading on those that will follow from conclusion to proofs, to inner ranges, and to higher paths of wisdom'.46 His conception of the teaching role of the Church left little room for State domination.

Gladstone, wounded by political defeat in relation to the Irish University Bill of 1873, frustrated by his inability to persuade his sister Helen to reconvert from Roman Catholicism to the Church of England, sickened by the conversion to Rome of his Cabinet colleague, Lord Ripon, in 1874, and accepting uncritically the biased interpretations of the day-to-day work of the Vatican Council spread by Dollinger, Acton and Mozley, issued his violently anti-Papal pamphlet in 1874, <u>The Vatican Decrees in Their Bearing on Civil Allegiance: A Political Expostulation</u>. He followed it up in the following year by an answer to the furore it engendered.47 In essence, Gladstone's attacks questioned the civil loyalty of Catholics and resurrected the ancient penal jibes of a divided allegiance. He demanded reassurances.

Replies were produced speedily and that by Bishop William Bernard Ullathorne associated Gladstone's stance with those of Acton, Dollinger and the early writings of <u>The Rambler</u>, <u>The North British Critic</u> and <u>The Chronicle</u>. Ullathorne's reply, indeed, was a classic exposition of the built-up frustration of Catholics who had striven for centuries to prove their loyalty to the State. 'What a descent from the <u>Church Principles</u> published by the same author in the year 1840', Ullathorne remarked.48 Mgr. Thomas Capel noted the 'singular bitterness in Mr Gladstone's manner of speaking of converts' in which he had endorsed the opinion of the <u>Contemporary Review</u> that 'no one can become Rome's convert without renouncing his moral and mental freedom, and placing his civil loyalty and duty at the mercy of another'.49 Throughout Gladstone's 1874 pamphlet he had confused the notions of 'authority' and 'infallibility'. Capel summed up the general feeling of Catholics when he declared: 'Every Catholic who reads Mr Gladstone's pamphlet must feel that a wanton, deliberate, and unprovoked insult has been offered to him and to his religion'.50 Even as disinterested an observer as the logical positivist, Frederic Harrison, remarked 'the hubbub about the Vatican Decrees is silly mimicry of (the) flagrant aggression of the military bureaucracy of Prussia ... I cannot but regard the Catholic side in this controversy as being, in its broad features, the side of liberty and moral independence'.51 The aristocratic 'old Catholic', William Clifford, Bishop of Clifton, encapsulated Catholic anger when he wrote:

> Nearly half a century has elapsed since the passing of Catholic Emancipation. During that period Catholic peers and Catholic judges and Catholic magistrates have administered justice on the bench; Catholic barristers have pleaded at the bar; Catholic soldiers have fought in the army; Catholics have served their country in every office of trust. During the whole of that period the public voice of the country has proclaimed that Catholics have proved themselves to be loyal. Nobody then has a right to put Catholics on their trial, and say that they shall

be considered guilty of a want of loyalty unless they can prove themselves innocent of the charge. Our conduct is before the world. We say we are loyal, and we claim it as a right to be taken at our word.52

The discussions at the Vatican Council took place at the moment that Gladstone's Elementary Education Act of 1870 was undergoing its legislative progress and at a time when for Manning it seemed 'the last hour of European institutions had struck'53 as he viewed the impact of the rapid secularisation of education in Italy.54 His passionate belief that Catholics had an obligation to present a Christian answer to current theories based on the exultation of the State became paramount in his thinking. The advent of Gladstone's Vaticanism attacks some few years after the Council, thereby entrenched the determination of all Catholics to sustain the fight for denominational education. Significantly, it had been the Catholic laity that had laid down the parameters of the struggle in 1870 - 'a system of popular education founded on the secular principle instead of being unsectarian would be sectarian in the most obnoxious sense to the community generally, and it would be especially unjust to Roman Catholics who under such a system would be compelled to support schools contrary to the plain dictates of their consciences ...'.55 In that statement we see the belief clearly delineated that, for Catholics, the teaching of all knowledge must be undertaken within a metier of Christian conviction. This stance was ever more manifest in the next thirty years as rivalry between board schools and denominational schools became acute: this rivalry forms the fourth development that finally secured the permanence of the dual system.

 Conflict raised its head in the years 1872-74,56 in relation to the stipulation of 1870 that no child in any State-aided school was to be compelled to receive denominational or other forms of religious instruction. Religious instruction had to be at the beginning, at the end, or at the beginning and the end of a school meeting, thus making it easy for children to be withdrawn if desired. The regulation had presumed that all forms of religious instruction could be confined to a set time or times in the school day. But what of 'the Catholic atmosphere' that not only permeated the whole life and organisation of a Catholic school but was the very <u>raison d'etre</u> of its existence? Statues were displayed in schools, prayers were said 'silently' at the change of lessons, hymns were often used as suitable material for singing lessons, religious or hagiographical passages were used in reading, writing and comprehension exercises. The Catholic teacher, herself, had an interpretative role that was uncompromisingly committed and if the teacher happened to be a religious brother or a nun or a priest the very sight of the religious habit or the clerical cassock would convey a distinct religious message. Chesterton was later to define this atmosphere: 'Every part of education has a connection with every other part. If it does not all combine to convey some general view of life, it is not education at all'.57 Given that philosophy, it was inevitable that the provisions of 1870 would prove to be incapable of forming a workable legalistic framework for parliamentary aid. Government increasingly had thus to turn a blind eye to the ignoring of the spirit of its own legislation. The protection of Catholic schools from 'the violation of religious liberty' and the recognition of 'the sacred rights of parental authority' were the abiding justifications of the Catholic party in all the debates about education until and beyond 1902.

Catholic determination reached its apotheosis in the general election campaign of 1885 in which the demand for rate-aid became particularly strident.58 The political action on the part of the bishops in this campaign was formally justified by the outspoken Bishop of Nottingham, the Oratorian Edward Bagshawe, when he claimed such action to be one of the highest duties of a bishop 'since the interests of God, of His Church, and of society, are more affected by politics than by anything else after the direct practice and teaching of religion itself'.59 Bishops and priests, he maintained, 'may most properly use in political action their rights as individuals, and their legitimate influence as leaders of their people'.

The Liberal Government was defeated on its budget proposals on 8th June 1885, and Gladstone resigned. After an abortive attempt of the Tories to form an administration, a general election ensued in which Chamberlain called for 'free schools' in return for an increased exchequer grant. The Weekly Register summed up Catholic fears of this 'unauthorised programme' when it declared on the 7th October that 'by accepting further assistance from public sources in order to make their schools free, Catholics will incur perilous risk of losing their schools altogether, because politicians, presumably hostile, may, by withdrawing State assistance, make the continued maintenance of the schools practically impossible'. The solution, the only solution, was rate-aid.

The Tory party, under the shrewd leadership of Salisbury, declared a willingness to re-open for investigation the 1870 settlement. Salisbury, in an electioneering speech in Newport on 7th October 1885, declared: 'I do claim that whatever Church or form of Christianity (Christians) belong to, they should be given the opportunity to educate the people in the belief of Christianity which they profess ...', rather than have to submit to 'a lifeless, boiled down, mechanical, unreal religious teaching which is prevalent in the Board Schools ...'.60

Cardinal Manning had pleaded in The Nineteenth Century, not for the abrogation of the 1870 Act which 'would be like proposing the repeal of the Gregorian Calendar', but for an extension, completion and fulfilment of the basic principle enshrined in the dual system and already firmly established by legislation. As a consequence, Catholics were to demand of all parliamentary candidates an answer to each of two questions: 'Will you place denominational schools on a perfect footing of equality with Board Schools? Will you vote for a Royal Commission to inquire into the operation of the Act of 1870?'61

The questions were ingenious. They implied no re-opening of the 1870 settlement, as such, and they associated all denominational schools, Anglican and Wesleyan as well as Catholic, in their disarming queries. Before the middle of November 1885 even close followers of Chamberlain had been willing to pledge their vote for an enquiry. The campaign, vigorously pursued by the bishops in messages to the faithful throughout the election period and in the columns of the press, bore fruit. The Irish Party gave its support. T.P. O'Connor's <u>Manifesto</u> of 23rd November 1885 spoke of the Liberal menace to the future of denominational schools, in which 'under the name of free schools' Liberals had begun 'an insidious attempt to crush the religious education of the country, to establish a system of State tyranny and intolerance, and to fetter the right of conscience, which is sacred in the selection of the school as in the free selection of one's church'.62

The intervention of the Catholic bishops and of the Irish Party in the election campaign on the schools issue, and the direct support that intervention earned from many leading Anglicans, helped to produce a political stalemate in which the Tories, with the volatile support of the Irish members, sustained a majority of three over the Liberals. Tenuous as the outcome seemed to be, it was sufficient to enable Salisbury to establish the Cross Commission to enquire into the working of the Elementary Education Acts in England and Wales. Manning was appointed a member of that Commission.

Edward Norman has seen, in its educational policy, the public emergence of the Roman Catholic Church at its most visible. The effect of that policy was to consolidate clerical influence in the Church itself because of the necessity for a centralised scheme of action and a co-ordinated programme.63 Fed upon the watchwords of 'parental choice', 'liberty of conscience' and 'a fair deal for all the nation's children', the irrevocable nature of the dual system was acknowledged and, indeed, further entrenched by the Act of 1902 which finally abolished the school boards and provided a proper measure of financial support for all schools. For Catholics the struggle after 1902 was no longer to be a fight for existence but for a greater share of the national and local resources.

In the centenary year of the achievement of Catholic Emancipation, it was possible for Cardinal Bourne to claim for Catholic schools a further role, the tasks of the preservation of the nation's Christian character and the upholding of the standard of its Christian morality. Bourne saw the special mission of the Catholic Church 'in the second century of recovered freedom' to be 'to strengthen and uphold that Christianity which is based and rooted in belief in the divinity of Jesus Christ our Lord' and to maintain, 'in the country, the tradition of Christian moral life.'64 This new *consus fidelium* was to reach its apotheosis in the views of Cardinal Arthur Hinsley, writing at the outbreak of the Second World War when the millenium seemed to have arrived. Echoing the earlier sentiments of Manning, he claimed to speak for Christianity itself:

> our traditional English education demands that the children of a Christian people have by Divine Law a right to a full Christian education; that Christian parents have a twofold right and duty, both natural and supernatural, to preserve this priceless inheritance; that Christian children are in no sense the property of a state which has no religion or which is pagan and atheist; that secular instruction is not of such supreme moment as the formation of citizens to be Christians; that parents have an inalienable right to decide on the selection of teachers to whom their children will be entrusted; that the poor as well as the rich in all justice must have this same right and liberty.65

All the traditional claims are there: parental rights and duties; the demand for social equity and for financial justice. To these is now added, however, a profound sense of mission within which they are located, a crusade for the preservation of Christian teaching itself in the teeth of increasingly hostile, secular and materialist attitudes.

In 1944, the Roman Catholic bishops would have endorsed Fr. John C. Heenan's view that R.A. Butler must have slept with a copy of **Mein Kampf** under his pillow to have saddled the Church at the end of a devastating war with an immediate threat to that freedom of conscience and those minority rights which ecclesiastics had striven for years to uphold.66 Archbishop Bernard Griffin, indeed, considered the people had been tricked in 1944 because Butler's wide-ranging education measure had been introduced by a 'consensus' National Government that by its very nature had prevented minority groups from presenting their case within a traditional framework of parliamentary and political democracy. Butler could not claim to have an electoral mandate for such action. Griffin reaffirmed unequivocally that 'as loyal members of the State, and as taxpayers equally with others, (Catholic) parents claim that they should not be allowed to suffer because of their consciences, but should be granted equal facilities with other members of the community'.67 Nevertheless, Griffin resolved with his episcopal confreres that the financial burden of building new schools in a reconstructed English and Welsh educational system would have to be shouldered: the survival not only of the Catholic Faith but of Christian attitudes themselves would otherwise be at risk.

With the emergence of comprehensive reorganisation in the 'sixties', the financial debt of the Roman Catholic Church in England and Wales for the building of new schools soon exceeded fifty million pounds. The enormity of servicing such a sum prevented the Church from devoting attention to its other pressing social concerns. The Second Vatican Council (1962-65), despite its re-examination of religious attitudes and its debunking of institutional shibboleths, had little effect upon the case for the preservation of denominational schools. Indeed, it strengthened the argument in their favour. Mass attendance figures in England and Wales in 1965 were running as high as 50 per cent of the Catholic population and, as such, were one of the highest in the world. The Council, by an emphasis upon the importance of personal and family responsibility for religious growth and commitment, associated with the rights of conscience, endorsed those concepts of 'wholeness', 'unity' and 'spiritual integrity' which lay at the heart of the nineteenth century's philosophy of Catholic education. The growing urgency of ecumenism enhanced the need for religious formation and sought to strengthen Christian attitudes to encounter threatening social manifestations of modern society - abortion, euthanasia, genetic manipulation, violence, unemployment. Indeed, the age-old adherence to Christian teaching was now seen to be the only antidote to a long list of moral and social horrors. At its source was the continuing belief in the importance of a future life after death.

It is significant that during the Council the spokesman on education of the English and Welsh Roman Catholic bishops, Mgr. George Andrew Beck, emphasised that the continuing role of Catholic schools was not to sustain a sort of out-moded or out-dated ghetto sub-culture. Rather, it was to take 'the full richness of faith out into the community, to shed new light on truths which whatever discipline they belong to, reflect the one eternal truth that is God Himself'.68 This foreshadowing of a strategy for Catholic education in the twentieth century perhaps only reformulates the teaching that the seven-year-old Andrew learned at his mother's knee - being a Catholic is an attitude, not an act.69

NOTES AND REFERENCES

1. Thomas, Gordon, Desire and Denial, Grafton Books, 1986, p.232.

2. Ampleforth Abbey, Bishop Hedley's Address on School Work. Delivered at Ampleforth College on the Re-opening of Studies, 28th August 1877. At the time of his Address, Hedley was the Auxiliary-Bishop of Newport and Menevia.

3. von Arx, Jeffrey Paul, Progress and Pessimism, U.S.A.: Harvard, 1985, pp.68-9.

4. Sharratt, Bernard, 'English Roman Catholicism in the 1960s' in: Hastings, Adrian (ed.), Bishops and Writers, Anthony Clarke, 1977, p.128.

5. Wiseman, Nicholas, The Religious and Social Position of the Catholics in England, London, 1864, p.9.

6. Norman, Edward, The English Catholic Church in the Nineteenth Century, O.U.P., 1984, p.29.

7. Ibid., p.33.

8. Wyse, Thomas, 'Education in England', *The Dublin Review*, II, 3, Dec. 1836, p.12.

9. Ibid. See also p.34.

10. Macauley, Ambrose, *Dr Russell of Maynooth*, Darton, Longman and Todd, 1983, pp.68-9.

11. *The Dublin Review*, V, 9, July 1838, p.77.

12. Ibid., XIV, 27, Feb. 1843, p.177.

13. Morris, John (Canon), 'Popular Education in England' in: *The Dublin Review*, L, 99, May 1861, p.61.

14. Ibid., p.63.

15. Ibid., p.70.

16. *The Dublin Review*, LII, Nov. 1862, pp.117-18.

17. Altholz, Joseph L., 'The Political Behaviour of the English Catholics, 1850-1867' in: *The Journal of British Studies*, U.S.A.: Connecticut, Nov. 1964, pp.89-103.

18. McClelland, V.A., 'School or Cloister? An English Educational Dilemma, 1794-1889' in: *Pedagogica Historica*, XX/I, 1980, p.108.

19. Hickey, John, *Urban Catholics*, Geoffrey Chapman, 1967, p.88.

20. Manning's *Pastoral Letter* of 8th June 1865. See also McClelland, V.A,, *Cardinal Manning: His Public Life and Influence, 1865-1892*, O.U.P., 1962, pp.26 et seq.

21. Gladstone Papers, British Library, Manning to Gladstone, 7.3.1870.

22. Norman, Edward, op. cit., p.177.

23. The Dublin Review, February 1840, pp.243-4.

24. Other examples are Worksop, Glossop, Alton, Cheadle, Cossey, Brentwood, Whalley, Scarisbrick, Rainhill, Skipton, St. John's Wood, Bermondsey, Weybridge, Grace Dieu, Whitwick, Mount St. Bernard's Monastery, Marlinscroft, Oshaldeston, Poole, Dover, Brough, Tixal, Grantham, Castle Eden, Newport and Blair's Seminary, Aberdeen.

25. The Dublin Review, February 1840, pp.243-4.

26. See Leetham, Claude, Luigi Gentili: A Sower for the Second Spring, Burns and Oates, 1965, passim.

27. See Newman, J.H., A Letter Addressed to His Grace the Duke of Norfolk on the Occasion of Mr Gladstone's Recent Expostulation, London, 1875, p.20.

28. Leslie, S., The Oxford Movement, 1833 to 1933, London, 1933, p.62.

29. Gorman, W.G. Converts to Rome, London, 1910.

30. The Rambler, December 1848, p.236.

31. Capes, J.M., To Rome and Back, London: Smith, Elder and Co., 1873, p.233.

32. Watkin, E.I. Roman Catholicism in England from the Reformation to 1950, Oxford, 1957, p.200.

33. The Rambler, December 1848, p.238.

34. Ibid. p.241.

35. Ibid. Letter published from Frederick Oakeley, then teaching at St. Edmund's College, Ware, 11.12.1848.

36. For a full analysis of this venture see McClelland, V.A., 'The Liberal Training of England's Catholic Youth: William Joseph Petre (1847-93) and Educational Reform' in: Victorian Studies, XV, 3, 1972, pp.257-77.

37. The Dublin Review, 239, 506, p.327.

38. Manning, H.E., 'The Catholic Church and Modern Society' in: The North American Review, reprinted in Miscellanies, III, London, 1888, pp. 309, 322.

39. See McClelland, V.A., 'Gladstone and Manning: A Question of Authority' in: Jagger, P.J. (ed.), Gladstone, Politics and Religion, Macmillan, 1985, pp.148-70.

40. Montagu, Rt. Hon. Lord Robert, M.P., Expostulation in Extremis: or, Remarks on Mr Gladstone's 'Political Expostulation' on the Vatican Decrees in their Bearing on Civil Allegiance, Burns and Oates, 1874.

41. Capes, J.M., op. cit., p.225.

42. Ibid., p.226.

43. Ibid., p.218.

44. Gladstone, W.E., The State in its Relations with the Church, London: John Murray, 4th edn, 1841, vol. II, p.8.

45. Macaulay, T.B., 'Gladstone on Church and State', reprinted in his Critical and Historical Essays, London: Dent, edn 1909, pp.271 et seq.

46. Manning, H.E., The Rule of Faith, 2nd edn, 1839, p.45.

47. Gladstone, W.E., Vaticanism: An Answer to Replies and Reproofs, 1875.

48. Ullathorne, W.B., Mr Gladstone's Expostulation Unravelled, Burns and Oates, 1875, p.16.

49. Capel, J., A Reply to the the Right Hon. W.E. Gladstone's 'Political Expostulation', Longman, Green and Co., 1875, 3rd edn, p.8.

50. Ibid., p.47.

51. Ibid., p.65.

52. Clifford, William, *Catholic Allegiance*, A Pastoral Letter of 25th Nov. 1874, p.6.

53. Barry, W., *Memories and Opinions*, London: Putnam, 1926, p.85.

54. McClelland, V.A., *English Roman Catholics and Higher Education 1830-1903*, The Clarendon Press, O.U.P., 1973, p.243.

55. Westminster Archdiocesen Archives, *Proposed Declaration of the Catholic Laity*, 1870, pp.7,8.

56. For a full discussion of the problem, see McClelland, V.A., 'The Protestant Alliance and Roman Catholic Schools, 1872-74' in: *Victorian Studies*, VIII, 2, 1964, pp.173-82.

57. In *The Universe*, 8th August 1930.

58. See McClelland, V.A., 'The "Free Schools" Issue and the General Election of 1885: A Denominational Response' in: *History of Education*, 5, 2, 1976, pp.141-54.

59. *The Tablet*, 1st August 1885.

60. *The Weekly Register*, 10th October 1885. Report of Salisbury's speech at Newport on 7th October 1885.

61. *The Tablet*, 3rd October 1885.

62. *The Times*, 23rd November 1885.

63. Norman, Edward, *Roman Catholicism in England*, O.U.P., 1985, pp.76-7.

64. Bourne, Cardinal Francis, *Education and Morality*, Burns, Oates and Washbourne, 1929, p.22.

65. Hinsley, Cardinal Arthur in his *Pastoral Letter* for Trinity Sunday, 1940.

66. Heenan, J.C., *The Catholic Herald*, 10th March 1944.

67. de la Bedoyere, M. *Cardinal Bernard Griffin*, Rockliff, 1955, p.45.

68. *The Catholic Herald*, 5th July 1963.

69. See my argument in 'The Church and Religious Education' in: Cumming, J. and Burns, P. (eds), *The Church Now*, Gill and Macmillan, 1980, pp.109-20.

and violent political separation. This manifested itself in a highly romanticised and idealistic view of the country's past, and, in particular, an almost religious memory of the period of national liberation associated with 1916-22. It also gave further support to the power of the Catholic church and allowed it to use the comparison with Godless Britain to argue for a national ideology built on a publicly expressed foundation of Catholic beliefs with respect to morality and values.

The new prosperity of the 1960s stimulated change with surprising speed, and in ways that in retrospect would appear to have been inevitable. To begin with there were a great many important and fundamental social developments, in education, health care, and welfare generally: but to these can be added the emergence of individual consumerism with its attendant motor cars, foreign holidays and new houses; a much wider and more cosmopolitan range of leisure pursuits such as restaurants, nightclubs and sports facilities; and not least a flowering of the arts. Almost as dramatically the 1980s can be seen as a reversal of many of these latter trends with an economy in recession, high levels of unemployment, the accompanying social problems such as drugs, broken marriages, rising crime rates, and the return of that peculiarly Irish spectre, emigration.

During both of these periods of change, and to some extent as a consequence of them, there has developed within Ireland a debate about the fundamental nature of Irish society, about such underlying issues as ideology, image and identity, and about those individual characteristics which separate it and make it distinguishable from other societies. The very existence of such a debate is a signal that these basic ideas are unstable and changing, and that within the society there are a great many cultural ambiguities and complexities of identity. It does nothing to help resolve these tensions that they are often presented publicly in the form of easily maintained stereotypes. There is clearly a dilemma about how to join the modern world of industry and advanced technology, while at the same time maintaining in a real and vibrant form the valuable, distinctive and defining national characteristics from the

5
EDUCATION, RELIGION AND CULTURAL CHANGE IN THE REPUBLIC OF IRELAND

Seamus Dunn

INTRODUCTION

The 1960s and 1970s represented a time of profound innovation and renewal for Ireland in its cultural and economic life. This was immediately followed in the 1980s by a recession which, while reversing much of the economic progress, had little obvious effect on social and cultural change. A number of national and international forces contributed to the momentum of the first set of changes. These included the country's entry to the European Economic Community in 1973; the Vatican Council in 1962; the arrival of Irish national television, also in 1962, and the access, partly as a consequence, to the influence of the international mass media and its entertainment culture; the rapid economic change leading to a period of comparative prosperity. In a more negative sense, there was also the counter-balancing blow to this growing national feeling of self-confidence caused by the violence in the North of Ireland.

The consequence of economic change was an opening up of Irish society to ways of thought and behaviour that were dramatically different from those experienced in the past. Ireland seemed for the first time prepared to abandon its commitment to an indigent culture which was deeply rooted in a complex and apparently inseparable mixture of nationalism and Catholicism. This had produced a society with an almost xenophobic isolationism, one which placed great emphasis in particular on the need for a cultural and social separation from Britain, a spiritual separation to echo the comparatively recent past. The long, essentially unsuccessful, campaign to revive the Irish language is the single most important example of this. One immediate and understandable consequence of this uncertainty or loss of confidence has been a rush by some commentators to support and argue for a return to the symbols and fidelities of the past. Fennell,1 writes as follows:

> This ... produced the boom years of the 60s and led to a general ideological reaction against the nationalist program inherited from the revolution. The Gaelic revival was neglected and tacitly shelved. 'Catholic' became an unfashionable word and the Irish identity was declared to be non-Catholic. Things English came into fashion again ...

Although there has been some disagreement about how powerful its influence has been, the continuing violence in the North has remained within the consciousness, or at least on the edge of the consciousness, of the people of the Republic as a highly visible and not to be ignored symbol of the failure of the society to make any headway with its oldest problem. Some dimensions of the conflict, including its echo of the country's violent past, the re-emphasis on divided feelings and suspicion about the impress of Britain in Irish affairs, and ambivalence about the endangered Gaelic cultural inheritance, all add to the uncertainty evident in the debate about the national identity. It was the desire to face up to the problem of the North in particular which provoked the government of Garret Fitzgerald in the 1980s to attempt to implement what has been called a <u>constitutional crusade</u>. His analysis led him to the view that both parts of the country must find constitutional solution to the problems of separation of mind and of aspiration. He argued that the necessary components of this solution, for the Republic, included the generation within the society of a deeper tolerance of diversity in its constitution and laws, and in its daily and religious life. This would include an acceptance of pluralism and of its constitutional consequences, the freedom to act in conscience, and the clear and unequivocal separation of church and state. Pluralism was conceived of as a way of arguing for the equal value of all citizens in both parts of the island, whatever their religious, racial or socio-cultural backgrounds.

The most immediate and intractable barrier in the way of this crusade was the difficulty in reconciling such changes with the crucial and powerful position of the Catholic church within the society. The church while not publicly disagreeing with the diagnosis has tended to argue against, and so to frustrate, any attempts at change which seemed to it to challenge traditional values. Pluralism might be acceptable, but only if it did not imply any dilution of Catholic values. Even before the 1980s there was evidence of anxiety within the church about many aspects of the new world. Although not all were unique to Ireland, there had been a sequence of overt changes and attempted changes in Irish public life, of which this crusade was only a single manifestation. This had involved, among other things: the modification of the <u>Ne Temere</u> decree on mixed marriages by Pope Paul VI in 1970; the lifting of an age-old ban prohibiting Catholics from attending Trinity College, Dublin, also in 1970; the removal in 1972, following a referendum on the matter, of article 44 of the constitution which had given a special place to the Catholic church in Irish life; a succession of failed attempts to get family planning acts through the Dail, eventually succeeding with a parliamentary bill in 1979 and an amendment in 1985; and a national debate on the future of Ireland called <u>The New Ireland Forum</u> in 1983.2 Although the Catholic church was not opposed to all of these, it found the overall trend worrying, especially when placed beside what it perceived as a more general public laxity in moral affairs. This anxiety manifested itself in the victories by the supporters of Catholic values in two national referenda relating to the issues of abortion and divorce.

These defeats, discussed below, were of particular significance since they signalled an attempt to retreat, in moral and social if not in economic terms, from the new Ireland of the 1960s and 1970s.

Irish Christian Culture

The economic recession with its accompanying social problems, depression and loss of confidence, has helped to strengthen and support this desire to return to traditional values and to defend those aspects of the society which were formerly perceived as its foundation stones. The visit of Pope John Paul II in 1979 was an important stimulus in this process. The deep reserves of loyalty and commitment to the Catholic church, both in itself and as a symbol of emotional and social security, have acted to provide support for these signs of reaction.

The most overt form of this has been a series of highly organised, professionally run campaigns by groups of lay Catholics in relation to two attempts in the early 1980s to change the constitution. The first campaign, in 1983, was in favour of adding to the constitution an amendment that would make it impossible for an Irish legislature ever to pass laws allowing abortion in any circumstance. Since abortion in any form was already illegal, and since no political party had shown even the most remote interest in changing the law in this matter, this campaign was widely interpreted as a deliberate attempt to make the constitution even more Catholic in its provisions. The second campaign was an attempt to amend the constitution to allow a form of divorce in 1986. The general case against such developments was made in terms of the Catholic view of the *Family*, and the belief that this involves opposition to any legislation which would permit such things as contraception, divorce, homosexuality and pluralism: this last is usually interpreted as meaning secularism.

Whatever the intentions of those involved in the campaigns to support traditional Catholic views, the results were intensely disturbing for those who thought that the old antagonisms and religious prejudices of the past had disappeared from Ireland. An almost hysterical climate was produced and the whole process 'opened wounds in the Irish body politic that had in recent times seemed entirely healed'.[3] The Protestant churches argued publicly and forcibly that, whatever their own views on these matters, the demand that the constitution of the state should be used to protect Catholic versions of society and of morality represented a one- dimensional, exclusive and unacceptable view. For the first time since the founding of the state there was a no-holds-barred public confrontation between those arguing for an Ireland that protected Catholic morality in its constitution and those, including almost all Protestant interests in the state but by no means restricted to these groups, arguing for a liberal pluralism. Although in the event the first of these interests won the battle, many commentators have argued that the evidence in the figures suggests that they may have lost the war.4

THE INFLUENCE OF THE EDUCATIONAL FACTOR: THE BEGINNINGS

The dramatic nature of these changes and controversies in Irish society of necessity have affected the educational system. In order to understand how education has mirrored developments, it is necessary to pay rather more attention than usual to historical developments. The history of education in Ireland, like so many other aspects of its existence, is coloured and touched at all points by its long and complex relationship with Britain. More generally all aspects of the separate cultures of the two islands have become intertwined and confused over the centuries in ways that are still not always clear, although the colonial nature of the relationship has ensured that the influence of Britain (and British culture) has always been a very powerful one. At various times in history British policy on cultural matters has ranged from a comparatively mild assimilationist approach to the completely destructive ideology of the Penal days,5 when a series of laws, passed at the end of the seventeenth century, had as their aim the removal of all rights to property, religion and education from the native Irish. However, despite the many centuries of mutual influence and interpenetration, the two cultures have managed to remain, if not intact, distinct and separate and often antagonistic.

The long-term nature of the relationship has meant that the crucial strategy in the struggle for dominance has been a cultural one, and the most important element in this has been the replacement of the Irish language with English. And it is precisely in this process that the importance of education has always been recognised. Seamus Deane describes with quotations how the assimilationist policy of the early seventeenth century was perceived at the time. Interestingly, the optimism displayed in these quotations about the power of education reflects much modern controversy:

> ... the Irish septs be dissolved, that the Irish be moved into the towns, mingled with the settlers, educated in English, in grammar, and in science ... whereby they will in short time grow up to that civil conversation that ... (they will) ... perceive the foulness of their own brutish behaviour compared to theirs, for learning hath that wonderful power of itself that it can soften and temper the most stern and savage nature.6

It is not surprising then that the long history of schooling in Ireland is irretrievably, and to this day recognisably, mixed up with colonial history. For example, the earliest schools established under Act of Parliament were the parish schools of Henry VIII, the avowed purpose of which was to introduce a knowledge of the English language among the native Irish. The inevitable result of such a policy was that in time the English language became associated with power, influence and affluence: it became the language of legal, political, cultural, liturgical and economic life. The Irish language, on the other hand, became associated with disaffection, defeat, poverty and ignorance. When the Irish eventually gained independence in 1922, this frail, almost dead, language was, not unexpectedly, perceived as the most important link with the Gaelic past and therefore as the symbol of national identity. Ironically, the principal means to be used by the new state towards the reversal of the past, and the revival and restoration of the language, was once again the educational system.

Apart from language and general culture, the most

obvious and ineradicable difference between the two countries was religion. This was of great power in itself but it also became part of the symbolism of distinctiveness in that the commitment to Catholicism among the Irish was in part political; and this included its value as a token of opposition to the English state-supported church. Thus religion and politics were inevitably conflated from the earliest times, and for the Irish much of their political sense of themselves as a nation then and now included Catholicism.

THE NATIONAL SCHOOL SYSTEM

The first wide-ranging attempt to regularise educational provision in Ireland was the founding in 1831 of the <u>National School</u> system by Lord Stanley, then the chief secretary for Ireland. This was initiated with the provision of a sum of £30,000 by the British House of Commons. Before this the incidence of primary schools around the country varied considerably. This variation extended not only to the quality of the schools, some of which were described as <u>hedge schools</u> because of their lack of physical premises, but also to their geographical spread in that some parts of the country had no schools at all. Many of them were also of controversial origin in that they had been created specifically for the purpose of converting the Irish to Protestantism.7 This experience of education as a vehicle for proselytisation continues to influence, to some extent, Irish views about control of schools, school curricula, and such matters as religiously integrated schools.

The new National School system was intended as an acceptable general system which all creeds could support. Although it was legislated for and funded by government it was in many ways a locally managed system. The resources made available were administered by a central Board which consisted of seven Commissioners representing the main religious denominations. These were the <u>Commissioners of National Education</u>. This Board had the power to help with the costs of building schools, appoint inspectors, establish model schools, contribute to teachers' salaries and provide (and produce) school books. However, at local level the schools were under the management of some important local person, often a clergyman.8

This system has been recognised as one of the earliest experiments in the provision of widespread education by the state, and was the forerunner of much of what is today considered the normal duty of the state with respect to education. The clear intention was that the schools should be non-denominational, but not secular. It was hoped that if children from the different religions were educated together they would learn mutual tolerance and respect.9 There was to be no hint of proselytisation and all creeds were to be treated equally. With regard to the non-religious part of the curriculum it was felt that no difference need be made between the denominations. Religious education, however, was to be dealt with at a special and separate part of the day, when each denomination would meet with its own local clergy, who had right of access to the premises.

As an aid to this process special school texts were produced. These were carefully monitored by both Catholic and Protestant clerics to ensure that they were both non-denominational but clearly Christian in character. The texts themselves in terms of quality were a great improvement on anything that had gone before them, and they quickly acquired a very high reputation and were much in demand in England and in the colonies, much to the annoyance of commercial publishers.10

This pluralistic non-denominational ideal did not last very long, however, and one by one the various denominations found fault with it. Pressure groups from the churches forced amendments on the government, the results of which were to remove from the system the fundamental aim of a non-denominationalist curriculum. For example, the Presbyterians argued that allowing Catholic clergy into schools implied the promotion of popery, and that the curriculum did not deal directly with the Bible. Their pressure quickly made an impression and in 1840 a variation on the system allowed for a new school type which was essentially a Presbyterian school. Among the conditions of this were that only clergymen of their own denominations could enter these schools, so excluding Catholic priests and, almost inevitably, Catholic pupils, representing the majority of the people who were Catholic. To begin with, the Catholic bishops had a majority in favour of supporting the new National School System. Indeed in 1841 Pope Gregory XVI encouraged Catholics in this support. There was at all times, however, a strong minority of bishops who opposed the system vehemently, mainly on religious grounds, although for some the British character of the schools remained a political difficulty. There was also, despite reassurances and to some extent in the face of the evidence, a fear of proselytisation. This minority eventually became a majority in response to movements within the church generally, and in particular because of the influence of the churchman Paul Cullen, first while he was based in Rome, and later when he became Cardinal and Primate of the Irish Catholic church. In the end, as a result of a long and unremitting struggle by the hierarchy, the system was transformed into an almost completely denominational one. It was because of the hard-won nature of this power that the Catholic church, later, was not disposed to allow any of it to be eroded and has continually and successfully refused to countenance any legislation which would interfere with clerical control of education.

When independence was established in 1922, the Board of Commissioners was abruptly disbanded and replaced by a branch of the newly founded Department of Education. Despite the controversies and difficulties it had laboured under, the National School system had a solid record of achievement during the ninety years of its existence, and many basic features of the present primary sector can still be traced back to it. When it was established only about half of the population could read and write, but by 1901 the figure was 86 per cent. There were by then schools in all parts of the country irrespective of their poverty or backwardness. The total number of primary schools increased from 1000 in 1834 to over 8000 in 1921, and this is made more significant by the fact that the population decreased by over 50 per cent between 1842 and 1921.11

INDEPENDENCE

Immediately independence had been achieved the Irish government placed the revival of the Irish language at the top of its priorities, as the most powerful symbol of its new independence. This revival was to be achieved mainly through the schools and a system of compulsory Irish language teaching and use. The procedures established to ensure that this would come about were based on the assumption that Ireland was one nation with a single culture that was both Gaelic and Catholic. Akenson,12 provides many quotations from politicians of the day which demonstrate this. In particular the wishes of the Protestant minority in the South were ignored, and this aroused a considerable amount of resentment. Bishops from the Church of Ireland made protests at the time, as did others, but this point of view was not given any weight.13 This early inability to influence the views of the majority in the South may have been instrumental in persuading the Protestant population that protest in their own interest was futile. This in turn may have given an essentially false impression as to how they felt about many issues which concerned them, particularly when the special position of the Catholic church was made manifest in policy and in law. The determination to insist on the compulsory re-establishment of the Irish language also acted to make the gulf between the people on the two sides of the border grow wider and wider.

The first 1922 constitution of the independent Free State of Ireland was in all essentials a secular one. Churches were not mentioned, and certainly no denominational special status. However, the very largely Catholic population and the power of the hierarchy ensured that nonetheless government ministers took great care not to offend the Catholic church. This de facto respect for the views of the majority religion later translated into the spirit of the new constitution of 1937, which not only referred to the special position of the Catholic church, but was more generally redolent of Catholic thought, especially in relation to such matters as fundamental human rights. With respect to education it refers, in Article 42, to the prior rights of the family as the <u>primary and natural educator of the child</u> and guarantees to respect the inalienable right and duty of parents with regard to the education of their children. This language echoes quite precisely the views of the Catholic church on matters of education. The church argues that parents have the primary right to educate, and that the rights of the state are confined to the provision of schools and the establishment of academic standards. In particular the state has no right to go against parents' wishes with regard to educational matters. The role of the church is to guide and advise Catholic parents on the proper education of their children. Parents have the right to ignore church advice, but on grave peril of their souls. This is not the place to examine the convoluted nature of this argument or to analyse its tendency to be circular.14 But it is worth pointing out that there is no evidence that the church has ever systematically tried to find out the opinion of parents about schools. Certainly until recently there were no forums such as parent-teacher associations or parent representatives on school management bodies.

The resulting influence and power of the Catholic church in independent Ireland can be seen still in its control over a great variety of social and welfare institutions, and in its ability to influence, albeit indirectly, the course of government legislation. The church owns and manages hospitals and orphanages, and is intimately involved in almost all aspects of social welfare provision. In particular it owns and runs the great majority of the country's schools. It has been argued by Whyte,15 who has written the most comprehensive book about the relationships between Church and State in Ireland in this century, that this does not mean that the church has any direct governmental or legislative power, and that in fact the political leaders rarely consult with the church on matters of policy. He does not argue that there is a 'separation of Church and State', but describes the relationship as one of 'aloofness between Church and State'. However there is evidence that its hidden influence has always been powerful enough to frustrate government legislative intentions when these were considered unacceptable to the church.16

After partition in 1922 the educational systems in the North and South of the country, more or less identical up to then, diverged quite radically. The North began to develop a system based on local authority control, which, though providing for a considerable level of clerical and church representation and influence, was nonetheless amenable to local opinion and a measure of local control. In the South there was complete centralisation in the sense that the newly founded Department of Education in Dublin ran the system administratively and there was no attempt to create a local authority structure. This replacing of the Board of Commissioners is described by Akenson as '... substituting for an academic and professional oligarchy, an unfettered bureaucracy'.17

For a great many reasons, the first forty years in the South was a period of general stagnation in educational development. The system did not evolve or modify its structures, its curricula, or its manner of working in any significant or important way. As a result it became moribund and out of date.18 Two factors are thought to have been of particular significance in this lack of development. The first was the inevitably conservative power and influence of the church in education. The history of the struggle for control of education in the nineteenth and early twentieth centuries meant that it was accepted that the church would fight hardest on this issue. So after independence the state was correspondingly reluctant to interfere. This was certainly true of successive ministers of education, many of whom not only made no attempt to dispute policy and development matters with the church, but actually favoured and approved of a system which left the church in charge of education. General Mulcahy, Minister of Education 1948-51 and 1954-57, is quoted as follows:

> The State approach to education in the Irish Republic is one which unreservedly accepts the

supernatural conception of man's nature and destiny. ... it is determined to see that such facilities as ecclesiastical authorities consider proper shall be provided in the school for the carrying on of the work of religious education.19

As a result of this refusal to interfere with any important aspect of the day-to-day management and decision-making in matters of schooling, there was no change agency within the system. Because of the need to remove the traces of the colonial history, education was conceived of as a way both of regenerating the Gaelic past, and of protecting and supporting the Catholic and Gaelic nature of the society. By their very nature such aspirations tend to look back rather than forward.

The second reason why there was little interference, which to some extent followed from the first, was that the system was administered from the centre by a highly dedicated but rigorous and unimaginative bureaucracy. This was concerned primarily with maintaining the system, ensuring that it functioned efficiently, and trying to improve the procedures for regenerating the language. It is necessary to say that this approach was eventually acceptable to all the churches, including the Protestant churches. They also wished to keep their own schools because of their small numbers, and also as a protection from the effects of the **Ne Temere** decree and subsequent Catholic legislation with regard to mixed marriages. (This required that the agreement be secured from the Protestant partner to the marriage that the children be brought up as Catholics.)

Probably the first sign that the system might be about to change was the publication in 1965 of the report **Investment in Education**. This is described later, in more detail, as an important milestone in the dramatic transformation of the Irish educational system in the 1960s and 1970s. For this reason its description of the system at that time is important. On page three it states:

> The structure of the system of education in Ireland owes much to its history. It is in general an aided system. The state does not

itself operate the schools but assists other bodies to do so. Most of the primary and secondary schools are under clerical management. ... The major portion of public expenditure on education in Ireland is borne by central government funds.20

It was not just the primary schools which were controlled by the church. The secondary schools in the country had emerged in no planned or systematic way, and when the state was established all of these were privately owned, with the great majority of them owned by religious orders. This system was allowed to continue, with the state taking on, in the words of Investment in Education, the major portion of the expenditure on education, but with a very minor role in the ownership and control of the schools themselves.21

It can be and has been argued by the church that, had the church not been in a position to provide buildings, the state would have found the task almost impossible and that the result would have been a much more impoverished secondary system. From the point of view of the religious they had to provide the resources which the state could not afford.

> The burden of providing secondary education in Ireland rests on the shoulders of the religious, generally speaking. They bear the expense that normally is borne by the state. ... So long as the state is poor this arrangement for secondary education will exist in Ireland.22

Uniquely in this respect the Church in Ireland is still responsible for educational provision, as it has been from the beginning of Christian Irish history. One important consequence of this was that the number of places available in such schools was severely limited, and so a large proportion of the population did not attend a secondary school of any sort. Since secondary schools were also fee-paying, this also helped to ensure that those who did manage to be accepted tended to come from the better off sections of the community.

There was, however, one set of schools in Ireland

which was in a completely different situation. Schools in this set were given a variety of titles in different parts of the country, but they were all essentially technical schools.23 In 1930 a bill was passed to bring these all together under one system of management. As a result they were all renamed Vocational schools, and this is described by Fitzgerald as '... the only significant reform (in education) in the first 40 years of independence'.24 These schools were quite unique in that they were organised by Vocational Education Committees linked to local authority. Thus they were subject to an element of democratic control. They were also meant to be multi-denominational and sometimes were, although many of the committees were chaired by priests and had Catholic chaplains, ensuring that there was in some cases at least a degree of clerical influence if not control. In general terms they had low status and were usually considered to be inferior to the clerically run secondary schools. They were also to some extent thought of as dangerous in that they were 'state' schools and had a degree of autonomy.

By the 1960s the Republic of Ireland had about 600 secondary schools, almost all run by religious, and about 250 Vocational schools run by the Vocational Education Committees. A great majority of these schools were small and single-sex. With regard to the curriculum, this too was set in a well-defined and essentially unchanging mould during the first 40 years of the state. Mulcahy in 1981 writes,

> Despite the changes of recent years, at no time during the past 15 years or indeed at any time since the setting up of the Department of Education in 1924, has any sustained assessment and critical analysis been undertaken in regard to the overall purposes and programmes of post-primary education in Ireland.25

This judgement applied equally to the primary sector until 1971, when a new primary curriculum was established. This was in line with more modern developmental notions about the purpose and methodology of primary education, in that it changed the emphasis from the content of the curriculum to the children and their learning processes.

SOCIETAL AND EDUCATIONAL CHANGE

The role which education plays and has played in Ireland in promoting or suppressing movements for change is obviously dependent in many ways on the attitude of the Catholic church. Since education has always been to some extent controlled by the church, it is a profoundly important formative agency in the development of the national way of life. In the great majority of schools, the Catholic ethos is cherished and promoted, especially with respect to issues of morality and values, and this influences and helps to form views on such controversial issues as pluralism, the rights of minorities, attitude to violence in all their manifestations, and so on. Because of all this it might be expected that Irish society would project a deep mistrust and suspicion of any movement for change in these areas. It is therefore all the more surprising that in the 1960s and 1970s there was a strong process of secularisation at work and that this appears to be still active, if reduced.26

Whatever the influence of education in the development of these more general social changes, including the process of secularisation, it is significant that the educational system has itself changed considerably during the same period. 1962 was a crucial and perhaps even the introductory year for this process. Irish television was introduced, the Vatican Council began in Rome, and a trail-blazing research study of Irish educational needs was sponsored by the government and carried out with support from the OECD.27 However, as if to echo the past, the Minister of Education in that year, when asked about the need for new schools in new residential parts of Dublin, felt able to reply:

> Recognised Secondary schools are private institutions and so the initiative in establishing them does not lie with my department.28

The title of this important report, Investment in Education, is an indication not only of its content but of an assumed educational ideology. It created, for the first time, a complete statistical base for the existing system of education, and tried to forecast or project future figures so that some attempt could be made to begin long-term planning. It also sought to examine the future needs of industry and commerce, and to argue for a pattern of educational growth which would support those needs. The fact that certain government decisions about education almost immediately made these figures inaccurate is of less importance than the impetus the report gave to the continuing need for the compilation and management of such statistics, and for the need to connect educational change with economic development. From an ideological point of view it argued for a model of the educational system as an intrinsic part of the existing economic system, which could, if managed properly, contribute through its education of the people to a more productive economy. Education, it argued, should be planned and organised in such a way that the money spent on it produced a maximum output in economic terms.

The whole tone of the document was in itself an innovation in thinking about education in Ireland. It contained no agonising about the language, or about Gaelic culture, or any reference to the spirit of the past. It was instead an economics-based, hard-headed look at the actual condition of education with respect to the physical state of the schools, the number of children receiving education, and the basic quality of that education. Brown describes this aspect of it as follows:

> So instead of an Irish educational document reflecting on national identity, on the revival of Irish and on cultural imperatives of one kind or another Investment in Education dissected the social facts of Irish education, to reveal the class and geographical components of the system, setting out its human deficiencies for all to see.29

The picture which it painted was a disturbing one.

The educational system as a whole was depressed and under-funded with a badly run-down physical plant, a primary school system which failed many of its pupils and a class-based highly selective system at second and third level. The report made it clear that if the country wished to move into the new economic world of modern industry and commerce, the educational system demanded a great deal of extra money, energy and planning.

From a long-term point of view one of the most important immediate consequences of the report was the establishment of a Development Branch in the Department of Education, and this became the centre of the reform movement of the next decades. Also, almost immediately after the report, in 1966, the then Minister of Education (D. O'Malley of Fianna Fail) made what was probably the most dramatic and significant statement about education since the state was formed. He announced that the government intended to instigate a programme of development which would allow 'equality of education for all' and 'free education for all'. This was later reinforced by a statement that equal opportunity in education was 'our most urgent social and educational objective'.30

The process of putting this egalitarian aspiration into practice began almost at once, and over the next few years the structure and demography of education in Ireland was changed completely. In particular the newly founded Development branch, because of its financial muscle, was able to interfere in matters of organisation and structure in a previously unprecedented way. The table on page 108 helps to put the growth in the second level provision into perspective. It refers to the two years 1964 and 1980.31

In an enormous burst of energy there followed a sequence of changes which left hardly any facet of the Irish educational system untouched. These included a massive refurbishment of the physical plant to allow for the great increase in numbers,32 the promotion of new ideas about curricula at both primary and secondary level,33 the provision of greatly increased financial aid for students at university level, proposals about merging the two

Dublin universities, and radical innovation in the area of technical education at both second and third level.34 Perhaps the most clear measure of the change was that educational estimates rose from £16 million in 1957-58 to £44 million in 1967 and £49 million in 1969.35

		Pupils	Schools	Teachers
Secondary	1964	94,644	650	5,213
	1980	200,626	524	11,740
Vocational	1964	30,576	260	1,826
	1980	59,606	242	4,790
Others*	1964	-	-	-
	1980	25,894	56	1,684
Total	1964	125,220	910	7,039
	1980	286,126	822	18,214

* 'Others' refers principally to the new comprehensive and community schools created since the 'free education for all' statement.

The development in the provision of buildings is of particular interest in trying to understand the role of the churches in Irish society, and in education. It involved a massive extension of the system of second-level schools to cope with the huge influx following the 'free education for all' decision. This involved amalgamations of existing small schools into larger units, new buildings, extensions to existing schools and new types of schools. Before this, many small towns would have at least three small second-level schools: that is, a vocational school owned and managed by a local education committee, at least one boys' secondary school run by priests or religious brothers, and at least one girls' secondary school usually run by nuns. The promotion of schemes for cooperation or amalgamation or for the setting up of forms of comprehensive and community schools in such situations involved difficult, protracted and not always successful negotiations. However, the end result was that many new schools and many amalgamations were formed. At the same time new schemes for the creation of more representative management structures were worked out. Although the result of this was that the church representatives usually had a majority, for the first time parents and teachers, as well as in certain circumstances local authority representatives, became members of boards of management.36

The process of change has continued into the 1980s with a change in the emphasis, away from restructuring the overall system, towards more internal issues such as curriculum and pedagogical change,37 change in examination procedures,38 and a more general attempt to make the process of schooling more relevant to the modern world of high technology, unemployment and the need for industrial and commercial skills. In this it is reflecting more general European concerns about education.39

There was surprisingly little opposition from the church to these changes, given the scale and radical nature of much of what was happening. Randles,40 who writes from a position of sympathy with the church, seems to suggest that what disagreements there were did not result from what was being proposed so much as from the way it was being implemented. She cites in particular what she perceived as lack of planning and consultation, and the increasing power of the Department, arising from its new financial muscle, to interfere in the process. Akenson, who has little such sympathy with the church, argues that the hierarchy was quite happy with the new situations because:

> ... in return for massive dollops of money the church has surrendered no powers of any significance. It still controlled directly all the Catholic primary and academic secondary schools, and priestly chairmen still dominated the Vocational Educational Committees.41

It seems fairly clear that the most important reason for the absence of serious disagreements, at least in public, between Church and State is the private consultations which are carried on between the Catholic hierarchy and the Department of Education whenever any major new development is being considered. It also appears to be the case that these are now better organised than before and are carried out with some care. This ensures that any proposals which are likely to cause public difficulty are negotiated by the parties beforehand. In this way the church has quite unique influence.

> The most frequent and continuous topic for discussion revolves around the policies which raise structural or managerial questions; chief among these is the issue of access to the system, equality of opportunity and the publicly-managed vocational system. ... The overwhelming popular support for the free education scheme however gave the Catholic bishops little or no room for manoeuvre on these issues.42

Another important factor which must concern the church is the fact that the numbers of religious personnel are declining generally, and so the number working in education is also much reduced. This means that church control is increasingly second-hand. This, along with the growth in the number of schools and the accompanying complexity of the system, has meant that the church has had to develop more systematic and organised procedures for ensuring that its view on educational matters are always available at all levels and with respect to all issues from the local to the national.

> In response to the state policy initiatives of the 60s the churches and the managerial bodies created umbrella groups at various levels to increase their efficacy in negotiations with the state. On the Catholic side these developments have increased the direct input of the bishops in policy formulation. The power structure has consequently assumed a more orderly and systematic form.43

Clearly, in such a situation, the limits of acceptable policy change and development are likely to be well established in advance, and are unlikely to be breached. As well such a procedure is unlikely to lead to any fundamental change in the power structure with respect to control and final decision-making. Although much of what has been written here refers to the Catholic church, the position of the Protestant churches in the republic has been different only in detail.

> The educational policy of the Protestant churches, expressed usually through yearly formal synods, would with some important exceptions correspond closely to that of the majority church; however Protestant churches generally would have favoured local popular control and would have given lay teachers and lay people a larger role in church education structures. On the basic issue of the existing clerical managerial system and private status of secondary schools, Protestant policy would not have differed from the state position of the Catholic church.44

All of this has described the outer structures, or the measurable bare bones and statistics of the wide-ranging changes in education. The less tangible but possibly more significant consequences arise from apparent changes in attitudes among the young with respect to the values and moralities of the past. The importance of this is underlined by the fact that in 1984 more than 50 per cent of the population was under 25 years of age.45 Opinion polls and social surveys suggest that there have been important changes, especially among the young, both in behaviour patterns and in attitudes towards such issues as church attendance, sexual morality and drug-taking.46 As well as this the curriculum has changed in line with more general movements in Western Europe generally.47 For example, changes in the economy and the emergence of the new microchip-based technology have led to the demand for more vocationally oriented education, and this has been supported by a recent growth in the establishment of the microchip technology industry in Ireland. It is possible also to look at the results of this period of change as representing a failure of imagination and of nerve on the part of the Catholic hierarchy.48 One way forward for the hierarchy was to move with the changes, to try to influence them directly and on the hierarchy's own terms. A large part of the theoretical underpinning of the period has related to the notion of pluralism and how it might enhance and enrich Irish life. In the main this has promoted such essentially Christian ideals as the importance of individuals, freedom of conscience, rationality and truth. The church, by joining in the debate about these issues and by trying to relate them to its own views on morality and on social behaviour, could have provided support and leadership and sympathy. By opposing the processes at work in the new society, which were extremely powerful and not in themselves anti-Christian, the church proved ineffective on its own behalf. Instead of simply pointing backwards it might have helped to understand and illuminate the past with reference to the issues of the day. The hidden curriculum of the new education was particularly invisible to the church, and in placing its emphasis on the need to maintain control of the structures and the management of education, it missed what may have been the more important and significant business that was going on inside.

NOTES AND REFERENCES

1. Fennell, Desmond, The State of the Nation: Ireland Since the Sixties, Dublin: Ward River Press, 1983, p.15.

2. The New Ireland Forum, Proceedings and Commissioned Papers, Dublin: The Stationery Office, 1983.

3. Brown, Terence, Ireland: A Social and Cultural History, London: Fontana Press, 1981, 2nd edn 1985, p.347.

4. Brown, Terence, op.cit., pp.346-7.

5. Wall, M., 'The Age of the Penal Laws' in: Moody, T.W. and Martin F.X. (eds.), The Course of Irish History, Cork: Mercier Press, 1984.

6. Deane, Seamus, Civilians and Barbarians, Field Day Pamphlet No.3, Derry: Field Day Publications, 1983, p.6.

7. Bowen, Desmond, Souperism: Myth or Reality?, Cork: Mercier Press, 1971; and Bowen, Desmond, The Protestant Crusade in Ireland, 1800-1870, Dublin: Gill and Macmillan, 1978.

8. The literature on the National schools is now quite extensive and is growing, but there is no single up-to-date source. For general information see: Akenson, D.H., The Irish Education Experiment, Routledge and Kegan Paul, 1970; and Whyte, J.H., Church and State in Modern Ireland, 1923-1970, Dublin: Gill and Macmillan, 1971.

9. The notion of using the schools to promote mutual understanding in Ireland, especially in the North, is again very current. See: Dunn, Seamus, 'The Role of Education in the Northern Ireland Conflict', Oxford Review of Education, 1986, 12, 3.

10. Goldstrom, J.M., 'The Correspondence Between Lord John Russell and the Publishing Trade', Publishing History, 1986, 20.

11. Akenson, D.H., op.cit.

12. Ibid.

13. Parkes, Susan M., Kildare Place: The History of the Church of Ireland Training College, 1811-1969, Dublin: Church of Ireland Training College, 1984.

14. Clarke, D.M., Church and State: Essays in Political Philosophy, Cork: The University Press, 1984; Dunn, Seamus, 'The Education Debate in Northern Ireland: the Integrated Option', Studies, Dublin: 1986, 75, 299.

15. Whyte, J.H., op.cit.

16. There is by now a growing literature on church-state relations in Ireland. Whyte, J.H., op.cit., is still the standard reference: but see also, Brown, Terence, op.cit.; Akenson, D.H., 1970, op.cit.; and Browne, Noel, Against the Tide, Dublin: Gill and Macmillan, 1986.

17. Akenson, D.H., A Mirror to Kathleen's Face: Education in Independent Ireland, 1922-1960, Montreal and London: McGill-Queen's University Press, 1975, p.31.

18. Fitzgerald, Garret, Towards a New Ireland, Dublin: Torc Books, Gill and Macmillan, 1973, p.47.

19. Whyte, J.H., op.cit., p.20.

20. Investment in Education: Report of the Survey Team Appointed by the Minister for Education in October 1962, Dublin: The Stationery Office, 1965, p.3.

21. See Investment in Education, op.cit., p.78. For example, in respect of National (that is Primary) education in 1961-2 the ratio of expenditure attributed respectively to public funds, the schools and the parents was approximately £13.1 million to half a million to one-third of a million.

22. Quoted in Randles, Sister Eileen, Post-Primary Education in Ireland 1957-1970, Dublin: Veritas Publications, 1975, p.57.

23. See Akenson, D.H., 1975, op.cit. Most of these Technical Schools resulted from the Agricultural and Technical Instruction Act of 1899, which empowered local authorities to plan programmes of technical and agricultural instruction.

24. Fitzgerald, Garret, op.cit., p.48.

25. Mulcahy, D.G., Curriculum and Policy in Irish

Post-Primary Education, Dublin: Institute of Public Administration, 1981, p.1.

26. See the chapter on Secularism in Modern Ireland in: Clancy, Patrick, et al., Ireland: A Sociological Profile, Dublin: Institute of Public Administration, 1986; see also Ryan, Liam, 'Faith under Survey', The Furrow, 1983, 43, 1; and Kirby, Peadar, Is Irish Catholicism Dying? Dublin and Cork: The Mercier Press, 1986.

27. See Investment in Education, op.cit.

28. Quoted in Randles, Eileen, op.cit., p.89.

29. See Brown, Terence, op.cit., p.250.

30. Randles, Eileen, op.cit.

31. The figures for 1964 are taken from Investment in Education, op.cit. and those for 1980 from the Department of Education, Statistics Report, 1980-81, Dublin: The Stationery Office, 1981.

32. See Fitzgerald, op.cit.; also O'Buachalla, Seamus, 'Church and State in Irish Education in this Century', European Journal of Education, 1985, 20, 4.

33. Crooks, Tony and McKernan, Jim, The Challenge of Change: Curriculum Developments in Irish Post-Primary Schools, 1970-1984, Dublin: Institute of Public Administration, 1984.

34. Coolahan, John, Irish Education: Its History and Structure, Dublin: Institute of Public Administration, 1981.

35. Randles, Eileen, op.cit.

36. See Randles, Eileen, op.cit.; also O'Connor, S., 'Post-Primary Education', Studies, Dublin, 1968, 57, 227.

37. Crooks, Tony and McKernan, Jim, op.cit.

38. Coolahan, John, op.cit.

39. Ibid.

40. Randles, Eileen, op.cit.

41. Akenson, D.H., 1975, op.cit., p.149.

42. O'Buachalla, Seamus, op.cit.

43. Ibid.

44. Ibid.

45. Crooks, Tony and McKernan, Jim, op.cit., p.5.

46. See n.21.

47. Crooks, Tony and McKernan, Jim, op.cit.

48. Kirby, Peadar, op.cit.; see also Connolly, Peter, 'The Church in Ireland Since Vatican 2', **The Furrow**, 1979, 30, 12.

6

CHRISTIANITY - NATIONAL IDENTITY AND EDUCATION IN POLAND

Stanislaw Litak and Witold Tulasiewicz

INTRODUCTION

Though officially Christianity did not reach Poland until nearly three hundred years after it came to England or Germany, her conversion is well within the main European tradition. Her history can be cited as an example of coexistence of a largely unified centralized church with a central state government, carried on for the most part without a major conflict between the parties. Education from the start was provided by the Church and was expected to be denominational, in fact the first secular secondary school was not founded until the second half of the eighteenth century. Secular education, with modern not narrowly denominational curricula being introduced on a wider scale by the Commission for National Education in the 1770s, did not have time to prove itself since within a few decades both Church and State received the setback of the partitions of the country. However, it should be noted that for most of its existence the Commission, staffed by ex-Jesuits and Piarists was very much under Church supervision.

In the nineteenth century when secular education elsewhere in Europe became widespread, in Poland it was not always Polish education, thus giving the Church and private agencies though themselves persecuted, the opportunity to step into the breech ensuring the identity of interests of Church and, in the absence of State, nation, with no domination by either. After 1918 in independent Poland the separation of the two was proclaimed and expected, with the State taking over the role of provider of education. On the other hand religious education was freely available throughout the country for all taught by lay teachers in the primary school at the expense of the State. It was also available in a number of private denominational establishments, continuing an historical tradition, not only at primary and secondary but also at tertiary level, as in the case of the Catholic university of Lublin.

The post-Second World War separation of Church and State therefore is not a new phenomenon, but with religious education at first continuing to be available in secular state schools. It was not exclusively the Party's laicization programme, but also the Church's own design in the political reality of the 1970s to withdraw from state assisted provision, with priests on state payrolls in school, and to teach a full denominational religion outside the school in churches and catechist centres, once again in keeping with post-partition tradition of the country.

As a result of sharing a common fate with the nation at the hands of foreign occupying powers Christian presence in Poland has always been more pervasive, affecting not just ordinary lives and morals, but becoming identified with national feeling; indeed to some extent even with the State and State interests, with the two much more equal as partners at times, pursuing common policies when mutually advantageous. This chapter, by examining some of these issues, goes beyond an account of provision of schooling and devotes rather more space and prominence to the wider concept of religious education and national identity.

FROM THE MIDDLE AGES UNTIL 1795

Poland officially converted in 966 AD,1 the year in which its first nationwide ruler, Mieszko I, was baptized through the intermediary of Poland's southern neighbour, Bohemia. The first Polish bishopric in Poznan, founded in 986 AD was a soke of the Holy See, thus placing the country firmly within the orbit of Roman Christianity. The arrival in

Polish Christian Identity

Poland of Wojciech, Bishop of Prague, in 966 AD and his missionary activity among Poland's northern neighbours, the Prussians, and subsequent martyrdom on 23 April 997 led to the establishment of Poland's first ecclesiastical province. Pope Silvester canonized Wojciech and erected Poland's metropolitan see in the city of Gniezno in 999 AD. By the middle of the twelfth century the provincial structure was almost complete, consisting of the archdiocese of Gniezno and eight dioceses. This original structure proved surprisingly stable, surviving unchanged until the partitions of the country in the eighteenth century and in some instances after them. As the population became converted parishes were established, the main period of growth occurring in the thirteenth and fourteenth centuries. The number of monasteries too grew rapidly, up to the end of the thirteenth century there were some 300 male and female centres, particularly Benedictine and Cistercian, later a number of mendicant orders were added, with their female counterparts. In 1253 the second metropolitan see was erected in Riga for the territories of Livonia and Prussia and including two dioceses in the hands of the Teutonic Order which did not become Polish until 1466.

Up to the first half of the fourteenth century Poland was a monolithic state both in nationality and denominational terms, inhabited by Roman Catholic Poles. This situation changed during the reign of Casimir the Great (1333-1370) who annexed southwestern Rus,2 with its Ruthenian population and an established (since 988 AD) Eastern Orthodox form of Christianity. The accession to the Polish throne of Wladyslaw Jagiello (in 1386), after a period of personal union led to the political union (in 1569) of Poland and the Great Duchy of Lithuania. These two countries together formed, until the partitions, the so-called 'Commonwealth of the two Nations', territorially the biggest state in Europe, excluding Russia. In the first half of the seventeenth century the Commonwealth had an area of over 990,000 square kilometres. This shrank to some 737,000 square kilometres just before the first partition in 1772. At the same time the Polish-Lithuanian state became a multinational and multidenominational state, inhabited by Poles, Ruthenians and Lithuanians, in that order, a large number of Jews and significant minorities of Germans, Latvians, Russians, Tartars and Karaite Jews. Eighty per cent of the population of the Great Duchy were Orthodox Ruthenians.3

As a result of the influx of Poles into Ruthenian lands a further Latin rite metropolitan see was erected in 1375 in Halicz (later transferred to Lwow) with five dioceses and one archdiocese. It was Jagiello who was responsible for the permanent ecclesiastical structure of the Great Duchy of Lithuania. Her dioceses (the first in Wilno (Vilnius) in 1387 to which were later added two further bishoprics) were placed under the jurisdiction of the metropolitan of Gniezno. Thus the metropolitan province of Gniezno extended over a vast area of territory from Wroclaw in the southeast to Smolensk in the extreme east, linking the Polish and Lithuanian parts of the Commonwealth in one ecclesiastical whole.4

Alongside the Roman Catholic Church in Poland and the Great Duchy there existed then mainly in Lithuania until about the end of the sixteenth century an established Eastern Orthodox Church. Conversions among the Ruthenians did not start until the union in 1595 of a number of Orthodox bishops with Rome, ratified by the Synod in Brest Litovsk in 1596. It must be emphasized that until this union the Orthodox population of Poland and Lithuania enjoyed absolute religious freedom. After Brest the Orthodox hierarchy had been briefly outlawed, but as early as 1620 de facto, and by 1632-1635 formally, its legal status in the country was restored. The new Uniate (Greek Catholic) Church, however, faced serious difficulties in the early days of its existence, which intensified during the time of the Cossack insurrection which started in 1648. Firstly the Commonwealth-Cossack war had not only a socio-political but also a religious aspect. It was in a sense a religious war between the Cossacks defending their Orthodoxy and that of the Ukrainians, and the Commonwealth, whose government officially acknowledged the supremacy of Roman Catholicism, but defended, in this conflict, the Uniate Church's right of existence. Secondly, the Uniate Church though also Catholic and acknowledging the supremacy of Rome did not enjoy parity of status with the Latin Catholic Church. In the view of the Polish nobility it was a peasants' church, a halfway house between Catholicism and Orthodoxy. Not surprisingly it did not grow significantly until after the Moscow Wars and the peace treaty of Moscow of 1686. By the beginning of the eighteenth century, however, all Orthodox dioceses with one exception, had become Uniate, more or less voluntarily. It must be noted, however, that this growth took place at a time of increasing religious intolerance in that part of Europe, following the wars with Sweden, Brandenburg, Transylvania and Moscow. Moscow's newly discovered power assisted by Polish Uniate policies, placed the Orthodox Church in Poland under the jurisdiction of the Patriarch of Moscow. This gave the Tsar the right to intervene in Warsaw on behalf of Orthodox believers, at the same time allowing him the opportunity to meddle in purely Polish internal affairs. Matters would come to a head during the reign of the last Polish king, Stanislaw August Poniatowski,5 when Catherine II,6 could enlist the Orthodox subjects of the Commonwealth of the two Nations as her allies in anti-Commonwealth policies. Meanwhile the Uniate Church became progressively more latinized which further alienated many of the faithful. Moreover it was the Roman Catholic Church which was the principal confession in the country, and it was its bishops who played a prominent political role in Commonwealth affairs. They all sat in the Commonwealth Senate, while only the Uniate metropolitan archbishop had acquired that right by 1790. He was however, allowed to occupy only the last seat (after the most junior Catholic bishop) on the bishops' bench in the Chamber. This example confirms that by the end of the eighteenth century the different denominations which existed side by side in Poland did so not without conflict, even though with the exception of a Jewish pogrom, largely by the Cossacks, without a major religious war or persecution. Religious tolerance was officially guaranteed by the so-called Warsaw Confederation of 1573.7

The Reformation was not particularly successful in Poland,8 affecting mainly the German minority and a part of the anticlerical section of the Polish szlachta.9 The peasant and petty nobles majority in the country were too conservative to embrace the new creed. However, the Reformation made a permanent impact on the school system, adding to it, particularly by establishing a number of prestigious Lutheran grammar schools (gimnazja), the first in Elbing (1535). The Moravians followed suit with a school in Leszno. There was also the Arian academy in Rakow. In a sense the Reformation and Renaissance coincided in Poland, bringing about an unprecedented flowering of the arts, especially literature, notably the works of the two Lutheran writers, Rej,10 and Kochanowski.11

The counter-reformation in Poland was spearheaded by the Jesuits who arrived in the country in 1564.12 However, since the diocesan and parochial organizations of the Church were hardly touched by the Reformation, it was this organization which served as the tool of the post-Tridentine Reform of the Church in Poland13 and its ensuing spate of polemics with the Reformation. More importantly, however, the Reform enabled the Polish Church to acquire its specific characteristics which suited the political system in the country, known as the 'noblemen's democracy'14 and its denominational relations. The school system maintained by the Church played a significant role in propagating the Polish democracy ideas.

As in other countries, so in Poland too the school system was a church creation. In the Middle Ages education was provided in cathedral and collegiate schools. From about 1350 onwards a growing network of elementary parish schools was also available.15 In the first half of the sixteenth century schools run by religious orders blossomed out, to begin with those of Jesuits, later Piarist and other orders, and schools maintained by the University of Cracow, called academic colonies. Both the monastic and academic schools were secondary.16 By the time of the first partition in 1772 there were 104 monastic schools with some 27,000 pupils in Jesuit schools alone, and altogether some 35,000 secondary pupils chiefly the sons of the szlachta. Most of the schools were free. At the same time the parish schools (Samsonowicz claims 4000 schools of all types by the end of the 1500s,17) decreased in number.18 The academic level of monastic schools too, declined by the second half of the seventeenth century, mainly due to their inability to assimilate the new science and philosophy teaching. In Poland the political difficulties, wars with neighbouring countries in the north and east, the growing economic crisis and religious intolerance further aggravated the general situation of the time. The revival started in the early eighteenth century with a reform initiated in the Piarist schools and linked with the name of Stanislaw Konarski.19

In the seventeenth century Polishness was becoming more and more synonymous with the Catholic religion. In the Commonwealth it was the accepted thing that Poles and Lithuanians must be Catholic, the Ruthenians were Orthodox or Uniate and the Germans - Protestant. The nobleman's Sarmatian szlachta culture was closely identified with Catholicism,20 a trend reflected in the country's foreign policy during the sixteenth and seventeenth centuries when Poland was invariably ranged on the side of the Habsburgs or in the papal camp. Attempts to join up with France were unsuccessful, while the Russian party only increased its influence during the Wettin kings' rule (1677-1763).

In the sixteenth, but especially the seventeenth century until the Age of Enlightenment, Poles increasingly started travelling to Italy (especially Rome) to study, whereas previously Paris and German universities were preferred. Only the Reform, completed in 1783, of the two Polish universities in Cracow and in Wilno by the Commission for National Education, Komisja Edukacji Narodowej,21 Europe's first ministry of education, in 1773, and the reformist tendencies of some bishops put a stop to study travel by Polish clergy to Rome.22 From the fifteenth century onwards when the University of Cracow ranged itself on the side of the Council Party,23 there was never any doubt about the fullest loyalty of Poland to Rome. Arguably the reason for this may be the fact that Poland had not been in the forefront of theological debate. Also, Cracow University (founded in 1364) after a successful fifteenth century started to decline in the sixteenth. A similar fate befell the Jesuit University of Wilno (founded in 1578). Indeed not until 1784, by then in Austrian Galicia, was a full university founded in Lwow by the Emperor Joseph II in place of the Jesuit college existing there previously.24 Thus, there was little room for intellectual debate in the Commonwealth which may have rattled her unshaken loyalty to Rome.

The school reform of the Commission for National Education,25 was thus an attempt to revive the flagging fortunes of the country: a political, economic and intellectual revival. It was initiated in the belief that a modern, patriotic education of the largest possible number of youth of <u>all</u> classes could help save the Commonwealth. The reform, secular in origin, continued similar earlier efforts of Jesuit and Piarist teachers and of the King himself, who in 1765 founded in Warsaw the Knights School (<u>Szkola Rycerska</u>), Poland's first non-denominational school. The <u>Statutes of the Commission designed for the Academic Estate and Schools in the Lands of the Commonwealth</u> published in 1783 were a pioneer achievement unparalleled in Europe.26 Its future development however was peculiarly Polish. The Commission was initially responsible to the King. However, according to the 1791 Constitution, the Primate of Poland was a member of the highest executive body of the country - the 'Guardians of Rights', as 'the head of the Polish clergy and <u>president</u> of the Commission for National Education',27 (our emphasis). In this way the highest educational office in the country was firmly linked with the highest ecclesiastical authority. It is difficult to speculate if the character of the Commission changed from a secular body to a religious one as a result. Nevertheless it was once again an institution peculiarly suited to Poland, a country in which the Primate was the person next in importance to the King himself. He acted as regent during the King's absence and during elections. Be that as it may, the undoubted achievement of the Commission was that it created its <u>own</u> school system in which all secondary schools were linked with a university (or in its own terminology: main school, <u>szkola glowna</u>).

Unfortunately, there was no time to reorganize the elementary sector, the education in the parishes. These schools remained in the hands of bishops, although the Sejm (Parliament) of 1789 installed civil-military committees whose task it was to see that parish priests did not neglect their duty of maintaining parochial schools.28 The instruction reports of the Commission's inspectors on financing, staffing and the curriculum make riveting reading.29

AFTER THE PARTITIONS

As a result of the three partitions (in 1772, 1793 and 1795) Poland lost her independence,30 her territory divided up between Russia, Prussia and Austria. The three occupying powers tried to control the Church and to limit its influence, in particular by breaking up its organizational links - diocesan contacts across the three frontiers. The nineteenth century was marked by Polish attempts to regain independence through conspiratorial activity at home and forging alliances with friends abroad. Napoleon Bonaparte was initially welcomed as the greatest foreign hope, the creation of the Duchy of Warsaw in 1807 seen as a nucleus of a future Poland. After the Congress of Vienna in 1815, on parts of the territory of the former Commonwealth (and the Duchy of Warsaw) there arose the Kingdom of Poland (commonly known as Congress Poland), the Great Duchy of Poznan and the Free City of Cracow (the Cracow Republic). All these newly created states and especially Congress Poland with time became bastions of independence movements, including armed action which spilled over into former areas of the Commonwealth under direct foreign occupation. The main insurrections were the 1830 November uprising in Congress Poland, the 1846 and 1848 uprisings respectively in Cracow and Poznan, and the January uprising of 1863, as a result of which two of the territories lost their autonomy (Cracow and Poznan) and the hitherto separate administration of Congress Poland (already severely reduced after 1832) came to an end. In 1874 its name was changed to that of 'Vistula Region': the name of Poland disappearing from the geographical maps of Europe.

Polish Christian Identity

The political changes were accompanied by changes in the diocesan network.31 The number of dioceses actually increased but the ecclesiastical links across the occupied territories were cut. A number of monasteries, in Austria already in the eighteenth century, in Prussia and Congress Poland not until the nineteenth, were expropriated for political and economic reasons and suppressed. They continued to exist, however, without hindrance until the November uprising in the former Commonwealth areas occupied by Russia, and not made over to Congress Poland.

Gradually the Russian and Prussian occupants began to confiscate all remaining Church property in their territories, including Congress Poland - although the Austrians were less involved in this. Clergy were paid stipends by the occupying state becoming virtually state employees and bound by state laws and regulations. The numbers of Latin rite clergy were deliberately kept down. The agreement of the Russian authorities was required for the appointment of priests to parishes. Between 1863 and 1875 clergy were confined to travelling within their parish boundaries only. Bishoprics were left vacant, and the construction and rebuilding of churches and the formation of new parishes in Russia severely curtailed. The 1847 Concordat between the Tsar and the Holy See was never put into effect.32 In Prussia too Church activity was disrupted, especially after 1871 during the period of the Kulturkampf,33 when attempts were made to Germanize the Church itself by insisting on religious instruction (catechism) being given in German, and fluency in the German language expected of priests in parishes with an entirely Polish population. Many priests were removed from office, most spiritual, pastoral and educational church life had to go underground.

The uprisings intensified the occupants' reprisals, on the other hand they made the Poles more conscious of their own identity. Education in particular was to become the main instrument to bring up a young generation loyal to the occupants.34 In Prussia, less so in Austria, schools introduced German as the language of instruction. In the former territories of the Great Duchy, on the other hand, Polish education continued not only in the University of Wilno and the Krzemieniec Liceum in the southeast, but also in Roman Catholic secondary and elementary educational centres. These were of course the only areas of the Russian Empire with a developed network of schools, set up by the Commission for National Education some seventy years earlier.35 In the Duchy of Warsaw and the Kingdom of Poland the Commission's work was also continued. The University of Warsaw was founded in 1816,36 and a substantial number of secondary and elementary state schools were established. This promising expansion of Polish education both in the Congress Kingdom and the occupied territories in the east was stopped after the November uprisings. The University of Warsaw was closed in 1831, that of Wilno in 1832. The entire school system of Congress Poland was amalgamated with the Russian system. This continued until 1861 when Polish school administration was restored in Warsaw. Under Aleksander Wielopolski,37 a number of private elementary schools were started by the nobility and the clergy. In 1862 Wielopolski reformed the schools again to give them a Polish national character. This reform was suspended when after the January 1863 uprising the system was once more merged with that of Russia and indeed totally Russified in respect of the language of instruction, history and literature syllabuses in 1873. This was incidentally also the time for some expansion of vocational schools as industrialization progressed in the country.38 While the Polish character of education was being lost in Russia, in Galicia, under the terms of autonomy meanwhile granted by the Austro-Hungarian monarchy (in 1867) the Universities of Cracow and Lwow became once more Polish and Polish/Ukrainian respectively.

During the entire period of occupation the Roman Catholic clergy played a vigorous part in keeping alive a Polish identity. In the absence of a Polish state the Polish Church took over the missing leadership function. The motto 'a Pole is a Catholic' was universally accepted, especially in the mainly non-Catholic Prussian and Russian societies. Priests took an active part in the struggle for independence, fighting in the uprisings or preaching from church pulpits. Many theological college graduates went straight into fighting units, not only in Congress Poland but also in areas incorporated into Russia. The clergy's main role, however, was to kindle religious patriotic feelings through open and underground activity, such as preaching patriotic sermons, organizing festivals of national remembrance especially so during the period just before the January uprising in churches in Warsaw and Lublin.39 Patriotism became the hallmark of Polish religiousness. As a result many clergy were arrested and deported.

With the exception of the Orthodox Church, the other denominations fared no better than the Catholics. In the first instance the Uniate Church was to be eliminated. The move started in 1839 with the Tsar liquidating the Church in the Russian occupied (eastern) territories. The same measure was then applied in Congress Poland in 1875, the property going to the Orthodox Church. Despite the persecution and reprisals, for Polish nationals at least, but they were joined by others, living in the entire territory of the former Commonwealth of the two Nations, the Church became a rallying point for action to keep their national identity. Repressive measures had an almost opposite effect, spurring the people to demonstrate their Polishness. A number of female religious orders came into being which conducted their national activities clandestinely among factory workers and peasants in the countryside. In order to save the threatened Polish culture, priests organized and joined socio-cultural and economic discussion groups, a movement also supported by the rising tide of temperance societies especially in the Poznan region and later in Congress Poland.

Towards the end of the nineteenth century as a result of all this Latin Church activity in support of Polish national consciousness,40 a conflict of interests, leading to clashes, arose between Poles and Lithuanians and Ukrainians and Poles. For the link between national feeling and religion developed in Lithuania as well as in Poland. Lithuanian priests too were patriotic. The only difference was that in the one Catholic group there were Polish, in the other Lithuanian patriots. Indeed the first leaders of a national movement in Lithuania were priests, while the Ukrainians whose ancestors had rejected the Uniate Church in the days of the Commonwealth now increasingly identified with it. The Uniate Church became their national Church. These complicated (and uniquely intense) national and ecclesiastical problems were to intensify further during the two World Wars with Lithuanians and Ukrainians fighting for their own national independence.

INDEPENDENT POLAND

In 1918 Poland regained her independence.41 The territory of the new Republic represented 53 per cent of the area of the Commonwealth at the time of the first partition (388,390 square kilometres). The new Polish state came into being from parts of the former Commonwealth which had been divided by the three occupying powers. The main task therefore was to unite the different parts into a single state organism, with its distinctive administrative, legal and educational systems. The Second Republic, like the Commonwealth before the partitions, too was a multinational state. According to the 1931 Census Poland had a population of 31,916,000, of whom only 64.7 per cent were Poles. There were 16.0 per cent Ukrainians, 9.8 per cent Jews, 6.1 per cent Byelorussians and 2.4 per cent Germans. In theory all the nationalities were equal in law; however, the conflicts which were beginning to emerge at the end of the nineteenth century continued. A disturbing feature was the rise of antisemitism, which had in large measure an economic cause. The national structure of interwar Poland was reflected in its denominational makeup. The Poles were predominantly Roman Catholic, the Ukrainians and Byelorussians were Greek Catholic (Uniate) or Orthodox, the Germans were mainly Lutheran and the Jews professed Judaism. The so-called March Constitution of 1921 guaranteed all citizens freedom of conscience, but article 114 of it stated that

> as of the confession of the overwhelming majority of the nation - Catholicism occupies the leading

place among denominations equal in law.42
A similar clause appeared in the second (April) Constitution of 1935.43 The fact that on the whole only the Poles were Roman Catholic turned any nationality conflicts automatically into inter-church and interdenominational ones. There were difficulties too with the changed status of the Orthodox Church which had to yield its privileged position under the Tsar in the former Russian territories to the Roman Catholic Church. Some of the Orthodox bishops were alleged to be disloyal to the Polish state authority. On the other hand the Roman Catholic hierarchy demanded the return of the former Latin and Uniate rite monastic buildings and churches as well as lands confiscated by the Tsarist government and given to the Orthodox Church. Many of the Orthodox churches built under the previous regime in major Polish towns and cities to propagate the creed were pulled down.44
The Concordat with the Vatican of 10 February 1925,45 and the papal bull of 28 October of the same year (Vixdum Poloniae Unitas)46 were of tremendous significance for both Church and State. The Concordat regulated relations between the State and the Church, while the bull determined the borders of the old and created several new dioceses, thus abolishing the ecclesiastical structure of the partitions and creating one suited to the changed conditions of the Second Republic. There were five metropolitan sees, with Gniezno the seat of the Primate, plus twenty dioceses. The Uniate Church was left with its existing structure: one province (Lwow) and three dioceses, with one further Armenian Uniate archdiocese which had been located in Lwow since the seventeenth century for the Catholic Armenians. In addition to the parishes and the dioceses of the Church there were many monastic orders whose influence was on the increase. The Concordat and the Constitution together guaranteed the Church in Poland a particularly strong status. Despite this, however, unlike in several western Catholic countries, there never emerged a distinctive Christian-Democratic Party in Poland. The Work Party, Stronnictwo Pracy, (SP) founded in 1937 was small and its activities

confined to the Greater Poland region in the west which had a tradition of Catholic social thought. Efforts to found a Catholic Peasant Party were no more successful. Catholics were, however, active in the Polish People's Party, <u>Polskie Stronnictwo Ludowe</u> (PSL) and the nationalistic National Democratic Party, <u>Stronnictwo Narodowe</u> (SN), the latter especially influential among the Catholic clergy. It is further characteristic that although the majority of PSL members, including its leader, Wincenty Witos,47 were believers, the Party itself was strongly anticlerical. The reason for this was thought to be the influence of Polish <u>szlachta</u> culture whose outlook was appropriated by the modern farmers after the land reforms. The anticlericalism of the nobility despite its attachment to the Church goes back to the Middle Ages and especially the Ages of the Reformation and Enlightenment. Between the wars thus there existed in Poland a curious dislike for Christian Democracy;48 at the same time the Primate (August Hlond) himself tried to prevent priests from engaging in political activity, in which during the period of the partitions they had participated especially keenly in the former Austrian (Galicia) and Prussian (Greater Poland) provinces and in Silesia. Hlond tried to place the Church above politics to secure freedom for its religious activities, an effort for which he was accused of playing into the hands of the right wing <u>Sanacja</u> parties.49 However, mindful of its contribution to the preservation of Polish culture during the partitions, the Church tried to strengthen its privileged position in the country further by having Catholicism recognized as the state religion. This was not to happen, although the Church saw eye to eye with the government on most aspects of internal and external policy. All national festivals, for example the Anniversary of the 3 May Constitution (1791), were linked with Church holy days.

As in the past the Church during the interwar period continued its socio-religious work <u>via</u> the parishes, religious orders and other organizations united since 1930 in the Catholic Action, <u>Akcja Katolicka</u>, programme. Some 300 different newspapers and magazines were published yearly plus a large printing of socio-religious books and brochures. The Catholic Action, particularly influential in the countryside, organized religious festivals and pilgrimages to shrines such as that of the Black Madonna in Czestochowa. Purely cultural recreational work too was carried out with visits to national historical and nature sites, the Church organizing literary, drama, even vocational groups, the latter especially in farming areas, as well as sport activities.50 After 1937, courses were organized for the discussion of social problems from Catholic sociology's point of view. Their main aim was to improve religious life, and to raise cultural levels especially in the country. In southeastern Poland (Little Poland) this activity was more appreciated by the population than elsewhere. There were some 614,000 members of Catholic Action in the 1930s.

The Church was also responsible for religious instruction in state schools, in all of which, except in the higher education sector, after the Concordat the subject was compulsory. Provision for all other denominations of course was also made. There was teaching activity too in Catholic schools, both primary and secondary, general and vocational, orphanages and schools for the handicapped, most of these run by religious orders,51 especially the Jesuits who maintained four prestigious grammar schools, including the ancient boarding school at Chyrow. It was a feature of interwar Poland that in the secondary sector the number of private schools was slightly higher than state schools, but only a number of them were strictly denominational. The distribution was geographical with many Catholic schools in Silesia. An important event was the opening in 1918 of a Catholic University in Lublin (KUL),52 through the efforts of Father Rodziszewski, whose main aim was to provide higher education for a new Catholic intelligentsia capable of taking a clear stance in the country against the ideas of positivism and scientism, becoming increasingly popular at the time among the wider intelligentsia whose own position was characterized by an indifference if not actual hostility to the Church.

Polish Christian Identity

THE SECOND WORLD WAR

The attack on Poland by Nazi Germany on 1 September 1939 followed by the Soviet invasion seventeen days later put an end to the country's independence. Pomerania, Greater Poland, Upper Silesia and a part of Masovia were incorporated into the Reich, while Central Poland was transformed into the General Gouvernement with its capital in Cracow. After the German attack on the USSR most of the formerly Polish eastern territories occupied by the Soviet Union formed the two Reich Commissariats: East (Wilno) and Ukraine. Lwow became part of the General Gouvernement and Bialystok was incorporated in the Reich. These territorial changes again disturbed the diocesan borders which made Church administration difficult, however the legal status of the Polish Church provinces had remained as it was in 1939. Thus the Church as it did in the nineteenth century continued to provide a unifying factor.

Immediately the Church joined the fight53 against the occupying power, its clergy supporting the right wing underground political organizations, like the Action for Polish Victory (September 1939) which became the Polish Home Army in 1942. It fought with the partisan armies, stored arms in churches and monasteries, hid leaders wanted by the Gestapo, tended the sick and wounded. It also protected Polish religious art treasures and provided both premises and staff for underground education. It saved not only Polish lives, but several thousands of Jews from extermination. Some 60 priests were shot and a number sent to concentration camps for helping Jews. In their sermons, as far as possible priests kept up Polish spirits.

During the war the Nazis started a determined policy of fighting the Church in territories outside the original Reich itself, where in fact in 1938, anti-religious activity was much reduced - first of all in Austria, then especially in Poland. Religious life thus had to continue in conditions where normal Church organization had ceased. The fight against the Church assumed different forms in different parts of the country, but in most areas it could be said to be a fight against Polishness too, since the Germans were well aware of the closeness between Catholicism and Polish culture and national consciousness. In the first instance national leaders: political, intellectual and spiritual were to be eliminated. All universities and secondary schools were closed with their staff imprisoned or indeed executed, the two universities suffering most being Cracow where the first arrests started on 6 November 1939 and KUL Lublin on 9 November. In Lwow 24 professors were shot in 1941. Several bishops and large numbers of clergy were imprisoned. The fight against Polish culture led to the total closure of primary schools in territories incorporated into the Reich; they were left open though with a reduced curriculum (the teaching of Polish history, geography and culture was prohibited) together with some vocational schools in the General Gouvernement, whose population was intended to provide a semi-skilled labour force for Nazi Germany. Hundreds of thousands of young Polish workers were deported to the Reich right up to 1945. In the General Gouvernement some theological seminaries were allowed to function.54 As a result of this, university and secondary school teaching went underground in a systematic, well organized action55 in which priests too played a part, seminaries also went underground, as did the theological faculties of universities, thus ensuring the supply of new recruits for the priesthood. Underground education was even carried out in concentration camps.

In the incorporated Warthegau (Greater Poland provinces) anti-religious action was most intense. Almost from the start Catholics were segregated on national and linguistic lines. During 1940/41 1025 Polish priests were arrested.56 Some German Catholics living in the area were also persecuted. Altogether it is estimated that 19 per cent of diocesan clergy were murdered and an even higher percentage of church buildings and equipment (libraries, archives) completely destroyed.57

THE REPUBLIC AFTER 1945

The Nation and Church started the postwar period materially devastated, but morally intact. Neither

Polish Christian Identity

had contemplated any form of collaboration with the Nazis, there was no doubt about the patriotic integrity of the entire nation. Postwar Poland differed significantly from interwar Poland.58 After the Teheran, Yalta and Potsdam agreements her territory was shifted some 130 miles to the west, however the country as a whole found itself squarely within the Soviet sphere of interest. Poland lost most of her lands east of the river Bug, but was compensated by parts of Silesia, West Pomerania and East Prussia, which she had lost in the nineteenth century or earlier. Her total territory was reduced to 312,700 square kilometres (1968 count), that is some 80.5 per cent of her 1939 area. Her population in 1945 was but 24 million. The immediate postwar years were characterized by vast population shifts, Poles from the eastern territories settling in the new western and northern areas, whose German population had either fled earlier before the Soviet advance or was forcibly repatriated after the Potsdam agreement of July 1945. As a result in terms of nationality, Poland became an even more homogenous state, indeed in the early sixties she was almost exclusively ethnic Polish, with 98.6 per cent of her population Polish, as in the early Piast period one thousand years earlier. At the same time too the Catholic Church achieved a bigger majority compared with the other religious denominations.59 Of the thirty-six non-Catholic religions registered in Poland in 1985 only four were numerically significant: the Orthodox Church with 852,000 members, the Lutheran (Augsburg) Protestant Church with 75,000, Polish Catholics with 48,330 and Old Catholic Mariavites with 25,000 members. The remaining religions number no more than 60,000 individuals altogether.60 The Uniates are not listed separately, but figure among the Orthodox or Catholics. In 1972, after the final Vatican agreement which in several cases based itself on the old medieval and reformation period ecclesiastical provincial structure of the country, Poland was divided into 26 dioceses, with in 1985, 8101 parishes61 compared with 5889 parishes in 1946. Despite this growth by one-third, Polish parishes tend to be large with one church on average per 40 square kilometres of territory. The

135

number of parish priests grew from 10,300 in 1945 to some 22,040 in 1985,62 serving of course a meanwhile much bigger population of some 38 millions. Female vocations in religious orders, however, decreased most dramatically in that period with the loss to the secular state of children's homes, most of the existing Catholic schools and other educational establishments.

The war resulted in far-reaching socio-political changes in the country - in Poland in particular the two forces of Communism and Catholicism came face to face, after the liberation of the country (mainly) by the Red Army. The USSR also lent her strong support to the formation of the reconstructed Polish Communist Party on 5 December 1942. Among the population as a whole however, traditionally religious, the Polish Workers' Party, Polska Partia Robotnicza (PPR) did not gain much influence, despite proclaiming its own antifascist record in the fight for independence. There was reluctance on the part of the population to join the Party, a fate which had also affected membership of the left wing People's Army during the war, partly because of Church support for the Home Army.

The government of the future Polish People's Republic, Polska Rzeczpospolita Ludowa (PRL) developed from the nucleus of the Association of Polish Patriots formed in the USSR in March 1943, and was completed by the formation of the interim Government of National Unity in June 1945 in which the Communists held the key portfolios. The internationally unsupervised 1947 elections to the Sejm improved the Communist position further. Towards the end of 1948 the unification of the PPR and the Polish Socialist Party, Polska Partia Socjalistyczna (PPS) to form the PZPR, Polska Zjednoczona Partia Robotnicza (The Polish United Workers' Party) as in other central and eastern European countries gave the left an unassailable position and sole power in the country's government. A similar earlier act of unification of youth groups in July 1948 led to the emergence of the Association of Polish Youth, Zwiazek Mlodziezy Polskiej (ZMP), (the Universities' Association of Academic Youth ZAMP, united with ZMP in 1950) - which however collapsed in 1956 because of a singular lack of popular support. Its place was taken by two older organizations, the ZMS, Zwiazek Mlodziezy Socjalistycznej (Association of Socialist Youth) and ZMW, Zwiazek Mlodziezy Wiejskiej, (Association of Peasant Youth) and the reformed Scouting Association of Poland, ZHP, Zwiazek Harcerstwa Polskiego. ZHP, no longer the prewar ZHP whose ideology was Christian, united with ZMP in 1950,63 but retained some of the international scouting trappings which made it more acceptable to Poles.

The period from 1948 until October 1956 is known as the Stalinist period, during which the Party liquidated or subordinated all other political groupings. Regardless of the new Polish Constitution of 1952 (which was changed several times between 1954 and 1983) it also suppressed those political and ideological views and sentiments of individual citizens with which it was not in total agreement. Various charity, social and religious organizations not to its liking fared no better.

In 1948 a strong ideological offensive was mounted against education. The school system was to be changed according to Soviet models. Thus the new school programmes64 introduced in the school year 1949/50 were based on Marxist-Leninist ideology, with all syllabuses reflecting this ideological character with their 'construction of socialism in Poland' perspective, on lines similar to or identical with those prescribed in USSR and other satellite countries.65 Educational work in the secondary and tertiary sectors relied on ZMP leaders' help and organizational structure support in schools and universities. ZMP in turn acted on guidelines suggested by the PZPR. Religious education was systematically removed from school curricula, a campaign in which the newly formed, in 1949, Friends of Children Society, Towarzystwo Przyjaciol Dzieci (TPD) with the ostensive purpose of supporting the development of primary and secondary schooling played a leading role. By 1957 only 20 per cent of schools still taught religion.66 Textbooks were for the most part translated versions of Soviet school books, especially in history, literature and art and civics. In this way Polish education was virtually cut off from Western influences (and centres of learning) with which it had been associated over the last 1000 years. Almost all cultural and scientific institutes were either closed down or transformed and reorganized to conform with the new ideological trends in the country. All teachers were compulsorily retrained. In the economy teenage secondary school pupils were conscripted into a semi-military organization, called the General Action of Help for Poland (1948-1955) to help with economic construction and reconstruction. Indeed, the spontaneous enthusiasm of the young and old for this task was interpreted and given out as enthusiastic support for the PPR Party and its programme. The Church was affected by the unilateral abrogation of the Concordat by the government on 12 September 1945. The Ministry of Education circular of 13 September 1945 however stated that

> religious instruction is a compulsory subject in all public and private schools which are in receipt of state or local government grant for pupils whose religion is one of the confessions recognized by the state.

However,

> pupils whose parents do not wish them to receive denominational religious teaching in school are exempt from this subject.67

Thus, denominational religious teaching was available in grant-aided schools at that time.

As before the war the Church did not wish to play too active a part in internal politics despite the interest in some Catholic circles for such action and some encouragement from state officials. The Central Commission of the Polish Episcopate stated on 22 October 1946 that it 'saw no right conditions to form a political party' to stand in the forthcoming Sejm elections.68 The Church has in fact remained an independent force, above party politics avoiding the various pitfalls participation in civic elections might lead to and keeping to this line, to this day. The 1952 postwar Polish Constitution confirmed the separation of State and Church, article 82 states:

>The Church and other religious associations may freely fulfil their religious functions. It is unlawful to prevent citizens from taking part in religious activities or services, it is likewise unlawful to compel anyone to engage in such activities and services.

It goes on:

>The Church is separate from the State.69

The reopening of the Catholic University KUL 'above ground' (it had of course functioned 'underground') in November 1944,70 as the first Polish University to do so in territories relinquished by the Germans was an important educational event, as well as a religious landmark. On 24 March 1945 the first issue of <u>Tygodnik Powszechny</u>, a Catholic weekly published for the intelligentsia by the metropolitan curia in Cracow appeared.71 A more popular monthly <u>Znak</u> has appeared since 1946, which like the <u>Tygodnik</u> too, stopped publication between 1953-1956. By 1947 there were 30 Catholic press titles being published. The Church also restarted its educational work. In 1947 there were 54 Catholic secondary schools run by religious orders72 whose curricula were those of the state schools, but where a 'distinctive Catholic spirit' prevailed. The abysmal economic situation in the country after the Nazi occupation (Poland lost nearly 40 per cent of her national wealth and more than 6 million of her people) caused the Church authorities at their first postwar bishops' conference in June 1945 to set up a national headquarters of the <u>Caritas</u> organization supervised by the Episcopate's Charity Commission. Until taken over by the State in January 1950 <u>Caritas</u> with the Church support carried out a nationwide reconstruction and aid programme for the needy and sick members of society, particularly children. In 1946 <u>Caritas</u> was running 256 hospitals, 183 children's homes, 743 kindergartens and hundreds of other centres with financial support from abroad.73

The Church played a leading part in the integration of the western and northern territories ceded to

Poland under the Potsdam Agreement. The problem there was that the settlers from eastern Poland came into contact with the autochthonic population, which although conscious of its links with Poland, had for generations existed within a German state. This meeting of different national groups often led to serious conflict, aggravated by the often insensitive policies of the State and the bureaucratic property measures of local government. As a result the majority of the population later emigrated to the Federal Republic of Germany attracted by the higher living standards and other inducements. The tragedy was, that unlike the ethnic Germans living in these territories, this population had remained there after 1945 in expectation of Poland. If sections of the autochthonic population did nevertheless choose to remain in Poland, then the Church must be given much of the credit for keeping them there. For example, in the years 1948-1956 when many of the ethnic youth had difficulty in being accepted by educational institutions of the state, the Catholic University of Lublin and Catholic secondary schools would admit them. Also conflicts among the heterogenous newcomers from the east themselves, were often soothed by Catholic clergy which came west in large numbers.74 Indeed, priests were recruited and trained from among the local population of these lands. Changing the diocesan boundaries to fit the new state frontiers posed a political problem for both Church and State. With the shift to the west, the major portions of three eastern Polish dioceses had become Soviet territory. With the Catholics emigrating this caused no difficulty, indeed these three ecclesiastical borders still have not been settled. In the western and northern territories, however, there existed after 1945 a fragmented German and Czech ecclesiastical structure which had to be adjusted to the new political realities. The then primate, Cardinal Hlond, created five interim 'apostolic administrations' in 1945, in Wroclaw, Gdansk, Opole, Gorzow and Olsztyn, which continued until after the ratification by the <u>Bundestag</u> of the Polish-Federal German Republic Treaty on 7 December 1970.75 On 28 June 1972 six new Polish dioceses were finally erected, a national act in the interests of both the Church and the State.

Before that happened, however, during the Stalinist period there were serious clashes between the two authorities,76 a phenomenon not unknown in the other socialist democracies. Anti-church activity was intensified by the ZMP and PZPR in the media, after the Holy Office of the Vatican on 20 June 1949 threatened to excommunicate Catholics who had become members of the Party or who collaborated with it; not an easy definition to decide on. The State in turn passed a number of decrees, laws and regulations of an anti-ecclesiastical character, such as one concerning the registration of monastic orders. The State confiscated all lands belonging to the Church, with the exception of parish-owned properties. It thus took over hospitals run by the Church especially those by nuns and curtailed the activities of other Church organizations. The Church was blamed for 'impeding the reorganization of ecclesiastical administration in the new territories', an 'antipatriotic' act. At the same time pressure was put on the Church authorities to sign an agreement with the State, indeed a joint commission was formed to look into controversial questions. In order to exert greater pressure on the bishops and senior clergy, the younger clergy and lay Catholic workers were played out against their leaders. Thus as early as September 1949 a priests' commission was formed within the ex-combatants' League of Fighters for Freedom and Democracy (ZBoWiD), a body completely under Party control. The commission tried to enlist priests who had actively fought during the occupation and who had been imprisoned by the Germans, as well as those who were just critical of the Church hierarchy. There was active in addition another group, formed earlier in November 1945 around the magazine *Dzis i Jutro* (Today and Tomorrow),77 which in 1947 transformed itself into the publishing house PAX which in fact publishes its own Catholic daily paper to this day. The PAX papers were condemned by the majority of Catholic editors and journalists as not conforming to Catholic press standards. The decision caused a row, since not only were the editors of the two papers not invited to attend; but the papers could not be faulted on Catholic doctrine. This political act was made because it was suspected in Church circles that the PAX group, in trying to mediate between Church and State, was really supporting Communist Party policies. This suspicion was confirmed when a few days before the December 1948 PPR-PPS Congress already mentioned, which voted for the unification of the two parties, the Dzis i Jutro group, no doubt in order to retain its political influence, spoke out clearly in favour of the socialist order in Poland. All this brought a violent reaction from the majority of Polish Catholics.

Noteworthy is PAX's Publishing Institute (1949) which has rendered important service to Christian culture in Poland by publishing umpteen millions of copies of valuable Polish and translated works, which in many cases would have had no chance of appearing in print otherwise. On 9 February 1952 the PAX Parliamentary Group was formally constituted, with B. Piasecki, a pre-war right wing radical nationalist party chief, as its leader.78 Ever since 1948 PAX has adopted Marxist socio-economic and political doctrines, reserving its right, however, strongly to proclaim a Christian world view and moral outlook. Its particular stance includes the thesis of pluralism within socialism, not readily acceptable to the Party. PAX was fearful of the rise of the ZBoWiD Commission of priests, though small, as competitors and distanced itself from its unprincipled attacks on the Church hierarchy, which in the early fifties still could prove dangerous to the Church in Poland. PAX therefore formed its own moderate association: The Commission of Catholic Intellectuals attached to the Polish Peace Committee with both a secular and clerical membership. It did join forces with its rival in 1953 as the Commission of Clerical and Secular Activists attached to the all-Polish National Front Committee.

This was still the time when the situation was difficult for the Church. On 14 April 1950 the new primate of Poland, Stefan Wyszynski,79 signed, with the entire Polish episcopate an 'Act of mutual understanding' with the Government,80 a decision much applauded by PAX. It was, in the circumstances, an act of realistic assessment of the situation by the

Church, which however was initially received with disbelief and horror by the Vatican. Its significance as a unique experiment in the entire communist world did not emerge until much later. The 'Act' which was a compromise solution did have some advantages for the Church, as it could be interpreted as a substitute for the abrogated Concordat. The episcopate undertook to call upon the clergy to respect the state authorities, to collaborate with them in the work of rebuilding the country, to prevail upon Vatican diplomats to stabilize the ecclesiastical administration in the new territories, and to support the cause of peace. The state government for its part guaranteed denominational religious instruction in state schools, and the freedom for students to participate in out-of-school religious practices and exercises, as well as the admissibility of religious practices in full public view, such as pilgrimages, processions and open-air services. It allowed the existence of Catholic schools with full educational rights under the law, the continuance of the Catholic University KUL as well as of the two Theological Faculties in the universities of Cracow and Warsaw, a Catholic press and other publishing activities. The Church was free once more to undertake charitable and catechist activity in the country. Catholic associations and religious orders too were safeguarded. The 'Act' condemned German 'revisionism', an expected patriotic commitment, while the episcopate for its part once more declared its full support for the integration of the new territories. The possibility of deferring military service for alumni of theological seminaries and the conditional agreement of the episcopate for its clergy to collaborate with the now state-controlled Caritas organization were mentioned in an appendix to the document.

Despite expectations or hopes, the 'Act' did not put an end to inter Church-State problems. Thus, on 9 February 1953 the State Council decreed that all new clergy, including bishops, must swear an oath of loyalty to the Polish People's Republic (PRL). Clerics found to be acting against State interests could be removed from office. In 1952 the authorities renewed their efforts to abolish religious teaching in schools, to close down denominational schools and to eliminate religious associations. There was again interference with the running of religious orders. Some priests and bishops were arrested. The state press renewed its attacks on the Church. In a particularly curious move, the State forced cathedral chapters in the new territories to elect 'chapter vicars' (there were no Vatican appointed bishops there till 1972) for these areas, an office invalid in canon law, while reluctant Church administrators were accused of disloyalty to the State and of disregarding the provisions of the 'Act of mutual understanding'. In this patriotic propaganda action designed to hurt the authority and national prestige of the Church the Party used the help provided by ZBoWiD priests and to some extent by PAX. The weekly Tygodnik Powszechy was closed down as a journal of the Polish curia; later it was taken over by PAX. In this not untypically Polish 'split', however, PAX continued personal contacts with the Primate, urging him to give in further to the State. The Party authorities meanwhile were more concerned with subordinating the Church to the State by weakening the moral authority of the hierarchy, limiting its influence and accelerating the process of laicizing Polish Society than with accommodation. In this the State did not succeed, because though the Church would give way in certain matters, it stood firm on its principles in which stand it could count on majority support. The inevitable internment of Wyszynski was in fact a defeat for PAX also. The new acting leader of the episcopate had to yield to the government demand to get all clergy, including bishops, to swear the oath of loyalty on 17 December 1953. Priests who refused were not allowed to continue in office. The aim of this was twofold: to challenge the Church and 'taint' it with collaboration and to get it to work with the State and Party, somehow. Because of these complex aims government harassment did not stop with the oaths, but continued with the closure of children's homes and schools still run by religious orders. The two Theological Faculties were transformed into the State Academy of Catholic Theology (ATK) and the Christian Theological Academy (CHAT). The teaching activities of KUL were curtailed. In these difficult times PAX managed to gain some influence in ecclesiastical matters, and tried, significantly with rather less success, to convert Catholics to its own ideology.

With the end of Stalinism the government gradually lost interest in denominational struggles, the general situation complicated by growing intra-Party difficulties, which culminated in the 1956 demonstrations by workers in Poznan and the Baltic ports. A breakthrough came in October of that year when Wladyslaw Gomulka, himself a prisoner in the years 1948-1955,81 took over as First Party Secretary. Within a few days he released Wyszynski from internment. The Primate quickly lent his full authority in support of the reforms which contributed greatly to calm the situation, enabling Gomulka to proceed with his new deal. In the new climate PAX's fortunes too slowly began to revive. After 1957 it was allowed to open provincial branches, having hitherto been confined to Warsaw. It split in the same year, giving rise to a new group (Za i Przeciw - For and Against), which under the name Christian Social Alliance (CHSS) is still active. Up to 1958 Church-State relations improved significantly, the Mixed (Joint) Commission resuming its deliberations. Religious education was allowed in schools as an extra-curricular subject. Though this did not last, the Church meanwhile had managed to establish its own network of catechist points where religious instruction is given to this day. Most of those imprisoned during Stalinism were released, there were posthumous pardons. Tygodnik Powszechny was restarted, Znak too reappeared, indeed this grouping was later allowed a small (limited in numbers) representation in the Sejm, under the name Znak. A number of Catholic youth, intelligentsia, social documentation and studies clubs were licensed, though admittedly only in a few major cities. The countryside thus continued to rely more on the direct impact of faith and church attendance. Some of the clubs came into existence as a result of subsequent splits within PAX and other political discussion clubs. Their activities, whether in the Sejm or in the more sociological domain however, are not far removed ideologically from those of PAX itself or of CHSS.82 All these groups including PAX's Publishing Institute may be said to be rather elitist, acting mainly on Catholic intelligentsia consciousness. Of their papers Znak and Tygodnik Powszechny are most closely linked with the Church establishment although neither can be said to influence the episcopate which continues to act completely independently. It keeps to this stance to demonstrate its continuing opposition to the frequent infringements by the government of the 'Act', in particular of the Church's principled demands, such as the army call-up of seminarists, and its condemnation of frequent cases of surveillance by Security Agents of Catholic institutions and their workers, expecially priests and KUL students; the latter often experiencing difficulty in obtaining employment, especially in teaching, after graduation. Even so, attempts to 'clericalize' KUL failed, it continues to have a high percentage of social science students of peasant and working-class origin, i.e. not the new Party intelligentsia.83 The repressive policies of the Party were certainly not unconnected with Cardinal Wyszynski's efforts to mark Poland's Christian Millenium, the thousandth anniversary of the nation's baptism in 1966, on a grand scale. Clearly, the Primate's aim to get through 'to every parish and every family in the land' was not welcomed by officialdom. However, it was the letter written by the episcopate to the German bishops in November 1965 in which the Poles' forgive and ask for forgiveness'84 which was taken as an act of national disloyalty, 'casting doubt' on the permanent character of the postwar Polish-German frontier. Since there has always been absolute unanimity in Poland on this point, the episcopate's action could be interpreted as profoundly damaging. Gomulka himself conceded that the bishops had made no 'concessions', but had used some 'unfortunate words'.85 After Gomulka's resignation in 1970 in the wake of growing academic and workers' unrest ('the seventies'), his successor, Edward Gierek,86 initiated a new policy vis-a-vis the Church. This was certainly influenced by the Treaty between the Polish People's Republic (PRL) and the German Federal Republic (FRG) of December 1970, as well as the general detente in Europe and the world and the Helsinki Accord. In

1971 official contracts between the PRL and the Holy See were started, which despite the authorities' refusal to allow the Catholic mass to be transmitted on radio (it has been transmitted since 1980) and the backlog in church construction, have improved Church-State relations in a way which made the Church a partner of sorts of the State Government and the Party. The First Secretary of the Central Committee of the PZPR and the Primate would meet, and the press would carry reports of discussions

> on topics of importance to the nation (and church) which should lead to all Poles uniting in the task of working for the welfare of the People's Republic.87

There were similar communiques before the Pope's visit in January 1979.88 In this new climate the Church was encouraged to conduct missionary activity outside Poland, including religious contacts with Poles abroad, urging them to keep their home links firm. This could have its uses with Poles abroad persuading their influential foreign friends to help the country. Educational and pastoral work in Poland itself too started again to increase, lay experts being invited to work in some of the episcopate's specialist commissions. The Church's voice can be heard condemning the morality of the government's atheization programmes in schools and universities or the army call-up of seminarians. Once again the Church reminds the nation of the greatest moments in her history, especially those not mentioned in official school textbooks (referring to Tsarist, also Soviet policies in Poland), which they accuse of distortion. The appraisal of workers according to their political party ideology records is also increasingly being pilloried, in a way unique in socialist democracies. The Church's authority increased out of all proportion not only at home, but also abroad, after the election of Cardinal Wojtyla as Pope on 16 October 1978. The Primate, Wyszynski, must have used his authority to help bring this about. He certainly did so later in his September 1980 Solidarity period sermon in which he called for discipline and calm, for negotiations to solve controversial socio-political problems of the nation (this in the face of criticism from some opposing quarters). The Pope's first official visit to Poland in 1979 was an event unprecedented in her history, described as a 'nationwide plebiscite'.89 The following years gave birth to Solidarity, an opposition and movement characteristically Polish in its origins, its passion, its dignified conduct and ultimate fate. Its impact cannot as yet be objectively assessed. However, its religious backcloth must be mentioned in this chapter; the sudden demand for all kinds of religious experience: conversions, invitations by miners and workers to priests to visit mines and factories. All these events were recorded by the State-controlled news media.

The State of Emergency on 13 December 1981 was a shock - but once again both the President of the Military Council for National Salvation (WRON), General Wojciech Jaruzelski and the Primate, Jozef Glemp, appealed for calm.90 There is no doubt that these voices were heeded, indeed were the more effective for being heard together. In recent years the Church's independent and measured approach to the many difficult problems of internal policies and the government and Party's desire despite differences for political and economic normalization have brought both sides together to attempt mutual contacts, while PAX has renewed its call for constructing a pluralist society within the existing socialist framework. The possibility of some rapprochement between Church and State for Poland's sake is seen in the regular meetings between the President of the State Council, Jaruzelski, and the Primate. Note the tenor of Jaruzelski's speech to the Tenth Congress of the PZPR on 30 June 1986:

> The realization of the constitutional principle of separation of church and state, the freedom of the churches ... to fulfil their religious functions; the citizen's freedom of conscience and religion, the equality in law and duties regardless of his attitude to religion, these are the important, humanistic and lasting achievements of People's Poland.

He went on to say that

> The Party desires good relations between state and all denominations. The often difficult dialogue with the Roman Catholic Church ... goes on ... it is necessary and it is constructive. In our common struggle for peace, condemnation of revisionism, care of our national environment, protection of national treasures, links with Poles abroad, concern for the moral health of the nation and the fight against social pathologies - there is more than enough room for collaboration.91

Of course, there have been declarations and unfulfilled expectations before. It must be pointed out that while the Church insists on the abandonment of the deliberate ideological 'atheization programme' of society by the State, the government and Party introduced at the end of 1986 a new school subject: 'Study of Religion' (Religioznawstwo), not Religious Studies, into the secondary school curriculum, the aim of which according to the Church and some prominent lay people is to show the falsehood of all religion, a clear case of atheization of the youth, confirmed by the fact that the 'syllabus is a copy of a similar syllabus taught in PZPR Party schools' and political courses. The syllabus, it is true, was not agreed with any religious studies institutes of note in the country.92 On the other hand a reading of the syllabus document itself reveals a moderate and objective treatment of the subject, albeit with the more detailed surveys of various religious dogmas and especially cults found in similar course books in the West missing. The history of the Catholic Church in Poland is dismissed in one page, the emphasis being on Christianity's social views and action.93

The Church has not remained inactive in the face of this challenge. It has taken great care to raise the educational level of its clergy and of its own teaching to keep pace with the rise of the general educational level of society after the war: the abolition of illiteracy, the high percentage of school leavers with full secondary courses completed in People's Poland.94 Pastoral work in the postwar period has been determined not solely by religious needs but by the concrete political situation of the country. This is the Church's answer to the Marxist challenge and materialist ideology of the Party in power. Laicization can only be challenged by an expanded form of ministry: the continuing improvement of religious education of society through a mass ministry, the link of important national historical events with a religious commitment, already mentioned. One of these major events was the commemoration and celebration of the third centenary of King Jan Kazimierz's proclamation of St Mary as the Queen of Poland. As during the original royal vows in Lwow, so in March 1956 St Mary was once again proclaimed Queen in the presence of one million pilgrims from all over Poland: the so-called 'Jasna Gora (Czestochowa) Vows of the Nation'. The Sacrum Poloniae Millenium Novena organized by Cardinal Wyszynski which began in front of the same miraculous portrait of the Madonna on the anniversary of the 3 May Constitution served the same purpose. Events to which the Party does not attach the same degree of national significance.95

THE SPECIFICITY OF POLISH RELIGIOUSNESS

The two above examples (there are many others) underline the strong Marian cult of Polish faith, whose origins go back to the seventeenth century. This was shaped by three main directions which have occurred in European piety of the seventeenth and eighteenth centuries and which have been enriched by specific Polish experiences. These are, firstly, the Spanish religious tradition marked by an excess of feeling which reached Poland with the Jesuits towards the end of the sixteenth century, secondly, the more rational, non-emotional type of French piety which came in the middle of the seventeenth century introduced by the missionaries of St Vincent a Paul, and thirdly, the austere type of German piety whose representatives in Poland were the priests of the Congregatio Clericorum Regularium in Commune Viventium which reached Poland at the end of that century.96 The Polish elements are very symbolic in the first instance: the Society of Marian Fathers founded in 1679 with its cult of St Mary, the only Polish monastic order founded before the partitions.97 It is precisely this Marian cult whose roots reach to the end of the Middle Ages, especially the Baroque, which in Poland led to the establishment of a multiplicity of places of pilgrimage, which increased again in the second half of the nineteenth century and especially after the Second World War, when Jasna Gora with its portrait of the Madonna became Poland's religious capital. Every year in August pilgrimages continue the precedent of the first one organized by the Warsaw diocese in 1711.98

The second feature is the popular nature of religion in Poland marked by a strong fideism and sentimentalism with a weak intellectual base. Thus, while some 90 per cent of Poles regard themselves as Catholic only about two-thirds of workers in the heavily industrialized regions claimed to know the basic articles of faith according to an inquiry conducted in the 1970s.99 Even more interestingly, 45 per cent expressed some doubt of these articles and some 50 per cent criticized the Church's moral teaching. Those who profess Catholicism practice pre-marital sex, divorce, even abortion. People do not pray daily, yet many of them visit the church frequently. There is a contradiction among many Polish Catholics, who despite a traditional attachment to their Church are ignorant or in disagreement with its teaching. It would seem that, much day-to-day Polish religion seems to be mere custom and usage, ready to burst into faith only during a mass pilgrimage. According to another inquiry in 1980 throughout Poland only 50 per cent of Poles go to mass on an ordinary Sunday (it was Sunday 23 November 1980) and 15 per cent of these took communion. This, but one feature of Polish religiousness varies in different parts of the country; Sunday church attendance being most frequent in the southern dioceses of Cracow, Tarnow and Przemysl!100

Another survey, published in Poland in 1983, shows the family, as in other Catholic countries, as the main religious educator. Parents are the example, and it is they who watch over their children's religious teaching before school and now also during school in the catechist centres. Especially in the countryside parents make quite sure their children do attend. There are differences according to the family's age, and a correlation exists between parents and children's observance, the latter are at their most religious before their 'teens, less in towns as teenagers than in the country. Mothers and both parents influence daughters, fathers tend to influence their sons. Urbanization and industrialization can hinder religion. Figures from Kielce show 61 per cent of youth as religious (71 per cent of their parents), in Warsaw the figures were 48 per cent and 63 per cent respectively. Atheists were 20 per cent (18 per cent of parents) in Kielce, 31 (25 per cent) respectively, in Warsaw.101

Religion is too complex a phenomenon to be reduced to figures, nevertheless the thesis can be put that farmers in the southeast are most religious, 100 per cent; it is they who supply most candidates for the priesthood. In the countryside the parish continues to be influential educationally and culturally. It is also a control agent for religious observance. Workers in large industrial centres which started after the war and who were country-born are more religious than the 'older' pre-war proletariat. The situation among the intelligentsia is complicated. Those with higher education know little about religion (Warsaw in 1980),102 at the same time there is a growing intelligentsia population which is very much committed. More intelligentsia now discuss church and religious problems. PAX certainly has made a significant intellectual contribution in this respect. There is in addition the emotional impact of a religious experience, children's first communion or ex-Marxists rediscovering religion. Here too there is the contradiction between an intensification of religion, a charismatic experience among the youth, and at the same time a growing general religious indifference. Noticeable since 1978/1980, the election of the Polish Pope and Solidarity, is a revival of religious commitment. The question whether it will last or whether it is linked to passing historical events cannot be answered as yet.

CONCLUSION

Clearly, there is a loss as well as gain for the Church. In the nationally strengthened yet religiously somewhat diluted state it presents a curious parallel to the simultaneously equally weakened and strengthened Polish variant of the dominant secular monopoly.103 It is not as if educational provision had been lacking. Though under-educated in absolute and formal terms until comparatively recently, Poland has not been uneducated in the non-formal religious education sense, of being educated in church and at home during both free and occupied periods of her history. These influences are not easy to quantify exactly, but they must be added to the total of Christian education provision in the Polish case. Informal education is also carried out by the Party. Though foreign occupations have weakened the country in international status, within itself the nation presents a stronger, spontaneous religious (overwhelmingly Catholic now) as well as an ethnic (now overwhelmingly Polish) commitment, which many other nations require more formal schooling to sustain. The Polish example now is not characterized by religious instruction in school. Poland has a stronger, more efficient religious education programme outside the schools than many other nations have within state-assisted schemes. The relative absence now of private denominational schooling is responsible for less obtrusive elitarism to develop, at least from that quarter, even though it is not altogether absent especially as an intellectual elitism factor. This too is far from being a source of unmitigated weakness in internal: national, social and religious terms, while the international nexus of her 'ideologies' adds a certain support when viewed externally, providing the safeguard of continuing survival.

NOTES AND REFERENCES

1. Recent useful accounts of the history of Poland in English are:
   Gieysztor, Aleksander, Kieniewicz, Stefan,

Rostworowski, Emanuel, Tazbir, Janusz, Wereszycki, Henryk, <u>History of Poland</u>, Warszawa: Panstwowe Wydawnictwo Naukowe, 1979;
Davies, Norman, <u>Heart of Europe: A Short History of Poland</u>, Oxford: Clarendon Press, 1984.

For the history of the Catholic Church see:
Kloczowski, Jerzy (ed.), <u>Kosciol w Polsce</u>, 2 vols, Krakow: Znak, 1968 and 1970;
Kumor, Boleslaw and Obertynski, Zdzislaw (eds), <u>Historia Kosciola w Polsce</u>, Poznan-Warszawa: Pallotinum, 1974-1979;
Kloczowski, Jerzy, Mullerowa, Lidia, Skarbek, Jan, <u>Zarys dziejow Kosciola katolickiego w Polsce</u>, Krakow: Znak, 1986;
Kloczowski, Jerzy (ed.), <u>Histoire religieuse de la Pologne</u>, Paris: Le Centurion, 1987.

2. Rus = Red Ruthenia, the area around the cities of Lwow and Halicz, now in 'Western Ukraine' of the Ukrainian SSR, as well as the four more westerly provinces within present-day Polish boundaries.

3. Gieysztorowa, Irena, Ludnosc, in: <u>Encyklopedia historii gospodarczej Polski do 1945 roku</u>, Warszawa: Wiedza Powszechna, 1981.

4. Litak, Stanislaw, <u>Struktura terytorialna Kosciola lacinskiego w Polsce w 1772 roku</u>, 2 vols, Lublin: Towarzystwo Naukowe KUL, 1979-1980.

5. Rostworowski, Emanuel, <u>Ostatni krol Rzeczypospolitej</u>, Warszawa: Wiedza Powszechna, 1966;
Zywirska, Maria, <u>Ostatnie lata zycia krola Stanislawa Augusta</u>, Warszawa: Panstwowy Instytut Wydawniczy, 1975.

6. De Madariaga, Isabel, <u>Russia in the age of Catherine the Great</u>, London: Weidenfeld and Nicolson, 1982.

7. Korolko, Wiroslaw, Tazbir, Janusz, <u>Konfederacja Warszawska 1573 roku, wielka karta polskiej tolerancji</u>, Warszawa: PAX, 1980.

Polish Christian Identity

8. On the Reformation in Poland see the following publications:
Krasinski, Valerian, <u>Historical sketch of the reformation in Poland,</u> 2 vols, London: Murray 1838-1840.
Tazbir, Janusz, 'Recherches sur l'histoire de la Reforme en Pologne 1945-1959'; in: <u>Acta Poloniae Historica,</u> <u>2,</u> 1959.
Tazbir, Janusz, 'Spoleczny zasieg polskiej reformacji', in: <u>Kwartalnik Historyczny,</u> <u>82,</u> 4, 1975.

9. <u>Szlachta</u>, one of five social estates in the Commonwealth of the two Nations, comprising about 8-10 per cent of the population, coming after the clergy (1 per cent), before the burghers (6 per cent), Jews and peasants. Despite considerable economic differences within the estate their fiscal, legal and political privileges which they inherited, did not divide the <u>szlachta</u> into different strata of nobility. Their privileges emerged by the end of the fifteenth century, eg., the bicameral <u>sejm</u> (parliament and <u>sejmiki</u> (local diets) in 1497, rights to tax exemption and the statutes: <u>neminem captivabimus</u> and <u>nihil novi</u>. Their legislative monopoly was used to wrest further privileges. The poor nobles had the same rights as their prosperous brethren: attendance at the local diets and electing the King. Their sole duty was to provide unpaid military service. Their privileges protected them from the King and the obligations of the modern state. Their varied fortunes posed problems for the Republic and contributed to its downfall. Access to <u>szlachta</u> was strictly controlled, the King's nominations had to be approved by the <u>Sejm</u>.

See also:
Fedorowicz, J.K., Bogucka, Maria and Samsonowicz, Henryk (eds), <u>A Republic of Nobles</u>, Cambridge: Cambridge University Press, 1982.

10. Mikolaj Rej, 1505-1569, fashioned the use of Polish in his writings.

11. Jan Kochanowski, 1530-1584, acknowledged as one of Europe's foremost poets of the time. Other arts

too flourished during this period.

12. For the history of the Jesuit order in Poland see:
Zalecki, Stanislaw, *Jezuici w Polsce*, 5 vols, Lwow-Krakow: Anczyc, 1900-1906;
Piechnik, Ludwik, *Dzieje Akademii Wilenskiej w latach 1600-1655*, 2 vols, Roma: Apud Institutum Historicum Societatis Jesu, 1983-1984.

13. Litak, Stanislaw, 'Kosciol w Polsce w okresie odnowy potrydenckiej', in: Tuchle, Hermann, Bouman, C.A., *Historia Kosciola*, vol.3, 1500-1715, Warszawa: PAX, 1985.

14. 'Noblemen's democracy': a characteristically Polish socio-political system which was completed in the sixteenth century, and in which the szlachta (see n.9 above) played the dominant legal role because of its monolithic structure (equality of all members of the szlachta). At the same time the power of the King was severely curtailed by the szlachta, according to the principle that the King too is subject to the laws. See:
Sucheni-Grabowska, 'Sejm w latach 1540-1587', in: Michalski, Jerzy (ed.), *Historia Sejmu Polskiego*, vol.1, Warszawa: Panstwowe Wydawnictwo Naukowe, 1984.

15. Skoczek, Jozef, 'Rozwoj szkolnictwa w Polsce sredniowiecznej', in: *Historia Wychowania*, vol.1, Kurdabacha, Lukasz, (ed.), Warszawa: Panstwowe Wydawnictwo Naukowe, 1965.

16. For Jesuit schooling in Poland see:
Piechnik, Ludwik, 'Przemiany w szkolnictwie jezuickim w Polsce XVIII wieku', in: *Roczniki Humanistyczne*, 25, 2, 1977.

17. Samsonowicz, Henryk, 'Polish Politics and Society under the Jagiellonian Monarchy', in: Fedorowicz, J.K., op.cit.

18. Litak, Stanislaw, 'Wandlungen im polnishen Schulwesen im 18. Jahrhundert', in: Engel-Janosi, Friedrich, Klingenstein, Grete, Lutz, Heinrich (eds),

Formen der europaischen Aufklarung. Untersuchungen zur Situation von Christentum, Bildung und Wissenschaft im 18. Jahrhundert. Wien: Verlag fur Geschichte und Politik, 1976;

Wisniowski, Eugenius, 'The parochial school system in Poland towards the close of the Middle Ages', in: Acta Poloniae Historica, 27, 1973; pp.29-43;

Litak, Stanislaw, 'The parochial school network in Poland prior to the establishment of the Commission of National Education', in: ibid., pp.45-65;

Olczak, Stanislaw, *Szkolnictwo parafialne w Wielkopolsce w XVII i XVIII w.*, Lublin: Towarzystwo Naukowe KUL, 1978;

Kowalik, Jozef, *Szkolnictwo parafialne w archidiakonacie sadeckim od XVI do XVIII w.*, Lublin: Redakcja Wydawnictw KUL, 1983;

Zapart, Andrzej, *Szkolnictwo parafialne w archdiakonacie krakowskim od XVI do XVIII w.*, Lublin: Redakcja Wydawnictw KUL, 1983.

19. For Konarski's school reform see:

Kot, Stanislaw, *Reforma Szkolna Stanislawa Konarskiego*, Krakow: Gebethner i Wolff, 1923;

Konopczynski, Wladyslaw, *Stanislaw Konarski*, Warszawa: Kasa im. Mianowskiego, 1926;

Grabski, Wladyslaw, Maria, 'Stanislaw Konarski, Problem genezy osobowosci nowozytnego reformatora', in: *Przeglad Humanistyczny*, XVIII, 1, 100, 1974;

Author's Collective, *Pijarzy w kulturze dawnej Polski. Ludzie i zagadnienia*, Krakow: Polska Prowincja Pijarow, 1982 (see especially: Jan Buba).

20. On Sarmatian szlachta culture, see:

Tazbir, Janusz, *Kultura szlachecka w Polsce. Rozkwit-upadek-relikty*, second edn, Warszawa: Wiedza Powszechna, 1979.

21. The Commission for National Education (rather than 'of National Education'), i.e. for a national revival, was Europe's first Ministry of Education when founded by order of the Sejm on 14 October 1773. It functioned until 1794 funded from confiscated Jesuit property. Among its achievements were the reorganization of two universities and 74 secondary

and over 1600 parish schools. Its main aim was to establish a national, secular system of education which would be open to the majority of the population with modern curricula in which both individual and national state requirements would be met. Its schools were open to girls as well as boys, subjects such as hygiene, midwifery, physical education were available in addition to the usual academic ones. Polish was the language of instruction in all its schools.

An Elementary Books Society set to work to provide a full range of textbooks for the Commission's schools. Its teachers were to be trained in state colleges and paid a national salary scale.

The Commission's attack on the Church's monopoly in education was seen as the means of undermining the long term prospects of the conservatives whose aim was to prevent change in the Commonwealth at all costs.

The spirit of the Commission's work lingered on long after the Commission itself had ceased to operate after the last partition. Polish education at the time was in advance of that in Russia and even in the other occupying powers. The Duchy of Warsaw's Board of Education made provision for universal secular primary education in 1819, at a time when in Austria education was still controlled by the Church, with Latin or German as the languages of instruction. These achievements were possible because of the work undertaken by the Commission for Education.

22. See:
 Kloczowski (ed.), Kosciol, op.cit., vol.2, pp.116-29.

23. The Council Party stood for the supremacy of the General Council over the Pope.

24. On Polish Universities before the partitions see:
 Lepszy, Kazimierz (ed.), Dzieje Uniwersytetu Jagiellonskiego, 1364-1764, vol.1, Opalko, Kazimierz (ed.), id. vol.2, Krakow: Uniwersytet Jagiellonski, 1964;
 Bielinski, Jozef, Uniwersytet Wilenski,

1579-1831, 3 vols, Krakow: Gebethner i Wolff, 1899-1900;
Kochanowski, Jan Karol, *Dzieje Akademii Zamojskiej*, Krakow: W. Anczyc, 1899-1900;
Finkel, Ludwik, Starzynski, Stanislaw, *Historia Uniwersytetu Lwowskiego*, 2 parts, Lwow: Senat Akademicki Uniwersytetu Lwowskiego, 1894.

25. On the Commission for National Education see:
Jobert, Ambroise, *La commission d'Education Nationale en Pologne 1773-1794, son oeuvre d'instruction civique*, Dijon: Imprimeri Darantiere, 1941;
Kurdybacha, L., 'The Commission of National Education in Poland 1773-1794', in: *History of Education*, 2, 2, 1973;
Kurdybacha, Lukasz, Mitera-Dobrowolska, Mieczyslawa, *Komisja Edukacji Narodowej*, Warszawa: Panstwowe Wydawnictwo Naukowe, 1973;
Grabski, Mieczyslaw, Maria, *U podstaw wielkiej reformy. Karta z dziejow Komisji Edukacji Narodowej*, Lodz: Wydawnictwo Lodzkie, 1984.

26. *Ustawy Komisji Edukacji Narodowej dla stanu akademickiego i na szkoly w krajach Rzeczypospolitej przepisane w Warszawie roku 1783*, introduced by Kucharski, Wladyslaw, Lwow: Ksiegarnia Naukowa, 1923.

27. Kowecki, Jerzy (ed.), introduced by: Lesnodorski, Boguslaw, *Konstytucja 3 maja 1791. Statut Zgromadzenia Przyjaciol Konstytucji*, Warszawa: Panstwowe Wydawnictwo Naukowe, 1981, gives a useful account of the Constitution.

28. See:
Mizia, Tadeusz, *Szkolnictwo parafialne w czasach Komisji Edukacji Narodowej*, Wroclaw-Warszawa-Krakow: Ossolineum, 1964;
Szybiak, Irena, *Szkolnictwo Komisji Edukacji Narodowej w Wielkim Ksiestwie Litewskim*, Wroclaw-Warszawa-Krakow-Gdansk: Ossolineum, 1973;
Mrozowska, Kamilla, *Funckjonowanie systemu szkolnego Komisji Edukacji Narodowej na terenie Korony w latach 1783-1793*, Wroclaw-Warszawa-Krakow-Gdansk-Lodz: Ossolineum, 1985.

29. See the series of:
Instrukcje dla wizytatorow generalnych szkol and Raporty generalnych wizytatorow szkol Komisji Edukacji Narodowej, published by the Polish Academy of Sciences (Polska Akademia Nauk), History of Education Section, by Ossolineum, in Wroclaw (etc.): 1976 etc., 1974 etc., respectively.

30. For a concise account of post-partition history of Poland see:
Kieniewicz, Stefan, Historia Polski 1795-1918, Warszawa: Panstwowe Wydawnictwo Naukowe, 1969.

31. For details see:
Kumor, Boleslaw, Ustroj i organizacja Kosciola polskiego w okresie niewoli narodowej, Krakow: Polskie Towarzystwo Teologiczne, 1980.

32. Boudou, Adrien, Le Saint-Siege et la Russie. Leurs relations diplomatiques au XIXe siecle, vol.1, Paris: Librarie Plon, 1925, contains the text of the Concordat.

See also:
Kumor and Obertynski, Historia, op.cit., vol.2 (see: Wincenty Urban).

33. Zielinski, Zygmunt, 'Wykonanie ustaw sejmu pruskiego z dnia 20 v 1873' in: Prawo Kanoniczne, 11, 1-2, 1968.

Kulturkampf: The Poles successfully resisted the pressures of Bismarck's anti-Catholic cultural action launched in 1873 after Bavarian and Rhineland Catholics joined the Empire, as well as the activities of the Prussian Land Commission which forbade the purchase of houses for speakers of Polish in Prussian-occupied Poland. Poles as Roman Catholics were affected, even if the Act was not directed exclusively at them. The use of Polish was forbidden in schools. Priests had to use German in and out of church. A number were arrested.

34. Wroczynski, Ryszard, Dzieje Oswiaty Polskiej 1795-1945, Warszawa: Panstwowe Wydawnictwo Naukowe,

1980.

35. The reformist measures of the Polish Commission for National Education were used by the Russian authorities to reform their own schools in the former Polish areas in the early part of the nineteenth century. Indeed only in these areas were the schools of acceptable standard. See:
Hans, Nicholas, 'Polish Schools in Russia 1772-1831', in: Slavonic and East European Review, xxxviii, 91, 1959.

36. Kieniewicz, Stefan (ed.), Dzieje Uniwersytetu Warszawskiego 1807-1915, Warszawa: Panstwowe Wydawnictwo Naukowe, 1981;
Garlicki, Andrzej (ed.), Dzieje Uniwersytetu Warszawskiego 1915-1939, Warszawa: Panstwowe Wydawnictwo Naukowe, 1982.

37. Poznanski, Karol, Reforma szkolna w Krolestwie Polskim w 1862 roku, Wroclaw: Ossolineum, 1968.

38. Miaso, Jozef, Szkolnictwo zawodowe w Krolestwie Polskim w latach 1815-1915, Wroclaw: Ossolineum, 1966.

39. Jablonska-Deptula, Ewa, Przystosowanie i opor. Zakony meskie w Krolestwie Kongresowym, Warszawa: PAX, 1983;
Rostocki, Wladyslaw, Skarbek, Jan, Ziolek, Jan (eds), Duchowienstwo a powstanie listopadowe, Lublin: Towarzystwo Naukowe KUL (to appear as Roczniki Humanistyczne, 18, 2).

40. Lossowski, Piotr, Po tej i tamtej stronie Niemna. Stosunki polsko-litewskie. 1883-1939, Warszawa: Czytelnik, 1985.

41. On Polish history between the two wars see especially:
Jedruszczak, Tadeusz (ed.), Historia Polski, vol.4, parts 1-2, Warszawa: Panstwowe Wydawnictwo Naukowe, 1984.

42. The 1921 Constitution: Konstytucja 17 marca

1921, 4th edn, Warszawa: Ksiegarnia Gustawa Szyllinga, 1921.

43. The 1935 Constitution: Konstytucja Rzeczypospolitej Polskiej, Warszawa: Ksiegarnia i Czytelnia Szyllinga, article 114, 1935.

44. Wyczawski, Hieronim Eugeniusz, 'Cerkiew prawoslawna w II Rzeczypospolitej', in: Zielinski, Zygmunt and Wilk, Stanislaw (eds), Kosciol w II Rzeczypospolitej, Lublin: Towarzystwo Naukowe KUL. 1980.

45. Lukomski, Stanislaw, Konkordat zawarty dnia 10 lutego 1925 r. pomiedzy Stolica Apostolska i Rzeczapospolita Polska, Lomza: Ksiegarnia 'Unitas', 1934. This volume has the French original text on pp.1-21, followed by Polish text and commentary.

46. For the text of the Papal Bull: ibid. pp.30-44.

47. Wincenty Witos, 1874-1945, Leader, Polski Stronnictwo Ludowe, PSL, Polish People's Party. Its right wing faction, Piast, was in government in the early and mid-twenties, inc. 1926. PSL's participation in the Centre Left Opposition in 1929 and the formation of the federated Stronnictwo Ludowe, SL, were not particularly popular and the post-war revival of its fortunes aroused some hostility in the USSR.

48. The Chadecja (Christian Democracy Group) was formed in 1902 to counter the popularity of Socialism and to moderate the influence of National Democracy. Especially active in Poznania and Silesia, it may be said to have led a renaissance of Polish Catholicism and reinforced its intellectual foundations. In power in 1923 in coalition with PSL. In opposition to the government of Pilsudski, called for a Convention of People's Rights, with PSL, Socialists (PPS) and National Workers' Party (NPR);
   Strzeszewski, Czeslaw, Rozwoj chrzescijanskiej mysli spolecznej w niepodleglej Polsce 1832-1939, Warszawa: ODiSS (Osrodek Dokumentacji i Studiow

Spolecznych), 1981.

49. Sanacja (Salvation) is the name given to the movement led by Jozef Pilsudski, 1867-1935, conspirator, army leader, Romantic nationalist, who seized power in 1926, and his followers. It ruled from 1926 until 1939 in an elitarian autocratic fashion. It had a strong dislike of Social Democracy.

There is no unanimity about August Hlond's, 1881-1948, relationship to Sanacja, but see:
Pietrzak, Jerzy, 'Czy kardynal Hlond byl zwolennikiem sanacji?', in: Zielinski and Wilk, Kosciol, op.cit.

50. Zdaniewicz, Witold, 'Akcja katolicka', in: Zdaniewicz, Witold (ed.), Historia katolicyzmu spolecznego w Polsce 1832-1939, Warszawa: ODiSS (Osrodek Dokumentacji i Studiow Spolecznych).

51. On the growth of religious orders between the wars, see:
Kumor and Obertynski (eds), Historia, op.cit., vol.2, part 2.

52. The Catholic University in Lublin, Katolicki Uniwersytet Lubelski (KUL) was founded in 1918. With over 2000 students it remains a unique institution with a first class publishing and research record.

53. For a full account of the Church's activities during the Nazi occupation see:
Zielinski, Zygmunt (ed.), Zycie religijne w Polsce pod okupacja hitlerowska, 1939-1945, Warszawa: ODiSS (Osrodek Dokumentacji i Studiow Spolecznych), 1982.

54. On Third Reich policies towards Poles and Poland, see:
Madajczyk, Czeslaw, Polityka III Rzeszy w okupowanej Polsce, 2 vols, Warszawa: Panstwowe Wydawnictwo Naukowe, 1970.

55. Krasuski, Jozef, Tajne szkolnictwo polskie w okresie okupacji hitlerowskiej, 1939-1945, 2nd ed.,

Warszawa: Panstwowe Wydawnictwo Naukowe, 1977.

56. The liquidation of Polish clergy is documented by Smigiel, Kazimierz, 'Zycie religijne w Kraju Warty', in Zielinski (ed.), Zycie religijne, op.cit. See also n.53.

57. On Polish losses during World War Two, see: 'Straty wojenne Polski w latach 1939-1945', Neuordnung Europas. Straty Polski w drugiej wojnie swiatowej. Walka z kultura, polska. Zburzenie Warszawy, Poznan-Warszawa: Wydawnictwo Zachodnie, 1960.

58. On post-Second World War Polish history see: Gora, Wladyslaw, Polska Ludowa 1944-1984. Zarys dziejow politycznych, Lublin: Wydawnictwo Lubelskie, 1986.

59. See:
Kloczowski, Mullerowa, Skarbek, op.cit., pp.376-8.

60. Euhemer, Przeglad Religioznawczy, Polskie Towarzystwo Religioznawcze, xxx, 3-4, 1986, Warszawa: Polskie Wydawnictwo Naukowe, 1986, Appendix 3, pp.439-40.

61. Euhemer, op.cit., Appendix 2, pp.437-8; see also n.59.

62. Euhemer, op.cit., Appendix 2, p.437; see also n.59.

63. Gora, op.cit., pp.254-78.

For a detailed account of Polish scouting, see:
Broniewski, Stanislaw, Calym swoim zyciem. Szare szeregi w relacji naczelnika, Warszawa: Panstwowe Wydawnictwo Naukowe, 1983;
Wyczanska, Krystyna (ed.), Harcerki 1939-1945, 2nd amended edn, Warszawa: Panstwowe Wydawnictwo Naukowe, 1983;
Dobrowolski, Piotr, Janik, Krzysztof, Pietras, Wlodzimierz, PZPR w procesie ksztaltowania socjalisty-

cznej kultury politycznej, Katowice: Uniwersytet Slaski, 1984 (Janik characterizes PZPR policy towards youth movements, pp.81-5).
64. Miaso, Jozef (ed.), *Historia wychowania. Wiek XX*, vol.1, Warszawa: Panstwowe Wydawnictwo Naukowe, 1980, pp.352-65.

65. Tulasiewicz, Witold, 'Cultural Identity and Educational Policy', in: Brock, Colin and Tulasiewicz, Witold (eds), *Cultural Identity and Educational Policy*, London and Sydney: Croom Helm, 1985.

66. Miaso, op.cit., pp.364, 382.

67. Miaso, op.cit., pp.305-6.

For a detailed account of the Church after the war from a sociological point of view see:
Potocki, Andrzej, *Diecezja przemyska w swe 600 - lecie*, 3 vols, Przemysl: Wydawnictwo Diecezji Przemyskiej, 1986.

68. Micewski, Andrzej, *Wspolrzadzic czy klamac? Pax i Znak w Polsce 1945-1976*, Krakow: Oficyna NZS UJ 'Jagiellonia', 1981, p.29.

69. *Konstytucja Polskiej Rzeczypospolitej Ludowej uchwalona przez Sejm Ustawodawczy w dniu 22 lipca 1952 r*, Warszawa: Wiedza Powszechna, 1986.

70. Ziotek, Jan (ed.), *KUL: Dzialalnosc Katolickiego Uniwersytetu Lubelskiego w czasie okupacji*, Lublin: KUL, 1983, p.21.

71. Turowicz, Jerzy, Adam Sapieha, 'A prasa katolicka', in: Wolny, Jerzy in collaboration with Zawadzki, Roman (eds), *Ksiega sapiezynska*, vol.1, Krakow: Polskie Towarzystwo Teologiczne, 1982.

72. Kumor and Obertynski, *Historia*, op.cit., vol.2, part 2.

73. Majka, Jozef, 'Caritas', in: Gryglewicz, Feliks, Lukaszyk, Romuald, Sulowski, Zygmunt (eds), *Encyklopedia Katolicka*, vol.2, Lublin: Towarzystwo Naukowe

KUL, 1985, cols.1333-6.

74. Klafkowski, Alfons, 'Stabilizacja i rozwoj administracji koscielnej ziem zachodnich wyrazem polskiej racji stanu', in: Zeszyty Naukowe Stowarzyszenia Pax, Warszawa: 30, 1.

75. Kloczowski, Mullerowa, Skarbek, op.cit.

76. The situation in the Communist camp is described by:
Turlejska, Maria, Zapis pierwszej dekady 1945-1954, Warszawa: Ksiazka i Wiedza, 1972.

77. Micewski, Wspotizadzic, op.cit.

78. Boleslaw Piasecki, 1914-1974, pre-war leader of Falanga, an extreme right wing and nationalist party which had followers among radical students. After the war, director of PAX, one of the organizations which took over the Church's social and cultural role.
Rudnicki, Szymon, Oboz Narodowo-Radykalny. Geneza i dzialalnosc, Warszawa: Czytelnik, 1985.

79. Micewski, Andrzej, Kardynal Wyszynski, prymas i maz stanu, 2 vols: no publisher, 1985;
Kakol, Kazimierz, Kardynal Stefan Wyszynski jakim go znalem, Warszawa: Instytut Wydawniczy Zwiazkow Zawodowych, 1985.

80. The text of the Act of Mutual Understanding and the Protocol of the Joint Commission of the Rzeczpospolita Polska and the Episcopate which followed it are published by:
Slowo Powszechne, Year 4, nr.104 (1090) of 17 April 1950.

81. Rakowski, Mieczyslaw F., Przesilenie grudniowe. Przyczynek do dziejow najnowszych, Warszawa: Panstwowy Instytut Wydawniczy, 1981, gives sketches of the First Secretaries of the Central Committee of PZPR: Gomulka, Bierut, Ochab, Gierek.
Wladyslaw Gomulka, 1905-1986, seen as representative of a 'Polish road to Communism', but surrounded

by hardliners. Toppled by the Kremlin during his first spell as Party Secretary. After arrest released during the 1956 Thaw and took office again. Had to resign his second term following serious workers' unrest in 1970.

82. In 1984 the Catholic Sejm group Znak changed its name to the Catholic Social Parliamentary Group (KSKP) with the same number of deputies.

83. An inquiry conducted by examining students' personal records revealed that between 1946-1980, of KUL students: 24 per cent were of working class, 30 per cent peasant/farming class, 6 per cent craftsmen, 33 per cent intelligentsia origin.

84. The text of the bishops' letter can be found in: *Materialy i Dokumenty*, 3rd edn expanded, Warszawa: Wydawnictwo Polonia, 1966.

85. Ibid.

86. Rakowski, op.cit.
Edward Gierek, First Party Secretary December 1970 until September 1980, best known for his ambitious economic modernization plans which proved disastrous.

87. The meeting referred to is the one before Gierek's visit to Italy and the Vatican in October 1977. See also:
Kakol, op.cit., p.88.

88. Micewski, *Kardynal*, op.cit., p.399.

89. Tyszner, Jozef, *Polski Ksztalt Dialogu*, Paris: Editions Spotkania, 1981.

90. For the proclamation of the state of emergency in English see:
Jaruzelski. Prime Minister of Poland. Selected speeches. Interview with Robert Maxwell and biographical sketch, Oxford-New York-Toronto-Sydney-Frankfurt: Pergamon Press, 1985, pp.33-4: Communique of the Supreme Council of the Polish Episcopate,

Warsaw, 15 December 1981.

91. 'Speech of the First Secretary of the Central Committee of the Polska Zjednoczona Partia Robotnicza (PZPR) at the opening of the Tenth Congress of the PZPR on 30 June 1986', in: Zycie Warszawy, nr.151 of 30 June 1986, p.6 (authors' translation).

92. There is a good deal of literature about this, eg. in the Paris emigre paper Polityka; but see:
Kloczowski, Jan Andrzej, 'Religioznawstwo: Zagrozenie czy szansa', in: Tygodnik Powszechny, Year 40, nr.45 (1950) of 9 November 1986, p.3.

93. Euhemer, op.cit. The 1986 issue prints a full account of the topic materials to be used in the syllabus: pp.281 foll. and 297 foll.; pp.197 foll. and pp.345 foll. discuss attitude changes to religion.

94. See:
Miaso, op.cit.

95. Kumor and Obertynski, Historia, op.cit., vol.2, part 2.

96. Gorski, Karol, Od religijnosci do mistyki. Zarys dziejow zycia wewnetrznego w Polsce, Lublin: Towarzystwo Naukowe KUL, 1962.

97. Sydry, Stefan, Czcigodny sluga Bozy, o. Stanislaw od Jezusa Marii Papczynski i jego dzielo w swietle dokumentow, Warszawa: Ksiegarnia Sw. Wojciecha, 1937.

98. On the significance of the Jasna Gora Czestochowa Sanctuary for Polish life see:
'Czestochowska Matka Boza', in: Encyklopedia Katolicka, vol.3, Lublin: Towarzystwo Naukowe KUL, 1985, cols.852-79.

99. Information about the contemporary religiousness of Poles has been obtained from studies and inquiries: see:
Piwowarski, Wladyslaw (ed.), Religijnosc ludowa.

Ciaglosc i zmiana, Wroclaw: Wroclawska Ksiegarnia Archidiecezjalna, 1983.

100. Ibid.

101. Ibid.

102. Ibid.

103. The term 'monopoly' is preferred to 'ideology'; see:
    Berger, Peter L. and Luckmann, Thomas, *The Social Construction of Reality*, London: Allen Lane, Penguin Press, 1967.

7

CHRISTIANITY:
CULTURAL POLITICS AND EDUCATION IN GERMANY

Winfried Bohm

HISTORICAL SURVEY

If it is true, as the Italian philosopher Benedetto Croce asserts, that Europeans cannot fail to be Christians, then this applies with special force to the German cultural tradition.

Ever since the emergence of an authentic German culture in the early Middle Ages, in the Carolingian Renaissance, this culture has been moulded entirely by Christianity; and the following centuries of cultural development as well as political organisation in Germany cannot be understood at all if they are not regarded as representing a permanent dialogue - assimilation as well as rejection - with Christianity. This is true in a positive as well as in a negative sense. The most awful eras of German history - consider for example the Thirty Years' War (1618-1648) - as well as the most remarkable achievements in the fields of architecture, art, literature and philosophy, are manifestations of Christian religious motives. Goethe's Faust or Hegel's 'phenomenology of the spirit' would not have been possible without Christianity. As regards the education system - from the pre-school years to University - its roots are all Christian. Its dynamic driving force has its origins in the Middle Ages, an impetus maintained in the Reformation and the Counter Reformation, and the idea of social equality for all which alone would legitimise the democratisation of education was first thought of in religious terms, i.e. as the equality of all before God.

German Christian Tradition

Even if one describes and interprets the cultural development in Germany since the Middle Ages as a continual process of secularisation, that is of de-Christianisation, it still cannot be disputed that on each occasion this cultural development was sparked off by Christianity. The thesis has, therefore, been advanced confidently: a cultural identity in Germany is neither historically nor currently possible if not mediated through Christianity and a Christian education, be this through affirmation, rejection or indeed critical debate.

Of course, if we formulate this thesis in such global terms, then we obviously have not gained much. For though this thesis may be true and indisputable, it is also much too general to inform the reader of the uniqueness of German culture and more specifically to enlighten the reader as to the significance of Christianity for German culture and education. In particular, it would say little about the present-day relationship between Christianity on the one hand and culture and education on the other.

Here, indeed, lie the difficulties of this contribution. The dimensions of this chapter impose rather narrow parameters. And if the picture that can be inserted in this framework is not to highlight a small and, therefore, deceptive fraction of the reality only, then it must be taken at such a distance that all small details disappear. We will, therefore, leave out statistical data and present no quantifiable material, for both would be meaningless without an interpretation, that is, without reference to wider contexts and general tendencies. It would seem much more informative and helpful if we concentrate on tracing one or two main historical lines, pointing out some global trends and shedding some light on the current relationship between the Church and the State as well as on the education system. With such a complex problem as that of the question of the significance of Christianity for the identity of German culture and education, it would in any case be quite impossible to make a completely objective judgement and it would be foolish to attempt to set parameters or provide lists of individual items which will quantify and measure this significance. At best, simply a pseudo-objectivity would be achieved.

Preferable to this is an assessment in which the subjectivity of the author's point of view is acknowledged, in which the criteria for the choice of arguments presented are clearly explained and in which assumptions, when they are made, are not given out as facts.

Alongside these difficulties, which are related to the topic in general, there are also some specific difficulties which concern Germany's history and political situation. In modern times there has been no unity between state and religion: since the Reformation which started on German soil, two separate denominations have existed, not always peacefully, in Germany - the Roman Catholic and the Protestant - and the problem of Church and State has always been the existence of a State and two Churches which in turn view this situation differently. However, not only on the religious front has Germany been a divided nation for about half a millenium. Politically too, after the decline of imperial power and the break-up of the old Reich (the Holy Roman Empire of the German Nation) she was torn and divided for centuries and not until 1871 was the Second Empire created and then only as a so-called kleindeutsche Losung - that is, leaving Austria and other German-speaking countries outside her borders. After the collapse of the Third Reich, born of Hitler's dreams of a 'greater Germany', Germany was once again divided into the eastern German Democratic Republic and the western Federal Republic of Germany. It is clearly impossible to make universal statements concerning the present topic which could apply to both parts of Germany in view of the great differences between the two German states in terms of their political and ideological systems and their economic doctrine. Moreover it is obvious that the political system in the GDR, which rests on the ideology of Marxism-Leninism, will tend to tone down the Christian contribution to German culture in the past and to dismiss its influence even more in the present day.

These difficulties mean that, as regards historical development, we will concentrate on these general trends which, despite all disunities in religious and political spheres, apply to German culture and education as a whole. In view of the existence of two German states today we will concern ourselves with the Federal Republic of Germany and discuss in particular the legal solution of the relationship between Church and State and the influence of the Church on education. This attempt at an overall view can, it must be said again, only be described as incomplete. The author hopes that he will not be too biased and that he can present some material which will make clear the specifically German orientation of the problem discussed in this volume.

If one wants to explain to a foreign reader the unique relationship between Church and State in Germany one must go back to the original unity between the Church and the social order in the Middle Ages.1 Some historians have used the metaphor of two concentric circles to show that in the Middle Ages the Church and State existed as two separate powers, but that the two organisms, the two spheres of life - secular and spiritual - coincided so closely that the Civis Christianus could only be conceived in terms of the identity of Christian and Citizen. The State was seen and interpreted as an extension of the body of the Church. In these circumstances it is obvious that education could only be conceived as determined by the Church.2 Furthermore, what applied to the rest of Europe in terms of the content of education also applied to Germany and this grew from a symbiosis of Graeco-Roman scholarship and Christian belief.

The unique synthesis of Graeco-Roman learning and Christian faith is represented at the height of the Middle Ages by scholasticism with its fusion of ancient philosophy, natural theology and revelation. The University of Cologne was an outstanding centre of this thinking. To be sure this thought edifice contained from the start the spiritual dynamite which would lead to its collapse. When Thomas Aquinas spoke of the two great books of revelation: the book of the Holy Scripture written in Hebrew and Greek which contained the WORDS of God and the other, the book of nature written in the language of mathematics which contained the WORKS of God, what could be more obvious than to study both books separately and thus to separate science and religion, knowledge and faith. This separation process was completed very slowly, achieving its widest extent in Germany in the nineteenth century: Feuerbach, Marx, Virchow, Freud and Nietzsche are its outstanding exponents. As far as the link of Christian teaching with ancient philosophy is concerned, it was Luther who, at the beginning of the Reformation reproached the Catholic Church precisely for doing this: it has conceded to 'the accursed heathen' Aristotle greater influence on Christian belief than the only legitimate source: the word of the Bible.3

The Reformation in Germany has led not only to a religious split, but also to a restructuring of the relationship of Church and State: the so-called territorial Church. As it became clear that the two denominations could not be re-united either by a reconciliation or by force, the only solution was a state of parity of coexistence of Catholics and Protestants. The religious peace treaty of Augsburg (1555) may indeed have brought some peace between the disputing denominations, but this was established at the cost of religious DUALITY: from then on - following the principle cuius regio eius religio - there was indeed religious unity in individual German territorial states, her cities and principalities, but in the German Empire as a whole parity existed, that is the legal equality of two existing churches: Catholic and Protestant. This development clearly encouraged the process of disintegration of the German Empire. However, it also initiated the first moves towards the present situation of religious freedom in the country. Paragraph 24 of the religious peace treaty of Augsburg conceded the right of emigration for religious and conscience reasons and after the heat of denominational passions of the Thirty Years' War had cooled down, the Instrumentum Pacis Osnabrugense (1643-1648) which reinstated the concepts of tolerance and freedom of conscience introduced them into modern European Law. This distinctly German contribution to the development of basic human rights comes historically and theoretically well before the Anglo-American contribution. It can be no surprise therefore that the coexistence of Christians of two denominations has given rise to early ecumenical efforts. It may suffice here to recall Leibniz and his idea of the future union of all Christians.

If we are accustomed today to set the Counter Reformation against the Reformation and see this as an act of aggressive retaliation by the Catholic Church against the Reformation in the period between 1555 and 1648, then we are merely using an idea devised by the Prussian (and Protestant) historian Leopold von Ranke. For accepting this idea may obscure the fact that the period was not characterised solely by the Catholic landowners' desire to suppress the Protestant faith, but also by an intensive renewal of the Catholic Church itself, largely the result of the Tridentine Council and the efforts of the Jesuit Order. This other side of the so-called Counter Reformation must not be ignored when trying to visualise the significant influence of the Reformation and the Counter Reformation on German culture and education.

Although Luther himself was basically sceptical about the role of education,4 in that he attached much more importance to grace than to human judgement and freedom,5 he still fought with all the force of his authority to persuade the secular rulers to preserve the old schools and establish new ones. He also urged the priests to look out for competent teachers and schoolmasters and required parents to send their children to school. This was necessary, for with the dissolution of the monasteries, the Reformation had led to the closure of monastic schools and with the disappearance of ecclesiastical rule many of the Church schools also had disappeared. The universities too declined, because the Church no longer provided for them and because the Reformers inveighed continuously against the scholastic teaching methods and against the primacy of theological knowledge over belief.6 It was Erasmus who remarked critically about Germany: 'where the Reformation flourishes, culture and education wither away'. Since Luther had placed the Bible at the centre of Christian life, he was concerned that everybody learned to read God's word for themselves. Thus the main aim of Luther and the Reformers was an elementary education for everyone and the establishment of a school for the people: the *Volksschule* or elementary school. Luther was not the creator of the elementary school in Germany - subsequent political and national pressures were needed to bring this about - but he did provide an extremely important impetus to the establishment of a general elementary school in Germany.7 Together with his colleagues Philipp Melanchthon and Johannes Bugenhagen he prepared the organisational structure of the general elementary school. Melanchthon's school plan for Saxony, his 'sachsischer Schulplan' of 1528, served as a model for many German school regulations. Even more important, however, were Luther's efforts in the service of the German language (and with it the realisation of a precondition for the emergence of a German elementary school for everyone). This he ensured by his translation of the Bible and the compilation of his 'pocket' catechism, the <u>Kleine Katechismus</u>, and his German hymn book. In this context it must be said that even if Luther did not create the New High German language, it was through the medium of the above books that the common language used at the time in the chancelleries of princes became a popular and acceptable vehicle of everyday communication.

In a different way from Luther, the humanist Melanchthon devoted his interest to the secondary schools and universities. More so than Luther he was concerned with a synthesis of Reformation and Humanism. This synthesis received its clearest expression in the motto written by Johannes Sturm above the entrance to his grammar school in Strasbourg: <u>sapiens et eloquens pietas</u> - a thorough study of Latin combined with a deep faith. Some of the Protestant secondary schools became world famous: alongside Sturm's school in Strasbourg, the Gymnasium Schulpforta near Naumburg and most particularly the so-called <u>Tubinger Stift</u>, the Tubingen school foundation from which many leading men in the whole field of German culture have come forward and which later became one of the birthplaces of German idealism - Holderlin, Schelling, Hegel amongst others.

As regards the universities, most of which until the Reformation bore the legal, economic and educational imprint of the Church and which together with the imperial patronage had also obtained a papal charter, the situation changed considerably with the development of three territorial Churches. The local rulers now founded their own universities, indeed without papal dispensation, for example in Marburg (1527), Konigsberg, East Prussia (1544), Jena (1558), Giessen (1607), Kiel (1665). Older universities which accepted the new religion were reformed accordingly, for example Leipzig, Tubingen, Heidelberg. Seen in general terms these universities lost their universal and international character and ran the risk of becoming purely regional institutions.

If one acknowledges the Counter Reformation as not just a counter reaction to the Reformation, and accepts its origins as being rooted in a religious self-renewal of the Catholic Church, then its beginnings must be sought not in Germany, but in Italy and in Spain.

If this internal reform of the Church was to succeed, two evils of the time had first to be defeated: the material wealth of the Church and the dissolute, worldly conduct of its priests. The path of renewal shown by the mendicant orders on the one hand, and the mystics on the other, was also taken in theological and church-political terms under Pope Paul III and was transformed by church officials into concrete programmes at the Council of Trent (1545-1563). Even though the resolutions of this council only reached Germany very slowly and were implemented very hesitantly (not without irony it was said that the journey of the Council's resolutions from Trent to the diocese of Cologne took 200 years) - considerable efforts were made in the cultural and educational areas by the Catholic side, not confined, moreover, to the reform of the education of priests. Alongside Luther's successful catechism of 1529 there appeared the catechism of Petrus Canisius (1555), the first German Jesuit. His catechism was regarded as the basic school text for the German Catholic youth for more than two centuries.

Indeed it was the Jesuits, who devoted themselves, with all their energy, to Catholic education. In this their interest was primarily directed at secondary schools; similarly to the way the Congregation of Ursulines founded by Angela di Merici devoted its efforts especially to secondary schools for girls.

Unlike as in the case of the Protestant elementary schools the Jesuits put the use of the mother tongue behind that of Latin. The efficient organisation of their schools and the fine quality of their teachers brought about a rapid expansion of Jesuit schools and a deservedly high prestige; around 1600 the three largest Jesuit colleges on German soil, those in Cologne, Trier and Munich, each had over 1000 pupils. In the same way as the Protestants, the Catholics too founded universities intended as antipodes to the universities of the Reformation. One of the most famous of these university foundations is to this day the University of Wurzburg.8

Without pursuing in detail the history of the German education system in this chapter we have to point out that in the following decades and centuries - against all talk of the impending laicisation of the school and the process of instruction9 - the extension and expansion of education would have been inconceivable without Christian initiatives and stimuli. It must be added, however, that these initiatives and stimuli were always linked to political interests or social needs, and that it was these which enabled the religious objectives to be realised in the first place. This applies to the expansion of elementary education, the education of the handicapped and to pre-school education, but applies also to the foundation of the science of education. In this connection the names of the two outstanding figures, Johann Michael Sailer,10 for the Catholic side and Friederich Daniel Schleiermacher,11 for the Protestant side,12 must be mentioned.

In order to lend sharper contours to the picture we wish to paint here, let us turn to an historical process which has led to a new alignment in the relationship between State and Church and which has added a social dimension to the relationship of the two denominations.

With the termination of the Holy Roman Empire of the German Nation and the breakup of German territory into many individual nation states, the two denominations no longer faced each other as corporations of the one state in legal terms. Catholics and Protestants were now drawn in numerical order into the political calculations as population groups - whether as majorities, minorities or as a political equilibrium. The social situation of the Catholics shifted considerably in the nineteenth century. After the occupation by Napoleon, the Catholics lost almost all their schools and colleges in the secularisation, the expropriation that is of all church and monastic property and its transfer to state ownership. This resulted in an educational backlog for the Catholics during the following 150 years. In the nineteenth century the cultural leadership in Germany passed most decidedly to the Protestants, who in the fields of literature and philosophy had already taken over that position in the eighteenth century. The great literary creations of the Weimar classical period and the great philosophical ideas of German idealism were nurtured on Protestant ground, while Catholic philosophy rigidified to a large extent in neoscholasticism and exhausted itself in a resistance to modernism. Only in the domains of music and the plastic arts did Catholics and Protestants counterbalance each other.

With the founding of the Second Reich in 1871, Catholics became a minority, also in population statistical terms. This inferiority, however, was not only a numerical one, but was in evidence also in their unequal distribution in town and country, in the professional structure and as mentioned earlier, in their educational levels. Catholics primarily lived in the country, they vastly outnumbered Protestants in agriculture, in mining (Silesia, Ruhr) and in the building trade. The educational lag had a tendency to rise reaching its apogee at university level. The Protestants were concentrated in the towns, above all in the larger cities in the north. They controlled the banks, the world of trade and transport, and they had a clear lead in academic life. Typically Catholic areas as for example Altbayern in Bavaria, Westfalia or the Upper Black Forest area remained for a long time a sort of pre-capitalist and pre-industrial reservation

In this new socio-political constellation (in respect of the relation of the denominations to each other) a decisive change occurred in 1849. The National Assembly deliberating in the Paulskirche in

Frankfurt decided to grant the churches the right to become self-governing, independent that is from the state. This article was then incorporated in the Prussian Constitution and was further included in the Constitution of the Weimar Republic in 1919, to be transferred again unaltered into the Constitution of the Federal Republic of Germany as indeed also into the Constitution of the German Democratic Republic.

THE PRESENT SITUATION

Before looking at the present situation more closely it is of course necessary to comment on how the two major Churches reacted to this state-granted independence and how they exploited their new freedom. Hegel's remark that the churches in Germany were 'woven into the very fabric of the state' is indeed correct, but this applies in different ways to the Catholic and Protestant Churches. Whereas the Protestant Church, due to its close ties with the highest authority of the state (going back to the Reformation) and its territorial division according to political power orbits was organised until 1919 on territorial lines into regional churches and maintained its close links with the state power, the Catholics early on (in fact as early as 1803, the date of the expropriation of the Churches) had started to assemble in associations and societies and to make full use of the social and political techniques of modern democracy. In this they were greatly helped by their status of world Church with the head of the Church in Rome, as well as by distancing themselves from their State, as indeed by their concentration on pastoral and social tasks. The Catholic part of Germany thus underwent a nearly hundred-year-long process of political and social emancipation marked, however, by a number of setbacks; above all the co-called Kulturkampf under Bismarck.13 The Protestant Church to be sure caught up with this development in one fell swoop in 1934 with the so-called Barmen Declaration.14 These different experiences, however, deterred neither the Catholics nor the Protestants from initially adopting a rather irresolute attitude towards the rising tyranny of Hitler in 1933-34 nor from maintaining on the whole an ambivalent relationship to the Third Reich. On the one hand the resistance of professing Christians, lay persons, priests, monks, nuns and bishops of both denominations to Hitler represents a glorious chapter in German history; on the other hand, however, indifference, tolerance and silence which the Churches adopted towards the National Socialist state cannot be denied either. These undoubtedly represent a rather dark chapter in German history.15

After 1945 the Churches in Germany presented a different face. In the spiritual-political vacuum which prevailed after the collapse of the Third Reich, both Churches could be seen as forces of pre-political integration, as defenders of a new democratic order, above all, as supporters of values, order and sense.

If we now look more closely at the question of how the relationship of State and Church and how the influence of the Church on culture and education has been shaped since the establishment of the Federal Republic, then it appears rather difficult to make firm and detailed statements about this. We shall concentrate on three aspects which will be used to illustrate the problem:

    1) The legal and constitutional settlement of the relationship of State and Church;
    2) The position and organisation of religious education in German schools; and
    3) A look at the future of the Church and Christian religion in Germany.

The relationship of State and Church in the Federal Republic is laid down in articles of the Constitution, articles which, as mentioned earlier, were taken over word for word from the Weimar Constitution, which go back to a long democratic tradition and which can be reduced to one common denominator: 'a free church in a free state'. The fundamental articles of the Constitution concern the basic right of religious freedom (article 4), the institutional guarantee of religious education (article 7, paragraph 3) and the portions of article 140 affecting Churches which incorporate the regulations concerning the legal position of the established State Churches, as set out in the Weimar Constitution and incorporated in the Federal Constitution.

The most important regulations in this are:
- a) the qualified legal power of the Churches and religious communities as 'corporations of public law';
- b) the guarantee of religious education as an accepted national curriculum subject in state schools;
- c) the endorsement of theology faculties in the universities;
- d) the institutionalised religious ministry in the army and in prisons;
- e) the levying of a Church Tax by the offices of the state finance administration;
- f) the general release of Church property from state-imposed taxes;
- g) the supportive cooperation of the state with Church welfare organisations;
- h) the guarantee of private schools and their support by the state;
- i) the protection of Sundays and religious holidays;
- j) the participation of Churches and religious communities in public radio and television.16

If we restrict ourselves here to the Constitution of the Federal Republic then this does not mean that we have overlooked the differing regulations in the constitutions of the constituent states (Lander). A full discussion of Germany's federal structure and the significant differences in view of the dominance of the federal law over the state (Lander) law, would, however, be too exhaustive.

In considering these matters the following points which concern the special cultural and political situation in the Federal Republic must be emphasised. For the state Churches (to which over 90 per cent of the population belong) as social structures, associations and societies represent opinions current in society alongside those of similar institutions. Their special public and legal status stems from the fact that they have had attributed to them a significant role in the area of education and schooling, in the field of social-charitable services and for cultural life generally in the past and present. In a ruling of the federal constitutional court the Churches were singled out as special spiritual forces of society. It was emphasised, moreover, that 'large sections of the population take from them (or rather their received teachings) the standards for their moral behaviour'.17 It is also emphasised that in the modern rationalistically oriented welfare state such as the Federal Republic, man is seen only in parts - as a citizen, or as a consumer - as a partner in economic and other processes. As against this the Churches and religious communities alone consider the whole person and the depth and value of his human existence.18

Foreigners often find strange the phenomenon of the Church Tax levied by the state and made available to the Churches. This effective and socially fair procedure for the collecting of Church dues which includes all citizens liable to taxation is justified by the fact that it represents a form of financing Church tasks, which is superior to all other models of financing. Moreover it does give the religious communities in the Federal Republic material security which is totally unknown in many other countries. It also allows them the possibility of long-term and generous budget planning.

One institution appears particularly suited to illustrate the role of the Church in matters of education and culture: the special position of religious education in state schools. In all state schools, with the exception of non-denominational institutions, religious education is an ordinary subject of the curriculum and is, therefore, guaranteed a place on the timetable with an appropriate allocation of teaching time. Religious education is taught under state supervision in full agreement with the religious communities. The licence to teach the subject is awarded to the teachers by the Churches: as missio canonica on the Catholic and as vocacio on the Protestant side respectively. Withdrawal from religious education is possible after the 14th birthday in most federal states. In the last few years a new school subject entitled 'Ethics' has been put in place of religious education to accommodate the withdrawals.19

Far more than the simple existence of this subject of the curriculum in state schools the content change of religious education over the last three decades has mirrored the changes which have occurred in the public's acceptance of the Christian religion especially with regard to its influence on the nation's culture. Generally in this connection it may be said that until the mid-1960s, religious education was seen as an accepted part of school education and was viewed as such also by educationalists and by bodies responsible for formulating educational policy. In the 1970s and 1980s, however, the religious and Christian dimension has been increasingly eliminated from discussions of the theory of pedagogy and writings of philosophers of education. Philosophy of education and pedagogy have become orientated more and more towards sociological theories and models. Analogous to this, religious instruction has been ignored in plans to restructure and reform the education system and has been left entirely to the experts in religious education.

The subject itself has gone through a number of significant changes which are on the one hand the consequence of this changed evaluation of it by the public and on the other hand an expected reaction of religious educationists to the neglect of the religious component, the 'de-religionisation' or rather the 'de-Christianisation' of educational philosophy and educational politics.

After the Second World War, due to the general climate of spiritual and moral doubt, the teaching of religion had turned to the theological positions of the pre-war years (such as Karl Barth's 'Church Dogmatics'). It saw its task primarily in the annunciation of the gospel, in furthering Christian teachings and in conveying Christian morals.20 The fear of overloading the lessons with exclusively religious syllabuses, as did occur when teaching religion in this way, on the one hand, and the advance of exegetic science in theology on the other, led to a transformation of religious education towards the end of the 1950s; from 'annunciation in the school' to a 'hermeneutic interpretation of the Bible'. Analogous to the task of the school generally as an interpreter of the cultural heritage, the teaching of religious education too had seen as its main task the interpretation of Christian tradition and its writings.21

In the mid-1960s the question was being asked whether the Bible needed necessarily to be at the centre of all religious education. This question was soon answered with a resounding 'no'.22 In the place of Bible interpretation was put an 'existential hermeneutics', a theme and problem orientated approach to teaching which no longer takes the Bible as its starting point, but rather the concrete world of the pupil and the specific and social problems of the young.23 The task of religious education was now being seen as explaining and understanding these concrete problems of the young in the light of the Christian tradition.

At the end of the 1960s curriculum debates of other school subjects began to influence religious education also, and this led paradoxically to a further diminution of the theological and religious elements in religious education. This tendency was further accentuated in the 1970s when curriculum theory findings were also applied to religious education. The leading question now was: which qualifications necessary for the mastering of real life situations can religious education pass on to the young generation? If such qualifications cannot (from within society) be formulated, then religious education can be seen to be outdated and ready to be taken out of schools. The perspective had, therefore, changed radically compared to the beginnings of evangelism. No longer was religious education to be tackled from a religious or theological point of view, but its legitimation was to derive exclusively from a relevance for social qualifications and social usefulness.24

It is not surprising that strong objections were raised against this kind of one-sided interpretation of religious education. Against such a conception the questions were asked whether the dignity of its content was not being trampled on, or whether the Scripture text may legitimately be 'adapted' to social functions. Similar objections were raised against efforts made to reduce religious education to a kind of socialisation substitute and to place it next to psycho- or socio-therapy. Similar well-founded criticism was made of suggestions to reduce the substance of religious education to the study of religion or indeed to introduce agnostic themes into the core of this subject.

After this examination of the state of religious education, the question about the relationship between private and state schools should be put. This question is easily answered - the problem of private schools just does not exist in the same way in Germany as in other European and non-European countries. Whereas in many countries the freedom of religion and the influence of Christianity on culture can be measured in terms of the flourishing or the suppression of private schools, in Germany this indicator is totally meaningless. The exceptionally small number, 5 per cent, of private schools in the entire system of general education may indeed be remarkable, but it has nothing to do with the fact that the state would suppress Church-controlled schools or that the influence of the Church on education in general terms is limited. Moreover, the above-mentioned articles of the Constitution affecting the legal status of the Church are so generous - we refer here to the constitutional guarantee of religious education in schools and the guarantee given by each of the states of the federation for the existence of theology faculties at universities - that the need for Church-controlled private schools simply does not exist. Most of the private schools in the Federal Republic are, therefore, not maintained on religious or ideological grounds, but rather from economic motives, as a receptacle for pupils who have failed in the state sector (drop-outs) - or for the realisation of special educational philosophies or teaching methods.

The creation of a Catholic university too has been hotly debated. The foundation of a Catholic university in the small Bavarian town of Eichstatt is not really a new foundation and is certainly not meant as a counter institution to state universities. It came about simply because of the amalgamation of a Catholic teachers' training college with a small Catholic theological college. Whether this

Catholic university will develop further to a standard equal to that of other famous Catholic universities is, at present, unforeseeable.

CONCLUSION

If in conclusion we try to glance at the future development of the Christian contribution to Germany's culture, then it does not seem easy to give a sure prognosis. On the one hand are observations which may tend to a rather negative judgement: church attendances (for both denominations) are falling, the taking of the sacraments of baptism and marriage is declining significantly, religious knowledge and the readiness to profess openly to one's belief is reducing. The place of basic Christian dogmas is being taken by Eastern religions or mythical ideas (eg. the teaching of reincarnation).

Against these rather negative phenomena, however, some positive ones may also be found. The dwindling congregations are replaced by a growing 'electronic church' in the mass media. The fundamental Christian value of love of one's neighbour is gaining tremendous popularity, especially amongst the youth, which results in a lively engagement for the needy members of society, the old, the handicapped and for the problems of the Third World. The loss of faith is counterbalanced by a growing religious nostalgia, again especially among the young. In the Churches themselves transformations are occurring,25 which overcome the restricting rationality and purely scientific theology and which open up the Church to areas which had so far been neglected and marginalised, such as aesthetics and politics. One only has to think of the strong influence German theology had and indeed still has on Latin American Liberation Theology. At the same time a new life is being born of the gospel at the basic level of existence, that is in small and very small communities. This renewal of the Churches from within is a reminder of some reform movements in the long history of the Church and should certainly not be underestimated.

If one wants to attempt a simple formula, then

one could say that the Christian religion is today far from being the only point of reference for German culture. On the other hand, it would be equally wrong to speak of the disappearance of Christianity as an upholder of culture. Christianity is, as it has always been, a pillar of German culture, indeed an important one, sometimes easily visible, at other, times rather obscured. This, however, corresponds to the reality of a pluralistic state and of an open society.

NOTES AND REFERENCES

1. See Maier, Hans, 'Staat und Kirche in Deutschland Historische und soziale Grundlagen' in: Zacher, Hans F. (ed.), Kirche und Politik, Dusseldorf: Patmos, 1982. For the period after the Second World War, see Mikat, Paul (ed.), Kirche und Staat in der neueren Entwicklung, Darmstadt: Wissenschaftliche Buchgesellschaft, 1980.

2. Schoelen, Eugen (ed.), Erziehung und Unterict im Mittelalter, Paderborn: Schoeningh, 2nd edn, 1965; Klaus, Petzold, Die Grundlagen der, Erziehungslehre im Spatmittelalter und bei Martin Luther, Heidelberg: Quelle und Meyer, 1969; Garin, Eugenio, Geschichte und Dokumente der abendlandischen Padagogik, vol.1: Mittelalter, Reinbek: Rowohlt, 1964.

3. Petersen, Peter, Geschichte der aristotelischen Philosophie im protestantischen Deutschland, Leipzig: Meiner, 1921.

4. Asheim, Ivar, Glaube und Erziehung bei Luther, Heidelberg: Quelle und Meyer, 1961.

5. The rather sceptical approach of genuine Protestant educational theories can be traced to this stance of Luther's, cf. Grisebach, Eberhard, Die Grenzen des Erziehers und seine Verantwortung, Halle: Niemeyer, 1924; Bohne, Gerhard, Grundlagen der Erziehung, 2 vols.; see Die Padagogik in der Verantwortung vor Gott, Hamburg: Furche, 1958-60; Kittel, Helmuth, Der Erzieher als Christ, Gottingen: Vanden-

hoek und Ruprecht, 3rd edn, 1961.

6. Luther himself referred to universities as 'dens of iniquity' in which there was 'little reading of Scripture and no Christian teaching taking place'.

7. Menzel, Rudolf, <u>Die Anfange der Volksschule in Deutschland Dargestellt unter besonderer Berucksichtigung der mitteldeutschen protestantischen Territorien</u>, Berlin: Volk und Wissen, 1958.

8. For a fuller account of the history of education in the periods of Reformation and Counter Reformation in Germany see Von den Driesch, Johannes and Echterhues, Josef, <u>Geschichte der Erziehung und Bildung</u>, 2 vols., Paderborn, Schoeningh, 1951; Reble, Albert, <u>Geschichte der Padagogik</u>, Stuttgart: Klett, pocket edition, 1981.

9. See Erlinghagen, Karl, <u>Die Sakularisierung der deutschen Schule</u>, Hannover: Schroedel, 1972. It is useful to distinguish between 'laicisation' <u>Sakularisierung</u>, as a long process of de-Christianisation, and 'expropriation' <u>Sakularisation</u>, the historical act of confiscation of church and monastic property by the State in 1803.

10. Professor of Theology in Ingolstadt and Bishop of Regensburg (1751-1832).

11. Professor of Theology and co-founder of Berlin University (1768-1834).

12. The origins of the study of education as a discipline in Germany are discussed by Menze, Clemens, 'Die Wissenschaft von der Erziehung in Deutschland' in: Speck, Josef (ed.), <u>Problemgeschichte de neueren Padagogik</u>, vol.1, Stuttgart: Kohlhammer, 1976.

13. Goyan, G., <u>Bismarck et l'Eglise: Le Culturkampf 1870-1878</u>, 4 vols., Paris: Perrin, 4th edn, 1922.

14. <u>Barmer Erklarung</u>, one of a series of declarations (1934-1935) of the <u>Bekennede Kirche</u>, a branch of

Protestantism which opposed the Hitler-supporting Deutsche Christen movement; representative of the reorganisation of German Protestantism.

15. For a recent account of the history of German Catholicism see Hurten, Heinz, Kurze Geschichte des deutschen Katholizismus 1800-1960, Mainz: Grunewald, 1986; and Schatz, Klaus, Zwischen Sakularisation und Zweitem Vatikanum: Deutscher Katholizismus im 19. und 20. Jahrhundert, Frankfurt: Knecht, 1986.

16. For details see Listl, Joseph, 'Staat und Kirche in der Bundesrepublik Deutschland', Stimmen der Zeit, 98, 1973, pp.291-308; Mikat, Paul, Religionsrechtliche Schriften, 1. Halbband, Berlin: de Gruyter, 1974; and Von Campenhausen, Axel, Staat und Kirche im deutschen Verfassungsrecht des 20. Jahrhunderts, in Zacher, Hans, F. (ed.), op.cit.

17. Decisions of the Constitutional Court, Entschiedungen des Bundesverfassungsgerichts, vol.6, Tubingen, Mohr, 1957, p.435.

18. For details see Scheuner, Ulrich, 'Die Kirche im Sakularen Staat' in Im Lichte der Reformation: Jarhbuch des evangelischen Bundes, vol.10, Gottingen: Vandenhoek und Ruprecht, 1967.

19. Fox, H., Ethik als Alternative zum Religionsunterricht, Trier: Spee, 1977; and Martin, Gerhard (ed.), Religionsunterricht - Ernstfall kirchlicher Bildungspolitik, Stuttgart: Calwer, 1984. For syllabus details of the subject of Religious Education see the collection of documents Religion am Lernort Schule. Kommentierte Dokumentation der Evangelischen und Katholischen Lehrplane in der Bundesrepublik Deutschland, Munster, produced by the Comenius-Institut, Dokumentation 5, 1984.

20. See Kittle, Helmuth, Evangelische Religions-Padagogik, Berlin: de Gruyter, 1970.

21. See Otto, Gert, 'Evangelischer Religionsunterricht als hermeneutische Aufgabe', Zeitschrift fur Theologie und Kirche, 61, 1964, pp.326 foll.; and

German Christian Tradition

Gert, Otto, <u>Handbuch des Religionsunterrichts</u>, Hamburg: Furche, 3rd edn, 1967.

22. Kaufman, Hans-Bernard, <u>Streit um den problemorientierten Unterricht in Schule und Kirche</u>, Frankfurt: Diesterweg, 1973.

23. Halbfas, Hubertus, <u>Fundamentalkatechetik</u>, Munchen: Calwer, 1968.

24. Lott, Jurgen (ed.), <u>Religionsunterricht</u>, Frankfurt: Diesterweg, 1983.

25. Alberigo, Giuseppe, <u>et al.</u> (eds.), <u>Kirche im Wandel</u>, Dusseldorf: Patmos, 1982.

Translated by:

Elizabeth Ashurst and Monika Shepherd.

8

SCHOOLING, IDENTITY AND DENOMINATIONALISM: THE AMERICAN EXPERIENCE

Ronald K. Goodenow

INTRODUCTION

The relationship between religion and public, that is to say non-private, schooling in the United States, always a matter of significant policy debate and political controversy, has received sharpened attention during the years of the Reagan Administration. The issue of school prayer and Bible reading, controversy over the treatment of evolution in textbooks, the rise of the 'fundamentalist right' in the Republican Party, and dispute over the tax-exempt status of fundamentalist non-denominational secondary level academies and post-secondary institutions have been in national headlines for several years. So, too, there has been controversy over the flight of middle-class children from public schools to non-denominational, 'broadly Protestant', and Roman Catholic institutions which often claim to maintain higher academic standards, more rigid discipline and closer attention to moral and religious values. Hallmarks of the Reagan years have been increased conflict among various groups over the nature of education and, in terms of national government policy, a retreat from post-World War Two goals of equality of opportunity and strengthening the federal presence in funding new teaching programmes. Powerful voices within the Administration would abolish the United States Department of Education, while in many quarters new links between the corporate world and the education sector are being forged, giving 'big business' and its values a stronger voice in public education.

Sectarian U.S.A.

In this climate, policy debate abounds throughout the nation. Proposals to introduce voucher plans, calls for the strengthening of programmes which teach values and appreciation for Western culture, and the divestment of Federal responsibility in some areas have been part of widespread national attention to the purposes and effects of public schooling. 'Reform' and 'excellence' have become the bywords of many commissions and pundits interested in change. There has also been widespread discussion - on the political right and left - about cultural pluralism, with many educators anxious to promote social consensus and a broad national civic responsibility in light of a growth in seemingly divisive 'interest group' politics. Whether America has become fragmented by class, ethnic or racial group, gender or special need, or indeed religious orientation, and whether public schooling has lost its status as what social critic Max Lerner once called 'the American religion' is of great concern. To many parents and group members, the issue is not consensus but maintaining religious or cultural identity and freedom, and obtaining for their children schooling of high quality. Whatever the case, Americans are confronting a situation that is international in scope. Many Western industrial nations must cope with similar multicultural pressures, including multidenominationalism, as the result of immigration, ethnic reassertiveness and economic change.

This chapter will offer a brief overview of the historic relationship between schooling and cultural identity issues in the United States, a nation of immigrants, focusing upon main themes in contemporary scholarship. In so far as there is an emphasis upon denominational education, the focus will largely be upon Roman Catholic schooling. Beyond this example of denominational education and cultural identity lies the diverse and growing sector of non-denominational, largely Protestant schooling. Both offer excellent 'windows' on the nature of American public education and on the vexing issue of what constitutes 'cultural identity' in a nation characterised through much of its history by a frontier attitude, massive immigration and internal migration, pervasive racism, significant regional differences, transformations in economic life and technology, and rapid urbanisation.

THE PRESENT MOMENT AS BACKGROUND

Contemporary statistics suggest that the current condition is more than a matter of debate among scholars, policy makers, politicians and diverse interest groups. There has been nothing short of major demographic change in the United States over the past twenty years. This has reverberated through the educational system. In the mid-1960s approximately 31 per cent of the American population lived in the South, 16 per cent in the West, 29 per cent in the North Central States, and 25 per cent in the North-east. By the early 1980s, the South's share of the population had risen to 34 per cent and that of the West to 19 per cent. Significant decline, however, affected other parts of the country dramatically. Thus, the proportion of the population living in the North Central region had dropped to about 27 per cent and that of the population living in the North-east to less than 22 per cent.

These population shifts have been accompanied by other changes in the racial and ethnic composition of the United States. Over the decade from 1970 to 1980, the white population of the nation increased by only 6 per cent, with this group declining as a percentage of the total population. Blacks came to represent 12 per cent of the population during this period and the Hispanic share expanded enormously, becoming concentrated in Texas, New York and California. The populations of American Indians, Filipinos, Japanese, Chinese and Koreans grew rapidly. In sum, minorities came to represent about 17 per cent of the total population. More significantly, they now constitute about 26 per cent of the school-age population and some authorities suggest that by 1990 minorities will make up a quarter of the total population and over 30 per cent of the children in schools. This population is increasingly urbanised and, in the larger towns and cities at least, multicultural. As put by two scholars of the issue 'new social contracts are being drawn'.1 Basically, the conservative South and West are growing in size, while the more traditionally liberal sectors of the

Sectarian U.S.A.

Mid-west and East are undergoing relative population decline and debilitating deindustrialisation, though some sectors of the North-east have seen significant technology-based prosperity. In most parts of the country, urban demographics are changing. Larger minority populations are gaining political control and exercising stronger power over schooling policies and choices about schooling in inner-city areas plagued by poverty. Though there is conflicting data regarding whether there has been an increase in people living at or below the poverty level, there is some evidence of growing maldistribution of wealth, something addressed cautiously in new national tax legislation. Urban, minority, rural and under-educated young people are placed particularly at risk, especially in light of the skills required for the new post-industrial economy. Ira Katznelson and Margaret Weir link market and social demographic factors usefully in a recent neo-liberal interpretation representative of current fears about the state of public education. Writing in support of a restoration of citizen interest in public schooling, and in opposition to current trends, they argue a relationship between residence, identity and schooling that points to the importance of inter-relating such factors when looking at the inter-section of ethnicity and education:

> More and more Americans, including members of the working class, have been able to purchase particular kinds of public schools by purchasing specific kinds of residence zoning to ensure their homogeneity. Housing and schooling markets have displaced educational politics as key forums of decision-making. As a result, public education, which had been the repository of egalitarian aspirations and opportunities, has become more and more a force for social division and inequality. Education and the market have become increasingly entwined.2

What is known about such relationships? What do current statistics on education say on the current status of public and private schooling? Before examining the first question, it is important to look at numbers.

The statistics of most importance are those concerning enrolments. In 1970, about 10 per cent of all school age youth attended non-public schools. By 1983, this percentage had increased to approximately 13 per cent. Although elementary and secondary enrolment dropped from about 51 million to 46 million in this period, much of this loss was in the public sector. Further, as put in one recent study,

> Since 1965 ... the private school sector has seen a revolution in tastes and composition. The number of Catholic schools has declined, dropping from 13,292 schools to 9,432 in 1983, for a 38 per cent decline in almost two decades. Enrolments too have dipped from 5.6 million students to 3.02 million (minus 46%). While parental preferences were moving away from Catholic schools, however, other private schools were opening and growing. Besides the expansion in the established, affiliated private schools, such as Lutheran, Friends, Jewish, Calvinist and Episcopalian, there has been enormous growth in a relatively new group of private schools - Evangelical or Fundamentalist Christian academies ... private, non-Catholic schools number 17,291 in 1984, for a new total of 26,723 - of which 65% are not Catholic. About 10,740 of these non-Catholic private schools are new Fundamentalist Christian academies.3

Behind these statistics are other interesting ones. Since 1970, for example, non-Catholic enrolment in Catholic schools has increased from approximately 3 per cent to 11 per cent due less to a radical ecumenism on the part of parents than to a new distribution of wealth and immigration patterns. Attendance cuts across racial lines, with many of these students being non-Catholic blacks, approximately 20 per cent of Catholic school enrolment being of minority background. Before probing current policy issues and implications surrounding these dramatic trends, it is useful to explore reasons why people historically have chosen religious schooling. Some of the main themes now emerging in scholarly litera-

Sectarian U.S.A.

ture to challenge conventional wisdom about the nature of religious and state-supported schooling in the United States will also be presented.

PATTERNS OF HISTORICAL DEVELOPMENT

The relationship between schools and religion has roots in both the evolution of formal education and the social demography of the United States. In the early nineteenth century, public support for private religious - virtually always Protestant - schools was common. As suggested by one historian,

> denominationalism made a virtue out of the mandated separation of church and state by stimulating the burgeoning church groups to vigorous competition in education, as well as in proselytizing.[4]

Indeed, this condition continued well into the nineteenth century, with a system of public education evolving only when it became apparent that new forces of industrialisation, urbanisation and immigration required forms of common schooling that could not be met by the fragmented and often poorly resourced private sector. This said, it has been widely recognised by scholars that mid-nineteenth century public schooling incorporated moral and class values oriented not only to nation building and emergent capitalist interests, but also to the non-sectarian Protestantism of many of the 'founding fathers' of public education, including Horace Mann (1796-1859), the first Secretary of Education in Massachusetts, and Henry Barnard (1811-1900), the first United States Commissioner of Education.

The persistence of Protestant private schooling and the rise of Catholic schooling in these circumstances has not been studied extensively by historians until recently. To some degree, this neglect is caused by the extent to which American educational historians have been oriented normatively to writing about the triumphs of a public education that seemingly overcame 'divisive' religious and other interests that would sooner or later be consigned to the junk heap of history.5 Another reason, at least in the case of Protestant schools, is that, in many respects, the nineteenth century saw less development than did the twentieth. The period since the early 1930s has seen a proliferation of Seventh-Day Adventist, Mormon, Baptist, Christian Scientist schools and those of other denominations sometimes seen either as on the 'fringe' of mainstream Protestantism or located in the 'backward' rural South. Though the major growth among some denominations, such as the Lutherans, took place in the nineteenth century, and others, such as the Presbyterians, have witnessed a steady erosion of schools, the Episcopalians, for example, have expanded their schools. Since the Second World War about 300 Jewish schools have opened, though many of these offer instruction only at weekends.6 Unfortunately, these developments have appeared either so marginal or have been so recent as to escape intense scholarly attention.

While the historical literature on Protestant schooling remains somewhat undeveloped, the subject of Roman Catholic education has begun to receive focused attention. This is a welcome change. Until recently, much of the historiography of Catholic education resembled that, ironically, of public education in that church historians dwelled uncritically upon the triumphs of Catholic schools and colleges, exaggerating their importance, impact and responses to oppressive Protestantism.7 The education of Catholics, then, provides a valuable opportunity to look at several major motifs in American educational history, including reform, a subject of considerable interest in the United States in the 1980s. As suggested by James Sanders, one of the leading contemporary authorities on the history of Catholicism and education, much of the Catholic response to public schooling results not only from their status as urban dwellers, but the fact that considerable modern educational and social reform has been directed at Catholics. Hence,

> Because of their immigrant status, their alien ethnicity, and their at least equally alien religious affiliation, they became the principal single object of educational reform. It was they

above all others who were to be re-formed through the schools.8

One of the most influential interpretations of the Catholic educational experience was made in the mid-1970s by Marvin Lazerson. A historian often identified with a radical revisionism which reinterpreted American educational history and criticised predominant liberal interpretations that saw the school as a main democratic force, Lazerson, Michael B. Katz, Colin Greer and others explored the intersection of corporate capitalist interests with the uses of the school for 'social control', elite formation and the inculcation of corporate values. Writing in the History of Education Quarterly, Lazerson set out several themes which have come to influence subsequent study of Catholic education, suggesting that much Catholic education has been a response to a growing systematisation of public education. This system incorporated ideas on patriotism, the family and work that were often alien to the world-views and economic interests of many Catholics, fostering a resistance to the non-sectarian Protestant values of the public schools that transcended religious concern. In the midst of social transformations in urban life, the workplace and, indeed, the character of the Church itself, Catholic schooling helped define associational or community life, serving as a buffer between the immigrant and new and remote forms of management and control and providing a means to develop economic security. Although many Catholics had to struggle with a church hierarchy that often exercised power from the top down and schools that sometimes overly emulated public ones, they learned to use their schools as mediating institutions, permitting them both to maintain ethnic identity and allowing compromises and transitions which would ease the burdens of assimilation. As various compulsory education laws, teacher certification requirements and other impositions forced increased standardisation, and the class composition of the Catholic community itself changed, Catholics became less different. They were also able, in many instances, to maintain important ethnic, community, family and religious values as they increased their political influence. This said, as William Reese wrote recently, 'the relationship between family, schooling, and economy remains one of the genuinely murky areas of educational history'.9

This murkiness is diminishing, for although it has not been able to fill in all the missing pieces, work like that of Lazerson and Sanders has released Catholic educational history from the constraints of innumerable earlier studies, the primary focus of which was upon narrowly defined studies of ethnicity, religion and conventional institutional or biographical history. Even though some of this older work has its uses, the way has now been opened for more complex approaches. Unlike the case of much modern social history, which, moreover, has relied heavily on quantification as its primary method, it invites the blending of social, cultural, religious, educational and economic history as well as comparative analysis. In shedding new light on such subjects as Catholic-Protestant conflict over textbooks in the nineteenth century, such as that which surfaced in pre-Civil War New York, it treats them as symptomatic of very complex sets of Catholic aspirations and responses, and not merely manifestations of religious warfare.10

As Sanders and others have found on the basis of comparative studies, these aspirations and responses varied from group to group and city to city. Some groups, such as Chicago Poles, were far more interested in parochial schools than other groups, including the Irish in Boston or the Poles elsewhere. Some cities, like Chicago, had a far higher percentage of Catholic parishes with schools than others, such as Boston, where Catholics made peace with Protestants early and rapidly found a place in the public schools, choosing to spend resources not on schools so much as on monumental churches. Locally, Sanders notes, Catholic educational power in the public education system was expressed through Catholic teachers in schools, the appointment of a principal or some other accommodation which encouraged a decision to send children to the public schools. In nineteenth-century St. Louis, he finds, parochial schools went into decline at the very time when public ones introduced German language instruction for their students. Noting examples such as this, where language as a manifestation of cultural identity may have been more important than religion, he makes the somewhat unusual (and crucially important) observation that there is not enough data to suggest exactly how much the public schools offended Catholic sensitivities, there often being exaggerated commentary from the pulpit or press which was then cited by scholars. Little, as Sanders and other historians have noted lately, is actually known about what individuals thought. Separating responses according to income level, the ability to be upwardly or geographically mobile, gender, age, ethnic group, location and other such variables is difficult. Within many nationality groups, as in the case of Italians or Poles, responses to public or, indeed, all formal schooling varied significantly amongst people emigrating from different parts of the same country; Polish immigrants in Buffalo, for example, representing several religious traditions. These are the kind of questions which contemporary historians are confronting.11 They are applicable to all groups which have established schools outside the public system.

The determination that constitutes identity and how it is expressed vis-a-vis denominational schools is therefore a difficult one. It is evident that until recently there was greater policy interest in using the schools for Americanisation than pluralism and that the 'one best system' of modern 'progressive' education which evolved in the United States put a premium on bureaucratic management, corporation-type efficiency, fostering middle-class values, and being sure that immigrants and others were properly assimilated and educated for emergent industries and orderly behaviour.12 Certainly, it is possible to agree with William Reese when he writes that:

> ethnic and minority groups often successfully resisted attacks on their culture and preserved their unique values while struggling against a system that was insensitive, if not hostile, to their needs.13

The degree to which these values were unique to

Catholics, however, is not clear because all immigrants had to adjust to the occupational and material values promulgated in the state-supported schools. One recent study suggests the importance of this issue, reporting of an immigrant group that has not been studied extensively, that:

> resisting the integration of their children into a secular school system, many Slavic immigrants preferred parochial education and familial values that prized morality, Catholicism, and <u>early entry into the labor market</u> (emphasis added).14

Stated slightly differently,

> Decisions about school probably reflected broad family strategies about social mobility. For example, in early twentieth-century Chicago, Italians and Poles sought to establish and maintain a culturally defined level of economic welfare through the acquisition of property. Hence, they took their children out of school relatively early and used their income to buy property. By contrast, Jews and Rumanians emphasised the social mobility of individual children, as opposed to the family unity, and kept them longer in school.15

Indeed, it may be in the study of many groups heretofore ignored by historians and in looking at the many kinds of institutions they established that important interpretive breakthroughs will be made. There has been, for example, virtually no work on the many Greeks, Hungarians, Puerto Ricans and other Hispanics who came to the United States and the institutions they have started or chosen to attend. Far more research needs to be done, moreover, on which institutions reflect 'identity', particularly in a nation the size of the United States. Should scholars look to elementary schools? High schools? Colleges and Universities? Language schools? Evening schools? What is to be learned from looking at the curriculum and content of instruction?

Some of this work is now being done. William Reese had been exploring the attitudes of immigrant

Sectarian U.S.A.

socialists to public schooling and various community education efforts in several cities, finding ample evidence of support for public schooling. Ronald Cohen and Raymond Mohl have done ground-breaking work on Gary, Indiana, which has the virtue of comparing the immigrant to the Black experience in an industrial city noted for its implementation of progressive education. Sanders and a few other scholars have begun to look at Catholic curriculum and textbook content, considering factors of ethnicity and race as well as religion.16 A recent anthology edited by Bernard J. Weiss includes both new work on unresearched subjects and a welcome focus upon the broad spectrum of institutions created by Catholics. Underlying many of the studies presented in the Weiss volume is an issue fundamental to understanding the intersection of education and cultural identity: the relationship of shifting patterns of identity to practical needs. In his summation of the importance of the material published in this book, Weiss makes several crucial points. The first is the importance of looking at diverse experiences, expectations and outcomes. The second is one that is found increasingly in new 'post-revisionist' conclusions on American educational history. It is that working class immigrants were not easily exploited victims totally unsophisticated in their responses to new conditions. They were neither oppressed successfully by powerful capitalist interests - which did indeed try to exploit their labour and tailor schools and other institutions to exercise social control, sometimes with the willing assistance of educators - nor were they easily manipulated by forces in the Church representive of hierarchical, class or ethnic interests.

Looking at the pragmatic functions of traditional values, Weiss writes that:

> The premigration values and institutions that persisted are viewed as effective adaptive mechanisms rather than as manifestations of a lack of cultural sophistication. Such an interpretation regards the immigrant ghetto as a sort of decompression chamber in the process of entry into the American mainstream, characterised

by social order, and emphasizes the immigrant's role as an active agent in determining his destiny rather than as a disillusioned and impotent subject.17

THE 1980S: CONFLICT OR CONSENSUS?

There is some irony in the fact that a nation which has led the world in the development of mass systematised education and technological development may be witnessing an erosion of faith in a public school system that has been an important component of national development and prosperity. Why has this happened? What can be learned from the history of ethnic and sectarian responses to schooling to explain this phenomenon?

In her recent history of contemporary American education, Diane Ravitch writes that by 1980:

> Catholics, Protestants, and Jews had become accustomed to working together in an ecumenical spirit on common problems. Although covert anti-Catholicism and anti-Semitism lingered, they had lost their respectability. In the rapid advance of urbanization and modernization, American society had become so secularized that the religious groups most likely to encounter bigotry were Fundamentalists, particularly Protestants and Jewish denominations that clung to biblical commands.18

Bigotry is one example, as are the sheer demographics noted at the beginning of this chapter. Politics is another. Just as the Nixon Administration sought to gain in the urban 'white ethnic' vote - one result being the Ethnic Heritage Act of 1981 which encouraged the development of ethnic studies programmes, new community efforts to celebrate diversity and other initiatives directed mainly at Western and Southern European populations - there is ample evidence that the conservatives who set policy in the Reagan Administration have sought to gain from a stress on evangelical Protestant values, playing to some degree on fundamentalist fears. The current influence of evangelists like Jerry Falwell and Pat Robertson is obvious. There is nothing subtle in the many comments of President Reagan on abortion, school prayer, and the impending 'Armageddon' or the emphasis his Administration has placed on supporting private schools and eliminating 'pornography'. Without doubt they appeal to moral values rooted deeply in fundamentalism and America's working class, rural and lower middle income populations.19

Yet, the issue of cultural identity clearly transcends domestic politics for it is one that is arising increasingly in many modern societies, where, as a corollary - note recent debates in Britain over religious expression and sex education in state schools - religion is linked to ethnicity and an emphasis on individual expression that challenge the assumptions and educational systems and structures of the modern liberal welfare state. Joel Spring, a historian of post-World War Two American education, often identified as a revisionist, is a frequent commentator on tensions between those various professional and economic interests supportive of state-supported education and those that would remain outside the system. As he analyses the many twentieth-century Supreme Court decisions which have increasingly affirmed the primacy of First Amendment Constitutional provisions which guarantee separation of church and state, he finds growing legitimacy for the establishment of separate schools.

There are several examples of cases before the United States Supreme Court which demonstrate this tendency. In the 1972 case, <u>State of Wisconsin, Petitioner, v. Jonas Yoder, et al.</u>, the Court limited the right of a state to require compulsory attendance, in effect placing the burden of proof on public educators to show that state education is the only sure means to the creation of good and productive citizens. Other cases have, even when restricting its practice, recognised the importance of religion. The Pennsylvania case, <u>Abington vs. Schempp</u> (1963), restricted Bible reading to courses on comparative literature or religion, the Court ruling that it was not legal to read Bible verses at the beginning of the school day as part of opening exercises. <u>McCollum vs. Board of Education</u> (1948), an Illinois case which led to a decision against released time for religious instruction within the public school, and Zorach vs. Clauson (1952), a New York case in which the Court permitted released time for out-of-school religious instruction, set the terms by which students could be excused school for religious instruction. Engle vs. Vitale (1962), another New York case, made in-school prayer illegal. Everson vs. Board of Education (1947) allowed public support of transportation of children to religious schools. In sum, modern dissenters from public schooling can take heart in the Court's tilt towards First Amendment Rights and do so with the belief that they are in full accord with good citizenship and historic national values. In light of the difficulty many groups and individuals have in separating religion and education, Spring sees conflict arising when religious groups are forced to send their children to school under compulsory education laws and then find that in-school practices are repugnant to their basic values. These values, he suggests, are not always manifestly religious. Sometimes, as in the case of the Amish or, earlier this century, when Jewish parents objected to the imposition of the Gary Plan of platooned vocationally-oriented progressive education in the New York Schools because they believed it would erode academic standards, the reasons have as much to do with vocational objectives as moral and religious values. To Spring, compulsion to a system that in effect serves interlocking public and corporate interests is the main issue.20

The perceived propensity of the Courts to set public policy, as in abortion, affirmative action and other cases, combined with national legislation on these subjects and on the rights of the handicapped and other special interest groups, appear to be social consensus - a frightening development for many professionals, liberals and others committed to the ideals of common schooling and equality of opportunity. Yet political scientists Paul Peterson and Barry Rabe argue that shifting patterns of federal and state responsibility, court decisions, group consciousness and other factors are leading to a new and more pluralistic America wherein democratic expres-

Sectarian U.S.A.

sion is finding new and, perhaps, healthy forms.21 David Tyack and Thomas James perceive a darker side, claiming that fundamentalist Protestants, who see schools becoming increasingly secularised and subject to the influence of Catholics, minority groups and others who do not share their values will follow precedence and, pursuing political solutions of their own, find common ground with the Reaganites. Tyack and James make an important point about shifting power as it relates to cultural identity in the United States when they write that:

> By the 1980s, some fundamentalists turned away from the public school system, which they regarded as secular or worse, instead holding that education was a parental duty and not properly a state function. This represented a retreat from their attempt to enforce their fundamentalist views on all children. But other religious lobbies and politicians in Washington and the states were attempting at the same time to reverse the Supreme Court's bans on prayer and Bible reading, thereby restoring religion to the public school by constitutional amendment. Majority rule on religion in public education was an issue that refused to go away.22

One way to understand this phenomenon is to look beyond the words of powerful politicians and even some of the moral-laden cliches (eg. that fundamentalist academies are 'racist') which often set or distort the boundaries of debate. Unfortunately, there has been little scholarship on the groups which are now establishing their own schools, or on the schools themselves. The field is left to journalists, other commentators and risks of historical analogy and moral fervour.

In a particularly helpful essay published in The Public Interest on Education, Peter Skerry reports on his visits to Southern fundamentalist schools which are often portrayed as being established simply to avoid desegregation. Noting that Christian academies are being established throughout the United States and acknowledging that some were obviously set up to avoid desegregation, Skerry contends that rejection of mainstream culture, state power and much of the confusion that surrounds public education, its content and methods, has encouraged this institution building. He found that many schools are generally small. They often provide much-needed day care, homey and pleasant environments, good facilities and a relaxed 'non-institutional' feeling. The Baptist schools he visited moreover, manifested a historically fierce independence from state authority and church hierarchy. Many seemed to represent grass-roots democracy, volunteerism and reliability, reactions in part to the 1962 school prayer ban by the Supreme Court, its elimination of the pledge of allegiance to the U.S. flag in <u>West Virginia State Board of Education v. Barnette</u> (1943) and the steady erosion of religious ceremony in the public schools. Skerry claims:

> Such changes are seen by fundamentalist parents as direct assaults on God and country, the pillars of their universe.

Basically lower-middle class and working class in background, these parents feel pressured by the many changes taking place in the United States over which they have little control. Though Skerry does not address economic issues directly, nor does he suggest that such schools do indeed offer enhanced opportunity, it is clear that the fundamentalists he met are like their Catholic counterparts. Many need mediating institutions which offer cultural protection, discipline and opportunities for their children to gain the skills necessary for social survival in a hostile society undergoing dramatic change. Certainly to many it is cultural maintenance - the preservation of values - rather than material gain or economic issues that is the key to survival. As in public education, the assumption is likely to be that achievement guarantees success.23 Such hypotheses will have to be tested in the future.

Another perspective on the flight to religious schools is provided by James Coleman's controversial study on private, mainly Catholic, education. Suggesting that the issue of racial segregation is a minor one, and that in some respects urban Catholic schools are more tolerant in accepting black students than their public counterparts, Coleman asserts that he found a higher level of discipline and fairness about discipline in non-public schools. Achievement levels, he reports, were higher in non-Catholic schools than Catholic ones and about equal to those produced by public schools. All in all, however, parents desiring more than achievement - a serious and orderly academic environment and stress on traditional values - had little to lose and, in terms of escaping conditions of modern urban public education, much to gain. If, as many suggest, there is a widespread perception that bussing and other desegregation programmes create confusion and disillusionment among urban parents, religious schools offer many a non-racist alternative not unlike the one offered by Christian academies. Again, an operant assumption would appear to be that achievement will foster success - an integral part of the ideology of success and progress in the United States.24

CONCLUSION

These are perplexing times for American education. One critic, who writes of the contemporary 'conservative restoration', has attempted to put matters in broad perspective when he observes that:

> One road to the school crisis of the 1980s was the 'legitimacy crisis' of the 1960s, worsening in the 1980s. Evidence of mass alienation from school and other institutions abounds. A major survey by Lipset and Schneider (1983) found confidence in society at an all-time low. The many school crisis reports of 1983 pleaded for national consensus. Reagan's Secretary of State blamed the Beirut debacle on dissent at home. In 1984, one school head accused long-haired teachers and the end of dress-codes from the 1960s of undermining discipline. Another big-city school chief lost her right to bar anti-war groups from school while she allowed in army recruiters. Paulo Freire's liberatory ideas

spread while another professor's essay on teaching Vietnam to students in the 1980s drew heated replies in a major journal. From the conservative side, one academic wrote the university's epitaph in 1983, killed by the egalitarian excesses of the 1960s.25

Other scholars, as noted above, have bemoaned the decline of consensus about American education, claiming that there is far less support for public education amidst the crises of the 1980s than during the depth of the Great Depression, when many of the main institutions of capitalist America were widely held in disrepute.26 When viewed in these broader perspectives, it appears as though the growth of non-denominational schooling and continued interest in Catholic schooling - often by non-Catholics - is anti-democratic, at the very least supportive of a trend towards 'privatism' that also features a divestment of public responsibility by the state - a main tenet of neo-conservative political philosophy. It *may* preserve values, the family and cultural and religious identity at the expense of social equality of opportunity, factors that are both illusory and real in the lives of many Americans.

Much of the traditional historiography of urban and public education has indeed claimed that religious schooling has represented undemocratic, sometimes elitist, often 'backward' and 'divisive' interests - that 'old' values are preserved at the expense of the young and their needs. Many democratic pluralists such as John Dewey have felt strongly that all children should attend public common schools for precisely these reasons. Yet, the history of the subject suggests that interest in denominational and nondenominational schooling is not necessarily what many scholars and philosophers have made it out to be. For one thing, there is ample research to show that public education has not always served democratic interests. It has certainly not always respected pluralism and the needs and aspiration of many ethnic and minority groups. It has, as many recent scholars have suggested, reflected white male Anglo-Saxon class interests, both in the promulgation of ideas on its own importance and in devising educational means to maintain social control and train elites and compliant workers for a rapidly changing economic system more interested in profits, and national security than equality of access to schooling and equality of opportunity. At a time of major demographic change, when economic transformation - from 'industrial' to 'post-industrial' - and when major revolutions in attitudes about race, gender and family are underway, the past may be reasserting itself in ways that are not entirely new. This condition creates dislocations, hardship and a sense of moral drift reinforced by changes in family life, the growing influence of mass communication, evidence of persistent and perhaps growing structural inequality, and an impoverishment of ideas about social policy on the liberal left. The quest for identity takes many forms, including the use of friendly institutions for protecting the young as social transformations take place.

Finally, current conditions require far more attention to cultural identity issues by scholars. Especially, this research must be very sensitive to individual and group aspirations within 'community' settings; a topic that is as difficult as it is illusive. As Barbara Finkelstein suggests,

> The explorations of educational historians reveal a pre-eminent interest in the evolution of educational structures rather than educational processes or consciousness. Typically, historians have paid more attention to educational history as it structures economic and political opportunities rather than as it organizes and evokes meaning, feeling, or even political action. Disinclined to examine the problematic nature of relationships between social structure and human consciousness, they have been satisfied to understand group consciousness simply as a reflection of labor force position, of religious and ethnic affiliation, of age, or gender. They make virtually no connections between the structures of education affiliation and the meaning of educational experience, that is, between social class, ethnicity, age, gender and the social, moral, psychological meanings, uses,

and consequences of education.27

The changes which are taking place in American education, then, are significant in many ways when the persistence of religious identity and the uses of religious schools are taken into account. Whether these changes reflect failure in the public sector schools is not clear in light of broader socio-cultural and political-economic developments, many of which are global in character. In this regard, it is possible both to develop new insights on the limitations of public schools as much as on a society whose democratic character permits alternative institutions as a means of expressing identity, a quest for social improvement and, it may be argued, cultural and social equality - even at a time when a major public institution seems under threat, and it is not clear that alternatives can foster more opportunity than the public schools. When viewed through the prism of contemporary debates and impression, those who support public schooling as a means of fostering equality and democracy may be alarmed. When seen against a historical backdrop, the phenomenon suggests the limitations of public schooling in a society immensely diverse, prone to rapid change and susceptible to the power of interests over which schools have little control.

NOTES AND REFERENCES

1. For this observation and the foregoing statistics see Marcus, Sheldon and Mulkeen, Thomas A., 'The New Urban Demography: Implications for the Schools', <u>Education and Urban Society</u>, 1984, <u>16</u>, pp.395-6.

2. Katznelson, Ira and Weir, Margaret, <u>Schooling for All: Class, Race and the Decline of the Democratic Ideal</u>, Basic Books, 1985, p.27.

3. Cooper, Bruce S., 'The Changing Demography of Private Schools: Trends and Implications', <u>Education and Urban Society</u>, 1984, <u>16</u>, p.430; see also Gemello, John M. and Osman, Jack W., 'Estimating the Demand for Private School Enrollment', <u>American</u>

Journal of Education, 1984, 92, pp.262-79.

4. Kraushaar, Otto F., American Nonpublic Schools: Patterns of Diversity, Baltimore: The Johns Hopkins University Press, 1972, p.20.

5. This historiographic tradition has been discussed by many scholars. For an excellent overview see Cremin, Lawrence, The Wonderful World of Ellwood Patterson Cubberley: An Essay on the Historiography of American Education, New York: Teachers College, Bureau of Publications, 1965.

6. For some additional background and citations see Kraushaar, op.cit., pp.19-51.

7. This point is discussed in Sanders, James W., 'Roman Catholics and the School Question in New York City: Some Suggestions for Research' in: Ravitch, Diane and Goodenow, Ronald K. (eds), Educating an Urban People: The New York City Experience, New York: Teachers College Press, 1981, pp.116-40.

8. Ibid., p.118.

9. Reese, William J., 'Neither Victims Nor Masters: Ethnic and Minority Study' in: Best, John Hardin (ed.), Historical Inquiry in Education: A Research Agenda, Washington: The American Educational Research Association, 1983, chapter 12; and Lazerson, Marvin, 'Understanding American Catholic Educational History', History of Education Quarterly, 1977, 17.

10. See n.6 above, for both references to this older work and introduction to some Protestant-Catholic struggles.

11. Sanders, op.cit. See also Sanders, James W., The Education of an Urban Minority: Catholics in Chicago, 1833-1965, New York: Oxford University Press, 1977;
Lannie, Vincent P. 'Church and School Triumphant: The Sources of American Catholic Educational Historiography', History of Education Quarterly, 1976, 16.

12. See: Tyack, David B., The One Best System: A History of American Urban Education, Harvard Universi-

ty Press, 1974, for an excellent discussion of the rise of the modern urban school system and its response to immigrant children.

13. Reese, op.cit., p.231.

14. Ibid., p.232;
Bodnar, John, 'Materialism and Morality: Slavic-American Immigrants and Education', Journal of Ethnic Studies, 1976, 3.

15. Katz, Michael B. and Hogan, David, 'Schools, Work and Family Life: Social History', Ch.15 in Best, op.cit.;
Hogan, David, 'Education and the Making of the Chicago Working Class, 1880-1930', History of Education Quarterly, 1978, 18.

16. Reese, William J., Progressivism and the Grass Roots, Routledge and Kegan Paul, 1986;
Cohen, Ronald D. and Mohl, Raymond A., The Paradox of Progressive Education: The Gary Plan and Urban Schooling, Port Washington: Greenwood Press, 1979;
Sanders, Urban Minority, op.cit.

17. Weiss, Bernard J. (ed.), American Education and the European Immigrant: 1840-1940, University of Illinois Press, 1982, xvi.

18. Ravitch, Diane, The Troubled Crusade: American Education 1945-1980, Basic Books, 1983, p.325.

19. The Ethnic Heritage Act is discussed in Lynch, James, The Multicultural Curriculum, Batsford, 1983, pp.29, 41, 132, 139; contemporary fundamentalism is placed in political context in Shor, Ira, Culture Wars: School and Society in the Conservative Restoration 1969-1984, Boston: Routledge and Kegan Paul, 1986, pp.18-20; and Tyack, David B. and James, Thomas, 'Moral Majorities and the School Curriculum: Historical Perspectives on the Legalization of Virtue', Teachers College Record, 1985, 86, pp.513-37.

20. These issues are discussed at length, and sources are cited, in Spring, Joel, <u>American Education: An Introduction to Social and Political Aspects</u>, Longman, 1978; also:
Spring, Joel, <u>The American School 1642-1985; Varieties of Historical Interpretation of the Foundations and Development of American Education</u>, Longman, 1986. Though this latest volume of Spring discusses current policy debates and 'conflict' amongst interest groups, there is little mention of the growth in non-public education sectors;
The Gary Plan, and attempts to introduce it in New York and elsewhere, is discussed in Cohen and Mohl, op.cit.;
For a useful overview of U.S. Supreme Court Decisions on Education see Fellman, David, <u>The Supreme Court and Education</u>, New York: Teachers College Press, 1960.

21. Peterson, Paul. E. and Rabe, Barry G., 'The Role of Interest Groups in the Formation of Educational Policy: Past Practice and Future Trends', <u>Teachers College Record</u>, 1983, <u>84</u>, pp.708-29.

22. See Tyack and James, 1985, op.cit.

23. Skerry, Peter, 'Christian Schools Versus the I.R.S.' in Glazer, Nathan (ed.), <u>The Public Interest on Education</u>, Cambridge, ABT Books, 1984.

24. Coleman, James, 'Private Schools, Public Schools and the Public Interest' in: Glazer, op.cit.

25. See Shor, op.cit., p.4. The 1960s climate, which emphasised dress codes, basic skills and other reactions to progressivism is discussed extensively in Ravitch, op.cit. See especially p.316.

26. See Tyack, David, Low, Robert and Hansot, Elisabeth, <u>Public Schools in Hard Times: The Great Depression and Recent Years</u>, Harvard University Press, 1984.

27. Finkelstein, Barbara, 'Exploring Community in Urban Educational History', in: Goodenow, Ronald K.

and Ravitch, Diane (eds), <u>Schools in Cities: Consensus and Conflict in American Educational History</u>, Holmes and Meier, 1983, pp.305-6.

THE ROLE OF DENOMINATIONAL BODIES IN EDUCATION IN THE DEVELOPMENT OF EDUCATION IN THE COMMONWEALTH CARIBBEAN

M. Kazim Bacchus

INTRODUCTION: THE YEARS BEFORE EMANCIPATION

The various Christian denominational bodies which operated in the Commonwealth Caribbean made an important contribution to the development of education in the region. Their work laid the foundation of the system of dual control of schools and considerably influenced the nature of the educational programmes which were offered, especially in the primary schools. Even though the West Indian Governments increasingly assumed financial responsibility for their educational services, yet for over a century or more the denominational bodies played a crucial role in the establishment and management of schools, in the appointment and even in the training of teachers. With independence the elected governments of these countries have increasingly assumed greater responsibility for all aspects of their own educational services but the denominational bodies are still not without some influence in this field.

The wealthier planters who originally controlled the local legislatures sent their children back to England for their education and were, therefore, generally indifferent at first to the formal instruction of the children of the poorer whites, the coloured, and the black population. The Established Church, the Church of England also totally neglected the spiritual needs of the non-whites, especially the slaves, and 'ministered solely to the white residents.' There were a number of reasons why it adopted this policy. First, it had a very close relationship with the planters and it was even suggested that 'the

West Indian sugar interests had gained control of the Established Church. The Church itself was in the grip of King Sugar.'1 As a result, the Anglicans initially tried not to do or say anything that might conceivably offend the plantocracy which was not particularly supportive of educational activities among the black population and was strongly opposed to the education, even the religious education, of the slaves. Because of its actions one historian accused the Church of England of having 'signally failed the Negroes in the Antilles.' For example, one of its resident clergymen 'weakly and callously' decided at the beginning of settlement in the region not to antagonise the planters by preaching the gospel to the blacks - an act which was later considered 'a great blot upon the Church'.

Further, the ministers of the Established Church received their stipends from the State and the level of remuneration was determined by the colonial legislatures which were dominated by planter interest. Therefore they were careful not to offend the planters since this might have adversely affected their own levels of income. Captain S. Hodgson in commenting on the importance of this fact, observed that:

> The clergy depend, in a great degree, for their existence on the different Houses of Assembly; their incomes can, at any moment be reduced or augmented; let them hesitate to acquiesce in any proposition submitted by the planters, and they are exposed to beggary, (in fact) to worse than beggary since the press, controlled by the same planters will inflict wounds upon their reputation which no time can cure.2

Consequently most ministers of the Church of England became staunch supporters of the 'status quo' in the slave societies of the West Indies. There were many direct attempts by the Anglicans to support the attempts by West Indian Assemblies to block or suppress the work of the dissenting missionaries. A few of the clergy were themselves slave owners and even Bishop Lipscombe, when he was first appointed to the newly created diocese in Jamaica in the 1820s, petitioned the Secretary of State for permission to own slaves.

The reluctance of the Anglican Church to involve itself in the education of the black population, including the slaves, has also to be seen against its overall attitude to the education of the poor during the eighteenth century. Essentially it accepted the view expressed in the <u>Gentleman's Magazine</u> in 1797 that:

> a little learning makes a man ambitious to rise ... [while] his ignorance is a balm that soothes his mind into stupidity and repose, and excludes every emotion of discontent, pride and ambition. A man of no learning will seldom attempt to foment insurrections or form an idle scheme for the reformation of the State.3

As late as 1803, the Bishop of London, under whose ecclesiastical jurisdiction the West Indies then fell, was pointing out that 'men of considerable ability' held the view that 'it is safest for both the Government and the religion of the country to let the lower classes remain in that state of ignorance in which nature has originally placed them'.4

This focus on education as an instrument of domestication and conformity continued for some time and up to 1839 the view of the Anglican Church on the education of the poor, as stated in its Blackwoods Magazine was still that:

> Ignorance is the parent of contentment ... the only education which could be fitly and safely given to the poor is a religious education, which renders them patient, humble and moral, and relieves the hardship of their present lot by the prospect of bright eternity.5

THE EDUCATIONAL ACTIVITIES OF THE QUAKERS

But even this situation, in which religious and general educational efforts among the blacks and especially the slaves were frowned upon, by the planters, the colonial governments and the Established Church, did not entirely deter attempts by some missionaries to meet what was seen as an obvious need. For example, in Barbados, according to Dr Sporri, some Negro children were being instructed and brought up as Christians as early as the 1660s, and by the 1670s the Quakers had taken the first major step towards the religious education of the black population on that island. In his 1671 visit to Barbados, George Fox emphasised to the Governor that the educational policy of the Society of Friends was that 'black people should be given religious instruction' and that the Quakers would seek to teach them 'the light', i.e. admonish them to be sober, to fear God, to be diligent and truthful to their masters and not to rebel. In 1672 when he addressed the 'Ministers, Teachers and Priests' in Barbados he posed an embarrassingly disturbing question when he asked:

> And if you be Ministers of Christ are you not Teachers of Blacks and Tawnies (Indians) as well as of Whites. For is not the Gospel to be preached to all creatures? And are they not Men?6

In addition to the religious education which they offered, the Quakers used their parish churches to operate schools which were obviously not meant for slave children but were open to all those who were free, including members of any religious group. In 1662 it was reported that one of their members, a Mr Heynes, was licensed to teach as a school master in a parish church. For the Quakers the instruction of the young in 'reading, writing and casting accounts' was essential both for worship and for the conduct of worldly affairs. As part of their education the children also had to memorise Fox's catechism and one student was reported, not only to have known 'the primer by heart', but 'can readily construe Latin Child's Lesson' and 'turn the Catechism and proverbs out of Latin into English. He can also read in the Hebrew Bible.'7

At the Bridgetown Quaker School scholars read from the New Testament while a Jewish usher taught Christian doctrine from Fox's Primer to several Jewish children. It was also agreed to instruct poor

Multidenominational Caribbean

children free of charge 'and to turn no Child away upon the account of money', But in addition to the general education being provided through instruction in the basics of reading, writing and casting accounts, 'the school books and teaching that the Quakers provided for the children of all faiths in Barbados, acted as potent proselytising devices for the Society.'8

The planters were very disturbed by the educational activities of the Quakers and did everything to frustrate their efforts. In 1696 they succeeded in getting the local legislature to pass an Act which restrained anyone on the island from teaching school unless he had taken 'the oaths of supremacy and allegiance' and had a special licence from the Governor to teach. Both these requirements were aimed at curbing the educational activities of the Quakers. In fact a number of other steps taken by the planters made it difficult, if not virtually impossible, for the Quakers to continue the educational work among the black population.

RENEWED EFFORTS BY THE MISSIONARIES

These early educational efforts by some missionaries eventually subsided because of planter opposition, and it was not until some years prior to emancipation and during the post-emancipation years, that they were revived and intensified. There are two major reasons why this renewed contribution which the missionaries made to education in the West Indies was important. First, even though these activities were mainly religious and initially of a part-time nature, they had objectives and had achieved outcomes similar to those of the formal educational systems which eventually emerged in most of these territories. They, in fact, laid the foundation for the administrative structures and the educational programmes which continued to be offered in the primary schools in most of the British West Indian colonies for the next century. Secondly, their educational efforts were fairly comprehensive and included the provision of various types of schools to suit the convenience of different sectors of the population. Among these were 'field' schools, Sunday schools, evening and adult schools, trade schools, 'estate' or 'plantation' schools, independent schools and finally regular primary and secondary 'day' schools. As Rooke reminded us, these missionaries were not only priests: they were 'pragmatic pedagogues', and their evangelising efforts which 'extended from the pulpit and classroom into everyday life' could be 'best understood ... as part of a broad educational process known as "civilising" in the nineteenth century.'9

Most missionaries refused to accept the view which was then shared by many, that the moral standards of the slaves, among whom they hoped to do most of their work, could not be improved and pointed out that those who criticised the Negroes for their 'passions and vices'

> have applied no other instrument to elicit the virtues they have demanded, than the stimulus of the whip and the stern voice of authority ... They have required moral ends without the application of moral means, and their failure ... leaves the question of the capacity of the Negro untouched, and proves nothing but their own folly.10

They saw that the only way by which the slaves' moral improvement could be achieved or the assumption about their characters lending themselves to improvement could be properly tested was through providing them with religious and moral education. To some individuals, improving the moral and social conditions of the 'ignorant negro' was simply a matter of bringing them into contact with 'a more civilised people', that is to say 'the European'. If this were to happen, as Dalton suggested, 'we shall soon see how rapidly his tastes, his habits, and character became modified by such communion.'11 But the missionaries did not accept the view that the spiritual condition of the Negro could be improved by a process of moral osmosis. They saw the need for a more active intervention through formal instruction in the principles of Christianity. As a result, schools and churches in the West Indies, as R. T. Smith pointed out, came to be seen as 'the best instruments for the transformation of a rebellious slave population into a peaceful and obedient working class.'12

ATTEMPTS BY MISSIONARIES TO REDUCE PLANTER OPPOSITION TO THEIR EDUCATIONAL ACTIVITIES

The Missionary Societies were aware that most planters were, to say the least, 'unfriendly to their instruction' and often considered their preaching and teaching as 'endangering the public peace and safety'. The societies therefore attempted to instruct their field staff not to do or say anything that would make the slaves displeased with their masters, become discontented with their existing conditions or hope for amelioration, not to mention emancipation. The Anglicans warned their missionaries that, not only should they get the 'consent and approbation' of the relevant authorities before attempting to instruct their Negro slaves, but even when permission was granted they should, in their instructional programme, 'dwell most strongly and frequently on the great practical duties; of piety and obedience to their masters, contentment, patience and resignation to the will of heaven.'13 The Wesleyans were told that 'your sole business is to promote the moral and religious improvement of the slaves ... without in the least degree ... interfering with their civil condition'. For them the expressed intent of their work was to produce among the slaves 'a humble and subordinate carriage'14 and contentment with their station of life. Somewhat similar instructions were given to other missionaries and even the Baptists were warned, 'Do not intermeddle with politics ... Remember that the object of your mission is not to teach the principles and laws of an earthly Kingdom ... but the principles and laws of the Kingdom of Christ'.15 The Church Missionary Society (CMS) was even more emphatic about the nature of the religious education which its missionaries was to provide. It was to be one which would 'render the slaves diligent, faithfully, patient and useful servants ... the most valuable slaves on the estates'.16

But despite the precaution taken by most religious bodies, the planters continued to fear that their work, especially that of the 'dissenting' missionaries, was a threat to order and stability. They further felt that by allowing the missionaries to establish schools they would be driving another nail into the coffin of slave society which they so badly wanted to preserve. The Rev. John Smith had concluded in his report to the Directors of the London Missionary Society in 1818 that even those planters who did not question the intention of most missionaries to produce 'better' slaves, feared that even the most inocuous education was merely a first step towards creating a 'more self conscious group of subservients'. The planters argued that Christianity and slavery could not long exist together. In fact their view was that 'slavery must exist as it now is, or it will not exist at all'.17

Following the death in 1823 of Rev. John Smith, who was accused of involvement in the East Coast Slave Rebellion, the editor of the Colonist, a mouthpiece of the planters, put their views as to the education of slaves very clearly when he wrote an editorial castigating planters for not speaking out in time against the first advocates of education for the slaves. He pointed out that it should have been made clear that 'the missionary system is in fact, undermining the institutions and endangering the political existence of the Colonies'.18 As a Committee of the Jamaican House of Assembly, which was appointed to inquire into the cause of the 1831 slave revolt on that island, suggested

> the preaching and teaching of the religious sects called Baptists, Wesleyan Methodists and Moravians (but more particularly the sect termed Baptists), ... had the effect of producing in the minds of the slaves a belief that they could not serve both a spiritual and a temporal master.19

It was not that the planters were entirely unaware of the possible role of education in helping to produce a submissive black slave population and a pliant work-force. But they were very hesitant to take, what seemed to them to be the accompanying risks. Tannenbaum pointed out that 'the plantation owners opposed the preaching of the gospel on the grounds that it would interfere with the management of the slaves, make them recalcitrant, (by putting) notions of rebellion and freedom into their minds'. Therefore the suggestion that instruction in the Christian doctrine would make the slaves 'more obedient, and therefore more docile found little response among the planters'.20 Rooke made a similar point, noting that,

> the planters were ... unreceptive to an education which taught any form of equality between slave and master ... They saw social stability being threatened as much by the assumptions behind missionary education as by the practice of it. Doctrines of spiritual equality exposed the contradiction inherent in slave societies. As the planters correctly recognised, teach a slave he is lovable in the sight of God and he was bound to become uppity ... Teach a slave that Christ came to save all men and he will begin to wonder why some men deserve to own slaves while others deserve to be slaves.21

As a result of this scepticism by planters about the 'effectiveness' of education, even religious education among the slaves, the missionaries were frequently ridiculed and even physically harassed because of their work. The general atmosphere in these territories was one which deterred missionary activity, especially before the Moravians arrived on the scene. However, towards the end of the eighteenth century, there was a general thrust towards missionary work which emanated from the revival of religious enthusiasm in Britain. The Caribbean came to be regarded as a 'fertile field for British missionaries, a place where the word of God must precede and envelop all other aspects of learning'.22 This spurt in religious activities was further encouraged by the continuing belief then held by many key members of the Colonial Office, that religious education would be a crucial factor in any attempt at raising the moral standards and improving the social habits of the black population, especially the slaves. This was becoming more important as the pressure for emancipation increased and abolition was more clearly on the horizon. The British Government even indicated that it was prepared to help pay for maintaining 'an adequate number of clergymen and teachers throughout the West Indies ... if the revenues of the colonies are insufficient for this purpose'.23

To further show its commitment to supporting the educational activities of the various missionary bodies then operating in the West Indies, the British Parliament decided to compensate the Baptists and the Methodists for their chapels and other property which were destroyed by white vandals in Jamaica following the 1831 slave rebellion on that island. It wanted to ensure that the 'valuable services' of these missionaries would not be lost to the local population.

THE MAJOR EDUCATIONAL GOALS OF THE NEW MISSIONARIES WORKING IN THE WEST INDIES

Whenever it was provided, missionary education in the West Indies was 'deliberate, organised and systematic', with the most important objective of the missionaries being undoubtedly a religious one, i.e. to save the souls of the black population who were then mainly slaves. This overriding concern of the missionaries for the spiritual salvation of the slaves virtually overshadowed all their other concerns and this resulted in their ignoring, possibly even becoming insensitive to, the degrading social conditions under which the slaves lived. This was exemplified by one of the tales included in the book, **Missionary Stories**, which they often used in the education of the young. In the story a 'little negro' was made to repeat the following prayer

> O Lord, I thank thee for sending the big ship into my country and wicked men to steal me and bring me here that I might know and love thee. And now Lord Jesus, I have one great favour to ask. I pray thee to send wicked men with another big ship and let them catch my father and mother,

and bring them to this country, that they too may hear of thee.24

A second direct objective of the education provided by the missionaries was to help reinforce the existing social order and create stability within these societies. It has been suggested that social stability was not simply another latent outcome of the efforts at Christianising the slaves but a discrete and planned educational goal in its own right, 'secondary only to the major task of saving souls'. Most missionaries, according to Reckord, accepted the slave system 'as a manifestation of the mysterious workings of God'25 and carried out their educational activities, as much as possible, with the planters' interests or concerns in mind. So in the process of trying to save souls, the missionaries taught the slaves the importance of accepting their lot in society and 'to sustain injury with patience'. They also used the teachings of Christianity in an attempt to give legitimacy to the conditions under which the slaves lived. Commenting more generally on the role of religious education in slave society Stampp pointed out that

> through religious instruction, the bondsmen learned that slavery had divine sanction, that insolence was as much an offence against God as against the temporal master. They received the Biblical command that servants should obey their masters, and they heard of the punishments awaiting the disobedient slave in the life hereafter. They heard too that eternal salvation would be their reward for faithful service (even as slaves).26

But while the achievement of such stability was one of the major outcomes of the educational efforts of the missionaries, it would be quite unfair and incorrect to indict all of them as being 'compradors' of the planter class, having as their main objective the maintenance, through their religious and educational activities, of a subdued and servile non-white labour force for the plantations.

Multidenominational Caribbean

THE VARIOUS MISSIONARY GROUPS IN THE WEST INDIES

Among the more important missionary groups that were then operating in the West Indies were the Anglicans (Church of England), the Roman Catholics, the Moravians, the Methodists, the Baptists, and the London Missionary Society and it would now be useful to examine separately their specific aims, activities and achievements.

The Church of England - the Established Church

As indicated above, the early record of the Anglican Church in the religious education of the 'lower orders' of West Indian society left much to be desired. In 1625 the first Anglican rector sent out to Barbados only remained on the island for a year, being disgusted with the conduct of the population. However in 1652 the earliest known reference was made to the existence of 'educational institutions in the Caribbees' conducted by the Anglicans in Barbados. This would have meant that their ministers taught schools in addition to their 'weekly prescribed duty of catechising children'.

The Anglicans gradually became more interested in the education of the black population. In 1794 Bishop Porteus, Bishop of London and Head of the West Indies Diocese, established the Incorporated Society for the Conversion and Religious Instruction and Education of the Negro Slaves in the West Indies, a society which really did not become active until the early nineteenth century when it began to send missionaries to the West Indies. In St Kitts the Society did not restrict its work to the instruction of slaves and by 1833 there were 78 whites, 368 free and 1,583 slave children in its 6 day schools, 38 estate schools and 9 Sunday schools.

In addition, the Church of England authorities established the Society for the Propagation of the Gospel in Foreign Parts (SPG) which was very active in educational matters overseas, but not among slaves. Between 1711 and 1785 this Society dispatched about 353 missionaries and many school teachers and doctors to Anglican stations in British America, including the British West Indies. It was also to the SPG that the Codrington estates were endowed and so, in addition to the College and the secondary school which were established out of the funds provided by Sir Christopher Codrington, the Society was also responsible for education of the slaves on those estates. The SPG later began to improve the educational work among its slaves partly because it was felt that the education with which they had been provided so far, was largely responsible for their non-participation in the 1818 insurrection. Progress was even more marked with the appointment of a Director of the Negro Schools on the estates. The school day was lengthened from two to four hours. Children began to attend school between the ages of four to ten years, and in 1828 the Society gave orders that the estate children should remain at school until they were twelve years old. However, religion and the reading of the Scriptures were the only two subjects on the curriculum since writing and arithmetic were excluded at the Society's direction. Needlework was later added to the subjects taught to Negro girls and it was said that, on leaving school, the students 'were inundated with religious tracts', which helped them to keep up their reading skills.

The SPG also had missionaries in the Bahamas but here too they did little or no work among the slaves because of the opposition from the slave owners. The situation gradually improved and in 1738 an SPG sponsored Charity school was opened in New Providence but it catered mainly for white children, especially the poor whites, although a few Negro children were admitted.

In 1799 the Anglicans also organised the Church Missionary Society (CMS) to work specifically among the slave population which the SPG, the already established evangelical arm of the Church of England, had failed to do. The CMS wanted to include both clergy and selected laymen among its missionaries and began its work in the West Indies with a layman, William Dawes, a former Governor of Sierra Leone who settled in Antigua in 1813. The CMS worked on this island from 1815 to 1829 and even supported a school in Barbados - the National Charity School which was established in 1818 under the patronage of the Governor, Lord Combermere - by paying the teacher's salary. It admitted children between the ages of five and twelve, who attended from 9am to 4pm with a two hour break for lunch. The curriculum included the 'three Rs' and religion, the latter being taught 'in strict conformity' with the principles of the Established Church. While about half the number of children attending were slaves it was hoped that the others, who were mainly coloureds, would eventually become teachers to the slaves. This was partly the reason for the 'liberal' curriculum which was offered to some children. By 1825 enrolment at the school had reached about 160.

The Society also stationed missionaries in Demerara/Essequibo and by the turn of the nineteenth century began to work in Jamaica building schools and churches for 'the benefit of the servile classes'. It also sent out schoolmasters from Britain. Several attempts were made by the CMS to work with slaves and disbanded soldiers in St Vincent and Dominica but these efforts were not very successful. However by 1831 the Society had thirteen stations, a similar number of schools and eight catechists in Jamaica alone and its work expanded from then on, especially since it was able to secure Government financial assistance after emancipation.

Another missionary body attached to the Church of England which was engaged in educational activities in the region was Dr Bray's Associates which operated only in the Bahamas and Bermuda. The 'Associates' was established by Dr Thomas Bray who was also responsible for the founding of the SPG and the SPCK, the Society for the Propagation of Christian Knowledge. The Associates directed its attention mainly at educating free negroes and maintaining libraries in the West Indies and mainland America. In March 1793 it opened its first school, a day school, in Nassau and in accordance with its admission policy, free negroes were given preference over slaves. The view of the 'Associates' was that the free negroes were in the greatest need of education since, on the one hand, if the masters of slave children were interested in their education, they would have no difficulty in making the necessary provision for their slaves, while on the other hand, the whites, even the poorer ones, had much better access to education than the free blacks. By 1811 the Bray's School was therefore only admitting children of free negroes and it operated without serious interruption between 1793 and 1844. The teachers were all black because the staffing of the school benefited from the educated black Loyalists who came to the Bahamas after the American War of Independence.

The goals of the education that was provided were in line with those of the Church of England at that period, and the inspector was requested to see that

> the Children are properly instructed in the Principles of Christianity, and that the great and necessary Duties of Obedience and Fidelity to their Masters, and Humility and Contentedness with their Condition were duly impressed on their Minds.27

The curriculum was a religious and literary one, containing no practical subjects. In commenting on the effect of the education given by Dr Bray's Associates on the 'poor blacks and coloured population' Richards noted, in 1821, that those who went through the school were 'the best disposed Negroes in New Providence' while in the following year the Rev. Hepworth, an Anglican Missionary in the Bahamas, observed that the effect of their education

> already shows itself in the more orderly Demeanour and the more regular Attendance upon public Worship ... than in any of the numerous Sects with which this place abounds.28

The school was eventually operated on the Bell or Madras System of monitorial instruction and the curriculum also consisted mainly of the 'Four R's', religion, reading, writing and arithmetic. The children were catechised at least once and often twice per day and they usually listened to sermons from Mrs Trimmer's 'A Commentary on the Old and New Testaments'. Reading was mainly from the Bible, the Testament, Lewis' Catechism, and Prayer Books. In

1802-3 it was reported that the children knew their Catechism and were advanced in Arithmetic to 'Practice and Compound Interest'. But the authorities were always uneasy about these 'more advanced' subjects being offered at the school and after the 1802-3 examinations the following significant comment was added by the inspector: 'But I suppose the object of the Society is more to make them good Christians rather than good scholars'.29

In addition to the work of these societies other members of the Church of England became involved in education in the West Indies prior to emancipation. Bishop Porteus had always shown great interest in the education of the slaves and made efforts to encourage missionaries of a high calibre to go out to the West Indies, but without much success. As he explained to Lady Nugent 'clergymen of Character here ... can scarce be tempted by any Advantage, to go to the West Indies where they are in dread of the Climate'.30 Further in 1801 he even wrote to the legislators and plantation owners asking whether they would allow their slaves to be instructed in and converted to Christianity and be taught to read. These enquiries indicated that the Bishop was prepared to go beyond the eighteenth century position of the Anglican Church by departing from the practice of teaching 'religion without letters' to the slaves.

While the response to his enquiry was not very encouraging he nevertheless followed up the issue of education for the slaves and in 1808 put forward a draft plan for the education of the poor in the West Indies. In it he recommended the establishment of parochial schools in every parish of the various West Indian islands, where education was to be provided along the lines suggested by Dr Bell. The teachers were to be drawn from the local communities, including the employees on the sugar estates, and the schools were to come under the inspection, control and direction of the parochial clergy thereby laying the foundation for the spread of Anglicanism throughout these societies.

However, the plan fell through because the slave owners were still not yet in favour of any form of education for the slaves. Nevertheless he followed up with a circular to his clergy in the region recommending the establishment of Sunday schools conducted on the Bell system, for the instruction of the slaves. In 1823 the Anglican clergy in Barbados played a crucial role in the formation of an Association, the main concern of which was the Religious Instruction of Slaves. It called for religious education to be given to the slave population on Sundays and suggested that young slaves in particular should be compelled to attend. Due to pressure from the planters the Anglican clergy agreed that all instruction which they provided would be strictly oral.

The work of the Anglican Church in the field of education in the West Indies received a substantial boost with the establishment in 1824 of two Anglican dioceses in the region - one headquartered in Barbados and the other in Jamaica. This marked the real beginning of organised efforts of the Church of England to provide religious and general education in the West Indies. Bishop Coleridge, who was responsible for the Eastern Caribbean, became actively involved in the establishment of schools within his diocese. He displayed tremendous zeal in his work and his tenure was distinguished by 'remarkable progress', both in the affairs of the Church and in education. He was interested, not only in fostering the work of Sunday schools but also of day schools, and took under his superintendence the National Charity School in Bridgetown which, in 1812, was established under the patronage of Lord Combermere with the financial assistance of the CMS. In 1827 he also founded an elementary school for coloured girls and a girls' central school - both being located near to the National School which only enrolled boys. In addition he set about helping to improve the day schools in many parishes including the parochial school of St John and St Peter which served the poor whites. The whites in Barbados, whose numbers then equalled about one-sixth of the non-white population had most of the schools for themselves and Bishop Coleridge tried to break down the restrictions which operated against the admission of blacks and coloureds to some schools within his diocese.

Multidenominational Caribbean

Bishop Lipscombe who was sent to Jamaica was more concerned about raising the moral standards of the white population and showed less interest in the education of slaves. His application to the Colonial Secretary for permission to own slaves indicates how insensitive he was to the potential contribution which he, as the Bishop, might have been able to make.

The Church of England's activities in education extended to the other British Caribbean islands either directly or through one of its agencies. For example, around the 1820s, an Anglican school was established in Trinidad by the Rev. Tucker and his wife. This was the first coeducational school on the island and had an initial enrolment of 39 boys and 13 girls. The school, which was also operated under the Bell monitorial system, was specifically established to educate the children of the American black settlers who were the descendants of the black refugees that fled the turmoil of the American War of Independence. However, as late as 1835, it was noted that there was not one clergy, catechist, school or schoolmaster, connected with the Established Church operating in Port of Spain, Trinidad. The first public school in St Lucia was established in 1828 by the Anglican Church but it only continued its work for about two years owing to the lack of funds.

The Roman Catholics

The record of educational activities by the Roman Catholics prior to emancipation was poor, and as late as 1836 the Rev. Sterling noted that they 'appear to have no schools to which their own clergy attach the slightest importance'.31 Around 1832 Martin had observed that on the predominantly Catholic island of St Vincent the lack of education facilities 'has been a sore evil'32 while in Grenada although Roman Catholicism was the dominant religion, 'there was no established Roman Catholic school' before 1824. The only exception was a school, possibly a private one, operated mainly for the children of the free coloureds. As late as 1835 one observer of the Trinidad scene which also had a very large percentage of Roman Catholics, noted:

I am not aware of the existence of schools of any description (on the island). If they do exist, they are of very little moment.33

The poor record of the Roman Catholics in the provision of educational facilities, in the territories which eventually became part of the British West Indies, has to be seen against the fact that they had the longest experience of missionary and educational work in the region, starting with the earlier period of Spanish colonisation. They were in fact the only group which was allowed to conduct religious activities on the islands which were under Spanish or French rule. In the predominantly Catholic islands which were taken over by Britain from these nations, the education provisions available were in no way on par with those in the islands which, up to then, made up the British West Indies. More specifically the Catholic Church conducted little or no other educational activities among the slaves, apart from seeking to convert and baptise them into the faith. Even in the late 1830s when it began to take a more active role in the provision of education in Trinidad its initial policy was to educate the middle and upper classes to the neglect of the lower classes - a policy similar to that which was pursued in the Spanish American colonies. One of the reasons suggested for this approach was that

> the upper and middle classes would, on being employed, occupy more remunerative posts and their financial support of the Roman Catholic Church would be stronger. From this point of view the education of the lower orders was regarded as uneconomic.34

The reason for this policy was not only the close association which existed between the local Church leaders and the dominant groups in the island with a large Catholic population but also their general perception of the inability of the Negroes to benefit from any education. Since the mid-seventeenth century some of the Roman Catholic religious orders concluded that it was difficult to teach the slaves and even though they were usually christened, it was suggested that their minds were so 'crude and foolish' that it was nearly impossible to teach them to read and write. This observation was similar to the one made by certain well known Roman Catholic figures about the ineducability of the Indians and while the attitude changed over time it did not completely disappear.

With a generally negative attitude by many members of the Roman Catholic Church towards the educability of the Negro and with their experience mainly in providing secondary and higher education in the region, it was no great surprise that the existing elementary school facilities in the colonies with a substantial majority of Roman Catholics were minimal. As late as the 1830s it was said that a school established by Abbe Power for negroes was opposed by both the planters and his own Roman Catholic bishop, Dr McDonnell, who strongly objected to the poor being taught.

The British Government wanted to hasten the pace of educational development in the islands acquired from France and Spain, purportly to bring them on par with its older West Indian colonies, but mainly to ensure that the loyalty of their subjects was transferred to the new colonial ruler. At that time Roman Catholicism was identified with a foreign rival power, in this case mainly France, so the British Government was anxious to get the Church of England and other Protestant groups and later the Mico Trust participating in the education of the population in these islands, partly in an attempt to change the direction of their allegiance. The funds for the Mico Trust were provided in 1670 by Dame Jane Mico. Since the terms specified in connection with the original benefactor were not met, the money was used for the other stated purpose, i.e. redeeming poor slaves from the Barbary Coast. All the funds were not expended and by 1835 they had accumulated to £115,000. The British Government was persuaded to allow the funds to be used for the education of slaves, following the emancipation from slavery.

But the Roman Catholics, of course, were also anxious to maintain their religious dominance in these colonies and Coleridge, commenting on the situation in St Lucia, noted that every attempt at bringing together the French and English elements of the population 'has been openly thwarted by the Romish clergy'.35 They did not take very well to the efforts by other religious groups to intrude on what was traditionally their territory and moreover to seek converts from among their flock by attempting to educate them along Protestant lines in their schools. For example, the Anglican Bishop had insisted that all Protestant teachers introduce the catechism of the Established Church as a required textbook in their schools - an act which provoked protests and petitions from the Roman Catholics in Trinidad, many of whose children were attending these schools. However, the situation was not the same in all the islands and Trinidad, for example, presented a contrast to St Lucia where it was said that there was no evidence of religious animosity, with the Roman Catholic clergy being 'enlightened and liberal; [and] the same school contains English, Spaniards and French, [and] those who believe in and those who laugh at Transubstantiation'.36

Even the local Roman Catholic Church was not particularly anxious or ready to be involved in the education of the masses and in the islands in which the majority of the population subscribed to its faith, the Church 'threw its influence against State education' and would itself have nothing to do with it in the early years. It was noted that in Grenada the admittedly meagre funds set aside for schooling Roman Catholics were never used. A similar observation was later made with reference of the funds which became available for education by the British Government under the Negro Education Act, with the Catholics at first refusing to claim their share. On the other hand, they did object to the discrimination which seemed to have been operating against them in the dispensation of such funds. They were not even formally invited to participate in the parliamentary subsidy for Negro Education, and instead the Colonial Office asked the Mico Trust to work in those islands which had a predominantly Catholic population.

The Roman Catholics therefore attempted to oppose the educational efforts of the Protestants in those colonies like Trinidad, St Vincent, Grenada and

Dominica where up to 90 per cent of the population were Catholics. For example, when Dr Coke, the Methodist missionary, tried to secure financial assistance from the St Vincent legislature to establish a school for the Carib Indians remaining on that island, it was reported that his efforts failed because the Roman Catholic priests 'had infused ideas into the minds of the Caribs that the missionaries were spies'37 employed by the King. It was also noted when the Protestants attempted to provide schools in some of these islands, the Roman Catholic parents were strongly influenced by their priests against sending their children to receive instruction in such schools, especially when it was said that the schoolmasters insisted that the children learn, in the case of the Anglican schools, the catechism of the Church of England.

Such pressures were exerted by the priests even when there was no Roman Catholic school which the children could attend. Coleridge reported that in St Lucia where the Roman Catholics had 'no schools themselves ... they forbid any of their flocks to attend one in company with Protestants'. This resulted in parents who could afford it, sending their children to Catholic schools in Martinique, the United States and France. However they were said to have returned with 'French politics and French predelictions', submitting 'sullenly to English domination and look forward to a change'.38 It was a development which the new British rulers were not too anxious to encourage, and by 1825 a school was opened in St Lucia under the auspices of the Anglican bishop with the overall objective 'to advance towards an ascendancy ... both the religion and the language of Englishmen'.39

However, as education became more popular, the parents often ignored the pressures exerted by the priests and sent their children to whatever school was available in the area in which they lived. For example, three-quarters of the children attending one Anglican parish school in Grenada were said to be Roman Catholics. This situation gradually changed and when the Trinidad government began to encourage the establishment of independent schools, a number of these were opened up by the Roman Catholics, with the

Multidenominational Caribbean

priests themselves teaching in order to overcome the shortage of Catholic teachers. Then, as these schools became established, the Roman Catholic children transferred from the non-Catholic to the newly opened Catholic schools. In 1826, with the assistance of small Government grants, two 'Public Free Schools' were opened by the Catholics in Arima, Trinidad, which the local Carib population who inhabited the area attended 'in very large numbers'. In 1829 the Catholics also established a school at North Naparima in Trinidad, which was supported by funds that the curate raised 'by selling spirits at a profit'. In that year they also made efforts to set up schools in Grenada especially in St George's, but their efforts to provide popular education really began to acquire momentum a few years after the abolition of slavery.

The Dissenting Missionaries

Despite the hurdles which they faced it was the nonconformist sects, particularly the Moravians, the Methodists and the Baptists who were most active in educating and converting the slaves and also the free blacks and coloureds to Christianity. Their view of education for the poor and the disadvantaged substantially differed from those held by the Anglicans, and some of them, particularly the Baptists felt, as the Secretary of The Society for Bettering the Conditions of the Poor put it, that in the acquisition of literacy and numeracy skills, 'the poor have as good a right to ... instruction ... as the greatest and most elevated of their fellow subjects'.40 As a result of this attitude they came into frequent conflict with the sugar planters of the West Indies and even the State machinery. For example, the Government of the Bahamas passed the Act of 1821 which placed Methodists, Baptists and other dissenting preachers in the category of 'rogues and vagabonds', while Governor Metcalfe of Jamaica complained bitterly of the attitude of the Baptist missionaries accusing them of 'inciting discontent' among the Negroes and 'obstructing good Government'. Nevertheless, despite the objections, these missionaries pushed ahead with their work and carried on their educational activities, even when they experienced violent opposition.

The Moravians

Apart from some individual sporadic efforts, it took about sixty years, after the Quakers had first started their religious and educational work in the West Indies, before another organised group of missionaries - the Unitas Fratrum, otherwise known as the Moravians - came to work in these colonies. They originated from Germany and successfully established the first Protestant mission in the New World in 1732 in what was then the Danish West Indies. From here, they turned their attention to Jamaica where four of them arrived in 1754 at the invitation of two absentee planters, Foster and Burnham, who had themselves been converted to the faith. Their assignment was to provide religious instruction to the slaves on the private estates of their sponsors.

Following their initial efforts, the Moravians expanded their activities to Antigua (1756), Barbados (1765), St Kitts (1777), Tobago (1789), and St Thomas. In Antigua they at first began by 'instructing individuals in private' and met with some success, with their membership reaching the point where they soon had to build a new church. It was probably the first time that the slaves had white persons showing any interest in them and the Moravians' initial increase in their number of followers from among the slaves might have been due to this fact. The initial efforts at educating the slaves were not very successful partly because of their long working hours which left them with no time for schooling except at night and on Sundays. Hence one of the key institutions which the Moravians used was the Sunday School and they were also the first to establish evening schools in the British West Indies.

At first, aspects of their work had to be undertaken clandestinely since the planters objected to their teaching the slaves to read - even though the Scriptures were used as the only basis of their reading lessons. Since one of the main concerns of

Multidenominational Caribbean

the Moravians was 'to work within the framework of the society as they found it' and to give the planters no cause for alarm about their work, they only taught the catechism and 'Bible Studies' and strongly emphasised the importance of the slaves submitting to their masters' will and being totally obedient to their orders. As a result they eventually met with little opposition from the whites and were quite successful in convincing most planters about the salutary effects of their work. Owners of the neighbouring estates to those on which they originally worked were so pleased with the impact of their teachings on the demeanour of the slaves - teachings which stressed 'humility and submissiveness rather than resistance' - that they too began to employ Moravians in a similar capacity, providing for them the necessary accommodation to conduct their educational activities. Two Moravian brothers were also invited to Berbice in 1783 but there they were regarded with great distrust by the planters and the Directors of the Berbice Association who were particularly fearful of another insurrection following the Berbice Slave Rebellion of 1763. They therefore had to move to a more remote location to work among the Amerindians.

In 1822, the Moravians started to turn their attention also to regular schooling and by 1826 they increasingly concentrated their efforts in this field. Their schools were small - 20 to 30 pupils each - and were mainly attended by children of the freed coloureds and blacks while their Sunday schools were heavily attended by slaves. The teaching of religion and reading was the main focus of their educational efforts and they also later ran a Refugee School for orphan girls in Jamaica 'to rescue them from the evil ways of worldly pleasure' and prepare them for teaching positions in their schools or as 'servants in respectable families'.

They were also responsible for conducting seven estate schools in Jamaica, each with an enrolment of 60-100 pupils and they operated a number of small schools for free children, employing coloured women as teachers at a small salary. Prior to emancipation they had about 800 Jamaican children in all their schools, half of whom were slaves, the other half free with just over 400 attending day schools. Their settlements in St Kitts also had 900 children who had been taught to read in their Sunday schools. The total number of free children in their day schools was quite modest but they continued to work in this area until the abolition of slavery and the introduction of the apprenticeship system in 1834 when all children who were six years of age and under became free. From then on they began to intensify their efforts at establishing day schools.

The Moravians enjoyed the support of the more prominent whites and even at the Colonial Office they were considered 'the very best Missionary body the world has ever seen since the first Propagation of Christianity'.41 They therefore did not evoke much bitterness on the islands in which they worked, largely because they never publicly criticised the planters or adversely commented on the institution of slavery. But while they became respected for their 'quiet and inoffensive manner' the response which they had from the slaves was, on the whole poor, even though their success varied from island to island. By 1804, after fifty years of activity in Jamaica, they had only 938 converts and in Barbados it was said that they enjoyed no more success than the Quakers whose early efforts on that island were far from successful. The overall assessment by Bridges of their work was that it was 'respectable, harmless and generally ineffective'42 and as far as converting slaves to Christianity was concerned, their achievement, as Patterson indicated, could only be rated as fair.

The Methodists

The Methodists, whose missionary activities in the West Indies really started in the early 1800s, became interested in working in the region after Dr T.Coke's first visit to Antigua around 1786. There he found a Society of 2,000 members, mainly slaves, which was established by a convert, Nathaniel Gilbert. The Methodists were well received in Antigua and their work there met with a fair degree of success. They were able to provide financial support for the

Multidenominational Caribbean

English Harbour School Society which conducted schools in English Harbour, St John's and Parham and Methodist Sunday Schools soon proliferated throughout the island. By 1793 it was said that the Methodists had about 6,570 members in Antigua, most of them being slaves.

In St Vincent they became interested in converting to Christianity the Indians who had survived when the British took over the island. Dr Coke requested financial assistance from the local legislature for the purpose of constructing a school and dwelling house for a teacher or teachers who were to be engaged in 'the civilisation and pious education of the Caribs'. They were to be instructed in the English Language, the Knowledge of the Holy Scriptures and such other branches of education as may render them 'useful members of society, both in the religious and commercial world'. Despite the fact that there were two teachers available and ready to 'enter on the laborious task' of educating the Carib children their proposals had to be withdrawn because of opposition from the local Roman Catholic Church, which saw the proposed project as an infringement of their own territory.

In 1788 the Methodists began operating in Barbados with the main intention of working with slaves and around 1790 they opened their first chapel in Jamaica with a second one two years later. However, they were not very much liked there and encountered opposition generally from those who were against the instruction of slaves on the island. It was only in those areas where they were preceded by the Moravians that opposition to their work was somewhat muted. Monk Lewis was, for example, quite willing to give free ingress and egress to his several estates to the missionaries of any Christian sect but with 'the Methodists as always, excepted'. Nevertheless by 1820 they had over 59 missionaries stationed throughout most of the West Indian islands stretching from Jamaica to Trinidad and Tobago.

The first Methodist missionary who went to Demerara in 1805 was refused permission to remain in the Colony when he informed the Governor that he intended to instruct the slaves in Christianity. Nevertheless, three years later the Methodists succeeded in getting their work started. They also turned their attention to the Bahamas where the sect was introduced around 1800 by coloured and black individuals from the American mainland. Among them was one Preacher Paul who opened up the earliest private Negro school in Nassau for free and slave children and taught them the '3 Rs'. Around 1801, William Turton, the first missionary to be appointed to the Bahamas by the British Methodist Conference began open-air preaching in Nassau and in 1803, with the assistance of his wife he established a day school 'for the instruction of Youths'. He had hoped that the profits from this establishment could be used to assist their evangelising activities. By the end of the first year he found it necessary to enlarge the school so that he could obtain a livelihood without being dependent on Mission funds. In 1804 he applied to the Methodist Missionary Society in London for a second missionary to be stationed in the Bahamas and in 1805 he travelled to the 'Out Islands' and established a day school in Rock Sound in 1806. By 1820 he opened another school in Green Turtle Cay, Abaco where he himself taught from Mondays to Thursdays. The formal education activities of the Methodists in the Bahamas were limited but their overall contribution, as Rodney Bain noted, was very wide and their real educational work was outside the classroom.43

While the Methodists were specially interested in the religious education of the Negroes they preached to all who listened, with the result that their membership, while mainly black, also had a substantial number of coloureds and a significant minority of whites. They operated day schools, evening classes and Sunday schools and the attendance at these institutions was not only mixed in terms of the racial background, but also in terms of age, with both adults and children enrolled in their classes. Because of their appeal to all races the Methodists had many local whites, both men and women engaged in teaching in their schools. But their success among the blacks was quite modest and they were not as popular among this group as were the Baptists. Their support was mainly from the coloureds who came to form the bulk of the middle class.

Multidenominational Caribbean

Possibly one reason for their limited success with the slaves was the generally negative attitude towards the Negroes held by some key Wesleyan personnel. For example the Secretary of the Methodist Missionary Society had described the Negroes as 'intemperate, lazy, superstitious, promiscuous, shameless, debased and vicious'.44 Despite these perceived flaws in their character they were regarded as capable of improvement through the 'hallowing influence' of Christianity since it was 'ignorance' which was said to be basically responsible for these behaviours and attitudes. This meant that they saw the Negroes to be in great need of religious instruction which would lead them to acquire sound Christian virtues.

In their work the Methodists soon adopted a posture somewhat similar to the Moravians by attempting to be very conciliatory and supportive of the plantocracy. Their missionaries were advised to work within the existing social order and not to attempt to interfere with or change it. However despite this approach they were not very successful in winning the planters' support and in some islands anti-Methodist sentiments remained strong. As a result they were often subject to discrimination and persecution and their meetings restricted to daylight hours when the slaves were at work. In Barbados, opposition to their activities reached its peak between 1816 and 1823, when a Methodist chapel on that island was demolished and the missionaries subjected to serious harassment and intimidation by the whites. While the Moravians were seen as 'peaceful, moral, industrious and painstaking', the Methodists were considered 'cunning, intriguing, fanatical, hypocritical canting knaves'.45

The number of converts to Methodism, especially among the coloured population increased over time, and as it did white opposition to it grew. But like the Moravians, the Methodists did not made significant inroads among the slave population who, as was previously indicated, identified themselves more readily with and became very receptive to the Baptists. Nevertheless in 1829 there were 662 scholars at their Willoughby Bay School which included 136 slaves, 51 younger slave children and

Multidenominational Caribbean

the remainder free. Four missionaries continued to minister to schools in Parham, St Johns, Sion Hill, Willoughby Bay and English Harbour. By 1832 there were fourteen Wesleyan Sunday schools in Antigua, attended by 1,852 slaves and 40 free blacks. In addition there were about 610 infants in their estate schools and a substantial number of children attending their 'out-of-crop', that is to say seasonal, schools. It was suggested that it was because the missionaries, especially the Methodists, had done such a good job in the education of slaves in Antigua, that the Assembly there decided in 1834 to set all its slaves free rather than putting them through the optional four year period of apprenticeship.

The Baptists

A concern for education was written into the constitution of the Baptist Missionary Society (BMS) and this contributed to its active involvement in education in Jamaica, towards the end of the eighteenth century. Here the Baptists saw themselves as having a special role to perform or challenge to meet, trying to demonstrate the intellectual equality of the Negroes. Their work in the West Indies was mainly confined to Jamaica although they also operated in the Bahamas. The movement was unique in that in both islands it was started by coloured men from the American South. The individual responsible for the Jamaican mission was an ex-slave by the name of George Lisle (or Liele) who was previously a pastor in a Baptist Church in Georgia. His preaching was particularly effective among the slaves and poor free blacks and because of their strong appeal to and popularity with this section of the population, the Baptists at first suffered severe persecution. This however began to decline as their popularity increased. By 1780 Lisle had about 15,000 followers from different parts of the country, many of whom had previously been Methodists. He also had teachers of small congregations in the town and country and with the assistance of 'thirteen school masters' founded a school for instructing the children of Negroes.

Multidenominational Caribbean

Another follower, Moses Baker, who was also a Negro American, reported similar success in the conversion of slaves, although he too experienced a great deal of persecution. In 1814 John Rowe, the first missionary from the British Baptist Missionary Society, arrived in Jamaica to assist the efforts of the local Baptists and soon opened a day school for poor children in Montego Bay along with a Sunday school. Some slaves were also permitted to attend the day school. However, the lack of funds limited the scope of his operations. Another individual by the name of Lee Compare was invited to open a chapel and a school on the 'Whims Estate' but moved to Kingston soon after. By 1818 a chapel, which was also being used as a school house, was opened up in Ocho Rios.

The educational work of the Baptist Society really began to flourish in Jamaica with the arrival of three outstanding Baptist missionaries from Britain - James Phillipo in 1823, Thomas Burchell in 1824 and William Knibb in 1825. The first school for slave children in Jamaica was started by Knibb not long after his arrival and later a school for girls operated under the Lancastrian system of monitorial instruction was also established by Phillipo and soon had an enrolment of 294 girls. The 'British school' established by Knibb was under a plan 'exactly resembling the Borough School' where he had been trained. The attendance at this school was between 132 and 140 out of an enrolment of 182 - a figure which later increased to 224. A day school was established at Wilberforce which had a large congregation, and its enrolment of 90 children soon increased to 130. A Sunday school was also organised and the enrolment here rose from 247 to 475.

In addition Phillipo set up a private day school in Kingston for the more advanced education of pupils. In it he offered 'classical and literary' studies including such subjects as Latin, Greek and Hebrew and charged regular fees. He had an enrolment of between 140 and 200 scholars and the proceeds from this school were used to subsidise the operation of his Lancastrian school which offered 'gratuitous instruction' to children of the poorer classes, 'slaves or free'. But because of the resistance in the Society to 'mixed schooling' that is schools that were not organised on colour or status lines, the experiment was not very successful. A Sunday school that was started by him was popular enough to attract a number of pupils and Phillipo was eventually asked to establish a school and a chapel on virtually every plantation in his district.

The Baptists set up mission stations with chapels and day and evening schools in various parts of the country including Kingston and Spanish Town. By 1831 they had 42 mission stations, 14 pastors, 24 churches and 10,838 members. In addition to the 'British School' in Kingston there was another in Spanish Town with a School of Industry where various trades were being taught. Phillipo also had 'a small and fluctuating number of day schools' under his superintendence. Finally, attached to almost every Baptist mission station, there was a Sunday school for both adults and children and these together had a total enrolment of about 2,500-3,000 individuals 'of all classes'.

By 1833 the Baptists had schools in all the main coastal towns of Jamaica and they were the most successful of all the sects in educating the slaves and the poor and converting them to Christianity. One reason for this success was that because of their militancy against the planters, they were seen as strong allies of the downtrodden, especially the slaves, even though they denied expressing abolitionist sentiments. It was the stridency of their approach and their attempts to ignore the colour and caste divisions in the society that increased white opposition to their work. Some of the more influential inhabitants of Kingston were said to have called on Phillipo to remonstrate with him about his efforts to revolutionise the country by attempting to put Negroes on a basis of equality with white men. The Baptists were even blamed by the local planters for inciting the Jamaica Slave Rebellion of 1823 for which William Knibb and others were arrested, with Knibb eventually being expelled from the colony. All their chapels were destroyed following this insurrection, and participants in this act of vandalism included regimental officers of the militia, magistrates and even two rectors of the Church of En-

Multidenominational Caribbean

gland. The Baptists also made a small but important contribution to educational developments in the Bahamas. They conducted day schools for children, Sunday schools for both adults and children and as in Jamaica were popular among the Negroes, especially the slaves on whom they concentrated their efforts.

The London Missionary Society

The London Missionary Society (LMS) which was founded in 1795 by missionaries and laymen of several denominations, considered the establishment of a 'mission for the poor blacks' a few years after being formed. So in 1808 they sent out the Rev. John Wray to Demerara and Richard Elliot to Tobago to start missions. Wray soon established a school for black children at Le Ressouvenir which had a daily attendance of about 20. Five years later he was transferred to Berbice to start another mission there and in Demerara he was succeeded by Rev. John Smith who was later accused of and court martialled for complicity in the East Coast Slave Insurrection of 1823. After Smith's incarceration and death in prison, the Society took a few years before it resumed its activities in that Colony. Possibly, as a result of Rev. Smith's fate, these new missionaries were even more cautious in their activities of teaching the slaves, confining themselves to the moral and religious, and ignoring the development of such skills as reading, which Wray had attempted to teach.

The work of the LMS was mainly concentrated in the colonies which now make up Guyana. The precarious existence of their schools and the sporadic attendance of pupils were due mainly to the problem which faced all educational efforts in the Caribbean, namely that the bulk of the child population was made up of slaves who were not usually permitted to attend school during regular school hours. However by 1833, the missionary Ketley, while noting that 'progress was slow', reported a membership of 230 while in 1834 John Wray's chapel in New Amsterdam was attended by 401 children, 66 adults at sabbath school, 20 at infant school and 40 at the Winckel day school.

In reviewing the work of the missionaries, particularly prior to emancipation, one sees that despite their tremendous efforts at providing religious and general education, especially for the black population, their success could, up to that point, only be described as modest. They faced many obstacles, chief among which was the lack of support and often active opposition by the planters, especially prior to the 1830s. The view about their activities expressed by Dalton would have been shared by the planters. He suggested that while the missionaries might have been 'virtuous' in their intentions, 'their conduct was deficient in judgement and prudence' for, by their actions,

> They awakened the slave to a sense of his degraded position in the scale of mankind. They inculcated doctrines of equality and liberty at variance with the laws of existence ... They could not preach the doctrines of Christ crucified to men whose hearts were branded with the stamp of slavery without uttering anathemas against its injustice and inhumanity. They present the fruit of the tree of knowledge of good and evil to ever curious man and persuaded him to taste, eat and live.46

But the work of the missionaries undoubtedly had impact on the behaviour patterns and attitudes of slaves which was beneficial to the planters. Their teachings helped to reduce the incidence of stealing among their members, possibly even fostering a more favourable attitude to their work, and generally ridding them of some of the 'vice and foppery', which was said to have happened among the slaves who attended the Bethesda School in Antigua. Richard Watson, writing in the 1820s about the outcomes of the missionary efforts, suggested that

> by the simple force of religious instruction, by the habits of submission to the commands of Heaven, which has been formed, by the creation of conscience and the fear of God ... the jealousies, brawls, strifes, fightings which were the product of every day life among slaves on the plantation have been supplanted.47

But despite denials to the contrary, one of the latent outcomes of the education which they provided was to raise the slaves' aspirations and hopes for freedom. Dalton was correct when he pointed out that the colonists were misguided in calling for a future prohibition of all missionaries in the future on the assumption that

> by excluding the missionaries, they could succeed in extinguishing the desire for knowledge and freedom amongst the negroes. The desire once awakened is not to be repressed by penal enactments ... the slave [now] needed no teacher to make him aspire to the blessings of liberty.48

In fact 'the ideas of independence ... had long taken deep root in his mind' and led to a conflict between the slaves' desire for freedom, which was stimulated by their education, and the fear among the planters that education might lead to more slave rebellions. This was the source of a major dilemma and led to 'a sharp division between planter attitudes towards education and the missionary hopes of the results of education' which was the 'Christianisation of slaves'.49

The enthusiasm for learning revealed by those who attended their schools and churches was an important motivating factor for the missionaries. The dedication which many of them displayed in their religious and educational activities, despite the physical hardships, the abuses and persecution which they often encountered, in addition to the high mortality rates in the islands, revealed a substantial degree of commitment to their chosen task of bringing 'Christian enlightenment' to the non-white population. It was this persistence, coupled with the overall positive response to their work by their members, which contributed to whatever success they might have achieved. Commenting on the educational situation in British Honduras around 1832, Martin noted that

> though there are still a great number of people who can neither read nor write, yet there are also many in the classes to which these acquire-

ments were formerly unknown, who have made considerable proficiency.50

An achievement to which the educational facilities provided by the missionaries 'has certainly in a very great degree contributed'. These remarks would have been equally applicable to most of the other British Caribbean territories at the time.

The impact of their educational efforts was not confined to those attending 'schools', and it is known that many pupils attempted to pass on what they learnt to their parents and even to other members of their community, sometimes earning 3 to 10 pence per week for doing such teaching. The 'spill-over' benefits to the community were recognised and the Bishop even told a group of candidates for holy orders that every hour which a minister spent in a parochial school was a day gained for his after-ministry activities. He therefore suggested that these parochial schools should be among the most cherished objects of ministerial care

> since the benefits derived from them are incalculable; from the children it is reflected on the parents, from the parents it diffuses throughout the neighbourhood.51

As far as the adult non-white population was concerned, a substantial number of them not only became literate but, because of their education, were able to develop their leadership abilities, which allowed them to play key roles in the administration and organisation of the local church activities. The number of those who could read was increasing steadily, and in 1813 a clergyman from St Kitts reported that he had 'lately been making some enquiries as to the number of negroes, either slaves or freemen that could read [and] I found their number greater than I could have expected'.52 By 1820 it was even suggested that the missionaries were slowly bringing about, by their educational efforts, 'an alteration in the tone' of life in Jamaica and in the other West Indian islands. However, looking more at the total picture one finds that, as Latimer noted, while there was a nucleus of Christian slaves who had received some education from the missionaries the great mass of them had remained non-Christian and illiterate.53

In assessing the West Indian situation as a whole Gordon made a similar point by noting that 'pre-emancipation society was ... not in any sense an educated one'.54 The real foundation of a system of education for the masses based on full-time attendance at day schools had to await the abolition of slavery in 1834.

MISSIONARY EFFORTS IN EDUCATION IN THE POST-EMANCIPATION PERIOD

With the provision for Negro Education by the British parliament following the emancipation of slavery, the missionary societies rapidly extended their educational activities in the region, seeing the school as a nursery for the recruitment of future church members. They therefore set about erecting as many schools as they could afford, to establish their respective 'spheres of influence' over as large a section of the population as possible. The views of the Baptists, who were probably the most aggressive group in this 'scramble for souls', were clearly expressed by Phillipo who pointed out that

> The whole land is before us and when once we take possession of it, which we as a denomination are doing in a most unexampled manner, the warfare to a great degree will be over.55

The type of sentiment which spurred the missionaries into action in providing schools for their flock was expressed by the Rev. William Crookes who in a letter to his parent body said that he mourned and wept to see the parents of 'our children' having to send their children to schools where a creed 'other than ours' was being taught.

This 'indiscriminate eagerness' by Societies to expand their influence through the establishment of schools led to inter- and intra-denominational rivalry and discontent which was said to have replaced some of the group solidarity that existed, at least among some of the missionaries during the days of slavery. The Baptists reacted strongly to the initial entry of the LMS into what they traditionally regarded as their domain while they in turn were resented and envied by other missionary groups because their chief objective was to gain 'numerical strength'. The Church of Scotland was also accused of baptising apprentices 'wholesale' in Berbice. The Evangelical Magazine, in referring to these conflicts, felt it necessary to remind the missionaries that there was still much work to be done, 'very much land to be possessed', and that it was only 'the natural depravity in our own hearts' which prevented 'cordial union' and cooperation among the different religious groups. The Rev. Sterling had even criticised the practice by the missionary societies of using funds which they had collected, to build chapels rather than schools. As a result the rate of increase in the amount of school accommodation provided in Barbados, and possibly elsewhere in the West Indies, was greater than percentage increases in school enrolment between 1834 and 1844.

These conflicts that developed between denominations over the question of territoriality naturally spilled over to all their activities in the field of education as, for example, when they attempted to vie with each other for acquisition of the same piece of land, in order to get their schools in a district completed before other Societies. This led to unnecessary proliferation of schools in an area and even Latrobe had to remark that, 'as might be expected from the little connection that exists between the different missionary bodies ... schools are very unequally distributed over the surface of the island' (of Jamaica) with an 'utter destitution of the means of instruction in entire districts'. Even in the more accessible coastal areas 'large tracts of well populated country may be marked in which there are no schools at all'.56

The 'over-servicing' of some areas with schools eventually resulted in competition for students. Monitors of rival schools were often bribed to induce students to transfer to the school of the 'opposition' group. This expansionist policy by most of the missionary societies was obviously not always in the interest of the education of the children but with no central body or authority to coordinate these activities it was impossible to have a more rational allocation of school buildings within and between the various islands. The Governor of Trinidad, in commenting on the issue, noted that the anxiety to establish schools by the various religious bodies operating on that island 'appears to originate more in a spirit of rivalry or jealousy than to be regulated by any sound principle'. He went on to add that

> the establishment of a school in a particular quarter or district by one Church or Party is instantly followed by a like establishment by another Party without reference to the wants of the neighbourhood; and all come to the public chest for assistance, whether the number of their pupils amounts to 5 or 50.57

A major concern of the authorities during this period was to ensure that there was a peaceful transition from a slave to a 'free' society without any radical changes in the existing social order. For this it was necessary to get the population, including the children at school, to internalise those values that would lead to their willing acceptance of their 'ordained place' within the social order. 'Moral reformation' or 'moral elevation' among the ex-slaves was considered necessary to achieve this goal. Secondly, attempts needed to be made to ensure that the Negroes remained industrious and did not simply abandon their traditional roles but continued to work as labourers on the sugar estates. They also had to be taught to be 'responsible' and therefore 'reasonable' in their wage demands because without these qualities it was suggested that the whole economy of the region would eventually collapse.

By now the planters were generally willing to allow the various missionary societies to undertake the task of educating the Negro population because, in general, they also shared or accepted most of the social objectives of the planter class and could be 'trusted' to carry on as most of them had previously done, their moral and religious instruction 'with great deference to the understood needs of the social order'. For example, Caldecott noted that the fostering of the virtue of industry was a constant subject of pastoral advice during this period because no one knew better than the Churchmen the 'prime necessity of industrial habits' if the cause of religion was to prosper.58 Cox, a Wesleyan missionary, also repeatedly made the point that for the further development and maintenance of a civilised country the young needed to be 'trained to labour' and to acquire 'habits of application to industry' while Phillipo too indicated that he was convinced that if the Negroes were educated 'a more virtuous, enlightened and industrious people will nowhere exist'.59

Consequently the most important subject in the curriculum of the elementary schools became 'religious or scriptural instruction'. It was not only listed and taught as a separate subject but it also pervaded the entire instructional programme of all the elementary schools in the Caribbean. It was largely because the British Government considered that a religious and moral focus ought to be the major element in the education of the emancipated Negroes that it finally decided against secular control of education in these territories which was one of the options that it was considering at the time. The involvement of the Mico Charity in this educational endeavour was only made possible because, even though it was a non-denominational organisation, it was heavily committed to the same educational and religious goals as the missionary societies. Religious instruction and reading therefore came to occupy most of the time in schools and so important and closely integrated were these two subjects that many authorities came to regard them almost as the sum total of the curriculum that schools should offer free of charge to the children of the Negro population.

One controversy over the curriculum which developed with the planters was the teaching of practical subjects in the schools. The missionary bodies did not entirely lack interest in the subject of 'practical' or 'industrial' training although there was a marked difference among them as to the importance they attached to it. The Anglicans were probably the group that was most accommodating to the wishes of the planters to have the schools offer 'agriculture education'. For example, the Bishop of Barbados expressed much concern about the need to ensure that there would be an adequate supply of labourers for the sugar estates after the 'apprenticeship' period had come to an end. The Moravians were also very supportive of the idea of introducing practical instruction in their schools and did quite a lot in this area. In 1839 the Rev. Ellis, Superintendent of the Moravian schools in Barbados, suggested that young people ought to be trained in the habits of industry and 'even in early life' they should be taught the use of agricultural implements and be initiated into the mode of cultivating the soil.

The Baptists who, perhaps most strongly, felt that education should help to prepare at least some of the Negroes for occupational mobility outside the role of estate labourers, were also not against the principle of 'industrial training' even though they were opposed to the suggestion that it should be made compulsory and to the fact that it was restricted to agriculture which they saw as a means of prolonging the occupational relationships which characterised slave society. Nevertheless many of their ministers had plans to introduce the subject in their own schools although some of them later began to come around to the view that the betterment of the Negro could only take place by their escape from estate labour.

The Wesleyans while not openly objecting to the teaching of the subject were curiously silent on the issue. However, they had developed plans to introduce the Glasgow Moral Training System in their schools - a system which ruled out the possibility of combining literary education with agricultural instruction. In other words, agriculture or any other form of 'industrial training' did not form a part of the scheme of instruction which they advocated and in fact none of these practical subjects could have easily fitted into the comprehensive and integrated curriculum programme which they were proposing. While their scheme did not get off the ground their preferred educational strategy was indicative of the marginal importance which they attached to the teaching of agriculture in the elementary schools. As Burke pointed out, there was in these early days 'no modicum of agricultural training in their (the Methodists') schools' because they also shared the views of the Baptists that

> to prove the intellectual capacity of the Negro he must be allowed to absorb a type of literary education lest the study of agriculture tie him to his past condition.60

However, although some of the missionary bodies were not totally enthusiastic about the teaching of agriculture in schools they were all concerned with developing in the young Negroes a 'healthy' attitude to work. Some of them even felt that this could best be done through an active programme of religious and moral education because they feared that to insist on the teaching of agriculture would have deterred the 'apprentices' from sending their children to school since they still associated agriculture with slavery.

Another area of educational activity that was given a boost during this period, especially with some assistance from the Negro Education grant was that of teacher education. While the Mico Charity initially played the most important role in establishing Normal Schools in the region, some of the missionary societies also began to organise their own teacher training facilities, though in the majority of cases their numbers were very small.

On the whole, it was obvious that the work of the missionaries helped to provide a marked increase in the amount of educational facilities that were available throughout the region, especially in the post-emancipation period. Nevertheless only a small percentage of children of school age did receive the benefit of an education during this period. At no time would the number of available school places have been adequate enough, if those eligible to attend school all wanted to do so. It was estimated that only about 10 per cent of the total number of 'apprentices' and the younger children who were freed immediately on the passing of the Emancipation Act, were receiving some type of education and this was probably 'irregular, unsustained and intermittent'. The percentage attending regular day schools made up roughly one-third of those receiving some form of education but this figure increased substantially over the next few years. The Methodist Superintendent, Armstrong, noted that the subject of education had become so universally popular in the immediate post-emancipation period, that it ceased to be a matter of choice on the part of the missionary societies, whether or not they should establish schools at their principal stations. So despite what might, in actual numbers, be seen as slow progress, thousands of West Indian children were being introduced to some form of popular education and the idea of some elementary education for the children of the masses was gradually but irrevocably being accepted by the ruling class.

Apart from the unavailability or inaccessibility of schools, attendance and enrolment were low, not only because of the socio-economic conditions of the parents and the incidence of ill health among the children but also because of the negative attitude to education which some parents seemed to have later developed. Their former enthusiasm for having their children formally educated seemed to have waned as it became obvious to them that the education which was being given to their children was not providing them with the opportunity for occupational mobility for which they had hoped, nor with the skills which might have been of use to them in earning a living, especially outside the ambit of the sugar plantations. While there was much emphasis put on the quantitative increase in school places the issue of quality seemed to have been given less attention. There was the major and sometimes unquestioned assumption about the value to the ex-slaves of the knowledge and skills which the schools tried to impart. Their education was mainly intended to 'gentle the masses' by teaching them to accept their 'ordained' position in the social order and prepare them for the 'life hereafter'. The missionaries generally paid little attention to the kind of education that the parents wanted for their children and the kind that might help them to improve the physical, as apart from the moral quality of life in these societies. This was because they tended to ignore the role of education in social and economic mobility of the black population, though this concern was beginning to intrude on some of them, particularly the Baptists.

The poor quality of the education offered and the teaching methods used, dominated as the were by the monitorial system, came in for much criticism from independent observers. Even the Baptists began to recognise that the poor quality of the teaching was affecting their ability to keep their students at school and in 1844 they introduced a scheme whereby their teachers' salaries depended on the number of students which the schools could retain. But the conditions under which these teachers worked and their own low level of academic and professional training also contributed heavily to the poor performance of the students. Nevertheless, while the success of the schools seemed to have been uneven there was some general improvement among the students both in the 'common branches of instruction' and in their 'behaviour'. This was especially so for those who had come to school for the first time and did not 'know their ABC's'. As Bewley, the Methodist missionary observed, 'the results of the efforts of the missionaries varied considerably. In some instances children responded well, learned their lessons and improved morally; and in others progress was slow or non-existent'.61 Teachers placed considerable emphasis on cleanliness and tidiness among the children, and their personal appearance improved as a result of the insistence that they come to schools in clean and proper clothing. In referring to the students attending schools he observed that 'their apparel is clean and decent' and this no doubt had an indirect effect on the personal habits of the parents who had to prepare these clothes for their children and had to ensure that they took their baths before sending them off to school. While the claims made by the missionaries of the amount of moral improvement that took place among the children

Multidenominational Caribbean

as a result of their education was often exaggerated, some progress also seems to have been made in this direction. There were reported to be less incidence of 'lying and stealing' among those who had attended school and a general improvement in their 'manners'. They were supposedly more 'courteous'.

While some of the children later lost their ability to read because of the difficulty, especially in the less accessible rural areas, of obtaining reading materials on which to practise their skills, others were able to prevent this loss from occurring by their constant reading of the scriptural pamphlets that became available in many communities through the efforts of the various missionary societies. Others became exposed to reading materials outside the Bible and religious pamphlets, especially the newspapers which were becoming increasingly available locally through the efforts of the more educated coloured and black journalists. This wider reading began to raise the level of political awareness, at least among some of the masses, and partly resulted in an increasing dissatisfaction with the existing distribution of political power. With the ability to communicate, discuss and express their ideas, along with training for leadership roles both within the schools and the churches which some of them acquired, they began to agitate for changes in the existing political, social and economic system. And although the concessions granted to them at any point in time were marginal they were cumulative in their effect and provided increased opportunity for a few to rise up the social ladder. As early as 1837 the Secretary to the Governor of Antigua, a key position in the colonial bureaucracy, was 'an agreeable intelligent young man of colour' and in other territories like Jamaica, Trinidad, Grenada, Guyana and Barbados, the coloured and later the black population was gradually moving up the occupational ladder.

Others were able to further their education through the Normal Schools and became teachers and catechists and in some cases even ministers of religion. For example, a Baptist missionary report indicated, possibly with a slight exaggeration, that:

> Hundreds of youths of both sexes who, but for the moral and religious influence these schools have exerted, (on them) would have been ... the subjects of degradation and poverty (but instead) have risen to honourable distinction in the middling walks of life, whilst scarcely a year has passed but has witnessed the accession of many of them to the Church of God.62

The overall level of educational provision, however, still left much to be desired. In reviewing the educational situation in Jamaica during these early years - one which was probably quite similar to that found in most other colonies in the region at the time - it was noted that the educational facilities there were

> poor and limited in extent. Inter-denominational rivalry, the absence of Government inspection, ... lack of trained staff, together with the dishonesty of self-styled school proprietors claiming grants for fictitious schools, robbed the country of much real benefit (from these initial educational efforts). In many cases instruction was only nominal; the teachers were often 'ignorant, uneducated men not decently clad' and the children dirty and ragged.63

In addition to preparing some individuals for advancement in the Church and in the teaching profession, the education provided gave many of them the spiritual solace which helped them to endure the hardships which the society imposed on the Negro population. In other words it performed a 'cooling off' function among the masses. It did not however, as yet, seriously attempt to provide them with the skills needed to grapple with the economic realities of West Indian societies. The socialisation process on which the missionaries still attempted to focus their efforts was essentially geared towards building up among the young black population their acceptance of and moral support for, the existing social order, dominated as it still was by the economic interests of the white planters, and their own place on the lowest rungs of the social heirarchy.

Multidenominational Caribbean

The schools in the West Indies, Belize and Guyana continue to be operated partly by Government and partly by various denominational bodies. The percentage of schools run by any of these groups varies considerably from territory to territory. However in Guyana all schools were recently taken over and are now operated by the Government while in some islands nearly all schools have remained denominational. Over 90 per cent of all pupils between the ages of 5 and 12 attend these schools. Even in Government schools Christian religious influence still exists either in hymn singing and in morning and afternoon prayers.

The population of the region has remained quite religious and Church attendance, especially on Sundays and on holy days, is quite high. It is only Guyana and Trinidad that have a substantial number of non-Christians - mainly Hindus and Moslems - among the population.

NOTES AND REFERENCES

General Note

It is obvious that while a single term 'missionaries' was used to describe individuals from various religious sects carrying out educational and religious work in the West Indies, they were not, in any way, a homogenous group. Some were more 'elitist' in their outlook and tended to identify more with the interest of the planters. Others, like the Baptists, were more populist in their orientation and identified more closely with the poor blacks, especially the slaves.

It is difficult to specify the motivation among the various groups. Some were obviously pursuing their own economic interests. Others were more genuinely concerned with the spiritual welfare of their members and saw themselves carrying out a 'higher duty' in trying to 'save their souls'. They were therefore either not fully aware of, or refused to recognise the inconsistency between their concern for their followers and the compromises they made with the sugar planters about teaching the slaves to be content with their 'lot in life'. For the Baptists it might be argued that, because their missionaries, who originally came to work in Jamaica and the Bahamas, had a similar cultural capital to that shared by their followers, they were able to appreciate more fully the slaves' conditions and therefore found it easier to relate to them. On the other hand it can be said that, since the Baptists initially had no financial support from an overseas parent body, they had to depend heavily on their members to carry out their work and this was, to a large extent, responsible for the more populist orientation which they developed.

1. Hughes, H.B., Christian Missionary Society in the British West Indies During the Emancipation Era, unpublished Ph.D thesis, University of Toronto, 1944, p.109.

2. Hodgson, Capt. Studholme, Truth from the West Indies, London: William Ball, 1839, pp.35-6.

3. Hans, Nicholas, 'The Anglican Tradition in Education' in Usill, Harley, V. (ed.), Yearbook of Education, 1938, London: Evans Bros. Ltd., pp.778-9.

4. Ibid., p.779.

5. Quoted by Hans, Nicholas, op.cit., p.781.

6. Fox, George, 'To The Ministers, Teachers and Priests in Barbados', London (1672), quoted in Bridenbaugh, Carl and Roberta, No Peace Beyond the Line, New York: Oxford University Press, 1972, p.357.

7. Bridenbaugh, Carl and Roberta, No Peace Beyond the Line, New York: Oxford University Press, 1972, p.397.

8. Ibid., p.398.

9. Rooke, Patricia T., The Christianisation and Education of Slaves and Apprentices in the British West Indies: the Impact of Evangelical Missionaries (1800-1838), unpublished Ph.D thesis, University of Alberta, 1977, p.128.

10. See Watson, Richard, The Religious Instruction of Slaves in the West India Colonies, London: Butterworth & Son, 1824, p.7.

11. Dalton, Henry G., The History of British Guiana, London: Longman, Brown, Green and Longmans, 1855, vol.1, p.155.

12. Smith, Raymond T., British Guiana, London: Oxford University Press, 1962, p.145.

13. Instruction for Missionaries to the West India Islands, West India pamphlets, The Church Missionary Society of the Anglican Church, 1795, Sec.xvi, p.7.

14. Missionary Register, Wesleyan Methodist Missionary Society, November 1818, pp.484-6.

15. Baptist Missionary Society, Letter of Instruction, London, n.d., p.13.

16. Quarterly Chronicle of Transactions of the CMS 1815-20, 1:521, quoted in Rooke, Patricia T., op.cit., p.128.

17. See Phillipo, James M., Jamaica, Its Past and Present State, London, 1843, published by John Snow, p.429, originally quoted in Martyr of Erromanga, p.19.

18. Dalt, Vere T., A Short History of the Guyanese People, Georgetown, Guyana, 1966, p.254.

19. Reported in Harlow, V. and Madden, F., British Colonial Developments 1774-1834, Oxford: Clarendon Press, 1953, pp.584-5.

20. Tannenbaum, Frank, Slavery and Citizen, New York: Alfred A. Knopf, 1947, pp.82-3.

21. Rooke, Patricia T., op.cit., p.196.

22. Green, William A., *British Slave Emancipation: The Sugar Colonies and the Great Experiment 1830-1865*, Oxford: Clarendon Press, 1976, p.327.

23. CO 29/30, *Circular Despatch from Lord Bathurst to West Indian Governors*, dated 9th July 1823, Public Record Office, London.

24. 'The Prayer of the Little Negro' from *Missionary Stories*, 1842, p.7, quoted in Rooke, Patricia T., op.cit., p.158.

25. Reckord, Mary, *Missionary Activity in Jamaica before Emancipation*, unpublished Ph.D. thesis, University of London, 1964, p.13.

26. Stampp, Kenneth, 'Christianity in Slave Society' in Frucht, Richard (ed.), *Black Society in the New World*, Toronto: Random House, 1971, op.cit., pp.285-6.

27. Bain, Rodney E., *Education Policy in the Bahamas up to 1823 and its Determinants*, unpublished M.A. thesis, University of London, 1959, op.cit., p.182.

28. Quoted in ibid., p.212.

29. Ibid.

30. Wright, Philip (ed.), *Lady Nugent's Journal of her Residence in Jamaica from 1801 to 1805*, Kingston, Jamaica, 1966, p.xxxi.

31. CO 318/122, *The Sterling Report*.

32. Martin, R., *History of the West Indies*, London, 1837, vol.2, p.254.

33. Quoted in Bhagan, C., *A Critical Study of the Development of Education in Trinidad*, unpublished M.A. thesis, University of London, 1965, p.37.

34. Samarusingh, J.A.R.K., The History of Education in Trinidad and Tobago from Earliest Times to 1900, unpublished Ph.D. thesis, University of London, 1964, pp.134-5.

35. Coleridge, Henry, Six Months in the West Indies in 1825, New York: Negro Universities Press, 1970, pp.130-1.

36. Ibid., p.131.

37. Coke, Thomas, An Account of the Rise, Progress and Present State of the Methodist Missions, London, 1804, p.5.

38. Coleridge, Henry, op.cit., p.131.

39. Ibid., p.132.

40. Quoted by Hans, Nicholas, op.cit., p.780.

41. CO 318/152, Stephen to Hope, 11th November 1841, p.291.

42. Bridges, G.W., 'The Annals of Jamaica', vol.1, p.548. Quoted by Patterson, Orlando, in The Sociology of Slavery, London: MacGibbon & Kee Ltd., 1967, p.209.

43. Bain, Rodney, op.cit.

44. Rooke, Patricia T., op.cit., p.54.

45. Williams, C., Tour Through Jamaica 1826, p.37, quoted in Patterson, Orlando, op.cit., p.210.

46. Dalton, Henry G., op.cit., vol.1, p.323.

47. Watson, Richard, The Religious Instruction of Slaves in the West India Colonies, London: Butterworth and Son, 1824, p.22.

48. Dalton, Henry., op.cit., vol.1, p.323.

49. Rooke, Patricia T., op.cit., p.161.

50. Martin, R., op.cit., vol.1, p.158.

51. The Theological Tract, British Museum, 1269, pp.50-1.

52. Reported in Hughes, H.B., op.cit., p.185.

53. Latimer, James, 'The Apprenticeship System in the British West Indies', in Journal of Negro Education, vol.33, 1964, p.2.

54. Gordon, Shirley C., A Century of West Indian Education, London: Longman, 1963, p.18.

55. Underhill, Edward B., Life of James Murchell Phillipo, London, 1881, p.139.

56. Latrobe, C.J., Negro Education, Jamaica, Report to Lord Glenelg, 19th October 1837, Public Record Office, London, p.10.

57. CO 295/130. No.10, Governor of Trinidad to Secretary of State for the Colonies, 1st May 1940.

58. Caldecott, A., The Church in the West Indies, London: Frank Cass & Co. Ltd., 1970, first published in 1898.

59. Phillipo, James M., Jamaica: Its Past and Present State, 1838, op.cit.

60. Burke, Mavis E., The History of the Wesleyan-Methodist Contribution to Education in Jamaica in the Nineteenth Century 1833-1900, unpublished M.A. thesis, University of London, 1965, p.251.

61. Wesleyan School Reports, 1838, by T.H. Bewley, quoted in Ryall, Dorothy A., The Organisation of Missionary Societies and the Recruitment of Missionaries in the Diffusion of British Culture in Jamaica During the Period 1834-65, unpublished Ph.D. thesis, University of London, 1959.

Multidenominational Caribbean

62. <u>Baptist Magazine</u>, Baptist Missionary Society, 1840, p.270.

63. Government of Jamaica, <u>Report of the Department of Education 1950</u>, Kingston, Jamaica: Government Printers, p.2.

10
CHRISTIAN DENOMINATIONS AND THE DEVELOPMENT OF PRIVATE EDUCATION IN CHILE

Ruth Aedo Richmond

INTRODUCTION

The main focus of this chapter will be the specific contribution made by Christian churches and organisations to the provision of private education in Chile. While non-Christian religions have not been entirely absent from Chile's socio-cultural history, their general impact has been quite restricted and their educational influence small. This is clearly the case of the indigenous Indian people, such as the Mapuches, the Quechua and Aymara. It has been estimated that, out of a total of 468,000 Indians in 1970, just over one-fifth were non-Catholics. Native religions, however, have not themselves generated formal educational institutions; instead, formal education for Chile's Indian groups has been the outcome of efforts by either the Catholic Church or the State, although some evangelical activities conducted by Protestant denominations have had educational facets.

The dominant religious institution in Chilean history has been the Roman Catholic Church, which has left its mark upon the entire national culture and upon education in particular. The Catholic Church had sole responsibility for education in Chile prior to Independence. Much of the analysis which follows will constitute an overview of the main trends in the provision of private education by the Catholic Church since the formation of the Republic. Developments in Catholicism in Chile will be related to the educational role performed by the Catholic Church. In addition, the analysis will examine the growing but still minority churches of Protestant persuasion and the contribution they have made to the nation's private education.

CATHOLIC AND PROTESTANT SCHOOLS IN CHILE: FROM INDEPENDENCE TO THE SEPARATION OF CHURCH AND STATE IN 1925

During the first three decades of the nineteenth century, the Catholic Church in Chile was torn by a serious division between those who remained loyal to the Spanish Crown and those who transferred their allegiance to the new republic. Although Catholicism continued to be the accepted religion of the country, the Catholic Church was by no means wholly secure owing to the spread of Liberalism and the assertion by the new State of its power and jurisdiction. The eagerness of O'Higgins to develop the nation's education and his strained relations with the Catholic hierarchy go some way towards explaining the welcome given to James Thompson in the early 1820s. Thompson was a representative of the British and Foreign Bible Society who arrived in Chile in 1821 as part of a visit to several South American countries. O'Higgins took a great interest in the Lancasterian system of mutual instruction which Thompson promoted.1 With official Government support, Thompson established Lancasterian schools, in Santiago and Valparaiso, where the monitorial system was adopted. Foreign teachers, including two Protestants from England, were brought in to apply the Lancasterian method. In 1822, the Lancasterian Society was created with the support of several prominent citizens including O'Higgins.2 The Lancasterian schools, however, did not long survive the collapse of the Government. Without the protection and support provided by O'Higgins, the venture floundered; moreover, the Protestant aspects of the Thompson schools gave rise to considerable disquiet in Catholic circles.

The sense of insecurity felt by the Catholic Church was even greater when, between 1824 and 1830, its goods and properties were sequestrated by the Liberal Government. As far as education was concerned, the schools run by the Church were forced to close during this period and they did not reopen until the 1830s. While the fortunes of the Catholic Church certainly revived after 1830, there was to be no return to the position enjoyed during the colonial period.

The victory of the Conservatives in 1830 and the establishment of the Oligarchic Republic brought about the restoration to the Catholic Church of the goods and properties taken from it during the previous decades. This arrangement was conditional upon the Church agreeing to open primary schools and resume its educational duties. The Catholic religious orders already established in Chile (the Dominicans, Augustinians, Franciscans and Mercedarians) proceeded to open elementary schools in Santiago and elsewhere; secondary education, however, took longer to appear.

The precise relationship between Church and State was established through the Political Constitution of 1833. Roman Catholicism was recognised as the official religion of the Republic and the public exercise of all other religious faiths was prohibited. The executive power of the State was dedicated to the protection of the Catholic religion. However, to the great dismay of the Church and the Vatican, the Constitution asserted the State's right to exercise the powers of ecclesiastical patronage. Those powers were largely concentrated in the hands of the President, although the Senate and the Council of State had a role to play. The President, for example, had the power to nominate candidates for the highest ecclesiastical offices of the Catholic Church in Chile, but appointments were subject to the approval of the Senate. Thus, while there was no separation of Church and State, the superiority of the latter was clearly enshrined in the Constitution. This position was evident in the area of education, for the Constitution of 1833,3 established, through the doctrine of the <u>Estado Docente</u>, the fundamental and inalienable responsibility of the State for the nation's education. Clearly, therefore, the Church's monopoly of education was broken; the educational work undertaken by the Church in no way compromised the prior authority of the State in educational matters. It was only through the theory and practice of the Estado Docente that the very idea of private education could emerge distinctly; initially, all private education in Chile was that provided by the Catholic Church and private lay Catholics.

The amount of private schooling provided by the Catholic Church during the Autocratic Republic increased gradually. At the primary level, the Catholic Church continued to provide the overwhelming proportion of educational facilities; a small amount was provided by municipalities. The State had little direct interest or involvement in primary education during the 1830-1860 period; the dominant elites in Chile saw no justification for extending educational services to the mass of the people. The State's direct contribution to educational provision was more evident at the secondary level. Apart from supporting the Instituto Nacional and several provincial schools, the State preserved its right of administrative supervision and overall orientation over the nation's secondary education. In addition, small amounts of financial assistance were given by the State to Catholic schools and to private schools run by lay Catholics. Nevertheless, it would be a mistake to minimise the contribution made by the Catholic Church to secondary schooling during this period. The educational work of the Catholic Church was supplemented by the activities of newly-arrived religious orders, especially after 1834 with the re-establishment of the seminaries. The first to arrive were the French nuns belonging to the Order of the Sacred Heart (Sagrados Corazones, SS.CC.), who set up their first school in 1838 in Valparaiso, with a second school being established in 1841 in Santiago. These schools were devoted to educating girls from upper class backgrounds, with French language as a fashionable element of the curriculum. In June 1853, the creation of a normal school for women was approved by the Senate and the nuns of the Sacred Heart order were invited to operate this school. The curriculum for this normal school included reading and writing, religious education, sacred history and church history, Spanish grammar, arithmetic, sewing and embroidery.4 The male branch of the Sagrados Corazones in Chile also arrived in Valparaiso, where the fathers of this order set up their first secondary school in 1849. Their educational work was later extended to Santiago.

During the Bulnes administration,5 invitations were made to foreign clergy to undertake missionary activities among Chile's Indian populations in the south. In 1848, the first Capuchin missions from the Italian Provinces arrived in Chile. Their immediate activities focused upon missionary and educational work among the Mapuche Indians, who were by no means friendly or welcoming. In 1850, the Capuchins founded their first mission in Bajo Imperial (now Puerto Saavedra). Within two months of being founded, the mission had attracted 28 students, all of whom were Araucanian. The education given was basically the 'three R's' and the catechism. Eventually, the Italian Capuchins founded 20 missions, set up six elementary schools and opened boarding schools for Araucanian students which had an enrolment of 300 by the end of the century.

The ending of the prohibition on the Jesuits in 1850 opened the door for this Catholic order, whose name was particularly associated with educational work, to resume its activities in Chile. In 1856, the Jesuits' first school was opened in Santiago, the Colegio San Ignacio. Additional secondary schools were opened by the Jesuits in Valparaiso, Chillan and Puerto Montt within a short space of time. The Jesuits introduced their own educational programme into the Colegio San Ignacio; this programme, though academically rigorous, was different from that pursued in the Instituto Nacional. As a result, the students from the Colegio were unable to enter for the examinations conducted by the Instituto Nacional which were prerequisites for a university career. This situation raised many issues which fuelled the debate over 'Freedom of Education' (Libertad de Ensenanza), and stimulated some early thinking about setting up a Catholic university.

While the Jesuits and the Order of the Sacred Heart directed most of their educational work towards the upper echelons of Chilean society, the Brothers of the Christian Schools (Hermanos de las Escuelas Cristianas) focused their attention upon the poorer sectors of the population. From 1855 onwards, the

Private Education in Chile

Hermanos set up craft schools known as the Talleres de San Vicente in lower class districts of Santiago. Similar types of schools were established by the Dominicans. According to Fisher:

> The year 1869 saw the creation of the St. Thomas Aquinas Society for Catholic Education, from which emanated day schools, adult night classes and workshop courses for adolescents with vocational instruction for the shoe, cigarette, confectionery and pastry trades.6

The foregoing analysis of the educational contribution made by various Catholic orders during the Autocratic Republic supports the view that the Catholic Church was the dominant force in the field of private education. There were, of course, a number of schools run by Catholic lay individuals, the precise number of which is difficult to ascertain.7 The period of the Autocratic Republic, however, also saw the beginning of a new phenomenon in Chilean private education, namely, the setting up of schools with Protestant, rather than Catholic, connections. Though making only a very small contribution to the total provision of education in Chile, these schools were associated with significant development not only in Chile's socio-economic life but also with important legal and political changes. It must be remembered, however, that these 'Protestant' schools were not, at this time, comparable with the schools run by the Catholic Church, for they were not operated as Protestant church schools as such. Rather, they were schools founded and run by individual Protestants or by immigrant communities. An example of the former was Trumbull's free-school in Valparaiso created in 1847, while the latter is best illustrated by the schools in Osorno, Valdivia and Llanquihue set up in the early 1850s by German Lutheran immigrants.

Perhaps the most significant aspect of these schools was that they were allowed to open and operate at all, despite opposition from various Catholic quarters and despite the apparent constraints imposed by the Constitution. The de facto toleration of these Protestant schools was largely based on the fact that they were not evangelical in character and were designed to meet the educational needs of foreigners rather than Chileans. These foreigners, furthermore, came from countries which were deeply involved in Chile's commercial, industrial and agricultural development. In these circumstances, a form of wise pragmatism prevailed, it being considered counter-productive to give gratuitous offence to these foreigners by denying them the opportunity to have their children taught according to the language, religion and customs of their own countries. It must be emphasised that the <u>Ley Interpretativa</u> of 1865,8 gave legal approval to a situation which already existed but which needed regularising in order to remove doubts and uncertainties which could have damaged Chile's relations with major Protestant powers in Europe and North America. The <u>Ley Interpretativa</u>, by permitting freedom of worship in private establishments and by allowing private schools to be set up by Protestants for the purpose of educating their children, was a significant milestone in Chile's development of a more tolerant outlook. Religious toleration was typically associated with the currents of Liberalism and Radicalism which were gathering pace at this time.

In order to secure a proper appreciation of developments between 1865 and 1925, it should be understood that the <u>Ley Interpretativa</u> did not expressly permit or encourage the growth of Protestant missionary activity in Chile. The original justification of the Protestant-run schools which appeared after 1865 was to provide an education for non-Catholic foreigners in the country; they were not set up to spread Protestantism amongst the Catholic population. However, it so happened that, for a variety of reasons, some Chileans were attracted to the kind of education offered by the Protestant schools. Some Catholic Chileans with liberal or radical views, for example, were fearful of their children being indoctrinated by dogmatic Catholic priests and preferred the more secular but by no means irreligious education available in Protestant schools. The 1860s and 1870s were particularly notorious for the fierce antagonism between Conservatives and Liberals, each of whom deeply distrusted the motives and intentions of their opponents in educational matters. The ideological bias of history textbooks was an especially bitter focus of debate. Liberals such as Diego Barros Arana and Miguel Luis Amuntegui were anxious that private secondary schools should adopt the texts recommended by the University of Chile; these texts reflected secular and anti-clerical views which were anathema to the Catholic Church and its champion, the Conservative Party.9 In the context of these controversies, some of the Protestant schools appeared to be less objectionable to parents who disliked the Catholic Church's educational influence. Other reasons were also persuasive, for example, the Protestant schools were believed to offer a higher standard of education than could be obtained elsewhere in Chile. Some Chileans, especially within elite circles, saw foreign schools as more prestigious, and mastery of a second language was highly valued.

A prominent figure in the development of Protestant schools in Chile was Dr David Trumbull, an American Congregationalist pastor whose name is particularly associated with the **Escuela Popular** of Valparaiso which he set up in 1870. This school, which had had an unsuccessful forerunner during the earlier period, was created to provide primary education for the children of poor members of the English-speaking community in Valparaiso. Trumbull, along with other leading American and British residents, was concerned about the moral risks facing children in that thriving seaport; his missionary activities, therefore, were confined to saving the souls of young Protestants. The **Escuelo Popular** was a successful venture which survived long into the next century. The **Educational Yearbook** of 1933 gives the following characterisation of its activities:

> Public school methods, as developed in the United States, are followed in the **Escuelo Popular**, and the principals are women trained in that country. The central school has an attractive building, erected in 1910, which accommodates 400 pupils, and there are also accommodations in the building for twenty girl boarders and the

principal. The course begins with the kindergarten and continues for eight years. In the last years all the studies are in English. There is daily Bible instruction and all the upper-class students have Bibles. There are a number of branch schools in the city.10

Mention of the 'upper class students' points to a departure from the original character of the school; in addition, Spanish appears to have been used for some teaching in the initial school years. In 1933, there were 505 pupils enrolled in the main Escuela Popular in Valparaiso, with a teaching staff of 20, a quarter of whom were foreign.

The next major development regarding Protestant schools is associated with the name of a Methodist bishop, William Taylor. By being closely linked with the Methodist Church of the United States, Taylor's schools probably qualify as the first Protestant mission schools in Chile in any strict sense of that term. Two secondary schools were established in 1880: Santiago College and the Iquique English College. These schools, which were to be self-supporting, were designed for the children of the upper class families in the British and American communities. There is ample evidence to show that Taylor was initially approached by leading figures in the Chilean Government, including President Pinto and the Minister of Education, Amunategui.11 Their motives in inviting Taylor to establish his school in Chile cannot be separated from their desire to promote educational developments of a more secular and progressive orientation. Soon after its formation, in fact, Santiago College began to enrol Chilean children, especially from the families of upper class Liberals and from the emerging industrial bourgeoisie associated with mining wealth and the Radical Party. Under the direction of Mr and Mrs La Fetra, Santiago College rapidly gained a reputation for excellence and for progressive education based on North American pedagogical principles.12 The school, which catered for girls, was clearly Christian in orientation but was marked by a strong sense of religious tolerance. Great emphasis was placed on Christian character building.

Private Education in Chile

Towards the end of the 1880s there appeared in Santiago a boy's secondary school which was approximately equivalent to Santiago College. The Instituto Ingles was founded by the Presbyterian Mission. Like Santiago College, the language of instruction was English and eventually the children of Chilean nationals as well as those of foreign residents were enrolled. After several decades of operation, the Instituto Ingles was incorporated into the State system of education in 1926. However, it was accorded experimental status through its adoption of the Dalton Plan, whereby its association with pedagogical advances in North America was sustained. Around the same time (1930), the organisational basis of Santiago College also underwent a significant change. The links with the overseas board of the Methodist Mission were loosened and a separate national board of trustees was established for the school. The implications of these changes were that the school came to rely more upon local sources of finance; in addition, the school became less directly subject to ecclesiastical control.

The three and a half decades leading up to 1925 saw several significant developments concerning Protestantism in Chile. Following upon Taylor's pioneering work, for example, Methodism began to spread:

> Emphasis on self-support, development of a lay ministry, and the relatively low salaries of American missionaries, contributed to the very rapid growth of Methodism between 1893 and 1907.13

Beginning in 1890, several evangelical Protestant missions arrived in Chile, the most important being the Seventh-Day Adventists (1890), the Evangelical Baptist Convention of Chile (1892), the Christian and Missionary Alliance Church (1897) and the Salvation Army (1909). Another important development was the growth of local Pentecostalism, which triggered the growth of indigenous evangelical churches, often through splits within and separations from foreign missions. Pentecostalism, for example, was responsible for the split in the Methodists which led to the creation of the Methodist Pentecostal Church in 1901.

Developments in the area of Catholic private education between 1865 and 1925 must be seen in the broader context of changes and events in Chilean society. During this period, the power and influence of the Catholic Church clearly decreased in Chile. However, this relative overall decline and the various particular setbacks suffered, should not obscure the still considerable strength of the Catholic Church, for example, in educational matters. This period saw the Catholic Church experience several defeats on such issues as freedom of worship and liberty of conscience and witnesses a more rapid process to secularisation as revealed in new laws regarding marriage, burial and birth. The political champion of the Catholic Church, the Conservative Party, found itself confronted by highly articulate and determined representatives of Liberal and Radical opinion. While the Catholic Church was being challenged in the political-ideological arena, Catholicism was being assailed by currents of thought, such as Positivism, which undermined its claim to express the moral voice of the country. While the forces opposed to the Catholic Church were by no means united, their various efforts promoted the growth of secularism and helped to gradually strengthen the notion of a secular State. Eventually, the Catholic Church recognised the dangers associated with too close an identification with a particular political group, the Conservatives. The constitutional separation of Church and State in 1925 representated not only the culmination of a process of secularisation but also the willingness of the Catholic Church to accept a redefined role in Chilean society.

In educational terms, the 1865-1925 period witnessed a fierce battle which was closely linked with the 'religious question' in Chile. As has already been noted, the supporters of <u>Libertad de Ensenanza</u> could claim a victory of sorts but it was a victory which did not fundamentally compromise the essential character of the <u>Estado Docente</u>. Both principles survived and co-existed, although it was the latter which was more closely linked with the social and political trends of the period.

Private Education in Chile

Despite many challenges, struggles and setbacks, the provision of private schooling by the Catholic Church after 1865 continued to expand, partly through the activities of Catholic authorities and orders already in Chile and partly through the opening of schools by Catholic orders newly-arrived from abroad. Before examining this expansion, however, a significant new development in Catholic private education needs to be discussed. This development was the creation of a system of Catholic educational establishments parallel to the state system, that is, from the primary level up to and including the university level. The ultimate formation of this parallel system, which made feasible the complete education of young Chileans by Catholic institutions, was due to the creation of the Catholic University in Santiago in 1888. The driving force behind the foundation of the Catholic University was the Archbishop of Santiago, Mariano Casanova, who had long desired to utilise the opportunity presented by Libertad de Ensenanza at the higher education level. The Catholic University was set up, according to Galdames: 'to give a religious basis to professional studies'.14 The first faculty of the university was that of Legal, Political and Social Sciences, with an initial enrolment of 50 students. Soon afterwards, a course in mathematics was offered and in 1894 the School of Architecture was established, by which time enrolment had risen to 184 students. During the following years, an extensive range of faculties, schools and institutes was added to the Catholic University which came to represent a serious rival to the University of Chile, especially regarding the higher education of the country's elite.

The expansion of primary and secondary schooling under the auspices of the Catholic Church fulfilled a traditional duty towards education but also reflected the Church's determination to maintain as much influence as possible over the new generations of Chileans. As will be shown, the changing character of Chilean society forced the Catholic Church to devise a variety of educational responses. The old pattern of providing a humanistic education for the children of the elite and charity schools for the poor eventually gave way to a more diversified range of educational services.

According to data collected by Centro de Investigacion y Desarrollo de la Educacion (CIDE), total enrolment for primary and secondary schools in Chile in 1865 was 41,157, with 28,302 (68.8 per cent) in state schools and 12,855 (31.2 per cent) in private schools. Data for 1928 reveal a pattern of absolute increase but relative decline as far as private education is concerned. Out of a total enrolment of 588,036 pupils there were 519,100 (88.3 per cent) in state schools and 68,936 (11.7 per cent) in private schools in 1928. Apart from the discrepancies between CIDE's figures and other data available, this information has the further disadvantage of failing to separate enrolment in Catholic Church schools from that in other types of private schools. Indeed, the incompleteness and unreliability of much educational data and the absence of agreed-upon categories of analysis and classification conspire to render any account of the history of Catholic Church schools during the 1865-1925 period fragmentary and episodic.

The established Catholic orders continued their educational work in Chile. The Dominicans, for example, maintained a number of free primary schools, including at least four in Santiago and others in such towns as Concepcion, Chillan, La Serena, Talca, Quillota and San Felipe. Among the significant developments in this period was the opening in 1887 of the Colegio San Alberto Magno in Chillan, which offered both primary and secondary schooling to day and boarding students. The establishment in 1888 of the first chair of laws attached to the Colegio Santo Tomas de Aquino in Santiago attracted several prominent lecturers and considerable prestige. On this occasion, the Santiago newspaper, El Independiente, on 24 June 1888, offered its congratulations to the Dominicans for their promotion of Catholic education and Papal doctrine, and for being 'the first to react against state education, which carries tendencies towards atheistic education'.15 The most outstanding achievement by the Dominicans during this period was the creation of the Academia de Humanidades in Santiago in 1915. This school was claimed to be the first non-fee-paying private secondary school in Chile; in addition, it provided free primary education. During its first year of operation in 1916, the Academia de Humanidades had an average attendance of 190 pupils and a total enrolment of at least 250 pupils. Finally, in 1923, the Colegio Santo Domingo was founded in Valparaiso; this school continues to function to this day, as does the Academia de Humanidades.

Important educational developments undertaken by other Catholic religious orders include the founding of the Colegio San Agustin in Santiago in 1885 by the Augustinians and the creation of the Colegio San Pedro Nolasco in 1886 by the Mercedarians. The Jesuits continued to run the Colegio San Ignacio in Santiago, where many of the sons of Chile's traditional elites were educated. Another dimension of the Jesuits' educational work was their missionary activities in the south of Chile. As a result of a request by the Bishop of Ancud, two German Jesuits had established a religious house in Puerto Montt in 1859, where they attended to the spiritual needs of the German Catholic immigrants residing in that isolated part of the country, and opened an elementary school. Some time afterwards, a group of German nuns, Las Religiosas de la Inmaculada Concepcion (Mallinckrodt), arrived to assist the Jesuit fathers in their educational work.

The 1865-1925 period saw the arrival of several Catholic religious orders which were new to Chile and which brought with them several educational innovations. The Salesians, for example, were particularly associated with the development of technical and vocational education. Their schools were clearly not intended for the children of Chile's elites; they were designed to offer a more practical and useful education than could be obtained in the country's liceos. The Salesians began to provide agricultural education in 1895 and also undertook pioneering work in the field of commercial education. The Instituto Comercial Don Bosco was opened in Iquique in 1906 and similar institutes were established in Valparaiso, Valdivia and Punta Arenas. These educational contributions made by the Salesians were highly relevant given the contemporary arguments over the need for Chile to create an educational system suited to the economic development of the country.

Complementing the work of the Salesians were the educational activities of Las Hijas de Maria Auxiliadoras, the female branch of the Salesians in Chile. In 1895, the Salesianas opened a school in Talca devoted to vocational education for girls; courses in dressmaking, embroidery and drapery were offered free of charge, attracting many students. In 1904, a primary school, with attached workshops, was opened by the Salesianas in Punta Arenas; eventually, this establishment became a School of Domestic Services. In the next few years this order established a number of other schools for girls.

A rather different approach to education was shown by another Catholic order arriving in Chile, the Religiosos del Verbo Divino, sometimes referred to as the Padres de Steyl. This order first came to Chile in 1900 but the initial attempt to become established in Valdivia was unsuccessful, and so they transferred their mission to Copiapo, and set up their first Liceo Aleman in 1902. Seeking to avoid earlier mistakes, the Padres de Steyl modernised their approach to education by adopting the concentric plan, its emphasis on the sciences, and by integrating with the rest of the school system, including the state sector. The school proved to be a success, and the order expanded its educational work.16

These initial successes, however, did not satisfy the aspirations of the Padres de Steyl, for their foremost objective was the education of the country's elites. With this purpose in mind, they established a second Liceo Aleman in 1910, in Santiago, which quickly became one of the most prestigious schools in the country. Through its doors, and through those of other Verbo Divino schools, passed many of the new generation of Catholic leaders, especially those associated with the origins and development of Christian Democracy in Chile.

In vivid contrast with the educational orientation and activities of the Verbo Divino were those of the Capuchin missions in the south of Chile amongst the Mapuche Indians. The Italian Capuchins continued their work until the late nineteenth century, opening mission schools for young Araucanians. Faced by many difficulties, however, the Italian Capuchins eventually recognised that they could not satisfactorily fulfil their task and appealed to their fellow Capuchins from the German province of Bavaria to take their place. The Capuchinos Alemanes set about their difficult missionary and educational tasks with an approach which was better adapted and more sympathetic to the realities of Araucanian life. Considerable success was achieved, being reflected in the increased number of missions (24 by 1920), each of which supported a school; by 1929, there were 48 schools with an enrolment of over 4,000 pupils. Their work was supported by the efforts of the Hermanas de la Santa Cruz (Menzingen). The Hermanas opened their first school, for young girls, in Rio Bueno in 1901. While the fathers taught the Mapuche children as much as possible in the Araucanian language, the Hermanas conducted their lessons in Spanish. The education available in the missions was elementary schooling, supplemented by practical or vocational training (such as agricultural skills and handicrafts for boys and sewing and weaving for girls), plus moral and religious education.17

Clearly, the kind of educational work conducted by the Capuchin missions in southern Chile, especially the rural schools, was quite different from that undertaken by most private schools in the country and, indeed, by most Catholic private schools. It should be noted, however, that other Catholic congregations were involved in missionary and educational work among the Mapuche Indians.

An analysis of the educational work of the Catholic Church in Chile during the years between 1865 and 1925 would be incomplete without reference to changes in Catholic social doctrine and social action which began to appear from the 1890s onwards. The key event was the promulgation of the papal encyclical Rerum Novarum in May 1891. This encyclical represented Pope Leo XIII's attempt to point the Catholic Church in a new direction in response to deep changes occurring in the world, especially the development of industrial capitalism and the emergence of impoverished and exploited working classes which were beginning to build their own forms of organisation. The encyclical alerted both lay and ecclesiastical members of the Catholic Church to the urgent need to come to terms with these changes. Discussing the impact of Rerum Novarum, Loveman has correctly argued that:

> This critique of capitalist development did little immediately to influence the Latin American or Chilean Catholic hierarchy, but nonetheless provided doctrinal justification for initial efforts by progressive Catholic lay-persons and clerics to improve the lot of the working classes.18

The educational impact of the new Catholic social doctrine can be seen at two levels. Firstly, the new ideas had an influence upon the education of some of Chile's future Catholic leaders during the first two decades of this century:

> Based in the Jesuit college of San Ignacio, Father Fernando Vives de Soler and Father Jorge Fernandez Pradel influenced a group of future political leaders, priests and bishops who later played a leading role in the development of Chilean Christian Democracy. By 1917 Father Vives and his colleagues had established a 'Social Secretariat' and were engaged in unionization efforts among small numbers of workers in industry, transport, and commerce in Santiago.19

These initial efforts were strongly opposed by Conservative politicians and by Church leaders.

While Vives, Fernandez and others were seeking to educate Chile's future leaders in the precepts of the new social doctrines of the Catholic Church, a different kind of educational work was developed in association with social action programmes in working class communities. The Dominicans in Santiago, for example, began a programme of social and educational work in the working class barrio (shanty town), Yungay, as early as 1916. This programme included a dispensary, a free primary school, a distribution point for free clothing, and other forms of social assistance. Dominican nuns from the Congregacion de Albi came to help with the educational work at the primary levels and they also set up a liceo for girls.20 In addition, some Catholic congregations in Chile began to devise educational schemes for adults including women, and to provide various types of technical and vocational education for young people. Such educational strateqies as these were more attuned to the new ideas supporting social action than to traditional notions of charity.

THE CHURCH SECTOR OF CHILEAN PRIVATE EDUCATION: 1925-1985

The year 1925 marks a turning point in the relations between Church and State in Chile. The new Political Constitution of that year,21 brought many changes, some of which were consolidatory in character while others were genuinely innovative in the Chilean context. Article 10 (No.7), for example, gave constitutional recognition to libertad de ensenanza, compulsory primary education (recently enacted through the Law of 1920), and the State's 'preferential responsibility' for public education. The provisions regarding religious toleration in the 1865 Ley Interpretativa finally received constitutional expression through Article 10 (No.2):

> The Constitution insures to all the inhabitants of the Republic:
> Practice of all beliefs, liberty of conscience and the free exercise of all religions that may not be contrary to morality, good usage and public order. Therefore, the respective religious bodies have the right to erect and maintain houses of worship and accessory property under the conditions of security and hygiene as fixed by the laws and regulations.22

The greatest changes, however, came with the clear and definitive separation of Church and State, which was secured by means of an amicably arranged agreement negotiated between the Radical Government led by President Alessandri and the Catholic Church headed by Archbishop Errazuriz. As Mecham points out:

Chile thus earned the enviable distinction of being one of the few Latin-American nations that solved this delicate problem, not only without bloodshed, but in a spirit of good fellowship and hearty cooperation on both sides.23

This happy resolution was due partly to the accommodating personalities of the leading figures involved and partly to the recognition of mutual advantage in the disestablishment of the State and Church. The initial fears felt by the Catholic hierarchy were overcome when it was accepted that the Radical Government's proposals did not constitute an attack and were not a form of persecution. The separation of Church and State had long been a goal of the Radicals, who were attached to the belief that the State should be the impartial protector of all citizens' rights, with no particular church enjoying a privileged status above others in constitutional terms. The Radicals, moreover, were keen to end a situation whereby a secular institution, the State, was obligated to provide financial support to the Catholic Church. The agreement reached between President Alessandri and Archbishop Errazuriz, however, included provision for some financial assistance during a transitional period of five years, after which the Catholic Church would be financially independent. One of the most important points persuading the Catholic clergy of the benefits of disestablishment was the termination of the State's exercise of ecclesiastical patronage (patronato ecclesiastico), a change which received the Vatican's blessing. The 1925 Constitution:

> ... abrogated the government's right of patronage over ecclesiastical appointments and its veto privileges over the promulgation of papal decrees in Chile. The Church could establish dioceses, seminaries, apostolic vicariates, and religious communities without government permission, and all Church properties related to the exercise of cult were exempt from taxation.24

These changes, coupled with the juridical

recognition of the Catholic Church and of its religious orders and congregations, freed the Catholic Church from the irksome political interference in its affairs which the old State-Church system had brought. Disestablishment, furthermore, gave the Catholic Church the opportunity to extricate itself from political entanglements, especially from an increasingly damaging association with the Conservative Party. Obtaining unrestricted title to its extensive properties, securing constitutional acceptance of its role in education, and independence from the political world, the Catholic Church seemed to have gained from the disestablishment of Church and State in Chile. The fact that other religions and churches would henceforth enjoy the same formal constitutional and legal status, rights and duties did not seriously alarm the Catholic Church authorities by this time.

The changes in the 1925 Constitution affecting religion and education appear to have elicited a response from foreign and domestic Protestant churches in the years that followed. At least six Protestant churches, for example, began their evangelical activities in Chile in 1928-29 alone and during the next twenty years well in excess of thirty new Protestant churches appeared on the Chilean scene. Most were evangelical in character and Pentecostalism was particularly strong amongst the indigenous forms of Protestantism which sprang up.25 The growth of Protestantism in Chile can be observed in the following data: in 1920, Protestants constituted 1.4 per cent of the total population, 2.3 per cent in 1940, 4.0 per cent in 1950, 5.6 per cent in 1960 and 6.2 per cent in 1970.26 Somewhat different figures place the number of Protestants in Chile in 1900 at 21,000, just 0.7 per cent of the total population. By mid-1970, there were 741,000 Chilean Protestants (7.9 per cent), rising to 914,510 (8.9 per cent) in mid-1975 and to 1,116,460 (9.9 per cent) in mid-1980.27 According to Willems:

> there is a correlation between general cultural changes and growth of Protestantism. In Chile we found the heaviest concentrations of evangelical Protestants in areas whose social structure had

been most strongly affected by industrialization and urbanization. In 1960 41.7 percent of all Protestants were concentrated in the two most heavily industrialized provinces of Chile - namely, Santiago and Concepcion, which at the same time held 40.4 percent of the total population.28

Clearly, legal and constitutional changes cannot by themselves explain the growth of Protestantism in Chile. In addition to domestic socio-economic changes, various external forces also had an impact upon the development of Protestant churches. The twentieth century, especially after the First World War, has witnessed a considerable expansion of Protestant missionary activity throughout Latin America. The increased efforts of North American Protestant missions in particular coincided with the rapid and massive increase in the commercial, financial and political power of the United States in the continent. Accusations of cultural imperialism as well as of economic imperialism greeted these developments, but the evangelical and educational activities conducted by North American Protestant missions were defended by some Latin American educators. The views of both opponents (such as Alfredo Palacios of Argentina) and defenders (such as Gabriela Mistral of Chile) of the missions' work were expressed at the educational congress held in Montevideo in October 1925 under the auspices of the Committee on Cooperation in Latin America, a body set up by several United States and Canadian Protestant missions in order to coordinate their various activities.29 The Montevideo Congress made a number of recommendations regarding missionary education, including the six following:

> the school is recognised as an institution promoting social advance and democracy but the missions should attune their schools to each nation's system of education;
>
> the mission schools should be models of educational excellence;
> mission school education should promote interna-

tional understanding;

local leadership and administration should be encouraged;

attention should be given to rural education (farm schools), extension work and community service; and

coeducation should be encouraged.

Following this congress, fund raising campaigns were organised in the United States and Canada in order to support the educational efforts of the Protestant missions in Latin America. Much money was subsequently spent on improvements in school buildings during the 1930s. Prestigious educational projects, however, such as Santiago College, were beyond the capacity of most of the Protestant missions active in Chile; indeed, many of the smaller or less well endowed Protestant churches, especially the indigenous Pentecostal congregations, undertook comparatively little educational work, often limited to running Sunday schools.

Although it was run by a local board of trustees after 1930 rather than by an overseas mission board, Santiago College continued to provide a form of schooling which was considered typically 'Protestant' in character, or at any rate, it typified a certain kind of Protestant school. The new school buildings and facilities which the school enjoyed from the 1930s onwards reinforced its reputation for excellence. With both primary and secondary sections, Santiago College functioned as an elite school mainly for girls from upper class, well-connected backgrounds. Though clearly Protestant, the school imposed no religious test for students wanting admission; as a result, most students came from Catholic families and the religious education offered had no evangelical purpose or orientation. English was the main language of instruction and North American educational methods and materials were generally used. While many other Protestant mission schools in Latin America chose to conform to government educational programmes and to identify with national values and traditions, Santiago College preferred a more distinctive and independent approach, in effect outside of Government control and independent of Government support. If students wished to enter university, they were able to take examinations by arrangement with the Ministry of Education.

Over the years, Santiago College maintained its separate identity and, in the Chilean context, its distinctive approach to education. Its reputation for high quality schooling continues, as has its orientation towards leading trends in educational practice in English-speaking countries, especially the United States and Britain, for example an experimental programme based on Piaget's principles and a commitment to child-centred learning. An exchange system was arranged for Chilean teachers and British primary school experts in the 1960s.

The CIDE study published in 1971 provides a simple classification of Protestant schools in Chile and Latin America. The first category concerns those schools oriented towards education for excellence. Usually long-established and traditional, these Protestant schools offer an integral education, combining liberal, comprehensive and technical education, which seeks to help each individual student to fulfil his own potentiality. Santiago College clearly exemplifies this type of school.

The second category comprises Protestant schools which are geared towards evangelisation and indoctrination. The CIDE study distinguished two subgroups in this category: (a) small parochial primary schools associated with a particular Protestant church, and (b) Protestant schools, both primary and secondary, which are run by churches expressing more extreme Protestant doctrines. Examples of the latter include the schools operated by the Mormons and by the Seventh-Day Adventists. Though mainly established to fulfil religious purposes, the schools run by these types of Protestant churches nevertheless may provide a good secular education.

The CIDE classification of the traditional forms taken by Protestant schools also recognises the importance given to literacy work by Protestant churches. In addition, the CIDE study attempts to identify various educational features particularly associated with Protestantism, such as coeducation, sport as an integral part of the educational programme, and emphasis given to social sciences as well as physical and natural sciences. Moreover, the Protestant schools are said to promote democratic procedures and principles as part of a distinctive educational style which accepts and, indeed, encourages pluralism, nonconformity and individualism.

A more recent development occurring in Protestant education in Chile, also recognised by the CIDE study, has been the adoption of <u>concientizacion</u> as a basic method.30 Apart from new ideas circulating amongst Latin American educators and intellectuals, two factors have contributed to this tendency: first, the involvement of many Protestant churches in the 'theology of liberation' movement in Latin America and, second, the spread of Paulo Freire's psycho-social educational philosophy. <u>Conscientizacion</u> has had a broad and diverse impact. One example of its application was the creation in 1967 of the <u>Centro Audio-Visual Evangelico</u> (the Evangelical Audio-Visual Centre, CAVE) as an interdenominational agency for education, communications and community development. Lutheran and Pentecostal churches have participated in CAVE's programmes. In conjunction with the Ministry of Education, CAVE began an adult education scheme in the Bio-Bio region in 1968. Adult education centres were established and literacy work, suited to the educational level of the adults enrolled, was undertaken applying Freire's methodology. CAVE also took responsibility for training teachers in the techniques of adult education and its underlying philosophy. The Bio-Bio scheme set up workshops and technical centres from 1970 onwards in order to provide technical-vocational training for both men and women.

Clearly, Protestant churches in Chile have offered several kinds of educational services, ranging from elite schools such as Santiago College to non-formal adult education projects in remote communities. While there is no Protestant university in Chile (or in Latin America, for that matter), Protestant schools and educational programmes can be found at all other levels of the educational system.

These institutions, furthermore, qualify for the same kinds of State aid and treatment as Catholic schools. With perhaps 10 per cent of the total population now being affiliated with some Protestant church or other, Protestant schools can be expected to continue as an element of the overall educational system; however, their educational role is relatively minor and their educational services are rather uneven in quality and coverage. An indication of the comparatively small contribution made by Protestant churches to the nation's education was revealed by the census conducted by CIDE. In 1966-67, there were only 75 Protestant schools in the entire country, representing about 5.9 per cent of all denominational schools and just 3.3 per cent of all private schools.31 During the 1970s and early 1980s, there was no significant growth in Protestant schooling.

The Catholic Church, on the other hand, has continued to make a major contribution to the provision of Chile's education. The period of Chilean history after 1925 saw a rapid, though uneven, expansion of the State sector of education. While Catholic schooling, along with the rest of the private education sector, has not kept pace with this rate of increase, the Catholic Church has sustained its diverse educational activities in the face of more and more demand for schooling derived from demographic growth and the democratisation of Chilean society. The changes introduced by the 1925 Constitution, supplemented by other developments, served to define more clearly the parallel sector of education provided by the Catholic Church. At primary, secondary and university levels, the Catholic Church operated its own institutions and continued to add to its level of provision. Thus, in 1925, the Catholic University of Valparaiso was founded and was given State recognition in 1929; then in 1951 the Jesuits were invited by the Bishop of Valparaiso to take over the running of this university. In 1963 a third Catholic university, the <u>Universidad del Norte</u>, was established in Antofagasta, with branches in Iquique and Arica.

At the secondary level, different types of Catholic schools continued to function, catering for different strata and groups within Chilean society.

Private Education in Chile

The <u>Verbo Divino</u>, for example, sustained its involvement in educating children from Chile's elite circles. In 1950, a new <u>Liceo Aleman</u> was built in a well-to-do district of Santiago, to replace that which had been constructed during the First World War. Following a similar pattern, the <u>Religiosas del Sagrado Corazon</u> (Sacré Coeur) opened an elite school for girls in Apoquindo, a nearby district of Santiago, in 1957. However, the elite <u>liceos</u> mentioned above were not typical of all secondary schools run by the Catholic Church as far as the pupils' social backgrounds were concerned, however much the middle and lower socio-economic status schools might regard the elite <u>liceos</u> as models for imitation. Other differences to be noted include the wider dispersal of the non-elite secondary schools throughout the country in terms of distribution according to province and according to urban-rural areas; by contrast, all elite schools were urban-based with 56 per cent located in the Province of Santiago itself.

The diversity of Catholic denominational education is further revealed at the post-primary level by the expansion during the period after 1925 of several kinds of technical-vocational education. A significant development from the 1930s onwards was the founding of commercial schools for girls; the first such school was the <u>Instituto Comercial Blas Cana</u> run by the <u>Religiosas de la Casa de Maria</u>. Catholic orders, notably the <u>Salesianos</u>, continued to develop the field of industrial education, operating schools of different cycles of study; in the late 1950s only <u>La Gratitud Nacional</u> in Santiago offered the first two cycles lasting two and three years respectively, plus the third cycle which eventually led to the grade of technician. Even the <u>Mission de Steyl</u> (<u>Verbo Divino</u>) became involved in industrial education out of recognition of the educational needs of certain social sectors and through the impact of new ideas concerning social action and Catholic support of social democratisation. The period also saw the spread of <u>escuelas tecnicas femeninas</u> (technical schools for girls), mainly thanks to the efforts of the <u>Salesianas de Maria Auxiliadora</u>. In the field of agricultural education, <u>escuelas agricolas</u> (agricultural schools) were opened by the <u>Salesianos</u>, the

Hermanos de las Escuelas Cristianas, and the Maryknoll Fathers. While most escuelas agricolas were designed for boys, several agricultural schools for girls were also opened.

All these types of post-primary schools run by Catholic congregations became non-fee-paying schools after 1957 when the State decided to award them subsidies equivalent to 50 per cent of the cost per student in the state sector. At the same time, the State recognised the courses of study and qualifications provided by these private schools. By the time of the CIDE study, Catholic technical-vocational schools accounted for 80.2 per cent of the enrolment in the private sector of technical-vocational education. These Catholic schools had an enrolment of 16,614 in 1966-67.32 The census upon which the CIDE study was based identified 93 Catholic technical-vocational schools serving middle and low SES students in Chile; this figure represented 75 per cent of all such schools in the private sector. Between 1970 and 1973, technical-vocational education in private schools experienced a small decline (2.6 per cent) but between 1973 and 1981, a growth of 13.3 per cent was enjoyed.33

With regard to the provision of primary education, it has to be remembered that, ever since the Law of Compulsory Primary Education (1920) which was incorporated into the 1925 Constitution, the State has agreed to subsidise private sector schools, including those of the Catholic Church, which provide primary schooling. Between 1925 and 1950, the amount of subsidy gradually increased in rough approximation with the rate of inflation occurring in the nation's economy. Law 9864 of 1951, however, greatly increased the level of subsidisation and also improved the reliability of payment. Later, the Frei government tried to speed up the process of payment. In this way, the Catholic Church's traditional educational activities received the State's recognition and support and became better integrated into the national educational system, especially at the primary level. According to the CIDE study, there were 249,204 pupils enrolled in Catholic primary schools in 1966-67, representing 60.3 per cent of the total primary enrolment in the private sector.

Private Education in Chile

During the Allende period, despite many difficulties and conflicts between the Unidad Popular Government and the Catholic hierarchy, Catholic primary schooling continued to enjoy considerable support from the State. After the military coup, however, the Catholic Church discovered that its desire to maintain its educational services for the whole community, but especially for underprivileged sectors, came into conflict with a regime which had quite different priorities. The first years of the military junta brought home to the Catholic Church some of the disadvantages of a loss of financial independence. According to Smith:

> Despite promises by the military to place more emphasis on private education, they have not provided adequate grants for the maintenance of Catholic primary and secondary schools. This phenomenon, combined with delayed payments, chronic inflation, reduced subsidies when private funding has increased, and decreases in nutritional and health services have all severely hampered the ability of Catholic schools to set their own agenda and meet their previously announced commitments.34

In addition, the military regime has sought to impose ideological values and beliefs which have often been sharply at odds with traditional Catholic ideas and the new social doctrines of the Catholic Church. In recent years, the military government's policies of municipalisation and privatisation have had a great impact upon the nation's education; however, these policies were devised without any consultation with the educational community, including the Catholic Church, which certainly was not the intended beneficiary of these policies. Although the early 1980s saw a growth in the private sector of primary education, as measured by enrolments, the Catholic Church was not responsible for this increase. Instead, private institutions with orientations and purposes quite different from those pursued by Catholic schools flourished for several years.35 The social policies of the regime, coupled with the collapse of the economy, have severely constrained the ability of the Catholic Church to fulfil the need for primary schooling today, especially in poor urban and rural communities.

The story of the Catholic Church's provision of formal primary and post-primary schooling in Chile would be incomplete without reference to the important role played by several representative bodies and pressure groups which have been established to protect and promote the interests of individuals and organisations involved in private education. Catholic schools, in fact, were responsible for creating the first of these institutions, the Federation of Secondary Education Institutes (**Federacion de Institutos de Educacion Secundaria - FIDE-Secundaria**), in 1948. The basic idea behind this development was the perceived need amongst Catholic secondary schools to organise themselves on the basis of shared interests and to coordinate their relations with the Ministry of Education. The original pressing concerns of these Catholic secondary schools included the inadequacy of the level of State subsidisation which they received, often irregularly, and the financial difficulties of the Catholic Church as it tried to sustain its educational role in the face of increased demand due to rapid population growth. **FIDE-Secundaria**, in fact, exerted pressure on the Ministry of Education and the government of the day which bore fruit in the form of Law 9864 of 1951. The success of **FIDE-Secundaria** stimulated Catholic schools within different levels and types of education to follow suit; thus, in 1954 **FIDE-Tecnica** was created, in 1956 **FIDE-Primaria** was organised, and 1964 saw the foundation of **FIDE-Normal**. All of these federations initially represented Catholic schools only. In 1964, **FIDE-Secundaria** decided to modify its rules in order to include schools from the rest of the private sector of secondary education; in this way, the organisation's denominational character was terminated. Later, the other FIDE groups followed the same pattern begun by **FIDE-Secundaria**, including a two-fold division of membership into one category representing Catholic establishments and a second category representing non-denominational private schools and schools belonging to non-Catholic denominations.

Each FIDE undertook a similar range of activities, focused upon the following areas:

> legal services, including publicising and analysing laws, decrees and regulations, offering legal advice, and providing data regarding teachers' salaries and contracts;
>
> state subsidisation, particularly information on availability and procedures;
>
> pedagogical services, such as advice on new curricula and programmes, registration with the Ministry of Education, recognition of teacher qualifications, participation in educational planning, and publication of an educational journal;
>
> the provision of libraries and laboratories;
>
> collaboration with the Ministry of Education;
>
> pastoral services, especially geared towards promoting Christian teaching and values; and
>
> international relations with foreign agencies, inter-governmental institutions, and international educational bodies.36

While, as noted earlier, the FIDE groups abandoned their original denominational character, there can be little doubt that Catholic schools provided the dominant voice in each federation. The pressure group activities of the federations brought them into regular contact with the Ministry of Education. During the Frei Government, relations were relatively harmonious, but with the victory of Allende's UP coalition and the subsequent growth of fears for the future of private education, the federations adopted a more combative attitude. The FIDE groups, in close association with the Christian Democrats, led the campaign against all proposals which might result in the disappearance of private education in Chile. While many initial fears proved to be unfounded, the

ENU reform37 elicited a sharp response from the federations, which brought pressure to bear not only upon Allende's government but also upon the Catholic Church hierarchy, including Cardinal Raul Silva Henriquez. The defeat of Allende, however, did not bring a restoration of the kind of influence and access formerly enjoyed by the FIDE groups; instead, they were faced with a Ministry of Education which, under military control, was generally indifferent, if not unsympathetic.

Another representative institution which emerged within the private sector of Chilean education was the National Federation of Parent and Guardian Associations for Private Educational Establishments (<u>Federacion Nacional de Asociaciones de Centros de Padres y Apoderados de Establecimientos Educacionales Particulares</u> - FEDAP). This body, which coordinated the activities of parents' associations in private schools, was founded in 1951; initially, only Catholic schools were represented but in 1966 the particular denominational allegiance of FEDAP was ended in order to incorporate a broader range of private schools' parents' associations. Through FEDAP, the parents' associations in Chile's private schools acquired a national voice and a means of exerting pressure and influence upon the nation's central educational authorities. A representative from FEDAP, for example, served on the National Council of Education and within the Office of Financial Aid and Scholarships. During the Allende period, FEDAP worked closely with <u>FIDE-Secundaria</u> and the other FIDE groups in order to protect the interests of private education and to oppose the ENU reform. After the military coup, FEDAP continued to perform its representative duties within the constraints upon pressure group activities imposed by Pinochet's Government.

The post-1925 period in Chilean history brought several important changes in the character of the Catholic Church. The traditional, conservative role of the Church was by no means abandoned by significant elements both within the Church itself and in the Catholic community at large, but the period did witness the development, slowly at first but gathering momentum from the 1950s onwards, of a more

Private Education in Chile

dynamic and progressive involvement in the processes of social change. The beginning of modern social action tendencies within the Catholic Church in Chile have already been traced to the years leading up to 1925; these tendencies continued in the years that followed. Three main aspects of Catholic social action in Chile may be identified. First, there was the training of part of the nation's Catholic elite in the new social doctrines of the Church; according to Loveman:

> Anticommunism and sincere commitment to Catholic social doctrine provided the foundation of the education received at San Ignacio and Santiago's Catholic University by the generation of students in the late 1920's and early 1930's who would become the principal leaders of Chilean Christian Democracy.38

A second aspect of Catholic social action was the attempt by some members of the clergy, supported by lay Catholics, to provide programmes of social and educational assistance for the benefit of poorer sectors of the population; these multi-faceted programmes were designed not only to meet pressing needs but also to stimulate community involvement and the acquisition of practical skills. A notable example was the Casa Hogar San Pancracio, a major social, educational and technical project inaugurated by the Dominicans in Santiago in 1943. This project had many dimensions, including a fully-equipped medical centre, courses in accountancy, mathematics, dressmaking and domestic arts, a gymnasium, a printing-press and a theatre workshop.

A third aspect of Catholic social action was the attempt by some Catholic clergy to attract and cultivate working class leaders who would form an alternative to socialist and communist influence in the Chilean labour movement. One expression of this effort was the Chilean Trade Union Association (Asociacion Sindical Chilena - ASICH), an organisation founded in 1947 by a Jesuit father, Alberto Hurtado, with the purpose of training union leaders suitably oriented towards Catholicism and the Church's new social doctrines. Though having only very limited success, such attempts to develop a Catholic working class leadership reflected a genuine desire to redirect the Catholic Church away from its conservatism and elitism.

A major stimulus to the growth of social action doctrines in Chile was Pope Pius XI's <u>Quadragessimo Anno</u> issued in 1931. The same year saw the beginning of the first Chilean Catholic Action (<u>Accion Catolica Chilena</u>) circles which played an important role in spreading the new ideas concerning social justice. Significantly, several young members of <u>Accion Catolica</u> were involved in the breakaway from the Conservative Party in 1937 which led to the creation of the <u>Falange Nacional</u>, the forerunner of the Christian Democratic Party.

It has to be acknowledged, however, that the real growth of a wider acceptance of the social doctrines of the Catholic Church did not occur until after the Second World War and even then progress was slow. Surveys undertaken in 1940 and 1956 revealed many weaknesses in the organisation of the Catholic Church and in the strength of religious beliefs and customs in the country. According to Smith, one of these surveys found that:

> in urban areas of the country the concentration of the Church's efforts in terms of religious personnel and educational programs was focused upon the upper classes and a small minority of the middle class ... priests were not preaching the social doctrine of the Church at Mass or in Catholic schools (attended mainly by the rich), and the working classes still had the definite impression that the Church was not concerned with their interest.39

The situation in the countryside was worse, as suggested by the fact that the Conservative Party could rely upon a substantial rural peasant vote in elections. On the basis of these and other factors, Smith concludes that:

> no significant mutation of Catholic attitudes and behaviour in the direction of social and political reform had occurred before 1958.40

Nevertheless, certain trends and new developments soon began to bear fruit. Illustrative of changing conditions in Chile is the case of the Rural Education Institute (<u>Instituto de Educacion Rural</u> - IER), whose foundation in 1954 was inspired by a group of Catholics. The objectives of the IER were to provide education and training for Chilean peasants, to support and strengthen the peasants' communities and organisations, to help train peasant leaders, and to integrate the rural sector into the nation's overall economic development. With both state and private schooling in rural areas failing to meet the needs of the peasant population, the IER was designed to overcome this deficiency, especially through literacy programmes and training schemes for rural youth. Several training centres were established offering a range of courses in practical skills, literacy and community development leadership.41 Associated with the IER was a radio school which at one time reached over 1300 rural schools with an enrolment in excess of 82,000.42

While the operating expenses of the IER were partly offset by subsidies from the Ministry of Education and grants from the Ministry of Agriculture, help in meeting capital costs was obtained from a variety of domestic and foreign sources; from foreign governments such as Belgium, Holland, West Germany and the United States; from international bodies such as UNESCO, FAO and ILO; and from private donations, Catholic charities and US corporations. This package of support reflected the belief amongst the donors that the IER represented the type of rural educational institution which, in association with controlled agrarian reform, would help to avoid outbreaks of rural revolution in Latin America. In this sense, the IER became part of the anti-communist strategy being pursued in Chile and in the region during the 1950s and 1960s, forming the basis of the Christian Democrats' approach to adult education and the training requirements of schemes of agrarian reform and community development. As both a model and as an active participant, the IER constituted an important element of the Frei Government's policies concerning rural adult education.

Private Education in Chile

The Catholic Church's educational role underwent a major change in Chile and in Latin America during the 1960s as part of a dramatic transformation affecting the Church and its relations with the State, society and the secular world. While, as has been shown, Latin American countries had witnessed several applications of the new social doctrines of the Church, the Second Vatican Council (1962-1965) pointed the Catholic Church throughout the world in a new direction. A fundamental reorientation occurred which had its greatest impact in Third World countries and particularly in Latin America. The Second Vatican Council made a momentous choice whereby the Catholic Church disassociated itself from too close an involvement with the State and, instead, firmly aligned itself with demands for freedom and justice coming from the oppressed, the powerless and the poor. According to Smith:

> Vatican II officially reversed the long-standing Catholic tradition of the desirability of the union between Church and State, and it asserted emphatically that the Church 'must in no way be confused with the political community, nor bound to any political system' and that 'she does not lodge her hope in privileges conferred by civil authority'.43

The Church deliberately adopted a critical stance towards the State and particularly towards the structures of social, political and economic injustice upheld by authoritarian regimes which protected the privileges of the few at the expense of the rights of the many. The impact of the Second Vatican Council upon Latin America was profound, since it supported and legitimated the struggles for change and radical reform which many progressive Catholic leaders had been waging for many years. The Latin American Episcopal Council (<u>Consejo Episcopal Latinoamericano</u> - CELAM) warmly embraced the changes which Pope John XXIII had initiated. In 1968 a major conference organised by CELAM was held in Medellin which became famous for its articulation of what became known as the 'theology of liberation'. At Medellin:

150 bishops representing national episcopal conferences throughout Latin America issued a series of statements committing the official Church to a much more prophetic role of denunciation of concrete forms of injustice as well as a more active engagement in social action on behalf of marginal sectors of society. These bishops condemned the 'institutionalized violence' of the status quo that has long characterized Latin American political and economic structures, placing the responsibility for injustice on those who 'jealously retain their privileges' thus provoking 'explosive reactions of despair'.44

The Medellin conference left no doubt that the official leadership of the Church was actively to promote structural changes and liberating reforms rather than leave these vital matters entirely in the hands of others. This active role was to extend into the field of education. Not only were Catholic educational institutions of all kinds to spread the new spirit of social criticism, they were also expected to transform their own structures, method and practices in ways which promoted liberation rather than oppression. 'Education for liberation' became the watchword of the new approach which demanded continued expansion and improvement of education, greater equality of educational opportunity, and the diffusion of a 'spirit of criticism'. Existing educational systems were criticised:

because of their 'abstract and standard content', because they are oriented towards keeping the economic and social structures instead of changing them, because they insist on maintaining an economy based on a 'wish of having more' when actually the Latin American youth wants 'to be better' in the job of their self-realization by service and love'.45

Concern was expressed in the Medellin documents about the 'socio-economical segregation' typical of school systems with a fee-paying private sector which seemed indifferent to the need for social change.

305

Private Education in Chile

The continued relationship between traditional elite private schools and the Church was seen as a cause of embarrassment, while the absence of effective means for integrating private educational institutions into national educational systems was seen as an important handicap. As far as non-formal education was concerned, the Medellin conference openly recommended the methods of <u>concientizacion</u> associated particularly with Paulo Friere. Literacy work and 'liberating education' could not be separated in the new conception of Catholic education which through its critical spirit and its commitment to radical social change, found itself capable of conducting a meaningful dialogue with Marxist ideology and socialist movements which appeared to share similar goals and similar enemies.

The pronouncements emerging from the Second Vatican Council coincided with the victory of Eduardo Frei in the 1964 presidential election. Although several of the criticisms of traditional Catholicism were not entirely applicable to the Chilean case, these pronouncements received a favourable reception not only in Church circles but also in the Christian Democrat Government. Frei's political programme, the so-called 'Revolution in Liberty', seemed to include many practical expressions of the new commitment of the Church to social reform, so much so, perhaps, that the requirement that the Church adopt a critical perspective regarding all governments tended to be forgotten. The Medellin conference, however, gave added strength to those Catholics, both ecclesiastical and lay, who wanted the Church not only to take up a more independent position but also to respond more critically to the Frei reforms, which were by no means as radical as they first seemed and were presented. After Medellin, the Catholic Church in Chile was more clearly split between those who fully embraced the 'theology of liberation' and those who could not bring themselves to give up their traditional values and attitudes.

The post-Medellin divisions within the Catholic Church in Chile were expressed in the educational system, including the private sector. For example, the <u>Colegio Saint George</u> achieved some notoriety for its progressive curricular reforms, its introduction of the work-study principle, and its high level of politicisation. Some Catholic orders, especially the Jesuits, took seriously the argument that private schools should not be used to sustain social inequalities and unjustifiable privileges. According to Fischer:

> Exclusive Catholic schools, like St George's and San Ignacio in Santiago, initiated programs for institutional and administrative reform; concerted efforts were made to enrol and provide financial assistance to children of the lower classes, to revise the curriculum and emphasize the practical arts, and to transfer decision-making authority to the school community itself.46

Other forces in private education, however, such as the FIDE groups and FEDAP, could not countenance such educational innovations and also opposed the transfer of Catholic schools to the State even when this was supported by the Catholic hierarchy. These divisions within Chilean Catholicism and its approach to private education appeared during the later years of the Frei government but became most pronounced during the three years of Allende's presidency.

The Church's attitude towards the UP Government was complex. While accepting the constitutional legitimacy and authority of Allende's government, the Catholic Church nevertheless was uneasy about various aspects of the UP programme and joined with those forces seeking reassurance and security. Despite the reforming educational trends already noted:

> the Church remained steadfast in its adherence to the doctrine of libertad de ensenanza. Thus, in the face of the UP's preelectoral pledge to nationalize the country's educational institutions, the Church sided with oligarchical interests in promulgating the Democratic Statute of Guarantees.47

The Catholic Church, however, despite serious misgivings concerning Marxist ideology and militant socialism, did find some points of agreement with the

UP government's policies. Even in the case of the ENU, the Church's determined opposition did not blind it to the virtues of some aspects of the proposed reform. For example, the Church was increasingly interested in such educational principles as the combination of work and study, lifelong learning and greater educational opportunities for the mass of the population, but it found that the socialist orientation of these principles in the ENU was unacceptable.

During the Allende administration, the Catholic Church was unhappy with the restrictions on religious education in the UP's educational programmes. Moreover, the Church was highly critical of the Allende government for its apparent desire to impose a single ideological perspective upon the entire educational system. While the military coup put an end to the Church's fears regarding these particular tendencies, another set of problems and challenges quickly emerged. The Church, adopting a cautious and reserved attitude towards the military *junta*, at first believed that its basic interests and values would be respected. It quickly became clear, however, that no institution, including the Church, would be left untouched by the military regime and its policies. Thus, the imposition of military authority in Chile's educational institutions affected not only the State sector but also the private sector, including Catholic schools and universities. The *junta*, for example, nominated rectors for each of the three Catholic universities, which was unprecedented and, indeed, almost unimaginable in the context of Chile's educational history. The Chancellor of the Catholic University in Santiago, Archbishop Silva Henriquez, resigned in protest against this intervention and against the mass expulsion of students and teachers. In addition, the principle of the autonomy of private education was broken through the direct military intervention of the *Colegio Saint George*, whose progressive pedagogical practices and liberal, critical values were anathema to the military government. The application of National Security doctrines to the teaching of history and civics further alienated the Church.

By 1974, the Catholic Church, along with other religious denominations, was openly critical of the junta's repressive policies and its atrocious record on human rights. The ecumenical Comite Pro Paz (Committee for Peace) was organised, under the initial direction of the Lutheran Bishop, Helmut Frenz, to provide legal, economic, medical and social assistance to the victims of repression and their families. When, in 1975, the Comite Pro Paz was closed down, and Bishop Frenz expelled from the country, the Catholic Church created the Vicaria de la Solidaridad (the Solidarity Vicariate) in order to continue the programmes of assistance. At the parish level, schemes of educational aid were organised, especially for children whose parents could not otherwise afford to send them to school. Free schools were established, sometimes with secondary school pupils serving as teachers. Schemes to help dropouts, and to help graduates of primary schools to gain entry to secondary education, were also devised. Pre-school educational facilities were established. With increases in unemployment, courses offering various vocational skills were developed in poor districts. Many of these programmes operated with the assistance and support of local clergy but the active involvement of the residents of working class areas and shanty towns was crucial. As Smith points out, the financial independence of these schemes contrasts significantly with the financial dependence of formal Catholic schooling upon the State. This loss of financial autonomy became particularly serious during the second half of the 1970s, when private education had to endure cutbacks in state subsidisation; for the Catholic Church, these cutbacks had the effect of limiting its ability to provide more educational opportunities for needy pupils.

The military regime's repression of higher education resulted in the closing down of many institutes, research centres and deliberative bodies within the Catholic University; in addition, the availability of scholarships was restricted and enrolments declined. In 1976, the Academia de Humanismo Cristiano was created, with Archbishop Silva Henriquez as its president. As well as producing its own critical magazine, Analisis, the Academia became:

an important intellectual centre for critical research and discussion, among intellectuals who were excluded from the universities, in the social sciences, economics, health, education and agriculture, among others.48

However, despite keeping certain traditions and values alive, such institutions as the Academia were no substitute for a fully autonomous higher educational system.

The Directivas Presidenciales of 1979 began a process whereby the Pinochet regime elaborated a set of educational policies which changed the face of Chilean education and effectively terminated the historical sequence which had culminated in the Frei educational reform. The Catholic Church's response to the programmes of municipalisation and privatisation was one of alarm and criticism. Despite the fact that the new method of allocating state subsidies to private schools held out the promise of greater support to the private sector, the Catholic Church was opposed to the general spirit of the new educational reform as well as to many of its particular facets. In June 1981, the Conferencia Episcopal de Chile issued a pastoral letter which represents the most comprehensive attack on the military regime's educational policies by the Catholic Church. In this letter, the Catholic bishops called attention to the government's exaggerated emphasis on the values of individual effort and competitiveness; to the excessive importance given to the role of economic incentives in the motivation of students; to the complete omission of any explicit reference to the term 'democracy' within the new school curricula; to the lack of any mention of the importance of cultivating a critical spirit and outlook; and to the preoccupation with National Security which placed the new curricula in an ideological straitjacket. Above all, the bishops were concerned that, as there was no community participation at the local level, nor any participation by teachers, parents and pupils at school level, the reform appeared to be a deeply authoritarian measure introduced to reinforce the characteristics of the political system. In addition, the pastoral letter expressed the bishops' anxieties about the processes of municipalisation and privatisation:

> libertad de ensenanza does not imply the acceptance of just any mode of privatisation of the school system, for example that based upon the mere play of the economic market, in view of the negative consequences that could be produced in practice among schools which, given over to free enterprise, grow in an unequal way to the detriment of less fortunate sectors.49

Thus, the struggles by the Catholic Church on behalf of libertad de ensenanza have resulted in a curious and unexpected situation. Having survived the attacks by the anticlerical Radicals and the UP coalition's threats of nationalisation, the Catholic Church now finds its vision of Chile's future under serious challenge from a distorted version of the very doctrine it has promoted. There can be no doubt that the kind of private schooling which the Pinochet regime's educational policies have encouraged represents, from the Church's perspective, a serious degeneration.

Today the Catholic Church maintains a broad range of educational facilities and services, finding that it needs to defend itself, but the enemy has changed. For many decades, the Church was locked in fierce battle with the proponents of the Estado Docente, but it now finds that it is the structure and values of the free market economy, held in place by an authoritarian military regime, which are most threatening. That regime has effectively destroyed the Estado Docente, and in so doing has substituted the idea of education as a commodity for that of education as a social duty, a public responsibility of the whole community. By acting as a principled force of opposition, by offering protection to individuals and organisations which otherwise might have perished, and by keeping alive the notion of education as a social duty, the Catholic Church may eventually find that it has helped to perform a peculiar historical function, namely, the preservation of the seed of the Estado Docente in Chile.

Private Education in Chile

NOTES AND REFERENCES

1. For a study of the Lancasterian system in Latin America, see Robertson, James Alexander, 'Joseph Lancaster, James Thompson and the Lancasterian System of Mutual Instruction with Special Reference to Hispanic America', *Hispanic American Historical Review*, 1921, **4**, pp.49-98.

2. See Labarca, H. Amanda, *Historia de la Ensenanza en Chile*, Santiago: Imprenta Universitaria, 1939, p.86.

3. *Constitucion de la Republica de Chile: Jurada y Promulgada el 25 de Mayo de 1833*, Santiago: Segunda Edicion, Imprenta de la Opinion, 1845.

4. Labarca, H. Amanda, op.cit., p.129 and pp.137-8.

5. Manuel Bulnes: President of Chile 1841-51.

6. Fisher, Nelson, *Chile, the Evolution of an Educational System*, unpublished Ph.D. thesis, University of Nottingham, 1974, p.179.

7. Labarca, H. Amanda, op.cit., p.130.

8. Anguita, Ricardo and Quesnay, Valeria (eds), *Leyes Promulgadas en Chile desde 1810 a 1901*, 2 vols, Santiago: Imprenta Nacional, 1902.

9. See Woll, Allen L., 'For God or Country: History Textbooks and the Secularization of Chilean Society, 1840-1890', *Journal of Latin American Studies*, 1975, **7**, pp.23-43.

10. Inman, Samuel Guy, 'Latin America' in: Kandel, I.L. (ed.), *Educational Yearbook of the International Institute of Teachers College*, Columbia University, 1933, p.485.

11. Ibid., pp.459-60.

12. Labarca, H. Amanda, op.cit., p.167.

13. Barrett, D.E. (ed.), World Christian Encyclopedia, New York: Oxford University Press, 1982, p.227.

14. Galdames, Luis, A History of Chile, translated and edited by Isaac Joslin Cox, New York: Russell and Russell Inc., 1964, p.350.

15. Quoted in: Ramirez, Ramon, Los Dominicos en Chile y la Primera Universidad, Santiago de Chile, 1979, p.109.

16. Blancpain, Jean-Pierre, Les Allemands au Chili, 1816-1945, Bohlan Verlag Koln, 1974, p.777.

17. Ibid., pp.760-71.

18. Loveman, Brian, Chile: The Legacy of Hispanic Capitalism, New York: Oxford University Press, 1979, p.305.

19. Ibid., p.306.

20. Ramirez, Ramon, op.cit., p.134.

21. Constitucion Politica de la Republica de Chile: Promulgada el 18 de Septembre de 1925, Santiago: Imprenta Universitaria, 1925.

22. Mecham, J. Lloyd (ed.), Church and State in Latin America: A History of Politico-Ecclesiastical Relations, Chapel Hill: University of North Carolina Press, 1960, p.219.

23. Ibid.

24. Smith, Brian H., The Catholic Church and Political Changes in Chile, 1920-1978, unpublished Ph.D. thesis, Yale University, 1979, p.136.

25. Barrett, D.E., op.cit., p.229.

26. Tennekes, Johannes, 'Le mouvement pentecotiste chilien et la politique', Social Compass, 1978, XXV, 1, p.57.

27. Barrett, D.E., op.cit., p.226.

28. Willems, Emilio, <u>Latin American Culture: An Anthropological Synthesis</u>, New York: Harper and Row, 1975, p.368.

29. Inman, Samuel Guy, op.cit., pp.449-522.

30. Zachariah, Mathew, <u>Revolution through Reform: A Comparison of Sarvodaya and Conscientization</u>, New York: Praeger, 1986.

31. Brahm, Luis A., Cariola, Patricio and Silva, Juan J., <u>Educacion Particular en Chile. Antecedentes y Dilemas</u>, Santiago: CIDE, 1971.

32. Ibid., p.80.

33. Nunez, P. Ivan, <u>Las Tansformaciones Educaciones bajo el Regimen Militar</u>, 2 vols., Santiago: Programa Interdisciplinario de Investigacion en Educacion (PIIE), 1984, p.319.

34. Smith, Brian H., op.cit., pp.637-8.

35. The private educational institutions which have thrived in recent years have been privately-owned, profit-making establishments. The early 1980s witnessed the rapid growth of <u>conglomerados educacionales</u>, typically family businesses operating several schools for a profit-making purpose. These enterprises benefited greatly from the Pinochet regime's policies of privatisation, municipalisation and subsidisation. For further information, see Aedo de Richmond, R., <u>An Examination of the Significance of the Private Sector in the Evolution of Chilean Education</u>, M.Ed. thesis, University of Hull, 1986, pp.412-16; and Aedo-Richmond, R., Noguera, I. and Richmond, M., 'Changes in the Chilean Educational System During Eleven Years of Military Government: 1973-1984', in: Brock, C. and Lawlor, H. (eds), <u>Education in Latin America</u>, London: Croom Helm, 1985.

36. Brahm <u>et al.</u>, op.cit., pp.217-21.

37. Escuela Nacional Unificada (National Unified School). For a detailed study see: Farrell, Joseph P., *The National Unified School in Allende's Chile: the role of education in the destruction of a revolution*, Vancouver: University of British Columbia Press, 1986.

38. Loveman, Brian, op.cit., p.307.

39. Smith, Brian H., op.cit., pp.200-1.

40. Ibid., p.202.

41. Brahm et al., op.cit., p.230.

42. Freeburger, Adela R. and Hauch, Charles C., *Education in Chile*, Washington D.C.: US Department of Health, Education and Welfare, 1964, p.35.

43. Smith, Brian H., op.cit., pp.4-5.

44. Ibid., pp.69-70.

45. Cariola, Patricio, 'The Thought of the Church and the Future of Catholic Education in Latin America', *Religious Education*, 1971, LXVI, p.421.

46. Fischer, Kathleen B., *Political Ideology and Educational Reform in Chile: 1964-76*, Los Angeles: Latin America Center, University of California, 1979, pp.61-2.

47. Ibid., p.144.

48. Edholm, Felicity (ed.), *Education and Repression: Chile*, London: World University Service, 1982, pp.73-4.

49. Conferencia Episcopal de Chile, *La Reforma Educacional*, Santiago de Chile: Ediciones Paulinas, 1981, p.26.

A SCHOOL SYSTEM FOR AN INDIGENOUS RELIGIOUS MINORITY: THE KIMBANGUISTS OF ZAIRE

William M. Rideout, Jr.

In much of Africa, certainly in Zaire, churches and schools have been key institutions for the creation of new, and the reinforcement of old, minorities. The symbiotic relationship between these two institutions was designed and nurtured by the foreign missionaries who directed both. The successes thus achieved in Zaire during a period of some 80 years (1880-1960) prior to independence is indicated by the following figures: with a population of 13,174,883 at independence, Christians numbered 5,033,047 (4,220,439 Catholics and 812,608 Protestants) and there were 21,400 educational establishments with 1,533,314 students (of whom some 10,000 were foreigners) enrolled in Catholic (1,025,598), Protestant, excluding Kimbanguists (446,646), and secular schools.1 While the declared literacy rate of 65 per cent at independence was perhaps inflated, it is generally agreed that in sub-Saharan Africa only the Republic of South Africa and Ghana had literacy rates higher than Zaire. Through schools and churches, missionaries exerted a profound impact on the people of Zaire and they undoubtedly had more and deeper contacts with the Zairians than any other group of foreigners.2

Furthermore, the missionaries had power and prestige. The colonial structure in the Belgian Congo has often been characterised in terms of a trinity consisting of the administration, the Catholic Church, and large enterprises.3 It is not surprising that Zairians should have attempted to achieve recognition and equality with Europeans at least within the religious sector of the colonial structure. As soon as the missionaries arrived in Zaire they had begun to train the people not only to provide the service functions needed to establish and maintain the missions per se, but to educate the people as evangelists to work among their own tribesmen. Often the African evangelists were more successful in proselytising than were the foreign missionaries. Consequently, Zairians had knowledge and experience about missionary activities and quite naturally they considered the missionaries and their institutions as models which they, brothers in the faith, might successfully emulate through the establishment of their own religious sects. Understandably the history of Zaire is punctuated with instances of Christian-based African religious movements evolving and attempting to gain recognition from and equality with the foreign-dominated missions.

Most of these indigenous religious movements failed after experiencing an initial period of acclaim and expansion. Kimbanguism, however, serves as an especially unique instance where maturation brought continued development and renewed dynamism rather than decay and dissolution. After years of colonial persecution (1921-1959) Kimbanguism had, by 1974, achieved recognition from the Government of Zaire as one of three major Christian churches in Zaire, and full membership of the World Council of Churches as a Protestant sect.

The Kimbanguists have eschewed the usual minority options of secession or seclusion, have sought to assert and protect their minority status, and have actively moved to make themselves into a national religious majority. The church represents a movement on the part of the people to discover their religious selves much as Zairians have, under Mobutu's policy of 'authenticity', been trying to discover their 'political selves'.4

The dynamism of Kimbanguism derives substantially from its ability to Africanise the missionary model and especially the missionary school. While this chapter will briefly review the evolution of the Kimbanguist movement, it is the growth and development of this indigenous religious school system which will be its major focus.

HISTORICAL BACKGROUND

No region of Zaire has been as extensively exposed to European political and religious influence as Bas Zaire, that portion located between the Atlantic Ocean and Kinshasa. Since their first contact with the Portuguese in 1482, the Bakongo people, who inhabit parts of northern Angola and Cabinda as well as southern Congo/Brazzaville, have voluntarily, or under duress, been periodically evangelised. The first Portuguese Catholic missionary contingent arrived in 1490 followed by intermittent waves of secular priests, Jesuits, Franciscans, Augustinians and Capuchins. The early missionaries met with tremendous success. The Manikongo, the King of the Bakongos, was an early convert, along with most of his family, and he took the name of King Affonso. Subsequently other important Bakongo rulers were baptised and one of King Affonso's sons was trained in Portugal and returned home as a bishop in 1521.5

In view of the experiences of the second missionary wave in the nineteenth and twentieth centuries, it is fascinating to note that in this first missionary effort it was recognised early by King Affonso (sometimes referred to by the Portuguese as the 'black Constantine') and the missionaries that there were not, and probably would not, be enough missionaries to provide the religious instruction required, and that it would be impossible to send suitable Bakongos to Portugal for training. It would, therefore, be necessary to train the people in place. In 1509 a boarding school was established to provide religious instruction for 400 princes and sons of chiefs; a few years later this school was expanded to 1,000 pupils. At the same time a local system was established to provide for Christian education in the provinces with,

> native catechists as schoolmasters. Schools for girls were also inaugurated. The King went so far as to declare ... that 'everyone in his kingdom was to be educated'.6

At least in the central region of the kingdom, Christianity was the established state religion.

In spite of these accomplishments, by 1717 the last missionaries had withdrawn from the Bas Congo - what is now the Bas Zaire region. By the second half of the nineteenth century when the new missionaries penetrated these areas, they found ruins, some vestiges of mission influence in the local culture, and many crucifixes and crosses. Corruption, political intrigue, and the slave trade combined to destroy the power of the Bakongo Kingdom and its links with Portugal.7

As the new wave of missionaries and explorers sought to penetrate the African heartland by ascending the Congo River, it became apparent that a reliable line of communications had to be built across the Bas Zaire in order to by-pass the 300 miles of rapids on the lower river and connect the coast with Kinshasa, the port of entry to the great navigable stretches of the Congo River and its drainage basin. The combination of affording the shortest access from the ocean to the Congo basin and the need for chains of missionary stations to support and process supplies to new stations being established inland meant that Bas Zaire and the Bakongo people received the full impact of the missionary revival. The highest concentration of missions in Zaire was developed and has been maintained in Bas Zaire. This also meant that the bulk of the schools, and certainly the most advanced secular oriented education available to Africans, was first available in this region.

The culture clash which the Bakongos experienced, therefore, has been profound, and lengthy and prophetic movements had developed here even during the first missionary incursion. By the time of Simon Kimbangu's prophecy, the second foreign incursion had confronted the traditional Bakongo culture with three rather distinct impinging cultures, the colonial, the national or Catholic mission, and the foreign non-Belgian Protestant mission. As G. C. Oosthuizen has pointed out:

> Where the culture clash has been strongest ... independency is strongest; where a tribe has been studiously protected from the shock of culture clash ... independency is absent.8

The Bakongos, as noted, experienced a quite profound culture clash and after the Second World War were among those most actively engaged in independence efforts. It should not be assumed, however, that the foreign cultures were being imposed upon a totally resisting population. Balandier claims that the Bakongo people were one of societies in Central Africa best prepared for European contact, and adds:

> it must be noted how much this ethnic group sought at an early date to multiply its contact with colonial society.9

(author's translation)

In spite of the cultural confrontations and the suffering which accompanied European domination, the Bakongo's adaptation to the modernisation process was an obvious success.

THE PASSION OF SIMON KIMBANGU

Simon Kimbangu, a Mukongo, was probably born in 1889 at Nkamba, a small village north of Thysville (now Mbanza Ngungu), a commercial and administrative centre on the Matadi-Kinshasa railway. Kimbangu was educated by Baptist teachers and became a catechist for the Baptist Mission Society. His other jobs as a domestic in European homes in Kinshasa and near Nkamba and as a factory worker exposed him to prevailing urban as well as rural conditions in Zaire at that time in both indigenous and European milieux.
    In 1921, after experiencing visions in Kinshasa, Kimbangu sought to escape them by returning to Nkamba. However, he not only continued to have visions but experienced miracles as well. Finally, after having refused to obey the instructions he was receiving during these visions, he was warned in a dream that if he did not do as he was told and begin to heal the sick his own soul would be reclaimed. Propelled by this imperative Kimbangu began his faith healing and preaching from the Bible.10 The news of his religious activities spread rapidly throughout the Bas Zaire region, and people began to flock to

Nkamba at the rate of some 4,000 to 5,000 per day. First Protestant converts began to follow him and then Catholics also joined the movement. The roads and pathways to Nkamba were crowded with the sick hoping to be cured, and churches as far away as Kinshasa were emptied as people sought to see and hear the new prophet.11 Kimbangu's message was straightforward and strict; his basic precepts were the condemnation of fetishism, lascivious dancing, polygamy, smoking, and drinking.

> Dancing drums were destroyed, women of polygamous families were sent home, fetishes were burned or thrown away. This could not have been done by missionaries or the administration without a major uprising.12

There were elements of ancestor worship in Kimbangu's teachings, but his message was clearly one of Christianity as preached by the Protestants and taught in their schools although adapted to the local environment.

From March until October when Kimbangu gave himself up to the colonial authorities, the movement continued to spread until the pilgrimages and conversions led to extensive job absenteeism, to Catholic converts destroying rosaries and even attacking a statue of the Virgin Mary as an extension of Kimbangu's interdiction against fetishes, and to Congolese soldiers from the Belgian colonial military force, Force Publique, asking for leave in order to visit Nkamba, the New Jerusalem. Even excommunication or the threat of excommunication seemed unable to stop Catholic conversions. It was at that point, claimed Chome, in writing about the movement, that businessmen, industrialists and Catholic missionaries, the vast majority of whom were Belgians, demanded that the colonial administration intervene.13

Kimbangu was arrested, tried by a military court and sentenced to death. Shocked by accusations of glaring irregularities during Kimbangu's trial (the most flagrant of which was that he was tried by a military rather than a civil court which could not be justified, by the issue per se which was clearly religious rather than military). King Albert of the Belgians intervened and commuted the sentence to one of life imprisonment. Nevertheless, the three pillars of Belgian colonialism, the Catholic mission, business and colonial administration, including the military, had won. Simon Kimbangu was imprisoned in Lubumbashi where, thirty years later, he died in 1951. Followers of Kimbangu, according to some estimates numbering 37,000 heads of families, were dispersed throughout the country and were permitted to return to Bas Zaire only after independence in 1960, ending what the Kimbanguists refer to as their diaspora. The last governmental condemnations of Kimbanguists occurred in 1957.14

THE PERIOD OF PERSECUTION

Kimbanguism's sweep through the rural areas made suppression of the movement by the Belgian colonial administration practically impossible. Attempts to identify Kimbanguists were further complicated by the fact that the faithful generally returned to their former Protestant or Catholic missions and their continuing loyalty to Kimbanguism was kept secret. The movement did not die because the factors leading to its development and dramatic expansion remained unaltered. As Crawford Young has explained,

> ... the motor force in these movements was an apocalyptic reaction to a colonial situation which seemed beyond any secular remedy. The millennial vision provided the means for transcending a temporal situation which was intolerable yet beyond the power of the African to alter.15

While there is no question that the movement also developed or revived ethnic consciousness, the colonial administration's decision to disperse Kimbangu's adherents gave rise to its multi-ethnic orientation. Kimbanguists were deported not only to nearby areas which had not been infected, but pockets of them were relocated in every other province of the country. The deportees not only continued to practise their faith in secret but began to proselytise and to bear witness among the tribes located in regions where they were being resettled.16 Meanwhile the number of followers among the Bakongos also increased and expanded geographically into Congo/Brazzaville where French officials did oppose them, but with much less vigour than the Belgians.

During the 38-year period they were banned, the membership was often torn and shaken by the rise of other African-led syncretic or messianic movements which grew up in Zaire and often called themselves Kimbanguists or tried to draw strength from the movement by trying to associate themselves with it. One of the strangest incidents was the initial link between Kimbanguists and the Salvation Army missionaries who began to evangelise in Zaire in 1935. The Kimbanguists at first believed that the red letter 'S' on the collar lapel of Salvation Army uniforms stood for 'Simon' and that the movement represented a Kimbanguist reincarnated in European form. Once the Salvation Army understood what was happening and renounced Kimbangu, the association between the two groups collapsed.

By the 1950s, the religious channel for the venting of frustration tended to be supplanted by the modern, secular nationalism of the Abako, ...

the Bakongo tribal organisation which evolved from a linguistic and cultural movement into a political one.17 The problem facing the disorganised Kimbanguists was increasingly focused on what their political role in the growing nationalist movement in Bas Zaire should be. The leadership of the Kimbanguists began to be taken over by Kimbangu's sons while his wife, until her death in 1959, remained a source of inspiration and spiritual authority.

Joseph Diangienda, the youngest son of Kimbangu, was permitted to visit his father in prison just prior to his death and returned to Bas Zaire with the word that he had been selected by his father to lead the movement. Diangienda accepted the position and began to negotiate with colonial officials in an effort to have the ban against the Kimbanguists lifted. In 1954, he returned to Kinshasa from exile in Tshela to direct the movement. Special attention was given to making Kimbanguism known in Belgium and elsewhere overseas. In September 1957, Information on Kimbanguism and Prophetic Christianity - Kimbanguism-Statute, were published (in French) and in August of 1959 the government officially lifted the ban on Kimbanguism.18 At this point there were some 40 different Kimbanguist groups without common structure or links united only by a common bond to Kimbangu. Pulling the movement together, Diangienda, as Spiritual Chief of the Kimbanguist Church, officially founded the Church of Jesus Christ on Earth according to Simon Kimbangu, l'Eglise de Jesus Christ sur la terre, par Simon Kimbangu (EJCSK) in 1959. Adhering to a traditional type of organisational pattern, the EJCSK had organised according to two principles: division of work, and hierarchy and discipline.19

On the political side, the Abako party had consolidated its position as the party of the Bakongo, with its leader, Kasavubu, subsequently the first President of Zaire. Bakongo politicians obviously appreciated the influence of Kimbanguism and their efforts to capitalise on its political potential were illustrated by such things as the pictures which were circulated in 1959 in Bas Zaire showing Peter giving the keys of the kingdom to Kasavubu, on the instructions of Kimbangu.20 Indeed, two prominent Kimbanguists held significant political positions in early national governments. Emmanuel Bamba was Minister of Finance from May 1962 until June 1964 while Charles Kisolokele, eldest son of Kimbangu, served as Minister of Labour in 1961-62.

Thus, it was profoundly important to the movement when Diangienda through a basic declaration of the EJCSK in 1960 pronounced that the Church would not be associated with any political party. The EJCSK would promote peace, reconciliation and non-violence in a country menaced by politics. Good citizenship, which included political participation, would be encouraged but the choice of political parties within which members served would not be specified or influenced by the Church.21 The point was also strongly made that the Church was open to all who wished to join regardless of race, in keeping with Kimbangu's teachings. Significantly, no white was killed or wounded in the founding and suppression of Kimbanguism and there had been no anti-colonial revolt under Kimbangu's leadership.22

Diangienda added that the Church was not seeking material gains, that followers would not be advised against seeing doctors, but the Church would seek to spread the good news of Christ as the Protestants and Catholics did. EJCSK faith and doctrine would be centred on reading and explaining the Bible.23 Furthermore, Kimbanguists would support the ecumenical movement and would engage in a range of social action activities: building hospitals, dispensaries, child care and agricultural training centres, until then almost exclusively the domain of the foreign missions which received partial support from the government for these purposes.24 Aside from the revivalist type atmosphere of their worship services, similar in style and atmosphere to services in Baptist Churches with black congregations - and reflecting Kimbangu's own Baptist background and training, the Church had basically a puritanical orientation. The institution of Communion was not introduced until 1971.

KIMBANGUISTS' EDUCATIONAL COMMITMENT

Since reading the Bible and preaching was the model portrayed by Kimbangu, literacy has been of major importance to the Kimbanguists. As long as Kimbanguist children could attend the existing schools, there was little need for Kimbanguists to establish schools of their own. However, as the movement to grant clemency to the Kimbanguists began to make headway in the mid-1950s, known Kimbanguist children were expelled from schools. This forced the Kimbanguists to open their own school in 1956 and by 1960 priority consideration was being given by the movement to the building and operating of schools.25 Then as now, schools were generally constructed by volunteer labourers with students themselves participating actively. With perseverance and steady pressure, the Kimbanguists succeeded in getting the government to subsidise their schools on the same

325

basis as that applied to the Catholic and Protestant school systems. Following the pattern of the missionaries, the Kimbanguists also established a Bureau de l'Enseignement Kimbanguist (BEK) which serves as the general headquarters for their educational system, as the Bureau de l'Enseignement Catholique (BEC) and the Bureau de l'Enseignement Protestant (BEP) serve the Catholics and Protestants respectively.

While Kimbanguism has spread to the Central African Republic, Cameroon, Congo/Brazzaville, Zambia and Angola, the Kimbanguists had established few schools outside of Zaire. However, the rationale for the establishment of schools has expanded from simply providing schools for Kimbanguist children who might otherwise be deprived of education to being a key factor in proselytisation and to meeting the increasing demands for education necessary to lead a usefully participating life in the twentieth century. The importance of and the potential for proselytisation among the youth is indicated by the fact that in Zaire over 50 per cent of the population is estimated to be under 15 years of age. Indicative of the Kimbanguists' successes in educating its people are the results of a survey research study which found that only 30 per cent of the total Kimbanguist population in Bas Zaire had not been to school.26

Kimbanguist children are not required to go to Kimbanguist schools nor are children attending Kimbanguist schools required to be Kimbanguists. Religious discrimination of this nature would, of course, jeopardise the government's subsidisation of Kimbanguist schools, for although all religiously run schools are permitted to teach some religion, children are not required to participate if they do not wish to, and thus cannot be excluded for religious reasons. Therefore, while the Kimbanguists are not actively encouraged to proselytise and convert, as the national Catholic mission had been under the colonial administration, the Kimbanguists have fully realised how important a tool education is in the propagation of their sect. Following the model the European missionaries created some 80 years earlier, the Kimbanguists have employed it with at least equal vigour and success.27 In addition to schooling,

Kimbanguists have engaged in extensive social services in agriculture, healing, youth work and cooperatives. It is in a sense acculturation of a system - new (Kimbanguist) wine in old (missionary) bottles. The EJCSK's maintenance and expansion, and its promotion and support of such extensive social service programmes, are made possible through a tax of at least 10 per cent of income, paid in produce, labour or money, by Church members. Unlike their missionary models, they have never had access to significant financial assistance from external sources - a fact which makes their achievements even more impressive.

The question invariably arises as to whether or not Kimbanguism is a nationalist movement. The answer usually is rather predetermined by the definition one uses for nationalism. If one defines it as

> a consciousness, on the part of individuals or groups, of membership in a nation, or of a desire to forward the strength, liberty or prosperity of a nation ... 28

then one might well find the movement nationalistic. Such phenomena might be manifested in political, cultural, religious, and other areas with

> Political nationalism being a movement reclaiming for the nationals, the natives, an ever larger part of the direction of their own affairs, a movement which finally ends in independence for the people concerned.29

(author's translation)

In this light, Kimbanguism might well be considered as one of the initial manifestations or generators of national consciousness. Certainly it is important in the sense that it is a black movement, requiring no white direction or supervision, and Kimbanguism, its members add, 'is "our religion" because it was founded by one of our race.'30 (author's translation). In this instance, the 'religious self' would have preceded and prepared the way for the development of the 'political self'. However, as with the Catholics and Protestants, the latter term used in Zaire as a classification excluding Kimbanguists, Kimbanguism, while embracing all tribes within Zaire, has not eradicated all tribalism among its own constituents, although the Church has made great efforts to overcome the internal divisiveness that tribalism has generated. Kimbanguism, it must be noted, is also more than a national Zairian movement since its adherents are now found in at least eight other neighbouring African states. Moreover, whilst most members are Africans, the Church is not racist – it has admitted white members and assigned them positions of responsibility. In short, while not an instrument of Zairian nationalism it does promote Zairian national development and ethnic cooperation and demonstrates dramatically that Zairians can direct a dynamic and sophisticated contemporary missionary movement successfully even in competition with older, wealthier and larger foreign missionary movements.

The Kimbanguist school system which was first developed to train Kimbanguism's human resources when colonially dominated schools refused to do so, has also demonstrated to other Zairians that this could be accomplished by Africans. This effect would undoubtedly qualify as 'forwarding the strength, liberty or prosperity of the nation.' Today this is further shown by the fact that the leaders of the Church are fully committed to identifying their best secondary school students and helping them to obtain a university education.31 However, this task too is being undertaken on national rather than on tribal or regional bases.

Noteworthy for the Kimbanguist school system in Zaire is, first of all, the astonishing speed with which it has expanded from a system too insignificant to report in 1960 to a system in 1970 which at the primary level enrolled 161,433 students or 5.7 per cent of the national total and at the secondary level 13,640 students, or 5.9 per cent of the total enrolment.32 Present-day figures are in the process of compilation.

The second point is the Kimbanguists' emphasis on the primary school level which is related to the lower cost per pupil and to the use of teachers with lower qualifications and thus their greater availability. It is also significant that over 90 per cent of Zairian children aged 8 to 12 are attending primary school, and therefore, can be reached (and proselytised) through the school. This emphasis on primary education is also reflected in the Kimbanguist effort at the secondary school level. There, too, over half of those in the upper four grades (cycle long) were in the normal school stream which means they will become qualified to teach at the elementary level, or, if necessary, in the first two grades of secondary school. Students from the normal school stream in secondary school, can, of course, continue on in pedagogy at the post-secondary level, as can those enrolled in a general secondary stream.33 Training teachers, for primary schools, is a further key consideration.

The fourth striking element about the Kimbanguist system is that it adds to the existing imbalance of education opportunity in the country. Kimbanguist schools are concentrated in those parts of the country which already have substantially more schools than their percentage of the total national population would warrant. This, in a nation where education has been a major determinant in the achievement of upward social mobility, inherently has serious political implications. President Mobutu, well aware of this, stated in 1970,

> The harmonious development of the Republic demands that there be an equal geographical distribution of schools of all types. That policy is inscribed in the fundamental orientation of our economic organisation... 34

Kimbanguist schools were first eligible for government grants in the provinces approximately during the following years: Kinshasa, 1962; Bas Zaire, 1963; Shaba and Bandundu, 1966; Kasai Oriental and Kasai Occidental, 1968; Haut Zaire, 1969; and Equateur and Kivu, 1970. The speed with which the system grew in Kasai is not as surprising as it might have been had the Balubas not been voracious in their efforts to acquire education almost from the beginning of colonial rule. An added consideration of interest is that a disproportionate percentage of the educated elite in Zaire are either Balubas or Bakongos. This causes resentment by other tribesmen and it puts Balubas and Bakongos in competition with each other for the desirable elite positions time after time. Yet, in spite of this, the Kimbanguists today have an educational system which is probably serving more Baluba primary school children than it is Bakongo children. This would seem to indicate the extent to which Kimbanguism has detribalised itself. There is some indication that while initial expansion was opportunistic, efforts are now being made to assist in the national effort to upgrade the educationally deprived provinces, especially since the President announced that policy in 1970.35

TO NATIONALISATION AND BACK

The remarkably rapid expansion of the Kimbanguists' school system was not accomplished without difficulties. While the construction of classrooms was being achieved through the dedication and commitment of Kimbanguist congregations, problems began to surface with regard to teaching cadres required to operate the system. In the late 1960s, it was reported that BEK was experiencing difficulties in paying its teachers and there were also accusations of tribalism and incompetence within the Bureau.36 This was followed by a BEK move to licence teachers in the Kimbanguist system, a move which, it was claimed, was being made in order to replace non-Kimbanguist with Kimbanguist teachers.37 Apparently the Kimbanguists felt that the extra devotion and sacrifice which they might ask for and receive from Kimbanguist teachers, and could not expect from the non-Kimbanguists in their school system, would help them to overcome many of their problems, especially those of a financial nature.

At approximately the same time a further crisis hit BEK. Following the above-mentioned complaints about leadership problems Mayimbu-Mantuidy replaced

Mvwendi as Director General of BEK.38 This was followed some two years later by reports of a possible schism in the Church and an accusation from Kasai Oriental, heartland of the Balubas, that Mvwendi, still active within BEK, was favouring Bakongos.39 In short, the Kimbanguists were obviously not immune to the types of financial mismanagement and tribal problems which have continually plagued religious as well as political movements in Zaire. Nevertheless, it should be noted that the Kimbanguists continued to pursue the social and educational goals they had enunciated as being part of their religious mission. Diangienda met with Mobutu in July 1968, and outlined the agricultural and educational accomplishments of the EJCSK. He also emphasised willingness to associate Kimbanguist leaders in support of the social policies of the government.40

Meanwhile, governmental action in 1971 to nationalise the university system, while it did not directly affect the Kimbanguists, deprived the Catholic and Protestant systems of their universities (Kinshasa and Kisangani respectively) and was to be a precursor of further and more profound government intervention.

On December 30, 1974, the Political Bureau of the national party, the **Mouvement Populaire de la Revolution** (Popular Movement of the Revolution - MPR) nationalised the entire school system in Zaire and disenfranchised all previously existing and approved educational systems. At the same time, all religious education in the schools was forbidden in order to prevent

> the perpetuation of religious segregation practised, up until present, by the churches within their school networks.41

> (author's translation)

The government included within the nationalisation the Catholic Junior Seminaries (**Petits Seminaires**), traditionally used, among other things, to provide a mechanism for screening prospective candidates for the priesthood. Following nationalisation these schools were to follow the same curricula as other secondary schools. The BEP and the BEK did not have a comparable secondary school structure functioning to recruit their own future church leaders.

In spite of the impact created by nationalisation, Diangienda announced in 1975 that EJCSK had undertaken a 'vast' programme of development to benefit the entire population, without distinction of race or confession, by establishing farm cooperatives and a House of the People in Kinshasa, and had under construction a large hospital as well as a medical school, a school for pastors and another for masons plus welcome centres for the needy. In addition, EJCSK churches also served that function. Diangienda stressed that masons were working into the nights to complete these new units.42 Moreover, a school of Kimbanguist theology had been established similar to those founded by earlier missionary stations for the same purpose. This school was associated with a community agricultural centre. Students in school did not receive scholarships - they worked to provide for themselves and their families. Those who were not employed in the city worked on the farm. Thus, the school was self-sufficient.43

The nationalisation of the school system (primary and secondary) lasted from late 1974 to early 1977. The Catholics, as noted, with by far the largest school system in Zaire, began to withdraw teachers and administrators from their former schools by January 1975, and large numbers of Belgian missionary teachers returned home.44 The Political Bureau's concession which approved the teaching of religion after class hours but away from the schools did nothing to slow down the withdrawal of large numbers of religious personnel from the positions they had held in the pre-nationalised systems. Those leaving their former systems, and perhaps Catholics especially, felt they were being evicted. This conviction was further reinforced by the fact that in those schools established to prepare religious cadres, including the Senior Seminaries (_Grands Seminaires_) operated by the Catholic Church to train priests, the government had by 1972 already installed political party _Mouvement Populaire Republicain_ (MPR) committees to provide a sound civic and political training component for students. This political intervention was a festering sore but seemed to offend Catholics more than Protestants or Kimbanguists perhaps because the Catholic programme was more highly structured, concentrated and idiosyncratic. The Churches' unhappiness at losing their school systems was compounded by the fact that the nationalised schools were turned over to new managers who were very often incompetent and ill-prepared. There followed a general fall in academic moral standards in addition to the waste and loss suffered under the new management. The situation deteriorated so seriously and so rapidly that within two years the government was forced to call back missionary and religious personnel.45 In February 1977, a new agreement was signed between the State and the Catholic, Protestant and Kimbanguist Churches. It specified that:

a) The churches would be responsible for operating their own system but they would be placed directly under the overall supervision of the State.

b) By 1980 full financial management would be returned to the religious systems.

c) New religious schools would be established, as they had been prior to 1974, on the initiative of those responsible for schools in the various denominational education bureaux, but to obtain proper coordination and 'rational and reasonable' geographic distribution, a national planning service would be established to oversee school expansion.

d) All schools would receive national subsidies on a per capita attendance basis. In primary and secondary schools, however, Churches could, as under previous arrangements, benevolently contribute, as their means might permit, to the operation of the schools in their networks. The role of the Churches loomed even larger given the government's previous decisions which in 1971 ended provision of textbooks and classroom supplies, in 1972 cut all assistance other than 'what was required to keep the schools open' and in 1972/73 had approved the reinstatement of fees for the above expenses the government had ceased to fund.46

e) School inspection would be handled as it had been prior to nationalisation, except that those engaged would serve only within their own systems and would be called 'coordinators' rather than inspectors. They would, however, have direct links with national supervisory inspectors.

f) Churches would have the right to teach religion within their own networks. The State insisted, however, on reinforcing also the teaching of civic and political education in all religious systems.47

[Official State schools in Zaire do not teach religion.]

DENATIONALISATION AND PROGRESS

While the nationalisation of the Kimbanguist school system caused the Churches great concern, as it did for the Catholics and Protestants, it appears, nevertheless, to have also had some highly beneficial effects. As was noted previously, nationalisation came at the same time as the Kimbanguists were experiencing serious tribal infighting among their Bakongo and Baluba members within the BEK in the early 1970s. Like the Protestants, the Kimbanguists did not deliberately withdraw teachers from their nationalised schools (and unlike the Catholics neither group had a foreign cadre of school personnel operating within their systems). However, one of the constant troubles of the Zairian school system has been the loss of teachers, and without links with religious organisations which would address their problems and assure their pay, teachers formerly within the BEK and BEP systems left the profession in greater numbers than ever before.48 Thus, by the beginning of the 1976/77 school year, the government was desperately trying to staff the classrooms and the fact that neither BEP nor BEK had officially withdrawn teachers made little difference in the dismal recruitment situation. At any rate, from all indications, the temporary government occupation of the Kimbanguist school system gave the BEK a chance to put its own house in order.

In terms of their proportion of the national school system, the religious groups suffered a decrease. In 1974, it was stated that approximately 90 per cent of the schools were religiously run (Catholic, Protestant and Kimbanguist). By 1984, this had fallen to an estimated 80 per cent of primary and 65 per cent of secondary schools.49 It appears that the percentages shifted for the three systems as a whole roughly from Catholic in 1974 at 80 per cent to 70 per cent in 1984; Protestant from 15 per cent to approximately 17 per cent and Kimbanguist from 5 per cent to about 3 per cent. At the same time, however, the national system underwent powerful expansion between 1974 and 1984 even though the growth rate of all systems had previously declined gradually from 9.9 per cent between 1966/67 and 1968/69 to 3.4 per cent between 1970/71 and 1972/73.50 In the context of a national population which was estimated to have increased to 30,261,000 by mid-1982, primary school enrolment was projected to have increased from 3,219,554 in 1971/72 to 5,200,000 in 1978/79.51 If these estimated figures and proportions for each school system are fairly accurate, it means that the Kimbanguist system has remained rather stable in terms of total numbers of students enrolled by the BEK while the BEC system has added over half a million students to its enrolment, the Protestants just over 400,000 and the Official System by increasing from 10 to 20 per cent of the total added almost 1,000,000. This expansion was accompanied by increased government financial support which rose to an average of 20 per cent of the total annual budget - more specifically, from 17 per cent of the total in 1976 to 23 per cent in 1980.52

However, educational figures on Zaire must be used with great caution. David Gould, who has been studying Zaire for some two decades, commented when it had been reported that the number of teachers in Zaire had expanded from 37,300 to 143,400 between 1960 and 1975, then to soar to 230,000 by 1978, that perhaps as much as two-thirds of the educational payroll could be attributed to phantom teachers; the real figure would likely be well short of that total. While Gould's assessment may also be overstated, Mobutu himself, in arguing on behalf of his economic reform programme in Paris in 1978, noted that fictitious teachers on the payroll represented a major source of potential budgetary savings.53 The lack of a reliable data base on which to estimate educational costs and to plan national human resources, development needs and availabilities became so serious that the World Bank provided a credit to Zaire (Project Nr. 1519 OZR) to obtain the data and to re-establish a competent system for providing such data on a continuing national basis.54

Mobutu's programme of 'Zairianisation', announced in November 1973, provided the Kimbanguists with more national recognition than ever before. Here was a religious order functioning well which had already been basically 'Zairianised'. The 'radicalisation' move which followed during the next year, and provided the basis for the nationalisation of the school systems, probably contributed significantly to the rise in the prestige of all Churches and their personnel after the government was forced to ask the Churches to resume responsibility for their systems when it became painfully apparent that the government was totally unable to manage them.55 While all religious systems tried to re-establish their former schools, the task was staggering - as was the cost. In many cases, the schools had been plundered of textbooks as well as furnishings. In the worst cases, it was impossible to reopen the schools and they were abandoned by the religious groups formerly responsible for them.56 Without the external resources to draw upon, the Kimbanguists had an even more difficult time trying to rehabilitate their system and BEK's development slowed down. The Kimbanguist, Protestant, and Catholic Churches have remained free of the taint of corruption which affected the state. While the Churches have not been channels to power and influence, they have offered status and security.57

There is no doubt that the Kimbanguists have experienced a dramatic growth in membership since independence. It is currently estimated that 68 per cent of the national population of Zaire is Christian and that roughly two-thirds are Catholic and one-third Protestant (including Kimbanguists). Of the estimated 6,859,160 Protestants, it is difficult to identify the number of Kimbanguists. Their totals have been estimated at between 1,000,000 and 3,000,000. The most recent report available claimed they had 8,000 congregations with 2,000,000 adult members and 3,500,000 affiliated.58 The very nature of these figures is indicative of the fact that they are estimates. If the Church is at or near 2,000,000 adherents, then its growth has indeed been phenomenal. Transcending class, tribal and national boundaries, and developing its own hierarchical organisation under the leadership of Kimbangu's three sons, it has become a major religious, social and cultural factor in Central Africa.

CONCLUSION

There is no question that this religious minority is seeking to become a majority by becoming a church for all the citizens of the country and by being a church which will assist the nation to achieve its social and cultural objectives. There is also no question that the dynamic development of its educational system has been a (if not the) major factor in Kimbanguism's success. Finally, there is no question that the original missionary model may still be a relevant one providing that it is racially detribalised, that is with all tribes participating, with Whites admitted as well as Blacks, and de-Europeanised in its direction and management. For the Kimbanguists, independence has not suggested the separation of education and religion, rather it has offered a new opportunity to acculturate and nationalise the European missionary church/school model and infuse it with a new indigenous dynamism. This pattern is an interesting alternative to the more prevailing one of completely nationalising the school systems and separating them from religion.

The bond between formal education and religion has persevered in Zaire since its first exposure, and that exposure, too, occurred simultaneously. Education, even in the face of contemporary Zaire, where failure seems endemic for its people as well as its politics, remains one of the most cherished popular desires. Benoit Verhaegen, who has worked in and studied the educational systems in Zaire since before independence, noted:

> The idea remains intact that success in school can assure the greatest professional and social advantages and lead to the summit of the social pyramid. The school in Zaire is, in principle, and for sometime will be, open to all. For this reason, in a society which has become profoundly unequal and unjust, the school acts as a powerful equalising myth. All or almost all accept their disastrous situation and present inequality because there subsists for each individual the hope of change and promotion through the school. Education thus procures for the regime the greatest part of its legitimacy.59

Understandably, therefore, the school system has been the most rapidly expanding segment of the public sector.60 One still finds the otherwise incomprehensible situation where 49 per cent of 20-year-old cohorts could be found enrolled in the educational establishment in Kinshasa.61

It is, therefore, perhaps appropriate that the Churches, among the precious few institutions in Zaire which have remained uncorrupted by a regime which equates uncorruptibility with potential disloyalty, continue to remain fundamentally responsible for the operation of the educational system. Moreover, in a country where the adult literacy rate is at 15 per cent, one of the highest in Africa, the Churches are committed to making the Zairians literate for religious as well as socio-political reasons.62 And it is ironic that these same Churches provide the regime which often treats them as an enemy with the very legitimisation it needs. However, as Drachoussof, Vis and Sokal have written,

> ... Zaire's economic collapse is, at root, a political and essentially moral problem, and the solution, likewise, will require a strengthening of moral values - in the African context, this means religious values, whether traditional or Christian - and a radical political change.63

Kimbanguist Zaire

Perhaps in these circumstances, the Churches are powerfully placed ultimately to play a powerful role in the process of national revitalisation. Among them will be one unique member of the World Council of Churches, l'Eglise de Jesus Christ sur la terre par Simon Kimbangu, which has already combined some of the old with much of the new and has taken a foreign institution and made it its own. In the process it has and continues to use education, as other Churches in Zaire have historically done, to prove to its followers that their individual development and well-being are of critical importance.

NOTES AND REFERENCES

1. L'Office de l'Information et des Relations Publiques pour le Congo Belge et le Ruanda-Urundi, Le Congo Belge, Bruxelles: Imprimeries Dewarichet, II, 1959, pp.152-3.

2. Rideout, William M. Jr., Education and Elites: The Making of the New Elites and the Formal Education System in the Congo (K), unpublished PhD dissertation, Stanford University, 1971.

3. Young, Crawford, Politics in the Congo, Decolonisation and Independence, Princeton University Press, 1965, p.10.

4. Dawson, Richard E. and Prewitt, Kenneth, An Analytical Study of Political Socialization, Boston: Little, Brown and Company, 1969, p.17. The 'political self' was used by the authors to cover, 'an individual's package of orientations regarding politics ...' Through his relationships with the social world an individual develops 'political self'.

5. Aexelson, Sigbert, Culture Confrontation in the Lower Congo, Falkoping: Gummessons Boktryckeri, 1970.

6. Anderson, Efraim, Messianic Popular Movements in the Lower Congo, Uppsala: Almqvist and Wiksells Boktryckeri, 1958, p.33.

7. Aexelson, op.cit.

8. Oosthuizen, G.C., <u>Post-Christianity in Africa, A Theological and Anthropological Study</u>, London: C. Hurst and Co., 1968, p.30.

9. Balandier, George, <u>Sociologie actuelle de l'Afrique Noire</u>, Paris: Presses Universitaires de France, 1955, pp.103-11.

10. Chome, Jules, <u>La passion de Simon Kimbangu</u>, Bruxelles: Editions de Remarques Congolaises, 2nd edn., 1959.

11. Ibid.

12. Ibid., p.15.

13. Ibid., pp.27-9.

14. Beguin, Willy, 'L'Eglise de Jesus Christ sur la terre par le prophete Simon Kimbangu', in: <u>Le Monde Non-Chretien</u>, Paris, <u>22</u>, 89-90, 1969.

15. Young, op.cit., p.252.

16. Beguin, op.cit.

17. Young, op.cit., p.286.

18. Bazola, Etienne, 'Le Kimbanguisme', in: <u>Cahiers de Religions Africaines</u>, Kinshasa, II, 3, 1968.

19. Lasserre, J., 'L'Eglise Kimbanguiste du Congo', in: <u>Le Monde Non-Chretien</u>, Paris, <u>19</u>, 79-80, 1966.

20. Young, op.cit.

21. Bazola, op.cit.

22. Chome, op.cit.

23. Lasserre, op.cit.

l'Education, Kisangani: 21-22 Janvier 1978. The author points out that teacher attrition rates over a 3 year period 1968/69-1971/72 in Upper Zaire were highest - 99.6 per cent (out of a sample of 277) - in the government's official school system. While it was high in the religious systems too, it was less than in the official system. Moreover, it was easier for religious orders to replace those who left with comparably qualified teachers than it was for the official system.

49. Dafumu, Mukenge, Finalites, Objectifs et Modeles de la Formation des Enseignants du Second Degre en Afrique Subsaharienne, Contribution a l'etude comparee: Les cas du Nigeria, du Senegal et du Zaire, unpublished PhD dissertation, Faculteit der Psycholgie en Pedagogische Wetenschappen, Katholieke Universitet Leuven, 1984, p.444.

50. Ibid., p.452.

51. Huybrechts, Andre, 'Zaire Economy' in: Africa South of the Sahara, 1986, London: Europa Publications Ltd., 1986, pp.1024, 1029.

52. Dafumu, Mukenge, op.cit., p.539.

53. Gould, David, Bureaucratic Corruption and Underdevelopment in the Third World: The Case of Zaire, Elmsford, N.Y.: Pergamon Press, 1980, p.2.

54. Interview with World Bank representative, March 14, 1987.

55. Young, Crawford and Turner, Thomas, The rise and decline of the Zairian State, Madison: University of Wisconsin Press, 1985.

56. Interviews with Catholic clergy during 1981.

57. Young, Crawford, op.cit., p.121.

58. Barrett, David B., World Christian Encylopaedia, Nairobi: Oxford University Press, 1982.

59. Verhaegen, Benoit, 'Paradoxes Zairoises', Paper presented at the Annual Meeting, Canadian Association of African Studies, Quebec, May 1983, pp.2-3.

60. Young, Crawford, op.cit.

61. de St. Moulin, Leon, 'Kinshasa', in: <u>Revue Francaise d'Etudes Politiques Africaines Mois en Afrique</u>, Dakar: <u>6</u>, 9 Septembre 1971.

62. Huybrechts, op.cit.

63. Ibid.

12

AFRIKANER IDENTITY AND EDUCATIONAL POLICY IN SOUTH AFRICA

Alan Penny

INTRODUCTION

The cardinal premise of the new constitutional system is the distinction drawn between own and general (common) affairs. The new Constitution lays down in section 14 (2) that the matters mentioned in Schedule 1 to the Constitution, which include education at all levels, are own affairs of the White, Coloured and Indian population groups, respectively. This means that all educational matters that relate solely to a specific group, are own affairs of the population group concerned. The education of each of these population groups will therefore, as an own affair, take place within the context of the particular group's own culture and frame of reference.1

We believe that the teaching and education of the children of white parents should occur on the basis of the life and world view of the parents. For Afrikaans speaking children this means that they must be educated on the basis of the Christian/National life and world view of our Nation. In this life and world view, the Christian and National principles are of basic significance and they aim at the propagation, protestation and development of the Christian and National being and nature of our Nation. The Christian basis of this life and world view is grounded on the Holy Scripture and expressed in the Creeds of our three Afrikaans Churches. By the national principle we understand love for everything that is our own, with special mention of our country, our language, our history and our culture.2

Although separated by a period of thirty-five years these two statements reflect what are the dominant ideological premises underlying South African education today; its structures, philosophy, provision and curriculum. Embedded in a host of Apartheid legislation of which the Race Classification Acts and the Group Areas Acts form the cornerstone, and within the Black Homelands Policy, education is seen to serve a fundamental ideological function. It is seen as essential in leading the child through the mother tongue into the cultural and national life of his own people. Hence, one finds separate schools for the Afrikaans and English speaking white groups, the Coloured race group, the Indians and the various black ethnic groups, of which the Xhosa, Zulu and Sotho form the majority.

Three crucial and interrelated questions arise. The first, how has Afrikaner3 nationalist ideology viewed the educational system in the country over time, within its overall purpose of nation building? The second, what has been its philosophy in shaping and moulding the young (vorming)4 to become desired members of South African society? The third, deriving from the second, how is that society perceived? It would be naive to believe that the present shape and form of South African education emerged to some pre-designed master plan. Indeed, it is as much a consequence of economic forces and processes as it is of the political and ideological. In particular, the rapid industrial and economic growth of South Africa following the Second World War, the urbanisation of the majority of the white population and the emergence of the Afrikaner as a powerful force in the economy brought with it major changes. Similarly, South Africa's international position and its relations and status with regard to the rest of the world especially after the declaration of a republic has seen a steady 'integration' of the 'old enemy', the English speaking white South

Afrikaner South Africa

African, into the Afrikaner fold, now defined in terms of a broader South Africanism.

In order to address these questions it is necessary to appreciate two factors about the Afrikaner. The first is that his religion and, in particular, the three Dutch Reformed Churches have exercised an important influence and control over the political and educational history of South Africa. Calvinist in origin, this religion, a gospel of predestination of an elite and the divine authority of the state over the individual, is preached in its more extreme forms, providing a theological justification for <u>Apartheid</u>. Frequently the Afrikaner is likened to the Israelites of old.

The second is that the Afrikaner group within the South African context is small, threatened and has suffered repression. A fear of a loss of identity has been crucial in the creation of Afrikaner nationalism. Stemming largely from seventeenth and eighteenth century Dutch, Belgian and French immigrants, and from their contact with the indigenous tribes, their history is a history of conflict, of the subjugation and dispossession of the sub-continent's black tribes, of opposition to, followed by defeat by British Imperialism, and ultimately of 'victory' over that imperialism when in 1961 the country became a republic. This history has bred a distinctive people with a distinctive set of attitudes and beliefs which are themselves in a state of flux, given the changing nature of the context.

In the course of this chapter an attempt will be made to trace the emergence of the present educational policy in South Africa by focusing on the dominant ideologies which have shaped educational thought and practice. In particular, Calvinism and nationalism as they emerged in the policy of Christian National Education, and more latterly, the forces which have brought about an evolution in that policy will be looked at. It is important to keep in mind that this policy, originally designed for the preservation of the Africaner volk5 was imposed on all other South Africans without negotiation, as they were confronted with Afrikaner Nationalist notions of ethnic and racial exclusivity.

Afrikaner South Africa

In July 1939 the Federation of Afrikaans Cultural Organisations (<u>Federasie van Afrikaanse Kultuur Vereniginge</u> (FAK)), sponsored a Christian National Conference in Bloemfontein at which an Institute for Christian National Teaching and Education (<u>Instituut vir Christelike Nationale Onderwys en Opvoeding</u> (ICNO)), was formed. It was commissioned to formulate an educational policy (<u>Beleid</u>) which would embody the key tenets of Afrikaner Calvinism and Nationalism. In statements that followed, the Institute promoted mother tongue instruction and a Christian education

> based on Holy Scripture and formulated in the Articles of Faith of our three Afrikaans churches,

which would be nationally oriented, emphasising

> love for everything that is our own, with special reference to our country, our language, our history and our culture.6

When in 1948 the final FAK/ICNO document was published it also contained fundamentalist doctrines condemnatory of the theory of evolution and views supportive of the theory of predestination. The <u>Beleid</u>7 insisted too that history and geography were to be taught as divinely determined and that only teachers who were prepared to subscribe to these fundamentalist tenets were to be appointed. Whilst the more extreme of these demands were never adopted, the segregation of the two white language groups and the various black ethnic groups did follow, and a particular educational theory emerged to interpret, reinforce and promote this particular philosophy which is called 'Fundamental Pedagogics'. As developments have shown, the ideas embedded in this document have shaped South Africa's educational policies and practices for both whites and blacks. They are rooted in the racist ideology underpinning the Black Homelands Policy.

Afrikaner South Africa

THE ORIGINS OF CHRISTIAN NATIONAL EDUCATION

Since much has been written on the origins of a system of Christian National Education, the aim of this brief exposition is not to contribute original research on a wide ranging topic, but to provide a sense of perspective.

Practices which embodied a close relationship between church and school, as formulated in the Synod of Dort (1618/1619) were brought to the Cape by the early Dutch settlers. Amongst the edicts of that synod were those which decreed that a Christian magistracy was to see to the provision of an education by 'only orthodox Christians' and was to include religious instruction. By the time of the British Annexation of the Cape in 1814, a struggle similar to that which took place between Church and State for the control of education in Europe, had ended by the end of the nineteenth century in a centralised, state controlled system of education. A different pattern emerged in the two Boer Republics of the Orange Free State and the South African Republic (Transvaal), however, which were not conquered until 1920. There a church dominated pattern continued, and as Muir has shown, the relationship was even formalised in their respective constitutions.[8]

The Calvinist Roots

The struggle in the Cape, however, was significant in one important respect. It centred around the Fellowship of True Afrikaners (<u>Genootskap van Regte Afrikaners</u>). Launched in the Cape village of Paarl on August 14, 1875, its members

> Fastened on to the concept of Afrikaner people as a culturally distinct element within the population of South Africa: a blending of Hollander, German and Huguenot for the most part, knit together by two centuries of common history into a natural group fully identified with the South African soil and speaking a common language, Afrikaans.[9]

Crucial to the ideas of the group were those of a theologian, one S. J. du Toit, an admirer of the Dutch Calvinist theologian and politician, Dr Abraham Kuypers. Du Toit developed a coherent philosophy which sought to combine the cultural and political ambitions of Afrikanerdom and to fix them in a theocratic mould. The efforts to propagate the Afrikaans language were central in this, providing the cultivation of both a cultural and a national consciousness.

For the Genootskap, the starting point was the concept of Christian National Education which had first appeared in the Netherlands in the 1860s. The Genootskappers' programme aimed at the restoration of the church's role in education and the nurturing of Afrikaner culture through the development of the Afrikaans language. Both ideas found some degree of acceptance in the rural areas but they did not attract those colonists who regarded the Dutch language as necessary for the growth of their own civilisation, nor with those who rejected Kuyperian neo-Calvinism. The fact that the Afrikaners in the Cape lacked political control meant that the movement's attraction lay in the cultural rather than in the overt political arena.

On the other hand these ideas were elaborated in the two Boer republics, particularly after 1881 when for a short period du Toit became Superintendent of Education for the Transvaal. The import and significance of them has been disputed, however, and it has been argued that du Toit's attempts to persuade President Kruger to adopt Kuyperian neo-Calvinism as a systematic framework for Afrikaner politics were largely unsuccessful; also that it is unlikely that these principles provided the mainspring for the modern Afrikaner ideology of Apartheid.10 Nonetheless, S. J. du Toit is important, since he was responsible for some of the earliest Afrikaner statements of the 'chosen people' view, the providential thesis.

The evidence seems to suggest, therefore, that the emergence of an official policy of Christian National Education owed more to the continued growth of Afrikaner nationalism than to a residual form of Calvinism, and that the religious underpinnings of

Afrikaner South Africa

that policy came more as a later justification for that nationalism rather than as its wellspring.

The Nationalist Roots

Only a brief outline of the growth of Afrikaner Nationalism will be noted. As with the growth of most nationalist movements, the process was complex and diffuse, embedded in a matrix of economic, political and institutional forces. Prior to the Anglo-Boer War a major force behind its growth lay in Afrikaner reaction to British Imperialism. In particular, van Jaarsveld argues that it was the war between the Transvaal and Britain between 1880 and 1881 which gave form and content to the nationalism which had been latent in the Afrikaner people since before the Great Trek.11

This movement grew and flourished during the next twenty years, culminating in the Anglo-Boer War of 1898-1901. As de Villiers has pointed out:

> The Afrikaner consciousness which took root in the last quarter of the nineteenth century was stimulated in the Cape Colony, and particularly in the two Boer Republics, by the folly of the Jameson Raid (inevitably identified with Rhodes and British Imperialism). The misery of the concentration camps and Kitchener's farm-burning policy in the Anglo-Boer War, together with the way in which these came to be exploited in later years added to the emotion, as did the attempt of Milner to anglicise the people during the period of reconstruction following the war.12

After the formation of the Union in 1910 however, its growth can best be understood by seeing it as involving two key elements: first, inherent beliefs which were transmitted through oral traditions and folk memories, and which concerned such matters as the right to land and 'proper' political order; and second, derived or borrowed ideas of a more abstract political, philosophical and religious nature, which are grafted onto the base of the 'inherent' notions.13 In applying this to Afrikaner political thought, Giliomee singles out the strength of the need to maintain white supremacy and to reject inter-racial intercourse, and the belief that being

> the oldest or original white inhabitants (they) were entitled and indeed better equipped than the English to build a 'proper' political order for South Africa.14

He proceeds to show how ideas derived from the Netherlands during Kuyper's premiership (1900-1905) were included in Malan's premiership from 1948-1954: ideological pronouncements, and in particular, that God had ordained separate nations with separate political institutions, each with a unique destiny.

In summary, crucial in the growth of the Afrikaner nationalism after the Boer War were the following: First, the attempts by General Louis Botha (first South African premier), and Jan Smuts, later Field Marshal Smuts, prior to the First World War to promote a policy of reconciliation between the two white South African language groups within the structures of British Imperialism. Second, the decision to, and the consequences of, entering the First World War on the side of Britain. Third, the concentration of industrial capital largely under English control, and fourth, the economic and social impact of the post-war depression.

In addition, there were also important ethno-cultural issues involved, and citing McCormick, Giliomee states that it was the Nationalist ethno-cultural character and image and not its formal economic proposals which attracted voters and retained their loyalty.15 This image was promoted and fostered in a variety of ways, via party political platforms, party controlled newspapers and later the radio, and through direct intervention in the economy, through the establishment of the Afrikaner Economic Movement and the Reddingsdaad.16 Degenaar has described this process as follows:

> The ideal of Afrikaner nationalism to rule South Africa was not achieved politically in a vacuum. As organisational substructure was necessary and ... this was provided by the process of bureau-

cratisation of Afrikaner life which coincided with the processes of industrialisation and urbanisation. On the cultural level bodies such as the FAK, the Federasie van Afrikaanse Kultuurverenigings (the Federation of Afrikaans Cultural Organisations), played an important role. The Broederbond established this cultural front in December, 1929 ... Its wide range of activities is evident from the fact that by 1937 almost 300 cultural bodies, church councils, youth and student associations, charitable, scientific and educational groups had affiliated to it. (O'Meara)17. It stimulated interest in Afrikaans literature and encouraged the Afrikaner's participation in industry and business.18

It was from the host of shared political values, historical memories and myths about themselves that Afrikaner national consciousness emerged.

After the First World War the collective ethos was bureaucratised and its potency lay in the way it overcame particularist interests and forged a common cause, later embedded and sustained within the more insidious legislation of the late 1940s and beyond. Between 1948 and 1960 political power was consolidated and the declaration of a republic outside of the Commonwealth in 1961 to all intents and purposes represented the triumph of the Afrikaner, his church and his state over white and black resistance. From then onwards a call for wider white South Africanism emerged which coincided with an increase in the level of official state coercion.19 Stultz describes the process as follows:

> Until 1960 the purpose was to preserve Afrikanerdom, today it is the preservation of white South Africa from the forces of Communism through white unity and resolve.20

More recently and especially since 1976, to these forces have been added major forces of black nationalism, those of the African National Congress, all, according to official government pronouncements, bent at subjugating the white 'nation'. Apart from the popular grass roots opposition movements in the black townships, and the work of the official opposition within the white parliament, extra-parliamentary opposition to the South African government's policies have come from two major groups; the black trade unions and the mainline English speaking churches. The latter, particularly the Roman Catholic Church, the Anglican Church and the Methodist Church, have all raised doctrinal and ethical objections to Apartheid, and have made repeated calls for an equitable redistribution of the country's wealth, an end to all Apartheid legislation and state violence, and for the democratisation of the state. The extent to which these calls are supported by their members is uncertain, for it would seem that the maintenance of white economic domination and political security remains a priority for most English as well as Afrikaans speaking whites.21

CHRISTIAN NATIONAL EDUCATION IN PRACTICE

Whilst the origins of Christian Nationalism as it emerged in the 1930s and 1940s remained contested, consensus does exist about its subsequent nature, impregnated as it is with Nationalist political ideology. P. J. Coetzee, writing in 1968, encapsulates the existing dogma as follows:

> It is necessary for us to take all measures to ensure the diversity and separate development of different ethnic groups in the future. All factors which may exist to foster a growing-together and an integration into a greater unity in this country must be systematically removed, otherwise we shall not avoid the process of fusion. The whites still have a great calling in South Africa. There are millions of underdeveloped people of different ethnic groups in the country who are dependent on the help and guidance of the whites. But we can only give this if we see to it ourselves that we do not descend into the sewer of integration.22

Afrikaner South Africa

These racial prescriptions and the narrow interpretation of Calvinism have been widely analysed and criticised, particularly on grounds of its emphasis on racial exclusiveness, separation and the inherent inferiority of the 'non-white' peoples of the country.23

Schooling, in particular, has played a crucial role in the process of inculcating a broader white South Africanism based on these premises. Apart from the introduction of a variety of national rituals, signs and symbols into white schools, from a daily flag raising ceremony to regular quasi religious nationalist ceremonies at which the national anthem is sung and prayers are offered up for the state, the evidence is clear that it is through the curriculum that an uncritical one-sided conception of reality is propagated.24 In all-white schools compulsory 'Youth Preparedness', 'Guidance' and 'Bible Education' courses exist, whilst for boys, para-military cadet training is also included. Bible education is compulsory in all state white schools. In the so-called private schools, most of which are affiliated to or controlled by either the Roman Catholic, Anglican or Methodist churches, it might be expected that a different ethos would prevail. This is certainly what some of these schools endeavour to achieve, but in reality, in spite of their admission of a limited number of 'non-white' pupils, and their professed denominational affiliations, differences between them and schools in the white state sector are limited. This is for three main reasons First, the private schools enjoy considerable patronage from large mining and industrial houses, for whom they have provided many of their managerial leaders, and to which these leaders send their children for their education. Thus, they are closely identified with industrial and commercial capital, which is a key element in the values underpinning this broad South Africanism and the processes by which it has emerged. Second, all schools, whether black or white, private or state, are required to meet certain criteria to qualify for registration. Whilst these are generally concerned with the qualifications of staff, building, space and facility norms, and the length of the school day and school year, curricula requirements are also laid down which include 'Youth Preparedness', 'Guidance' and for boys, cadet programmes. At present, the majority of private schools appear to offer neither 'Youth Preparedness' nor the kind of guidance programmes presented in the state schools, but they do, however, have compulsory cadets. These programmes come under direct control of the military, under whom school teachers are commissioned and trained. Third, a problem common to all private schools concerns rising costs occasioned by a faltering economy and high inflation, and dwindling white numbers through the decline in the white birth rate. Very few black families can afford the fees charged. At the same time it is argued that the majority of the parents would be reluctant to pay these rising fees if the curriculum was regarded as radical in any way or did not afford their children a better than average chance of gaining access to higher education or white collar employment, through success in the Matriculation examination. In this respect, the public examination system exercises considerable control both through the syllabuses laid down and the kind of material rewarded by marks allocated to it.25 In practice, therefore, one finds the following four characteristics in the structure and content of education in South Africa, namely:

a system based on ethnic divisions;

unequal resource allocation among the various ethnically-based sub-systems;26

social curricula calculated to inculcate the state's interpretation of social reality, and to blind the young as to the nature of the country's major problems;

an authoritarian structure of educational management in which the teaching profession has very little say;27

How have these features been legitimated in practice? Inevitably this is not easily answered. However, in an attempt to do so the following part of this chapter will focus on:

- The influence of Afrikaner educational theory and philosophy: Fundamental Pedagogics and,

- The contribution of the work of the South African Teachers Council to the teaching of the ideology of Christian National Education.

FUNDAMENTAL PEDAGOGICS

The influence of Afrikaner educational theory and philosophy, commonly called Fundamental Pedagogics, has been much debated in South Africa. It is proposed here merely to outline its major tenets, methodology and claims and then to expose the links between this philosophy and Apartheid education. The main point to make is that it has extremely wide currency within Afrikaans-medium and controlled teacher education and training. As such it is extremely pervasive.

Secondly, Fundamental Pedagogics is ostensibly based on the work of the Dutch educationist, C. J. Langeveld, with alleged roots in Husserlain and Heideggerian phenomenology. It is seen as a part discipline of pedagogics and whilst there are differences of viewpoint within it, its proponents argue that Pedagogics is a science, indeed, the science of education. It is further argued that by using the phenomenological method:

> it is possible to discover pedagogic essences, knowledge of which will enable us to implement further authentic education.28

Viljoen and Pienaar describe this method as a series of steps, as follows (from page 32 of their book):

> (Step 1): The intuitive investigation of the phenomenon one has taken as one's point of departure.

> (Step 2): ... the preliminary suspension or setting aside of all faith, superstition, dogma, opinions, theories and philosophies of life and the world. This step is also called 'epoche' or

> bracketing.
>
> (Step 3): ... The next step is to separate the essential features of the phenomenon from the non-essential and incidental ... This is the eidos-seeking investigation into the essence (<u>Wesensschau</u>).
>
> (Step 4): Now the phenomenologist investigates the various modes in which the phenomenon manifests itself ...
>
> (Step 5): The investigator must now examine the categories he has designed and determine whether they are in fact ontic (irreducible) and universally valid ...
>
> (Step 6): The relationship between the various categories must be traced ...
>
> (Step 7): The hermeneutic act or act of description-interpretation ...

Having followed this description in steps, Landman and Gous argue that:

> pedagogical findings will (then) have achieved the qualities of truth, universality, validity, consistency, disinterestedness and lack of bias in all elements of science.29

In a study of the phenomenon, Gluckman argues that pedagogical writings are based on certain metaphysical and epistemological presuppositions and that these arise out of a belief in Afrikaner Nationalism and Calvinism.30 This leads, she argues, to a prescriptive form of education, based on the theocentric belief that:

a) God is the ultimate reality: He is universal and omnipotent;

b) all knowledge comes from God, and man comes to knowledge of God via the Bible, faith, feeling and intuition;

c) values are absolute and objective, and come from God;

d) God is the Absolute authority to whom man owes total obedience. But God has delegated his authority to man. Children must, thus, obey their teachers, parents and all others with authority over them.

It is clear that the concept of divine authority and human obedience is of major importance and this is taken up by Kilian when he asserts that the 'freedom' education can bring is only attainable when there is recognition of the authority of certain norms and standards which are to be observed in the course of human action.31 The difficulty noted and expressed by critics of the above, however, is that within this view of man and education:

> to act freely becomes equated with acting responsibly, and acting responsibly in turn becomes equated with acting in accordance with set norms and standards ... The individual who rebels ... is not only acting against the temporal de jure authority of the state but is defying the set norms laid down by a 'Higher Being'.32

A critical review of Fundamental Pedagogics, has argued that it has nothing to do with phenomenology, is nothing but 'the mystification of education and phenomenology', and that the misinterpretation of Heidegger and Husserl is 'totally irresponsible'.33 The writer accuses proponents of it of borrowing philosophic concepts in the hope of lending academic respectability to the 'science' and that:

> The setting in motion of the elaborate machinery of a 'phenomenological reduction' is a mere sham if it leaves the dogmas of Christian National Education as firmly entrenched after the reduction as they were before.

The writer continues:

> To the ideal of Christian National Education would seem to belong: a servile submissiveness to authority, a naive acceptance of bourgeois moralism, and the inculcating of a Calvinist Christian ideology.34

The third point to make is that Fundamental Pedagogic doctrines have underpinned much educational research in South Africa, research which has been uncritical of Christian National Education and which has taken the political status quo as it affects education unproblematically. In a review of educational research undertaken by Clark between 1973 and 1978, the writer found that of the six hundred and forty master's degree theses presented in education faculties, 84 per cent were written in Afrikaans, whilst 89 per cent of those written in English were presented at Afrikaans medium universities.35 Given that the overall ethos of these faculties is Fundamental Pedagogic, that every education student in these institutions follows a course in the subject, it is reasonable to assert that the ideology has wide currency. Clark further notes that from a close study of the thesis titles it was possible to conclude that:

> The focus was on the individual pupil or teacher or social group rather than on the national, including the multi-ethnic context ... wider social and political contexts having been ignored.36

It is perhaps significant, as Fouche has indicated, that Fundamental Pedagogicians too have confined their research to relatively harmless and trivial matters, ignoring questions of ideology, racism or authoritarianism. As she says:

> Any attitude critical of their teaching has been seen as emanating darkly from Communist forces, anarchists, etc. The question as to what rightly constitutes education as opposed to indoctrination has, understandably, been neglected.37

Afrikaner South Africa

Finally, it has been argued that the <u>Broederbond</u> appropriated the education system to the service of its Christian National education policy ideals.38 It was inevitable after 1948, once its members had acquired senior positions in the government and public service, including control of the various provincial departments of education, that Christian National ideology would begin to permeate the education system. The architect of Verwoerd's education system, a Dr. W. M. M. van Eiselen, was a leading member of the organisation. It was his commission's report of 1951 which laid the foundations for the Bantu Education Act No. 47 of 1953 and the Extension of University Education Act No. 45 of 1959 which placed on the statute books the complex structures of <u>Apartheid</u> education.39 Other members included senior academics in Afrikaans medium universities and a former head of the South African Broadcasting Corporation. It is clear that the close association between professional expertise and what was seen as service to the nation (<u>Volksdiens</u>), cannot have been mere coincidence, the manner in which the education system has been fashioned since 1948 strongly reflects Christian National ideology.

THE SOUTH AFRICAN TEACHERS' COUNCIL FOR WHITES

This is a statutory professional body which was established by Act of Parliament (Act 116) of 1976. Amongst other things all white teachers must acquire registration with the SATC before they are able to obtain a permanent tenured teaching post in a state controlled school. Registration is conditional upon signing assent to the SATC CREDO, the full text of which is reproduced in the notes below.40

According to the SATC Secretariat, the CREDO sums up the professional code of ethics of the Council and it is in terms of this that action can be taken in response to any complaints. By its very nature and form, the SATC through its CREDO exercises considerable control over the white teaching profession in a number of ways:

In the first place its explanatory power is fully Christian National as its references to the Christian and National character of education indicate. Though one might wonder how much of this is accepted in practice, the evidence taken from a summary of discussions on the CREDO by a large group of white, predominantly Afrikaans speaking school principals in late 1984 seems to suggest that the ideology is taken unproblematically.41 Secondly, whilst the SATC's professional powers are considerable, those cases it has heard since its inception and which have resulted in the dismissal of teachers have been brought in terms of teacher/pupil relations and the failure of the teacher to accept the authority of the school principal.42 Thirdly, by compelling all white teachers to seek membership and to sign the CREDO in order to obtain a tenured and permanent teaching post, the SATC is, in the words of one school principal, 'implicating many teachers in a lie'.

Thus, whilst this control might be termed 'benign', the CREDO differs little in essence from what was first stated in the 1948 Christian National Education policy document (**Beleid**) referred to earlier in the chapter. As such its power probably lies in its ability to define the relationships it enshrines, and these will remain unchallenged until, if ever, any overt action is taken to ensure absolute allegiance to the CREDO.

DEVELOPMENTS AND SHIFTS: PROBLEMS OF AFRIKANER EDUCATION POLICY

In attempting to assess the extent to which Christian National Education principles have been internalised, it is necessary to make the following six points.

First, the political policy of <u>Apartheid</u> introduced after 1948 has its roots in the Afrikaner's historical and cultural past. Educational <u>Apartheid</u> is an expression of political <u>Apartheid</u> and it is possible therefore to conflate the dominant ideology of education, Fundamental Pedagogics, with the political ideology.

Second, the Afrikaner Nationalist's assumption of political power in 1948 coincided with an economic 'take-off' within South Africa. As a consequence of the Second World War the country had begun to break free from the constraints of its connection with metropolitan Britain. In ideological terms this meant for the Afrikaner nationalist that apart from education functioning to maintain group and social cohesion and identity, it now also became necessary for it to impart the required skills to individual workers. This movement has been accentuated during the last fifteen years by the threat of international sanctions, the oil crisis and the moves by the South African government towards autarky. Studies of this development and the impact on education have illuminated the manner in which capitalist production relations have increasingly become legitimated within that of the ruling ideology of Christian National Education.43

Third, the evidence from official publications clearly indicates an official justification for separate group identities on the grounds that without the promotion of group differences, an intergroup conflict will arise. R. Muir has outlined this clearly as follows:

> South African society is legitimated by conservative politicians and academics as a functional and natural system of stratification not in crude racial terms, but in terms of cultural identity and of harmonious relations between groups. It is argued that the stratification system operates functionally to reduce conflict between groups.44

Fourth, education, it is argued, fits the white group to undertake the task of providing leadership and skills especially for the black groups. What is not stated is the implied cultural superiority of the whites. Nor is it stated that education is crucial to producing and maintaining the present social stratification. More recent studies of this, however, point not only to the cultural hegemony of Afrikaner and white culture in general45 but also to the emergence of a technicist ethos aimed at inculcating and encouraging the adoption of free enterprise values as a counter to the growth of socialism.46

Fifth, it is necessary to place developments in education within the dynamics of the political and economic structures of South African society as a whole, a practice opposed by the Fundamental Pedagogicians who 'bracket off' education and prefer to see it exclusively. Yet, as Buckland points out, by the middle 1970s it was increasingly being realised that:

> The schooling system was not producing workers with 'realistic' aspirations and 'appropriate' value systems required by industry, and the results of this 'inadequate harmonization' put society 'at great risk', on a 'road to disaster'.47

The South African government responded to this crisis by launching The Human Sciences Research Council (HSRC, based in Pretoria), de Lange Investigation into the state of education. Its findings represented a major ideological shift by the government as it sought to accommodate its ideologies to the forces of modernisation. Quoting Danziger, Buckland states that this represented a:

> clear shift from a justification of existing institutions in terms of their intrinsic value to their justification in terms of their instrumental utility of effectiveness Secondly, we observe a shift from cultural to political and finally economic institutions as the main focus for legitimating ideas.48

It would seem, as Buckland indicates, that the transformation of schooling from its origins in Christian National Education into a powerful force for modernisation was achieved by the infusion of a technicist ideology, by which goals of management efficiency and control were elevated above the previously explicit goal of the preservation of Afrikaner identity.49

Finally, what is clear, is that the relational patterns created by the ideology and practice of <u>Apartheid</u> have resulted in group definitions and in the structuring of relations between these groups. Ideological <u>Apartheid</u> is now seen to differ from

Afrikaner South Africa

actual <u>Apartheid</u>. The former is justificatory, continuing to express itself in official doctrines and appealing to the emotional myths of the past, the latter continuing to aim at the pragmatic development of a powerful white elite. It is the promise of economic security which appears to have attracted much white English-speaking support for the nationalist government. In this many of those English speakers who are practicing Christians have tended to clash with the views of their church leaders. For the majority of black South Africans, however, the total rejection of <u>Apartheid</u> Bantu Education, and of the Christian National ideology which underpins it, now includes also the economic system which reinforces it. As Dore has said:

> The effect of schooling, the way it alters a man's capacity and will to do things, depends not only on what he learns, or the way he learns it, but also on why he learns it.50

For the majority of whites, including English speakers, now part of a wider white South African nationalism, the threat posed by growing black demands, is not only a cultural one, but also an ideological one in both political and economic terms.

NOTES AND REFERENCES

1. <u>White Paper on the Provision of Education in the Republic of South Africa</u>, Pretoria: Government Printer, 1983, p.5.
   The South African Constitution Act was passed in 1983, came into effect in 1983 and gave rise to the Tricameral System. Blacks fall under General Affairs of the White House of Assembly. Indians have their own Chamber, called the House of Delegates and Coloureds (mixed race) also have one, called the House of Representatives. Thus the majority Blacks are still without own representation in the country, except in 'their' homeland parliaments.

2. Rose, B. and Tunmer, R. (eds), **Documents in South African Education**, Pretoria: Ad Donker, 1975, p. 120.

3. When using the term **Afrikaner** one has to bear in mind that not all Afrikaans speaking white South Africans are supporters of the Nationalists' policy of **Apartheid**. Some of the Government's fiercest critics, like Dr. Beyers Naude, Breyten Breytenbach or van Zyl Slabbert, are Afrikaners. Although the term has tended to become a blanket term to cover all who presently subscribe to the ideology of Apartheid, currently many English-speaking South Africans support the Government.

4. **Vorming** - Afrikaans for shaping and moulding. The term carries with it strong behavioural connotations.

5. Volk - Afrikaans for people.

6. Muir, R.K., 'Christian National Education', in **The African Studies Programme**, Occasional papers No. 4. Johannesburg: University of the Witwatersrand, 1968. Reprinted in: Rose, B. and Tunmer, R., op. cit.

7. Federasie van Afrikaanse Kultuur Vereniginge, **Christelike-Nasionale Onderwys Beleid**, Instituut vir Christelike-Nasionale Onderwys, Johannesburg, 1948.

8. Muir, R.K., in: Rose and Tunmer, op. cit., p. 112.

9. Davenport, T.R.H., **The Afrikaner Bond**, Oxford University Press, 1966.

10. du Toit, A., 'Puritans in Africa? Afrikaner 'Calvinism' and Kuyperian Neo-Calvinism in late nineteenth century South Africa', **Comparative Studies in History and Society**, 1985, 27, 2.

11. van Jaarsveld, F.A., **The Afrikaner's interpretation of South African History**, Cape Town: Simondium, 1964.

12. de Villier, R. 'Afrikaner Nationalism', in: Wilson, M. and Thompson, I. The Oxford History of South Africa, vol. 2, Oxford University Press, 1971.

13. Giliomee, H. 'Constructing Afrikaner Nationalism', in: Adam, H. (ed.), Africa: The limits of reform politics, Brill, 1903, pp. 83-98.

14. Ibid.

15. McCormick, R.L., 'Ethno-Cultural interpretations of nineteenth-century American Voting Behaviour', Political Science Quarterly, 1974, 2.

16. Reddingsdaad. This was an organisation set up to provide support for the Afrikaner poor whites. Redding comes from the verb red which means to save, daad means a deed; thus (National) Salvation Movement.

17. O'Meara, D., 'The Afrikaner Broederbond, 1927-48; class vanguard of Afrikaner nationalism', Journal of South African Studies, 1977, 3, 2, p.169.

18. Degenaar, J.J., The roots of nationalism, Pretoria: Academica, 1982.

19. de Villiers, R., op. cit.

20. Stultz, N., 'The politics of security: South Africa under Verwoerd, 1961-6', The Journal of Modern African Studies, 1969, 7, 1.

21. The overwhelming support given to the ruling party by white voters, English and Afrikaans speaking, in the 1983 referendum clearly suggests this. In addition, every white male in South Africa is conscripted into the South African army, where he is subjected to overt pro-government propaganda. An indication of the effectiveness of the political socialisation which occurs there, in the schools and through the media, is the relatively small number of conscientious objectors convicted each year. The home, school and community form a powerful 'conscience' in support of conscription, so much so that

conscientious objection is regarded as cowardice in many quarters. Good examples of the kind of literature which floods the media, schools and colleges, are: Paratus and Cadet/Kadet published by the South African Defence Force, and The Aida Parker Newsletter, published by Aida Parker, Auckland Park, Johannesburg.

22. Coetzee, P.J., 'Akkulturasie', in: Cronje, B. (ed.), Kultuurbeinvloeding tussen blankes en Bantoe in Suid-Afrika, Pretoria: van Schaik, 1968.

23. See amongst other general texts:

Moodie, T.D., The rise of Afrikanerdom, University of California Press, 1975;
Giliomee, H. and Elphick, R., The shaping of South African society, Cape Town: Longman, 1979;
Hexham, I., The irony of Apartheid: the struggle for national independence of Afrikaner Calvinism against British Imperialism, New York: Edwin Mellen Press, 1981.

24. This point is made by the authors of various papers in Education, Curriculum and Development. Hunter A.P., et al. (eds.), Johannesburg: University of Witwatersrand, 1983.

25. The examining of history is a frequently cited example and has been the focus of much critical comment by the white English speaking teacher associations and by the Black, Indian and Coloured Associations.

26. The following tables provide details of:

A. Per capita expenditure in Rands on education for each group:

Year	White	Indians	Coloureds (mixed race)	Blacks excluding independent homelands
1978/79	724	225	357	71
1981/82	1048	670	356	118
1982/83	1211	711	497	146

B. Total budgeted by central government for education:

1981/82	R566 million
1982/83	R668 million
1983/84	R911 million
1984/85	R1240 million

C. Population: percentage of each group

Year	Blacks	Whites	Coloureds	Indians
1983	73	15.3	8.9	2.8
1999	77.6	11.8	8.2	2.4

(projected)

D. Age Structure: 1980 (percentage)

Age	Blacks	Whites	Coloureds	Indians
0-14	43.7	28.5	36.5	39.7
15-64	53.8	65.2	61.0	57.7
65+	2.5	6.3	2.5	2.6

Race Relations Survey - 1985, **40**, Institute of Race Relations, Johannesburg, 1985.

27. Hunter, P., Unpublished Inaugural Lecture, Johannesburg: University of Witwatersrand, 1981.

28. Viljoen, T.A. and Pienaar, J.J., *Fundamental Pedagogics*, Butterworths, 1971.

29. Landman, W.A. and Gous, S.J., *Inleiding tot die Fundamentale Pedagogiek*, Johannesburg Pers, 1969, pp. 4-5.

30. Gluckman, H., 'The extent to which Calvinism and Christian National Education have influenced Pedagogical findings in South Africa', in: Beard, P. and Morrow, W. (eds.), *Problems of Pedagogy*, Butterworths, 1981.

31. Kilian, C.J.G. and Viljoen, T.A., *Fundamental Pedagogics and fundamental structures*, Butterworths, 1974.

32. Parker, B., 'Freedom and authority in Fundamental Pedagogics', in: Beard, P. and Morrow, W., op. cit.

33. Fouche, F., 'Pedagogics: the mystification of education and phenomenology', in: Beard, P. and Morrow, W., op. cit., p. 223.

34. Ibid.

35. Clark, A., 'Mapping an unchartered frontier: educational research and the HSRC de Lange Report', in: *South African Educational Policy, Analysis and Critique*, Faculty of Education, University of Cape Town, 1982.

36. Ibid., p. 32.

37. Fouche, F., op. cit., p. 30.

38. See for example:

   Carter, B., *The politics of inequality: South Africa since 1948*, Thames Hudson, 1962.

Marquard, L., The peoples and policies of South Africa, Chapter 8, Cape Town: Oxford University Press, 1962.

Wilkins, I. and Strydom, H., The Super Afrikaners, Jonathan Ball, 1980.

39. Published in Pretoria and printed by Pretoria: Government Printer.

40. SOUTH AFRICAN TEACHERS' COUNCIL CREDO

The teachers -

whose names are entered in the register of the South African Teachers' Council for Whites, are conscious of the high calling of their profession to educate the future citizens of their country;

believe that the ideals, aspirations, training and conduct of members of the teaching profession determine the quality of education in this country;

and therefore pledge themselves as teachers to honour and obey the laws of the country and to conduct themselves in accordance with the high ideals of their profession as expressed in this code.

The teacher and the pupil

A teacher -

practices his calling in an awareness that education in this country is founded on the Bible. He shall, nevertheless in the implementation of the policy in regard to the Christian character of education at all times respect the convictions of both parents and pupils in regard to religious education and religious ceremonies;

accepts that education has a broad national character that must be cultivated through the conscious expansion of every pupil's knowledge of the country, its language and cultural heritage, history, traditions and national symbols;

accepts character development as part of the task of education and promotes the highest moral standards by word and example;

undertakes as his professional responsibility the guidance of each pupil in his care in the pursuit of knowledge and skills and in the development of his full potential so that he may become a responsible and selfsupporting citizen of a democratic state;

recognises the individuality of every pupil, respects his personality, fosters a healthy environment for education and learning, exercises authority with compassion and refrains from words or actions which are destructive or negative; and

respects the right of every pupil to have confidential information about himself withheld at all times except when required by authorised agencies or by law.

The teacher and the parents

A teacher -

endeavours to maintain friendly cooperation with the parents of pupils in his care; and

does everything possible to uphold parental authority, to promote the pupil's confidence in his own home and to keep parents adequately informed about the progress of their child.

The teacher and the community

A teacher -

accepts the principle that the school serves the community and respect the customs and codes of the community as far as this is educationally justifiable;

accepts his responsibilities as a member of his profession to give guidance to the community in respect of the development of correct attitudes to and the advancement of education, as well as his personal involvement in communal and civic affairs; and

recognises that the teaching profession occupies a position of public trust, involving not only the individual teacher's personal conduct but also the interaction of the school and the community, and therefore his actions and conduct shall be of such a nature that he commands the respect of the community and enhances the image of the profession.

The teacher and his employers

A teacher –

is loyal to his employers by serving them to the best of his ability, obeying all their lawful instructions and regulations, and by conducting professional business through the proper channels only; and

refrains from discussing confidential and official matters with unauthorised persons.

The teacher's obligations to his colleagues and his profession

A teacher –

contributes his share to the dignity and public image of the teaching profession both by his exemplary personal behaviour and conduct and by his fair and loyal dealings with all other members of his profession;

accepts the authority and instructions of those who are placed in a position of authority without necessarily suppressing his own professional views or surrendering his professional independence;

accepts his responsibility together with all other citizens of the country for the development of sound public opinion and trust to promote party political or contentious aims; and identifies himself with his profession and its demands, inter alia by participating in educational activities and by keeping abreast of educational thought and development.

The CREDO is an official publication of the South African Teachers' Council for Whites. (Act No. 116 of 1976); Pretoria: Government Printer, 1976.

41. South African Teachers' Council for Whites, Symposium report AU2/11, 26 November, 1985, Pretoria: Government Printer, 1985.

42. Private correspondence with the SATC Registrar, J. L. Lemmer, March, 1986.

43. See particularly the papers in:

Kallaway, P. J., (ed.), Apartheid and Education, Johannesburg: Ravan Press, 1984.

44. Muir, R., 'Class, Race, Culture and Education', in: The Kenton Conference Proceedings, Lawrence, M. (ed.), Minabatho: University of Bophuthatswana, 1983.

45. See for example:

>Penny, A. J. and Millar, C.J., 'Staff and Student Perceptions of Academic Requirements: A Black South African University', in: Hunter, A.P., et al. (eds.), Education, Curriculum and Development, op. cit. (ch. 13).

46. Kallaway, P.J., op. cit.

47. Buckland, P., 'Technicism and de Lange; reflections on the process of the HSRC investigation', in: Kallaway, op. cit.

48. Ibid.

49. Ibid.

50. Dore, R.e-The Diploma Disease, Unwin, 1976.

INDEX

Africa 1, 11, 316, 317, 319, 322, 323, 326, 328, 337, 338
America (USA) 10, 11, 12, 14, 192-216, 231, 238, 276, 278, 290, 291, 292
America (Latin) 8, 10, 11, 12, 187, 286, 288, 290, 291, 293, 305
Antigua 229, 240, 242, 246, 250, 261
Araucanians 284, 285
Atheism 149, 152, 282
Augustinians 272, 283, 318

Bahamas 229, 230, 231, 239, 243, 244, 246, 249, 264
Bakongos 318, 319, 320, 323, 324, 330, 331, 334
Balubas 330, 334
Baptists 198, 208, 223, 224, 226, 228, 239, 244, 245, 246-9, 253, 257, 258, 260, 261, 263, 320, 325
Barbados 220, 221, 228, 230, 233, 240, 242, 243, 245, 254, 257, 261
Bas Zaire 318, 319, 320, 323, 329
BEC (Catholic Bureau) 326, 335
BEK (Kimbanguist Bureau) 326, 330, 331, 332, 334, 335, 336
Belgians 321, 322, 323, 324, 332, 347

Benedictine 68, 119
BEP (Protestant Bureau) 326, 332, 334
Bible 8, 39, 42, 47, 62, 75, 97, 175, 185, 192, 205, 207, 220, 227, 231, 241, 243, 261, 278, 320, 325, 345, 348, 355, 358, 371
British Baptist Missionary Society 246, 247

Calvinism 196, 239, 243, 347, 348, 349-51, 355, 358, 360
Caribbean 11, 12, 217-69
Catechism 3, 4, 5, 13, 118, 126, 143, 145, 151, 176, 177, 220, 228, 231, 237, 238, 241, 261, 274, 318, 320
Chile 8, 11, 12, 270-315
Christian National Education 347, 348-57, 360, 361, 362, 363, 364, 365
Christian Scientist 198
Church of England 10, 65, 68, 74, 75, 217, 218, 219, 228-34, 238, 248
Church of Ireland 58, 99
Church of Scotland 21, 22, 30, 34, 35, 254
CMS (Church Missionary Society) 223, 229, 230, 233
Cistercian 119
Communism 136, 142, 143, 360

Diangienda, Joseph 323, 324, 325, 331, 332
Dominica 230, 237
Dominicans 272, 275, 282, 286
Dutch Reformed Church 13, 347

EJCSK (Church of Jesus Christ on Earth according to Simon Kimbangu) 324, 325, 327, 331, 332, 339
Emancipation 63, 68, 76, 80, 217, 221, 232, 234, 236, 241, 252, 258
England 5, 6, 9, 10, 11, 12, 14, 15, 17, 21, 28, 39, 44, 47, 48, 57, 61-88, 117, 238, 292
English Language 95, 238, 243, 291, 292
Episcopal Church (Scotland) 21, 22, 23, 26, 30, 34
Episcopalian 196, 198
Estado Docente 272, 273, 280, 311
Europe 1, 2, 4, 5, 6, 9, 10, 11, 89, 109, 117, 170, 222, 316, 320, 337
Evangelical 196, 204, 279

FAK (Federation of Afrikaans Cultural Organisations) 348, 353
FIDE (Federation of Secondary Education Institutes) 298, 299, 300, 307
France 5, 10, 12, 48, 150, 236, 237, 238, 273, 347
Franciscans 272, 318

Free Church of Scotland 32, 34
Fundamentalist Christian 196, 207, 208

Gaelic 18, 31, 48, 91, 95, 99, 102, 106
Germany 6, 10, 12, 13, 14, 117, 120, 121, 126, 129, 133, 139, 140, 146, 150, 160, 170-91, 200, 275, 285
Grenada 234, 237, 238, 239, 261
Guyana 249, 261, 263

Hermanos 274, 275, 285, 296
Humanism 176, 281
Hungary 13, 202

ICNO (Institute for Christian National Teaching and Education) 348
Ireland, Republic of 2, 10, 11, 12, 84-116
Ireland, Northern 2, 6, 15, 38-60, 89
Irish 48, 91, 95, 99, 200
Irish Language 66, 67, 69, 74, 75, 80
Italians 201, 202

Jamaica 218, 226, 230, 233, 239, 240, 241, 242, 243, 246, 247, 248, 252, 254, 261, 262, 264
Jesuits 68, 117, 122, 124, 132, 150, 156, 157, 175, 177, 178, 274, 283, 286, 294, 301, 307, 318

Jews 120, 121, 129, 133, 155, 196, 198, 202, 204, 206, 220
Judaism 129

Kildare Place Society (Society for Promoting the Education of the Poor in Ireland) 38, 39
Kimbangu, Simon 319, 320-22, 323, 324, 325, 337
Kimbanguists 12, 316-44

Lancasterian system 247, 271, 312
Latin 2, 20, 121, 130, 178, 220
Latin Catholic Church 121, 128, 130
Leninism 137, 172
Ley Interpretativa 276, 287
Libertad de Ensenanza 274, 280, 281, 287, 311
Lithuanians 120, 123, 128
LMS (London Missionary Society) 224, 228, 249-53
Luther 174, 175, 176, 177
Lutheran 122, 129, 135, 196, 198, 275, 293
Lynn Committee (1921) 40, 41

Marxism 137, 142, 149, 152, 172, 306, 307
Martinique 238
Mercedarians 272, 283
Methodism 39, 58, 79, 222, 224, 226, 228, 238, 239, 242-6, 258, 259, 260, 352, 353

Methodist Missionary Society 245
Mico Trust 236, 237, 256, 258, 278, 279, 280
Missionaries 2, 147, 150, 218, 220, 221-64, 274, 277, 279, 283, 284, 290, 295, 316, 317, 318, 319, 326, 327, 332, 337
Monasteries 61, 126, 130, 150, 175
Moravians 224, 225, 228, 239, 240-42, 245, 257
Mormons 198, 292
Moslems 29, 263

National School System 96, 97, 98, 113
Netherlands 46, 347, 350

Papacy 8, 16, 74, 75, 92, 93, 97, 98, 147, 177, 282, 285
PAX 13, 141, 142, 144, 145, 148, 152, 166
Pentecostalism 279, 280, 293
Phillipo, James 247, 248, 253, 256
Piarist 6, 117, 122, 123, 124, 135
Poland 6, 8, 11, 12, 13, 14, 16, 117-69, 200, 201, 202
Portuguese 318, 319
Presbyterian 21, 22, 34, 39, 58, 97, 98, 198, 279
Prussia 6, 119, 125, 126, 131, 135, 160, 175, 177, 180

Quakers 196, 219-21, 240, 242

377

Reformation 170, 174, 175, 176, 177, 178, 180
Rome 76, 120, 123, 180

Salesians 283, 284, 295
Salvation Army 279, 323
Santiago 271, 272, 274, 278, 279, 281, 282, 283, 286, 290, 291, 292, 295, 301, 307, 308
SATC (South African Teachers Council for Whites) 361, 362, 371-4
SSCORE (Scottish Central Committee on Religious Education) 27, 28, 33, 36
Scotland 6, 10, 13, 17-37, 46, 48, 49, 51
SCOTVEC (Scottish Vocational Education Council) 29, 36
Secularism 2, 3, 4, 5, 6, 8, 9, 12, 23, 25, 27, 29, 31, 32, 39, 41, 69, 70, 71, 73, 77, 93, 97, 99, 105, 117, 118, 124, 136, 153, 158, 171, 175, 179, 202, 206, 207, 276, 277, 280, 318, 319, 323
Segregation 38, 39, 41, 42, 44, 49, 50, 51-4, 56, 57, 58, 134
Seminaries 4, 5, 6, 72, 85, 143, 146, 147, 273, 291, 331, 332
Seventh Day Adventist 198, 279, 292
Slavery 217, 218, 219, 220, 222, 223, 224, 225, 227, 228, 229, 230, 232, 235, 239, 240, 241, 242, 243, 245, 246, 248, 249, 250, 252, 253, 255, 257, 263, 319
South Africa 8, 15, 345-74
Soviet Union 8, 10, 14, 120, 122, 125, 126, 127, 128, 133, 135, 136, 137, 161
Spain 10, 235, 236, 237
SPCK (Society for the Propagation of Christian Knowledge) 230
SPG (Society for the Propagation of the Gospel in Foreign Parts) 228, 229, 230
St. Kitts 228, 240, 241, 252
St. Lucia 234, 237, 238, 239
St. Vincent 230, 234, 237, 243
Stalinism 137, 140, 144, 145

Tobago 240, 243, 249
Trinidad 234, 237, 238, 239, 243, 255, 261, 263

Ukrainians 120, 127, 128, 129, 154
Uniate Church (Greek Catholic) 120, 121, 128, 129, 130, 135

Valparaiso 271, 273, 274, 275, 277, 283, 294
Vatican 8, 73, 75, 77, 82, 89, 105, 135, 141, 142, 144, 306

Wales 6, 61-88

Zaire 9, 11, 12, 13, 15, 316-44

For Product Safety Concerns and Information please contact our EU
representative GPSR@taylorandfrancis.com
Taylor & Francis Verlag GmbH, Kaufingerstraße 24, 80331 München, Germany

www.ingramcontent.com/pod-product-compliance
Lightning Source LLC
Chambersburg PA
CBHW071143300426
44113CB00009B/1063